THE JEWISH MIDDLE AGES

THE BIBLE AND WOMEN
An Encyclopaedia of Exegesis and Cultural History

Edited by Mary Ann Beavis, Irmtraud Fischer,
Mercedes Navarro Puerto, and Adriana Valerio

Volume 4.2: The Jewish Middle Ages

THE JEWISH MIDDLE AGES

Edited by
Carol Bakhos and Gerhard Langer

SBL PRESS

Atlanta

Copyright © 2023 by SBL Press

All rights reserved. No part of this work may be reproduced or transmitted in any form or by any means, electronic or mechanical, including photocopying and recording, or by means of any information storage or retrieval system, except as may be expressly permitted by the 1976 Copyright Act or in writing from the publisher. Requests for permission should be addressed in writing to the Rights and Permissions Office, SBL Press, 825 Houston Mill Road, Atlanta, GA 30329 USA.

Library of Congress Control Number: 2023932641

Contents

Acknowledgments vii
Abbreviations ix

Introduction 1

Cultural Setting

Gender and Daily Life in the Jewish Communities of
    Medieval Europe
    Elisheva Baumgarten 13

Late Midrashic Literature

"If You Keep Silent in This Crisis" (Esth 4:14):
    Esther the Medieval Biblical Heroine
    Constanza Cordoni 35

Judith in the Hebrew Literature of the Middle Ages
    Dagmar Börner-Klein 55

Commentary

The Tradition of Eve in the Commentaries of Rashi and Ramban
    Gerhard Langer 73

Sarah and Hagar in Medieval Jewish Commentaries
    Carol Bakhos 91

The Voice of the Woman: Narrating the Song of Songs in
    Twelfth-Century Rabbinic Exegesis
    Robert A. Harris 103

The Irony of the *Eshet Hayil*: Proverbs 31:10–31 in
    Jewish Medieval Exegesis
    Sheila Tuller Keiter 133

Hasidei Ashkenaz

Representations of Biblical Women in the Writings of the
    Hasidei Ashkenaz
    Judith R. Baskin 153

Poetry and *Piyyut*

Biblical Women in the Hebrew Poetry of Al-Andalus
    Aurora Salvatierra Ossorio..173

The Female Figure Zion in the Liturgical Literature of
    Al-Andalus
    Meret Gutmann-Grün 189

Mysticism

The Development of the Feminine Dimension of
    God in the Jewish Mystical Tradition
    Rachel Elior...219

The Biblical Woman Who Is Not in the Bible:
    Feminine Imagery in Kabbalah
    Felicia Waldman 247

The Figure of Ruth as a Convert in the Zohar
    Yuval Katz-Wilfing 263

Art

Female Protagonists in Medieval Jewish Book Art
    Katrin Kogman-Appel 285

Bibliography...323
Contributors...351
Ancient Sources Index...355
Modern Authors Index..365

Acknowledgments

Several of the essays in this volume were first presented as working papers at an international "Bible and Women in Jewish Middle Ages" colloquium held in November 2014 at the Institute of Jewish Studies of the University of Vienna and funded through the generous support of the University of Vienna and the University of Graz. I wish to thank the organizers, Gerhard Langer and Constanza Cordoni, and the participants whose work and comments made for a fruitful experience, one that led to the vision and publication of this volume. The German edition, spearheaded by Gerhard Langer, appeared in 2020. While the content of that edition appears here, this is not simply a translated version of that publication. On the contrary, many of the articles have been heavily edited and amplified. A great deal of work and energy went into preparing this volume and many were involved in the process.

I wish to thank Anna Deckert for translating "Biblical Women in the Hebrew Poetry of Al-Andalus" from Spanish and Dennis Slabaugh for translating the following articles from German: "Judith in the Hebrew Literature of the Middle Ages," "The Tradition of Eve in the Commentaries of Rashi and Ramban," "The Feminine Figure Zion in the Liturgical Literature of Al-Andalus," and "The Development of the Feminine Dimension of God in the Jewish Mystical Tradition" (originally written in Hebrew).

I am grateful to the Women and the Bible series editors for their ongoing support. In particular, I thank Irmtraud Fischer for her patience and encouragement throughout this lengthy process and Mary Ann Beavis for her editorial scrutiny. The volume as a whole has benefited from her astute comments and interventions. Many thanks to Nicole L. Tilford at SBL Press for her assistance and to Esther Heiss for her work on the German edition. The UCLA Center for Medieval and Renaissance Studies, under the directorship of Zrinka Stahuljak, and the UCLA Renée and David Kaplan Center for the Study of Religion Fund provided financial assistance for which I am grateful.

Finally, I wish to thank Hannah Rosenberg for her technical and bibliographic support. I am most grateful to Ann Hasse and Megan Remington for their editorial assistance. Each in her own way improved the quality of the volume and made the tedious task of editing immeasurably pleasurable.

Carol Bakhos
Los Angeles, August 2021

Abbreviations

AB	The Anchor Bible
ABD	Freedman, David Noel, ed. *Anchor Bible Dictionary*. 6 vols. New York: Doubleday, 1992.
AJSR	*Association for Jewish Studies Review*
ʿArakh	ʿArakhin
ʿAvod. Zar.	ʿAvodah Zarah
ʾAvot R. Nat.	ʾAvot of Rabbi Nathan
b.	Babylonian Talmud
B. Metz.	Bava Metziʾa
Bekh.	Bekhorot
Ber.	Berakhot
BW	Bible and Women
BZ	*Biblische Zeitschrift*
CBQ	*Catholic Biblical Quarterly*
EJL	Early Judaism and Its Literature
ʿEruv	ʿEruvin
Esth. Rab.	Esther Rabbah
Exod. Rab.	Exodus Rabbah
Gen. Rab.	Genesis Rabbah
Hag.	Hagigah
HBS	History of Biblical Studies
Hor.	Horayot
HTR	*Harvard Theological Review*
Hul.	Hullin
ITQ	*Irish Theological Quarterly*
JBL	*Journal of Biblical Literature*
JSHRZ	Jüdische Schriften aus hellenistisch-römischer Zeit
JQR	*Jewish Quarterly Review*
JSJSup	Journal for the Study of Judaism Supplement Series
JSQ	*Jewish Studies Quarterly*

JSS	*Journal of Semitic Studies*
LeqT ad Esth	Leqach Tov on Esther
Lev. Rab.	Leviticus Rabbah
m.	Mishnah
Meg.	Megillah
Midr. Ps.	Midrash Psalms
Midr. Song	Midrash Song of Songs
Naz.	Nazir
Nid.	Niddah
Num. Rab.	Numbers Rabbah
OTE	*Old Testament Essays*
Pesaḥ.	Pesaḥim
Pirqe R. El.	Pirqe Rabbi Eliezer
PL	Patrologia Latina
PUSHD	Princeton University Sefer Hasidim Database
Qoh Rab.	Qohelet Rabbah
RB	*Revue Biblique*
RHS	*Religionsunterricht an höheren Schulen*
RTL	*Revue theologique de Louvain*
Ruth Rab.	Ruth Rabbah
S. Eli. Rab.	Seder Eliyahu Rabbah
S. Olam Rab.	Seder Olam Rabbah
Sanh.	Sanhedrin
Shabb.	Shabbat
SHB	Sefer Hasidim manuscript in Bologna. Margaliot, Reuven, ed. *Sefer Hasidim*. Jerusalem: Mossad Ha-Rav Kook, 1957.
Shem.	Shemot
Sifre Deut.	Sifre Deuteronomy
SHP	Sefer Hasidim manuscript in Parma. Wistinetzki, Judah, ed. *Sefer Hasidim*. With an introduction by Jacob Freimann. Frankfurt am Main: Vahrmann, 1924.
SJ	Studia Judaica
Song Rab.	Song of Songs Rabbah
SVTG	Septuaginta: Vetus Testamentum Graecum
Taʿan.	Taʿanit
TGl	*Theologie und Glaube*
TSMJ	Texts and Studies in Medieval and Early Modern Judaism

TTZ	*Trierer theologische Zeitschrift*
VT	*Vetus Testamentum*
WMANT	Wissenschaftliche Untersuchungen zum Alten und Neuen Testament
y.	Jerusalem Talmud
Yad.	Yadayim
Yebam.	Yebamot
ZDPV	*Zeitschrift des Deutschen Palästina-Vereins*

Introduction

Carol Bakhos

Part of an extensive international series exploring the reception history of female characters in the Bible with an eye toward gender-relevant biblical themes, this volume focuses on the different ways in which women of the biblical tradition are treated in Jewish literature of the medieval period. It does so within a variety of linguistic and cultural contexts, paying special attention to literature emanating from Ashkenazic circles.

During the medieval period, Jews were given considerable communal autonomy, affording leaders an opportunity to control the degree to which community members engaged in non-Jewish practices. Like their ancestors who lived under Hellenistic and Roman rule, Jews to varying degrees embraced and adopted the linguistic and cultural trappings of their milieu. Their reaction to the world around them was characterized by symbiosis and synergy, on the one hand, and discord and dissent, on the other. And as in the ancient period, adaptation and appropriation created tension within Jewish communities as Jews negotiated the extent to which they partook in the wider cultural world they inhabited.

While Palestine and Babylonia were the great centers in late antiquity, the focal point shifts in the Middle Ages to the north and west. Jews migrate from Italy to the north as northeast France and the Rhineland become important settlement areas and are called Ashkenaz, after the biblical grandson of Japheth and the son of Gomer (Gen 10:3). The Ashkenazim, whose principal language became the Yiddish that developed from German, clearly differ in culture and language from the Sephardim (from the Hebrew *sepharad*, Spain), who were residents primarily of the Iberian Peninsula (known as al-Andalus in the Islamic period) up until their expulsion in the fifteenth century. They spoke Judeo-Spanish (also referred to as Espanyol, Judezmo, and Ladino), which evolved over time to include words of Turkish and Greek origin, and, although fewer and fewer people speak Ladino, it is still spoken today, mostly in Israel.[1]

For many, the Middle Ages in general evokes a sense of the sinister and brings to mind a world of fear, superstition, and religious fanaticism. With respect to Judaism, one cannot help but recall the Crusades, charges of blood libel, and the desecration of the Host. It is a period marked by persecutions, pogroms, and expulsions. Yet at the same time, the Middle Ages was also a time of lively cultural exchange and heightened creativity not only for Jews but also Christians and Muslims.[2] When we discuss the lengthy span of the Jewish Middle Ages and the diverse geographic locations under consideration, the picture is rather rich and vibrant.

The great manuscripts of traditional literature originate in the Middle Ages; prayers, feasts, and celebrations find their definitive forms here. Our oldest extant fragments of the Talmud are from the tenth century. Genres stemming from the rabbinic period, such as scriptural exegesis in midrash and *piyyut* (liturgical poetry) are further developed. New genres arise, such as the verse-by-verse Bible commentaries, Talmud commentaries, law codes, organized prayer books (sg. *siddur*; pl. *siddurim*), philosophical treatises, and mystical texts. This is the era of the great commentators, codifiers, philosophers, and poets, including Rashi and Rambam, Ramban and Radak, Ibn Ezra and Ibn Gabirol, Joseph Karo and Yehuda Halevi, to name but a few. Many of modern Judaism's texts, theological ideas, and institutions emerged and blossomed more fully in this period.

In the Middle Ages, the Bible continued to play a prominent role in the flourishing of Jewish literature such as *piyyut*, midrash, mystical texts, and, naturally, commentaries. In addition to the Bible, noncanonical literature made its way into cultural creativity. Moreover, Christian and Muslim scriptural interpretive traditions impacted the course of that creativity. For example, the Judeo-Arabic retellings of biblical and postbiblical narratives

---

1. Tracy K. Harris, *Death of a Language: The History of Judeo-Spanish* (Newark: University of Delaware Press, 1994); Harris, "The State of Ladino Today," *European Judaism* 11 (2011): 51–61.

2. For examples of the heterogeneity of Jewish life and culture throughout a wide range of geographic locations in the medieval period, see part 2 of David Biale, ed., *Culture of the Jews: A New History* (New York: Schocken, 2002), 305–671; see especially Raymond P. Scheindlin, "Merchants and Intellectuals, Rabbis and Poets: Judeo-Arabic Culture in the Golden Age of Islam," 315–86 and Ivan G. Marcus, "A Jewish-Christian Symbiosis: The Culture of Early Ashkenaz," 449–518.

concerning figures such as Abraham, Joseph, Moses, King David and his son Solomon, Queen Esther, and Hannah and her seven sons reflect the medieval crosscultural exchange of Hebrew and Arabic literary traditions.[3]

Myth and legends permeate Jewish creativity of the period; narratives of the period attach themselves to long-known material and figures but also often to new or *newly*-discovered ones, such as the Maccabees, Josephus, Ben Sira, and Judith. The poems, narratives, and legal texts of the vast and varied medieval Jewish literary tradition take up an array of subjects and concerns from living in the diaspora under unfavorable political conditions to living according to Jewish law, from embracing non-Jewish ways and customs to shunning them. Biblical stories are adapted in the face of crusades and persecutions and pressed in the service of strengthening Jewish identity vis-à-vis the world at large.

The present volume concentrates on the medieval Jewish reception and appropriation of several female biblical figures and narratives pertaining to women. Eve, Sarah, Hagar, Rebekah, Zipporah, Ruth, Esther, and Judith, a figure not present in the Hebrew canon, are treated here as well as the exceedingly popular postbiblical figure Lilith. Several essays also deal with the nameless woman of valor from Prov 31. Zion as a lamenting and yearning woman is also examined, and attention is given to the feminine voice in the Song of Songs.

This volume is far from exhaustive. We are well aware that the treatments of some topics are overshadowed by others and that some are only described cursorily, if at all. For example, while reference is made to the

---

3. There is a great deal of literature on Jewish-Muslim symbiosis of the period. See, for example, Steven M. Wasserstrom, *Between Muslim and Jew: The Problem of Symbiosis under Early Islam* (Princeton: Princeton University Press, 1995); Shari L. Lowin, *The Making of a Forefather: Abraham in Islamic and Jewish Exegetical Narratives* (Leiden: Brill, 2006); Jacob Lassner, *Demonizing the Queen of Sheba: Boundaries of Gender and Culture in Postbiblical Judaism and Medieval Islam* (Chicago: Chicago University Press, 1993); and Marc S. Bernstein, *Stories of Joseph: Narrative Migrations between Judaism and Islam* (Detroit: Wayne State University Press, 2006). On the Muslim influence on Hebrew poetry, see the classic works of Raymond P. Scheindlin, *The Gazelle: Medieval Hebrew Poems on God, Israel and the Soul* (Philadelphia: Jewish Publication Society, 1991); and Scheindlin, *Wine, Women and Death: Medieval Hebrew Poems on the Good Life* (Philadelphia: Jewish Publication Society, 1986). See also Arie Schippers, *Spanish Hebrew Poetry and the Arabic Literary Tradition* (Leiden: Brill, 1994); and more recently Peter Cole, *The Dream of the Poem: Hebrew Poetry from Muslim and Christian Spain (950-1492)* (Princeton: Princeton University Press, 2007).

growth of medieval Jewish philosophy and the flourishing of *piyyut*, we have not included a separate essay on either subject.[4] With this shortcoming in mind, our purpose is nevertheless to illustrate the ways in which biblical women appear in medieval Jewish literature and, in turn, what their presence tells us about medieval Jewish cultural creativity.

Before the individual figures and their reception are analyzed, the chapter by Elisheva Baumgarten offers an overview of the position of women in medieval Ashkenaz.[5] She uses the example of Dulcia, a learned and enterprising woman who, after her violent death in 1196, is lauded by her husband, Eleazar ben Judah of Worms, in a series of verses based on Prov 31:10–31. Baumgarten shows that medieval women, after all, played an active role in society, business life, and religious affairs. Dulcia supported her husband, was a successful businesswoman, and was active in worship and charitable activities that provided for the needy. During this period Jewish women engaged in lively exchange with non-Jewish women (and non-Jewish men) and shared with them the fate of the increasing

---

4. The literature on medieval Jewish philosophy is enormous. For a general overview, see Daniel H. Frank and Oliver Leaman, eds., *The Cambridge Companion to Jewish Philosophy* (Cambridge: Cambridge University Press, 2003); for examples of how feminist approaches have contributed to the study of medieval Jewish philosophy, see Sarah Pessin, "Loss, Presence, and Gabirol's Desire: Medieval Jewish Philosophy and the Possibility of a Feminist Ground," in *Women and Gender in Jewish Philosophy*, ed. Hava Tirosh-Samuelson (Bloomington: Indiana University Press, 2004), 27–50; and Idit Dobbs-Weinstein, "Thinking Desire in Gersonides and Spinoza," in Tirosh-Samuelson, *Women and Gender in Jewish Philosophy*, 51–77. Material from the Cairo Genizah has greatly impacted studies in *piyyut*. See Shulamit Elizur, "The Use of Biblical Verses in Hebrew Liturgical Poetry," in *Prayers That Cite Scripture*, ed. James L. Kugel (Cambridge: Harvard University Press, 2006), 83–100; Ezra Fleischer, *Sirat ha-Kodesh ha'ivrit bi-yeme ha-benayim*, 2nd ed. (Jerusalem: Magnes, 2007); Laura Lieber, *Yannai on Genesis: An Invitation to Piyyut* (Cincinnati: Hebrew Union College, 2010); Aron Mirsky, *Ha-piyyut: Hitpathuto be-Erets Yisra'el uva-golah* (Jerusalem: Magnes, 1990); Michael D. Swartz and Joseph Yahalom, eds. and trans., *Avodah: An Anthology of Ancient Poetry for Yom Kippur* (University Park: Pennsylvania State University Press, 2005). Most relevant to our volume's interest in biblical women, see Ophir Münz-Manor, "All about Sarah: Questions of Gender in Yannai's Poems on Sarah's (and Abraham's) Barrenness," *Prooftexts* 26 (2006): 344–74. Münz-Manor examines two poems by Yannai (sixth century) through the lenses of contemporary gender and literary studies.

5. For an excellent treatment of women in medieval Levant, see Eve Krakowski, *Coming of Age in Medieval Egypt: Female Adolescence, Jewish Law and Ordinary Culture* (Princeton: Princeton University Press, 2019).

changes in the areas of marriage and family life as well as in the religious sector. Yet despite their great social, economic, and religious contributions, medieval Jewish women did not occupy communal leadership positions. The essay also demonstrates that while Jews occupied space with Christians and shared similar gendered frameworks, there were distinct cultural differences between them.

The next chapter explores how the biblical heroine Esther is depicted in several medieval midrashic texts: Pirqe de Rabbi Eliezer, Yosippon, Esther Rabbah, Midrash Psalm 22, and Midrash Leqach Tov. Constanza Cordoni shows how each of these texts throws different light on the story of Esther and, in turn, highlights the different concerns of the authors and redactors. The depiction of Esther is amplified in order to attest to her Jewish identity. Through narrative expansion, Esther prays for her own well-being and for her people. In Leqach Tov, for example, she is depicted as eating Jewish food as opposed to the food of the kingdom. She is moreover presented as someone who follows her uncle's advice, but also as someone who is capable of acting of her own accord, which aligns with rabbinic halakah.

Whereas Cordoni devotes her analysis to the figure of Esther, Dagmar Börner Klein turns to the figure of Judith in medieval texts. This is especially significant because the book of Judith, preserved in the Septuagint, does not appear in the Jewish Bible (Tanakh).[6] The work nonetheless enjoyed great popularity in the Middle Ages in Jewish as well as Christian circles. The first Hebrew version was transmitted by Jacob ben Nissim ibn Shahin in the eleventh century, who lived in Kairouan, Tunisia. In his version, the heroine's identity is anonymous but in other versions, such as the Maʿase Yehudit, Judith herself finally mentions her name. Other renditions include the Megillat Yehudit, which makes Judith the daughter of Mordecai and in doing so connects the narrative with the story of Esther. Judith is described as being especially true to the Torah. In the end, the Israelites here are then victorious not only over the Greeks, but also over the Romans under Caligula. A further addition to Megillat Yehudit connects Judith with the Maccabees and introduces the motif of the endangerment of brides by means of the exercise of the *ius primae noctis*,

---

6. For a survey of the textual tradition of the story of Judith, see Deborah Levine Gera, "The Jewish Textual Traditions," in *The Sword of Judith: Judith Studies across the Disciplines*, ed. Kevin R. Brine, Elena Ciletti, and Henrike Lähnemann (Cambridge: Open Book, 2010), 23–40.

that is, the right of the sovereign (or lord of a manor) to consummate a marriage. The authority figure who demands this "first night" is, in each case, killed. As an endangered bride, Judith herself now loses the strength to kill the king; her brother, Judah, must take care of this. The endangerment and salvation of young brides also becomes an important motive for lighting the lights at Hanukkah. According to Rashbam, this miracle was effected through Judith's deeds, whereby she then assumes a central role in the story of the Maccabees.

Late midrashic narrative expansions such as these addressed seeming contradictions in scripture, filled lacunae in the plot, and answered questions raised by the text's terse style. At the same time, they afforded far more creative opportunities to amplify scriptural stories and flesh out their characters than the commentary tradition that flourished in the medieval period. The chapters in the next section attest to this difference.

Gerhard Langer opens the section with an analysis of two medieval commentaries on verses pertaining to Eve. One of the most important voices of the Jewish tradition, Rashi (Rabbi Shlomo ben Yitzhak from Troyes, 1040–1105) mediates between medieval exegesis and late antique rabbinic interpretation. His commentary on the five books of Torah is a verse-by-verse treatment of the most important passages. His terse, running commentary consistently references rabbinic midrashic and talmudic material. Langer illustrates how Rashi draws on earlier traditions selectively and, wherever possible, conveys a less hostile tone toward women. According to Rashi, the woman is not made subordinate to the man. Rather, as a consequence of sin, she will, to be sure, desire the man but will not be able to live out her sexual lust whenever she wishes. This is what is meant by the punishment in Genesis that the man shall "rule" over the woman. The second commentator discussed by Langer is the multitalented Ramban (Rabbi Moses ben Nachman, d. 1270) from Gerona, who was a master of everything from mysticism to medicine and philosophy. He also took part in a disputation as a representative of Judaism. It is unseldom the case that he takes a critical position over against Rashi. This is true also in regard to Eve. To mention just one example, Ramban develops a special variant of the notion of the androgynous human being; the sexual union has for him, of course, the goal of procreating children, but it also points to the very specific relationship between man and woman. In contrast to the union among animals, the human union is the most meaningful and designed as a permanent bond. "To be one flesh" means to return to the originally intended unity. Langer shows that, despite the differences between the two exegetes, Rashi and Ramban both highlight the significance of proper conduct.

We see this emphasis on moral conduct in the way in which medieval Jewish commentators considered other biblical stories. Even if the Jewish forefathers and foremothers did not behave in an exemplary manner, we learn from their shortcomings. As evidenced in my own examination of the treatment of Sarah and Hagar in the works of David Kimchi, Nachmanides, Gersonides, and Obadiah Sforno, there is indeed a clear shift from the tendency in classical rabbinical texts to embellish their actions and whitewash their characters. Nachmanides, for example, even fiercely criticizes Abraham, who, in his view, should have stood up for Hagar. Kimchi, on the other hand, is of the opinion that Abraham surely would have reprimanded Hagar if he only would have known how she treated Sarah, thus illustrating a lack of uniformity among the medieval commentators. For comparative purposes, the essay also discusses several medieval qur'anic commentaries on Sarah and Hagar.

Robert A. Harris's contribution not only provides a wide overview of the development of twelfth-century Jewish interpretations of the Song of Songs but also points to important aspects of the development of medieval Jewish exegesis. He argues that the move from midrash to *peshat* characterizes the twelfth-century northern French rabbinic school, a move from the authority of the classical ancient rabbinic tradition to a more contextualized scriptural interpretation that included a combination of reason and grammar-based readings. Harris, furthermore, investigates these Jewish exegetical methods and concerns against the backdrop of developments taking place among Christian interpreters. In his analysis of commentaries on the Song of Song, Harris focuses on the commentaries of Rashi and Rashi's grandson, Rashbam (Rabbi Samuel ben Meir). Whereas for Rashi the Song of Songs is a love song by King Solomon who, in the language of a widow, narrates prophetically and thereby comforts Israel in its sorrow, Rashbam reads it as a sustained dialogue between a young woman and her female companions.

Sheila Tuller Keiter explores the rabbinic, medieval, and modern Jewish receptions of the famous poem *Eshet Hayil* in Prov 31. Before doing so, she gives a background to the biblical text and the challenges scholars face with respect to its dating. She observes that by the Middle Ages, Jewish commentators generally accepted the allegorical approach. For example, Saadia Gaon first reads the poem according to its plain meaning and then treats the poem metaphorically, identifying the *'eshet hayil* as the wise man. Others such as Maimonides note that the woman represents "the healthy body in service of the human equilibrium." Keiter also points to medieval Jewish commentators such as Abraham ibn Ezra, Joseph Kimchi, and the latter's son Moses, who read the poem at face value. Keiter ends her essay with a fascinating argument for considering how *Eshet Hayil* is for the rabbis a repudiation of King Solomon's sinful ways.

Judith R. Baskin's contribution deals with the representations of biblical women in the writings of the medieval *Hasidei Ashkenaz* (German-Jewish pietists), who were connected with Rabbi Judah he-Hasid (the Pious). This group of writers was active in the twelfth and thirteenth centuries in the Rhineland and expressed their faith and convictions in the texts they interpreted. Sefer Hasidim, their most significant work, reflects their attitudes toward women, sin, and sexuality, among other topics. Sexuality is seen basically as positive, and in marriage it is even greatly welcomed. At the same time, however, the masculine lust for women, whether only in sinful thought or lived out in a real way, presents a serious problem. The *Hasidei Ashkenaz* believed that this lust was caused by women. Therefore, pious men must limit their contact with women as much as possible, even in their own families. In the second part of the essay, Baskin explicates the means by which the authors of Sefer Hasidim signify specific biblical women and female personifications. Whereas some biblical figures such as Jezebel, Delilah, and Bathsheba serve as outstanding examples of the fact that women tempt men to sin, Ruth embodies commendable feminine qualities such as virtue, modesty, friendliness, reticence, and obedience to male and divine authority. The final section of Baskin's chapter discusses the extensive exegesis of the *Eshet Hayil* poem of Prov 31:10–31 by Rabbi Eleazar ben Judah of Worms.

The volume's next section focuses on poetry and to some extent *piyyut*. It also turns to another geographical region, al-Andalus, as the Muslims called the region of the Iberian Peninsula ruled by them between 711 and 1492. The two essays in this section highlight the interplay between Arabic and Hebrew poetry, Jewish theology and biblical narratives.

Aurora Salvatierra Ossorio offers an overview of the role of biblical women in medieval Hebrew poetry of the region. The reader is afforded a glimpse into the poetic byproducts of acculturation, particularly led by Jewish elite who imbibed the best of the Arabic literary tradition. Made the object of love and wine songs, the women of the Bible were extolled not for their intellectual acumen but above all for their beauty and allure. Despite their objectification, they exercised a certain power. To illustrate how Jewish poets integrated Arabic literary styles and genres, Salvatierra Ossorio turns to the consideration of the Song of Songs.

The next chapter also examines the role biblical women play in medieval Jewish poetry of the Iberian Peninsula. Meret Gutmann-Grün explores the theme of the feminine figure of Zion in liturgical literature and pays special attention to the use of the Song of Songs in the poetry of Ibn Gabriol (died 1070) and Yehuda Halevi (died 1141). Zion is an active feminine voice; she speaks but is also the addressee. She is the beloved, the bride of God. Zion is also depicted as the mother of the children of Israel. Guttman-Grün's analysis, furthermore, draws attention to common features of both liturgical and secular songs with respect to love motifs and the yearning for liberation from Exile.

The next section is devoted to kabbalah, Jewish mysticism. We begin with Rachel Elior's essay on the development and significance of the Shekhinah, the feminine dimension of God, over the centuries. She sketches how the notion of the Shekhinah in the rabbinic period is transformed in medieval works of the kabbalists, who were active between the end of the thirteenth century up until the end of the fifteenth century in southern France and northern Spain. In works such as the Sefer Habahir and the Zohar, the Shekhinah is depicted in relationship to God instead of just in relationship to the holy city and to the people of Israel. The Shekhinah is moreover placed in the world of the *sefirot*. Toward the end of her essay, Elior ventures a view of eastern European Hasidism and its founder, Israel Baal Shem Tov (Besht for short). In Hasidism, the hidden divine world of mysticism was carried into the wider community, and its influence is palpable today.

Felicia Waldman also underscores the significance of the Shekhinah in kabbalah, which transformed the rabbinic notion of God's presence in the world into the queenly personification of the Godhead. Like Elior, she demonstrates the different ways the Shekhinah is depicted, not least of which is the physical embodiment of the exile of the Jewish people. In the second half of her essay, Waldman devotes herself to one of the most colorful female figures in the Jewish tradition, Lilith, who appears in mystical texts. Her depiction ranges from a man-threatening and children-menacing female demon with ancient oriental roots to Adam's first wife to the sexual playmate of God. Lilith was rediscovered in contemporary feminist works and portrayed as a self-assured woman who resists patriarchal rule.

Yuval Katz-Wilfing focuses on the role Ruth plays in the Zohar, traditionally attributed to Rabbi Shimon bar Yohai, who lived in the second century CE, but according to the scholarly consensus it is a product of medieval Europe. Medieval Jewish mystics build on the rabbinic notion of Ruth as an exemplar of conversion and highlight the role she plays in the future redemption of God's people. The Zohar, as Katz-Wilfing demonstrates, gives voice to the esoteric dimensions of Ruth's conversion and in turn to the conversion process.

Katrin Kogman-Appel concludes this selection of essays with her offering on feminine protagonists in the book art of the Jewish Middle Ages and, in a certain sense, returns to the beginning of the volume and takes up the thread there, namely, the distribution of roles described by Elisheva Baumgarten and the intensive confrontation with Christianity, which also becomes perceptible in book art. Kogman-Appel concerns herself with two biblical characters, Rebekah the wife of Isaac and Zipporah the wife of Moses. Kogman-Appel's comparative analysis shows convincingly that the Ashkenazic and Sephardic representations of both women clearly differ from each other. In Sephardic representations, both women appear in active roles and determine decisively the fate of their people. The models for many of these regional representations are the images of the Virgin Mary, whose significance in the Christian world increases in this period. Just as Mary contributes decisively to the salvation of all Christians, Rebekah and Zipporah now also become central figures in Jewish salvation history in the Iberian haggadah cycles. The Ashkenazic examples, on the other hand, are not as culturally embedded and offer us less insight into the lives of medieval Jews. Rather, they represent values such as motherhood, education, piety, and, not least of all, the martyr's death in the face of the real experience of persecution and the danger of forced baptism. Thus, they become symbols for these central values and also models for religious action.

The essays in this volume attest to the various ways biblical literature is interwoven into the fabric of medieval Jewish cultural and religious production. In particular, we get a sense of how biblical women were depicted, and in turn we glimpse attitudes toward real and imagined women, attitudes that reflect regard for women and maintain traditional roles that privilege patriarchy yet at the same time subvert it. It is striking that the authors of our primary sources are all male and no doubt played a dominant role in Jewish life of the period. We would, however, be remiss to ignore that these images of women present us with a more complicated understanding of their role in medieval Jewish society and culture.

Cultural Setting

Gender and Daily Life in the Jewish Communities of Medieval Europe

Elisheva Baumgarten

In a poem written in memory of his wife, Dulcia (d. 1196), who was murdered together with their two daughters during an attack on their house, Eleazar ben Judah of Worms (d. 1232), a well-known author and leader of the German-Jewish community, describes the many deeds that made Dulcia a pious, God-fearing woman as well as an ideal wife and mother. Eleazar ben Judah modeled his eulogy on the last chapter of Proverbs (Prov 31:10–31), starting each line with a quote from Proverbs and then elaborating on Dulcia's own life. He begins:

> *Who can find a woman of valor* (Prov 31:10) like my pious wife, Mistress Dulcia?
> A woman of valor, her husband's crown, a daughter of benefactors
> *A God-fearing woman* (v. 30), renowned for her good deeds,
> *Her husband trusted her implicitly* (v. 11), she fed and clothed him in dignity,
> So he could sit among the elders of the land, and provide Torah study and good deeds.[1]

This is a slightly revised version of "Gender and Daily Life in Jewish Communities," in *The Oxford Handbook of Women and Gender in Medieval Europe*, ed. Judith Bennett and Ruth Mazo Karras (Oxford: Oxford University Press, 2013), 213–28. This essay has received funding from the European Research Council (ERC) under the European Union's Horizon 2020 research and innovation program under grant agreement No 681507, Beyond the Elite: Jewish Daily Life in Medieval Europe.

1. Two translations are available: Ivan G. Marcus, "Mothers, Martyrs and Moneymakers: Some Jewish Women in Medieval Europe," *Conservative Judaism* 38 (1986): 34–45; and Judith R. Baskin, "Dolce of Worms: The Lives and Deaths of an Exemplary Medieval Jewish Woman and Her Daughters," in *Judaism in Practice: From the*

Only a few dozen lines long, the account of Dulcia's deeds represents the fullest description of a medieval Jewish woman's life that has survived in any known source to date and is one of the only texts that describes a specific woman. In many ways it is representative of the Hebrew sources that have reached us from the Middle Ages. It was written by a man, and indeed we have no text written by a Jewish woman from the medieval period. It is most concerned with different aspects of religious observance, the paramount topic for many of the Hebrew texts preserved from this period. It connects medieval life to the Bible—a common practice among medieval Jews who saw themselves living in direct connection to biblical events.[2] And, of course, it was written according to the literary conventions of its time.

This essay builds from the details of Dulcia's life as described posthumously by her husband. While Dulcia was an atypical, elite Jewish woman, like typical Jewish women from her time period Dulcia was active in her community and local culture. Like other medieval Jewish women, Dulcia is presented first and foremost as a daughter, mother, and wife. These were the expected roles of every Jewish woman, and while there were certainly women who did not marry, these seem to have been few and there are almost no records of them. Dulcia was an active businesswoman and moneylender. Like many of her Jewish neighbors, she was also an involved member of her community. Finally, Dulcia died as the result of a Christian attack, although in this case the attack did not stem from anti-Jewish motivations per se; rather, her killers were two criminals in search of money. In fact, the city officials in Worms caught one of the criminals and executed him shortly after the event. However, the relationship between medieval Jews and Christians that is reflected in her murder illustrates the complexities of Jewish life in Christian Europe.[3]

Middle Ages through the Early Modern Period, ed. Lawrence Fine (Princeton: Princeton University Press, 2001), 436–37. I have combined both these translations with slight adjustments throughout the essay, relying primarily on Marcus's translation.

2. See my recent *Biblical Women and Jewish Daily Practice in the Middle Ages* (Philadelphia: University of Pennsylvania Press, 2022).

3. This has been the topic of much recent research. For some conceptualizations of this relationship, see: Kenneth Stow, *Alienated Minority: The Jews of Medieval Latin Europe* (Cambridge: Harvard University Press, 1992); Ivan Marcus, *Rituals of Childhood: Jewish Acculturation in Medieval Europe* (New Haven: Yale University Press, 1996); Israel J. Yuval, *Two Nations in Your Womb: Perceptions of Jews and Christians in Late Antiquity and the Middle Ages* (Berkeley: University of Califor-

The living conditions and cultural circumstances in which Dulcia lived are representative of a way of life that characterized Ashkenazic Jews (that is, Jews in medieval Germany and northern France) during the twelfth and thirteenth centuries when these communities were at their zenith. The circumstances of Jews in the Ashkenaz changed drastically at the end of the thirteenth and the early fourteenth centuries when many Jewish communities experienced severe attacks (in Germany, the Rindfleisch events of 1298) or expulsion (England 1290; France 1306; and finally Germany 1394, during the Black Death). Thereafter, Jews began to move to Poland and northern Italy in large numbers, taking their customs and way of life eastward.

In following Dulcia and her Jewish counterparts in twelfth- and thirteenth-century Ashkenaz, this essay sees Jewish communities as integrated into their Christian surroundings. Some aspects of Jewish life—activities within the synagogue, religious education, and marriage arrangements—were by definition only between Jews, but medieval Jewish men and women lived in more complex and integrated surroundings. Jews lived in close quarters with Christians and had many business dealings with them. Not only was space shared by Jews and Christians, but time was as well. The Jews lived within the rhythms of medieval cities, knowing the pattern of Christian festivities and often unwillingly adapting themselves to Christian time.[4] As part of the need to accommodate Christian circumstances, Jewish authorities even amended traditional restrictions regarding trade with non-Jews during non-Jewish holidays. Furthermore, Jews and Christians shared basic markets of materials and produce. They lived in the same climate, had access to the same foods, built their houses and made their clothes and their books out of the same materials.

Despite these shared aspects of time, space, and material culture—facets that historians have often overlooked or down played until recently—Jewish daily life was still distinct. Jews entered Christian space; Jews dealt and even dwelt with Christians; Jews and Christians shared ovens and wells. But these myriad interactions were accompa-

---

nia Press, 2006); Jonathan Elukin, *Living Together, Living Apart: Rethinking Jewish-Christian Relations in the Middle Ages* (Princeton: Princeton University Press, 2007); Robert Chazan, *Reassessing Jewish Life in Medieval Europe* (New York: Cambridge University Press, 2010).

4. Joanne M. Pierce, "Holy Week and Easter in the Middle Ages," in *Passover and Easter: Origin and History to Modern Times*, ed. Paul Bradshaw and Lawrence Hoffman (Notre Dame: University of Notre Dame Press, 1999), 161–85.

nied by other practices that emphasized the distinction between the two religious groups.

1. Family and Households

> *She is like the merchant ships* (Prov 31:14), she feeds her husband (so he can) study Torah,
> *Daughters saw her* (v. 29) and declared her happy, *her wares were so fine* (v. 18),
> *She gives food to her household* (v. 15) and bread to the boys ...
> *She extends a hand to the poor* (v. 20),
> Feeding her boys,[5] daughters, and husband.

Dulcia's life as a mother and wife was fairly typical. She was the mother of three children, aged fifteen, twelve, and six at the time of her death; most scholars suggest that medieval Jewish families had between two and four living children.[6] Dulcia most probably was in her mid-thirties when she was killed, which would indicate that she, like most Jewish women, had her first child in her late teens shortly after her marriage. As was common, the names in her family fit a known pattern by which Jewish women had names in local vernaculars (in Dulcia's case, the name is Italian, perhaps indicating her family's origin), whereas men had names that were more ethnic.[7] The house in which Dulcia lived principally sheltered her nuclear family but was also shared by some of her husband's students. Based on responsa literature, one of the few sources for details of living patterns, it seems that most couples, like Dulcia and Eleazar, lived independent of their parents, certainly after a few years of support. At times a Jewish couple settled next door to their parents, but each nuclear unit maintained an independent household.[8]

---

5. The plural "boys" indicates her husband's students. Dulcia herself had only one son.

6. Kenneth R. Stow, "The Jewish Family in the Rhineland: Form and Function," *American Historical Review* 92 (1987): 1085–110; Abraham Grossman, *The Early Sages of Ashkenaz: Their Lives, Leadership, and Works* [Hebrew] (Jerusalem: Magnes, 2001), 8 n. 32, 10.

7. Dulcia's daughters' names were Bellette and Hannah. See Baskin, "Dolce of Worms." Goitein shows the same pattern in Muslim Lands, see Shlomo Dov Goitein, *A Mediterranean Society: The Jewish Communities of the Arab World as Portrayed in the Documents of the Cairo Geniza* (Berkeley: University of California Press, 1983), 3:2–14.

8. Irving Agus has collected many of the tenth- and eleventh-century responsa

Medieval Jews lived in communities made up of individual families that were often related to each other. In most cases these communities obtained permission from local or regional authorities to dwell and work within cities. They were also often allowed the privilege of self-government as well as some economic autonomy. For the most part, northern European Jews lived within cities, although single families often lived in rural areas. Most larger urban centers had Jewish communities, and these communities grew throughout the twelfth and thirteenth centuries.[9]

Jews, like other ethnic, social, and occupational groups in medieval cities, tended to live in clusters. Since there were no ghettos before the sixteenth century, however, their neighborhoods were not exclusively Jewish. Jews lived in close proximity to their Christian neighbors, often within a single courtyard. Moreover, as different maps of medieval urban centers have demonstrated, the Jewish quarter was usually situated in the center of the city, close to the cathedral and other important civic structures.[10] Few recent studies have investigated the interior of Jewish homes, but physical conditions were likely similar to those of their Christian neighbors.

Gender divisions of labor within the Jewish homes were also similar to those among Christians. Like Christian women, Jewish women were, in theory, responsible for the care of their young children. Jewish mothers were first separated from their sons when they began their formal

---

and translated them into English. Within the section on the family there are many examples of living patterns, see *Urban Civilization in Pre-Crusade Europe*, 2 vols. (New York: Yeshiva University Press, 1965), 2:554–729.

9. For the privileges and their recipients, see Jonathan Ray, "The Jew in the Text: What Christian Charters Tell Us about Medieval Jewish Society," *Medieval Encounters* 16 (2010): 246–48. For rural communities, Michael Toch, "Jewish Peasants in the Middle Ages? Agriculture and Jewish Land Ownership in Eighth-Twelfth Centuries" [Hebrew], *Zion* 75 (2010): 291–312.

10. For example, see Matthias Schmandt, "Cologne, Jewish Centre on the Lower Rhine," 367–77; Pam Manix, "Oxford: Mapping the Medieval Jewry," 405–20; Werner Transier, "Speyer: The Jewish Community in the Middle Ages," 435–47; Gerald Bonnen, "Worms: The Jews between the City, the Bishop and the Crown," 449–57; all of which appear in Christoph Cluse, ed., *The Jews of Europe in the Middle Ages (Tenth to Fifteenth Centuries): Proceedings of the International Symposium Held at Speyer, 20–25 October 2002* (Turnhout: Brepols, 2004). For Provence, see Danièle Iancu-Agou, *Provincia judaica. Dictionnaire des géographie historique des Juifs en Provence médiévale* (Leuven: Peeters, 2010). Many of the descriptions of the cities are accompanied by maps that show the centrality of the *rue de juiverie* (Street of the Jews) or *Judenviertel* (Jewish quarter) and its proximity to central urban sites.

schooling, either at home with a tutor or in a local school often situated in the synagogue. Men were considered responsible for their sons' education and for making sure their sons had professions. Girls received their education from tutors within the home or from their mothers and other female relatives.[11] It was not considered fitting for fathers to be involved in childcare, and this belief was so strong that new widowers with young children could remarry during the seven-day mourning period after the death of their wives so that the new wife could immediately begin to care for their young ones.

Yet despite medieval texts that upheld ancient traditions about the division of labor, daily life did not conform in many cases to these theoretical ideals. Women were often said to encourage their children to study, and in fact, moral treatises praised women for ensuring that their sons and husbands studied the Torah. Fathers are reported not only as caring for their young children but as being responsible for their behavior, despite the clear instructions that these children should be in their mother's care. Cooking tasks and food preparation seem to have been considered as both men's and women's responsibilities, although women were especially conversant in laws pertaining to the preparation of food.[12] This more diversified division of domestic duties remained constant for many centuries, even as other aspects of Jewish families and communities changed.

2. Medieval Jewish Marriage: Practices and Reforms

Marriage created and solidified connections between families and between communities. The first lines of the poem about Dulcia state that she was the "daughter of benefactors," and she might have been born into an Ash-

---

11. Ephraim Kanarfogel describes the education process in *Jewish Education and Society in the High Middle Ages* (Detroit: Wayne State University Press, 1992). See also Marcus, *Rituals of Childhood*; Elisheva Baumgarten, *Mothers and Children: Jewish Family Life in Medieval Europe* (Princeton: Princeton University Press, 2004), 200 n. 45.

12. Judith Baskin, "Jewish Traditions about Women and Gender Roles: From Rabbinic Teachings to Medieval Practice," in *The Oxford Handbook of Women and Gender in Medieval Europe*, ed. Judith Bennett and Ruth Mazo Karras (Oxford: Oxford University Press, 2013), 38; Baumgarten, *Mothers and Children*, 154–65. For food, see Rabbi Jacob Mulin, *Shut Maharil (Responsa of Rabbi Yaacov Molin-Maharil)*, ed. Yitzchok Satz (Jerusalem: Machon Yerushlayim, 1979), 314–15, no. 199.

kenazic family of Italian origin; such families were often considered the most respectable in Jewish communities. Her marriage to a prominent rabbi reinforced, as did other marriages, ties between scholarship and ancestry. Dulcia and her husband Eleazar probably were also typical of most couples in that they married in their mid-teens. This age of marriage remained fairly constant until the early modern period.[13]

In both law and practice, Jewish marriage and divorce underwent a substantial revolution during the central Middle Ages, much as it did within Christian society, where marriage became universally recognized as a Christian sacrament. While these Jewish alterations were not quite as dramatic as Christian ones, which redefined the sacramental nature of marriage and the church's control over it, they were nevertheless still significant.

To begin with, the process of getting married changed, with the ceremony no longer split between engagement (*kiddushin* or *erusin*) and marriage (*nissuin*). Solomon son of Isaac, known by the acronym Rashi (d. 1105), references the financial wisdom of holding the two events together: one celebration saved parents a significant amount of money. However, there was an additional, even more substantial benefit to the new practice. Once a woman became engaged, even if she was a minor, she would need a formal divorce if the union was not completed with full-fledged marriage. Although some Jews continued to keep two separate rituals separated by months or even years up until the late thirteenth century, this system was slowly replaced by an independent engagement ritual that was socially binding but did not require divorce if breached. This period also saw the rise of a new profession as well, that of the matchmaker.[14]

Moreover, the combined betrothal and marriage ritual itself changed. Elliott Horowitz and Esther Cohen have suggested that, much like the sanctification of Christian marriage, Jewish marriage underwent a sanctification of sorts in the central Middle Ages. One of the seven traditional wedding blessings changed and the version accepted in northern Europe stated: "Blessed art thou ... Who sanctifies Israel by means of marriage and betrothal [*huppah* and *kiddushin*]." Also, instead of the biblical stipula-

---

13. Jacob Katz, "Marriage and Sexual Life among the Jews at the Close of the Middle Ages" [Hebrew], *Zion* 10 (1945): 21–54.
14. Avraham Grossman outlines the process of marriage in *Pious and Rebellious. Jewish Women in Medieval Europe* (Waltham, MA: Brandeis University Press, 2004), 49–67.

tion that two witnesses could declare the marriage, it became increasingly common for a marriage to be completed in the presence of a rabbi and a quorum (*minyan*) from the community.[15]

Process and ritual mattered a great deal, but the most important changes in marriage related to the contract itself. Most famous are the statutes attributed to Gershom ben Judah of Mainz (ca. 960–1028) known as "Light of the Exile," which determined that women could not be divorced against their will and that a man could not have two wives at once. Although scholars have devoted much of their attention to the latter statute relating to bigamy, the former also had formidable consequences as the requirement of women to consent to divorce was a significant change from accepted Jewish law; until this time men had been allowed to divorce their wives regardless of the women's desires.[16]

According to traditional Jewish law, a man could divorce his wife without her consent, whereas Jewish women could only demand divorce under a small number of instances such as their husbands' impotence or conversion to another religion. Women required their husbands' consent to the divorce. Gershom ben Judah's statute was revolutionary in that it limited men's ability to divorce their wives, requiring a formal writ of divorce given with the approval of a court and witnesses, a process that became more and more formalized throughout the Middle Ages. By the thirteenth century, divorce writs were often granted only if the rabbinic courts of three different jurisdictions agreed. As one fifteenth-century rabbi commented, these strict demands prevented the swiftness with which some men initiated divorce, increased the cost of divorce, and reduced its appeal. Legal authorities also made it harder for women to initiate divorces, especially women who were defined as "rebellious wives" because they refused to have conjugal relations with their husbands. In these cases, medieval rabbis changed a prac-

---

15. Esther Cohen and Elliott Horowitz, "In Search of the Sacred: Jews, Christians and Rituals of Marriage in the Later Middle Ages," *Journal of Medieval and Renaissance Studies* 20 (1990): 225–50. The biblical stipulation continued to hold, although some communities repeated the nuptial blessing; see Zeev W. Falk, *Jewish Matrimonial Law in the Middle Ages* (Oxford: Oxford University Press, 1966), 58–64.

16. Susan Mosher Stuard, "Brideprice, Dowry, and Other Marital Assigns," in *The Oxford Handbook of Women and Gender in Medieval Europe*, ed. Judith Bennett and Ruth Karras (Oxford: Oxford University Press, 2013), 148–62; Baskin, "Jewish Traditions"; Grossman, *Pious and Rebellious*, 68–101.

tice that had been accepted since the early Middle Ages. According to earlier tradition, these "rebellious" women were granted divorces and provided with money from the marriage contract (*ketubbah*). Thirteenth-century rabbis in northern Europe demanded that such women give up their *ketubbah* money, leaving these women in financial positions that were more difficult. As a result, they refused their husbands conjugal relations in order to pressure them to give them a divorce and thus maintain their financial rights.[17]

These restrictions in divorce developed at different paces from the tenth to the fifteenth centuries, first limiting men's abilities to divorce their wives, and only shifting in the thirteenth and fourteenth centuries toward diminishing women's ability to instigate divorce. Some rabbis suggested that wives had become more eager to divorce than before. Whether or not wives were in fact more rebellious, they were certainly less able to divorce their husbands after 1250 than before. Viewed in the context of Christian prohibition of divorce and growing emphasis on the sanctity of marriage, these changes suggest an ongoing "conversation" between Jews and Christians over the merits of marriage and the undesirability of its dissolution.

The practice of levirate marriage also changed during the central Middle Ages. According to biblical law, if a man died without offspring, his widow was either to marry his brother or reject him through the rite of *halizah* (whereby the widow removed her shoe, threw it at the brother-in-law, spat at him, and thereby freed them both from the obligation; Deut 25:5–10). Levirate marriage was practiced in medieval Ashkenaz, although many community leaders openly stated that *halizah* was to be preferred and suggested even in the eleventh century that a widow should not be forced to marry her brother-in-law. One twelfth-century authority, Rabbenu Tam (Jacob ben Meir, 1100–1171), even suggested that the practice of levirate marriage should be forbidden. Nevertheless, some brothers-in-law still refused to release widows from levirate marriage or demanded money in return for release, sometimes dragging out the cases for years.[18]

---

17. Grossman, *Pious and Rebellious*, 240–44; Falk, *Jewish Matrimonial Law*, 13–34; Jacob Molin, *Sefer Maharil: Minhagim*, ed. Shlomo Spitzer (Jerusalem: Machon Yerushalayim, 1989), 493.

18. Grossman, *Pious and Rebellious*, 90–101, summarizes the conclusions of Jacob Katz, "Yibbum veHalizah baTekufah haBetar Talmudit," *Tarbiz* 51 (1981): 59–106.

3. Economics of Marriage, Divorce, and Inheritance

The economics of family life also changed during the Middle Ages. Financial arrangements played a major role in marriage negotiations and the creation of new households. In the tenth and eleventh centuries, the bride's family usually provided a dowry at the time of marriage; the contribution of the groom's family to the household would come later when he inherited a share of family wealth from his father. In this way the business of marriage was seen as a mutual arrangement to which each side of the family contributed at different points in the couple's life. A woman without a dowry was unlikely to find a partner, and the higher her dowry was, the better the match she could make. This practice was not unique to medieval Jews, and at least the initial dowry payment mirrored similar practices among Christians. By the later Middle Ages, men's families no longer provided funds later in the marriage, but instead at its outset. With both parents contributing to a new household, Jews were better able to support their children in what had become, due to anti-Jewish restrictions, a more difficult economic climate.

In addition, the ownership of a woman's dowry, if she died soon after her wedding without any heirs, became a contested matter during the twelfth century. Did the groom's family inherit the money despite the failure to create a child—that is, a biological bond between the families? During the twelfth century, Rabbenu Tam instituted a practice according to which families whose daughters died shortly after marriage without offspring were entitled to the return of the dowry. Increasingly during the twelfth and thirteenth centuries, both families had the right to demand their money back if one of the partners died without offspring.

The financial situation of divorced women was perilous, especially those who divorced with young children. They were entitled to the sum stated in their wedding contract (*ketubbah*), a sum that was often set quite high but not fully redeemed in practice. They were also entitled to their dowries, but they often did not receive these monies since they had been the husband's responsibility throughout the marriage, and he often claimed the money had been lost. Divorced mothers did receive alimony, but they also had to support their children, until the age of six for sons and until marriage for daughters. As a result, many divorced women were left with little money, and in most cases they were also homeless as one of the immediate effects of divorce was their departure from the shared home. If they were young, they often became burdens on their parents. Remarriage was an option, especially because families were anxious that divorced daughters might seek sexual satisfaction outside of marriage. At the same time, there was some concern that remarried mothers might neglect the children from their earlier marriages. As a result, divorced mothers could not, in theory, remarry until their youngest child was more than two years old.[19]

In contrast to divorced women, widows fared better economically. Unlike biblical and late antique practices that offered widows a home and subsistence but left the bulk of their husbands' estate to their children, medieval widows were first in the line of inheritance and became the executors of their husbands' estates, whether large or small. In fact, many husbands explicitly designated their widows as their chief heirs in their wills, and the favored treatment of widows sometimes caused discontent, especially among stepchildren.[20]

4. Everyday Economic Activities

> Her labor provides him with books, her very name means "pleasant."...
> *See how her hands held the distaff* (Prov 31:19) to spin cords for (binding) books,
> Zealous in everything, she spun (cords) for (sewing) tefillin (phylacteries) and megillot (scrolls), gut for (stitching together) Torah scrolls.

Before she was murdered by intruders in her home, Dulcia was a prominent businesswoman, lending money and manufacturing some forty Torah scrolls. Eleazar ben Judah also states that Dulcia supported him from money she lent, something that seems to have been quite unusual in that he refrained from working and owed his upkeep to his wife. Most Jewish men worked at the same time that they were learning and teaching Torah. Yet it was not rare for Jewish women to be involved in trade, moneylending, and other businesses. Jewish women might even have specialized in working with Christian women. William Chester Jordan has demonstrated that Jewish women in Picardy often did separate business

---

19. Israel J. Yuval, "Monetary Arrangements and Marriage in Medieval Ashkenaz" [Hebrew], in *Religion and Economy: Connections and Interactions*, ed. Menahem Ben-Sasson (Jerusalem: Merkaz Shazar, 1995), 191–208; Baumgarten, *Mothers and Children*, 144–53.

20. Grossman, *Pious and Rebellious*. It should be noted that although Grossman has outlined many of these topics, research on them is still quite rudimentary, and I expect these conclusions to be modified and nuanced in future studies.

with Christian women, sometimes even forming partnerships with them.[21] Women's business was modest, their transactions usually amounting to only one-third the value of those of men.

Women from wealthy families were often given property, money, or jewelry as part of their dowries, and in some cases their wedding contracts stipulated that they possessed these goods absolutely with no oversight from their husbands. Some women ran businesses independent from their husbands, often with their brothers or other kin. However, most couples ran their family enterprises, however small or large, together. There is evidence that Jewish women, like men, often traveled for business, met with non-Jews, and actively pursued retribution in court for business deals gone awry.

Scholars have suggested three central explanations for the expanded role of women in the medieval Jewish economy. First, because northern European Jewish communities were relatively new (founded during the tenth century) and small, women took a more active role than that which has been attributed to them in other regions in late antiquity. Second, perhaps Jewish women expanded their economic activities in emulation of their Christian neighbors; it was common in medieval towns to find women, Christian or Jewish, in workshops, and markets. Third, Jewish women have been noted as being especially active in families whose husbands traveled and left family businesses under the care of their wives. This was, once again, not so different from Christian women. While travel to distant Muslim lands all but ceased after the attacks on Jewish communities that accompanied the First Crusade in 1096, intra-European travel was still a constant in medieval life, and both women and men traveled regularly. Although there are fewer texts that discuss women who traveled than those that discuss men's travels, the number of women who are referred to as traveling is surprisingly high.

As was true among Christians, the economic activities of women generated some negative comment. In the streets and shops of medieval towns and cities, Jewish women actively took part in local businesses, whether as widows, individuals, or partners with their husbands. But some rabbis worried about women's abilities to dispense large amounts of money and

---

21. William C. Jordan, *Women and Credit in Pre-Industrial and Developing Society* (Philadelphia: University of Pennsylvania Press, 1993); Martha Keil, "Public Roles of Jewish Women in Fourteenth and Fifteenth-Century Ashkenaz: Business, Community and Ritual," in Cluse, *Jews of Europe*, 317–30; Grossman, *Pious and Rebellious*, 117–21.

assume financial responsibilities. Such practices deviated from talmudic law and in fact blatantly contradicted it. While some rabbis and legal authorities attempted to limit women's involvement in economic matters, it seems that in practice women remained active partners in business, especially joint family ventures, well into the early modern period.[22]

5. Religious Practice

She looked for white wool (Prov 31:13a) with which to make tzitzit, *she spun*
with enthusiasm (v. 13b)
She foresees how to do many commandments, all who see her praise her
...
She freely did the will of her Creator, day and night.
Her lamp will not go out at night (v. 18)—she makes wicks.
For the synagogue and schools she says Psalms.
She sings hymns and prayers, she recites petitions ...
In all the towns, she taught women (so they can chant) songs.
She knows the order of the morning and evening prayers,
And she comes early to synagogue, stays late.
She stands throughout Yom Kippur, sings and prepares the candles.
She honors the Sabbaths and Holidays as well as Torah scholars.

At least a third of the poem about Dulcia is devoted to her religious activities. Her husband emphasizes her communal work such as feeding the poor, clothing brides, and preparing the dead for burial as well as her personal devotion and worship. He also notes her status within the community as a leader—she taught women in her community and in other cities how to pray and led the women in prayer. As the wife of a leader within a community that constantly searched for ways to increasingly sanctify their lives, Dulcia's religious activities were unusually extensive.[23]

---

22. Alyssa Gray, "Married Women and *Tsedaqah* in Medieval Jewish Law: Gender and the Discourse of Legal Obligation," *Jewish Law Association Studies* 17 (2007): 168–212; Debra Kaplan, "'Because Our Wives Trade and Do Business with Our Goods': Gender, Work, and Jewish-Christian Relations," in *New Perspectives on Jewish-Christian Relations*, ed. Elisheva Carlebach and Jacob J. Schachter (Leiden: Brill, 2011), 241–64; Elisheva Baumgarten, "Charitable Like Abigail: The History of an Epitaph," *JQR* 105 (2015): 312–39.

23. For the history of the Ashkenazic Pietists, see Ivan G. Marcus, *Piety and Society: The Jewish Pietists of Medieval Germany* (Leiden: Brill, 1981). Eleazar has been

Yet most of the deeds attributed to her were also recorded in connection with other women and in fact were characteristic of pious men who were not very learned.

Like Dulcia, who is said to have gone to the synagogue early and remained there until late, most medieval women attended synagogue regularly, not only on Sabbath but also on weekdays. Indeed, some sources suggest that women, like men, attended synagogue twice a day, and there are reports of servants and Christian business acquaintances coming to the synagogue to summon them for business matters. Archaeological evidence indicates that central medieval synagogues, some of which were destroyed during the First Crusade, did not have a separate women's section; rather women seem to have prayed within the main sanctuary in a part allocated for them. After the First Crusade, some synagogues were rebuilt with a separate room attached to the main sanctuary by small windows. A number of tombstones throughout the medieval period describe women who, like Dulcia, were leaders of women's prayers. These female prayer-leaders, like those who instructed other women on ritual activities, were often the daughters or relatives of male cantors.[24]

In the thirteenth century, however, women's synagogue attendance began to change, as it became more common for menstruating women to avoid synagogues. While eleventh- and twelfth-century sources note that only especially pious women might choose not to attend the synagogue during menstruation, this custom slowly became expected of all women. In some cases, some women prayed outside the synagogue, while others simply did not go to the synagogue at all.[25]

---

identified as a member of this group. For a different approach to this group and to women in this group, see Elisheva Baumgarten, "Who Was a Hasid or Hasidah in Medieval Ashkenaz: Reassessing the Social Implications of a Term," *Jewish History* 34 (2021): 125–54.

24. For women's synagogues, an issue that needs yet to be explored, see Richard Krautheimer, *Mittelalterliche Synagogen* (Berlin: Frankfurter Verlags-Anstalt, 1927), 110–12; Monika Porsche, "Speyer: The Medieval Synagogue," in Cluse, *Jews of Europe*, 428–29. Dulcia herself was such a prayer leader. Other female prayer leaders appeared on tombstones; see Grossman, *Pious and Rebellious*, 181.

25. Elisheva Baumgarten, "'And They Do Nicely': A Reappraisal of Menstruating Women's Refusal to Enter the Sanctuary in Medieval Ashkenaz" [Hebrew], in *Ta Shma: Essays in Memory of Israel M. Ta Shma*, ed. Rami Reiner et al. (Alon Shvut: Tevunot, 2011), 85–104; Moshe Rosman, *How Jewish Is Jewish History?* (Portland: Littman Library of Jewish Civilization, 2007), 131–54.

The synagogue and its vicinity hosted many other community and personal events, such as circumcision rituals, marriage ceremonies, and court proceedings. Marriage rituals took place in the synagogue courtyard and circumcisions inside the sanctuary. Moreover, in many Ashkenazic communities during the Middle Ages the sanctuary of the synagogue became a court of sorts, especially for the resolution of difficult or longstanding grievances. A community member, male or female, could interrupt prayers to demand that a grievance be addressed. Such interruptions suggest that women were formidable and confident actors in the public sphere.[26] Many medieval women also publicly manifested their personal piety. While Torah study was first and foremost the reserve of men, medieval Jewish women are noted in the sources as praying, giving charity, and fasting, much like many of the men did. Fasting was a common practice among medieval Jews for communal events as well as for personal penance or petitions. Many of these pious acts were also displayed in the synagogue.

Dulcia and women like her also instructed other women on matters of religious practice. These female leaders were usually mentioned as leading by example in areas that were part of female expertise, such as candle-lighting on the Sabbath or ritual purity practices related to menstruation. Women were also referred to as authorities on the rules of keeping kosher and as expert makers of ritual garments. Those mentioned by name are in almost all cases the sisters, wives, and daughters of rabbinic authorities. Some of them are said to have received their instructions from their male relatives. For example, Bellette, the sister of Isaac ben Menahem of LeMans (eleventh century), was said to have instructed the women in her community on how to prepare for immersing in the ritual bath. In Bellette's case, the author emphasized that she instructed the women of the community in her brother's name.[27] One can only wonder what other behaviors were recommended by these women who clearly had a position of authority, with or without their male relatives' consent.

In relation to holidays and daily activities, medieval Jewish women sometimes followed commandments that had been defined in ancient

---

26. Avraham Grossman, "The Origins and Essence of the Custom of 'Stopping the Service'" [Hebrew], *Milet* 1 (1983): 199–221.

27. Many of these women were already noted by Abraham Berliner, *Jewish Life in Germany in the Middle Ages* [Hebrew] (Warsaw: Ahiassaf, 1900), 8–9, which was a translation of his *Aus dem inneren Leben der deutschen Juden im Mittelalter* (Berlin: Benzian, 1871).

sources as the obligation of men alone. These commandments, known as "positive time-bound commandments," included hearing the *shofar* (horn) blown on Rosh Hashanah and participating in some of the rituals of Sukkoth and Passover. They also included wearing *tefillin* (phylacteries) and *tzitzit* (fringes attached to clothing).[28] The women who took these obligations upon themselves usually belonged to elite families, in which the men were also performing these commandments; this was, in other words, a religious practice that was governed not only by gender but also by class. In the eleventh and twelfth centuries, women notably insisted on their right to shoulder these religious obligations, but the practice had slowly eroded by the end of the thirteenth century and the early fourteenth century. By then, rabbinic leaders had extended many religious observance practices beyond the rabbinic elite and turned commandments such as phylacteries into an obligation practiced by all adult men and not just by a select few. Alongside these changes in male ritual observances grew a steady resistance to female participation. This growing restriction on female ritual practice was yet another area in which the gender relations within the Jewish communities seem to have mirrored Christian communities.[29]

Finally, despite the many religious activities of medieval women, it is necessary to note that women, no matter how central, pious, or important, were not represented formally in any community institutions. They were not members of the community courts, synagogue committees, charity collectors or the leaders (*parnasim*) of the community. These were all men, as were the legal authorities (often, in fact, the same men), and they saw women as subservient, in religious practices as in all matters.

6. Jews and Christians: Shared Spaces and Separate Realms

As noted at the outset of this essay, Jews conducted their lives separately within their own community institutions and frameworks as well as in conjunction with their neighbors. Not only did Jews and Christians live in close quarters and within the same material and physical culture; they also shared ideas and values. Gender-based divisions and understandings of

---

28. Bitkha Har-Shefi, *Women and Halakha in the Years 1050-1350 CE: Between Custom and Law* (Jerusalem: Hebrew University of Jerusalem, 2002); Elisheva Baumgarten, *Practicing Piety in Medieval Ashkenaz* (Philadelphia: University of Pennsylvania Press, 2014).

29. Baumgarten, *Mothers and Children*, 85–91.

daily labor and of religiosity were often shared, despite the obvious differences between Jewish and Christian theology and practice.

Time and space were simultaneously shared and distinct. Jews lived within the medieval Christian city and according to its rhythm. Jewish and Christian women, to some extent even more than the men, were in daily contact. Some Christians went into Jewish homes for business as this was the locus in which most Jewish business was conducted; other Christians, especially women, resided within Jewish homes as house servants, wet-nurses, or nannies. The church and the rabbis were very aware of this coresidence and attempted often to outlaw it or to control and contain it. Medieval sources regularly describe the presence of non-Jews in the house, whether lighting the fire on the Sabbath, cooking, or observing Christian holidays and rituals. Jews also entered Christian space, whether Christian houses of worship or neighbors' homes. Jewish children were left at Christian wet-nurses' homes, pledges were returned, and trade took place. Jews and Christians knew where to find each other—seeking each other out at home, at the synagogue, and in church. Some sources contain evidence of Jews and Christians sharing meals and exchanging gifts as well.[30]

Despite these shared aspects of time, space, and material culture, Jewish daily life also manifested differences between Jews and their neighbors. For example, despite shared urban space and similar daily rhythms, Jewish and Christian calendars rarely intersected: the two communities observed different weekly days of rest as well as distinct holidays. Daily rituals, like praying and fasting for both men and women, whether Jewish or Christian, indicated an immediate belonging to one community or the other. Food preparation is a good example, especially because many food issues involved women who dealt with servants, neighbors, and the actual tasks of cooking. Jewish laws of keeping kosher forbade the eating of certain kinds of meat. Even when the meat came from an animal that was considered kosher, the animal had to be slaughtered correctly by a Jew and certain restrictions applied to the way it was cooked. Animals were often raised by non-Jews in partnership with Jews before being slaughtered by Jews, who would subsequently sell to their Christian neighbors the animals that did not meet the Jewish ritual standards. This practice generated

---

30. Solomon Grayzel outlines Christian legislation in *The Church and the Jews in the Thirteenth Century* (New York: Hermon, 1966). Jacob Katz discusses some aspects of Jewish legislation in *The "Shabbes Goy": A Study in Halakhic Flexibility*, trans. Yoel Lerner (Philadelphia: Jewish Publication Society, 1989).

some interfaith tensions, as it could appear that Christians were consuming substandard meats rejected by Jews.[31] Feasts and fasts in both communities also emphasized Jewish and Christian differences. Medieval Jews and Christians fasted frequently during the year as part of the annual cycle and as expressions of personal piety and devotion. These fast days were rarely shared; Christians often fasted on Wednesdays and Fridays, whereas Friday was never a Jewish fast day and Mondays and Thursdays were. Jews fasted during the weeks after Passover; Christians fasted before and during Lent. The practical details of how members of both religions, male and female, observed these fasts marked differences between them. Fasting and festivity also dictated other mundane behaviors such as when one could or should wash oneself. Jews bathed on Fridays as a rule; Christians did not.

Material objects and culture also created distinctions. Jews and Christians kept separate cooking utensils as part of the food differentiation addressed above. Also, although Jews had their own distinctive ceremonial objects like Torah scrolls, phylacteries, prayer shawls, and *shofarot*, many of which were part of male ritual use, they did not possess or revere holy objects in the same manner as their Christian neighbors. Relics were present and regularly used by Christians not only in public church ceremonies but also at home; Christian processions honored saints' bones or other remains, and a cure for a sick Christian might be hastened with a rock from Jesus's tomb. When the number of sacred relics increased in Christian Europe during the Crusades, this material distinction between Jewish and Christian communities became further extended.

Medicinal materials were shared by Jews and Christians and, to a certain extent, were more the realm of women than of men, as women grew herbs and applied cures to their households. Although Jews and Christians shared markets and diseases, but religion made a difference here as well. Jewish and Christian doctors and midwives are known to have cooperated during this period, often consulting with each other. The medicinal substances used by practitioners of both religions were fairly similar, as most came from local environments or markets. Yet religious belief deeply informed how these substances were used—the formulae, the verses recited at application, even the theories that explained their effectiveness. And, of course, because medical practice so often involved matters of life and death, practitioners of a different faith were sometimes avoided or distrusted.

---

31. Grayzel, *Church and the Jews*, 42.

7. Conclusions

As noted by Judith Baskin, Jewish women were often excluded from traditional centers of learning and seem to have not participated in learned theological and theoretical conversations during the medieval period.[32] This was largely true of Christian women as well. Yet this exclusion does not seem to have affected Jewish women's sense of belonging, religious belief, or involvement in daily devotional activities. The Bible was especially central to Jewish (and Christian) women's sense of belonging. In contrast to other traditional texts that women were not allowed access to, the Bible was used as an educational tool and as a model. Examining the place of gender conceptions and women's activities within medieval settings, one is struck by both the distinctions and the similarities between the lives of Jews and Christians, and more specifically Jewish and Christian women. Nineteenth-century scholars imagined medieval Jewish homes as havens in a hostile Christian world. Today we see those homes as distinctly Jewish yet also comfortably embedded in Christian surroundings.

Jewish life in medieval Europe certainly entailed differences from the surrounding Christian culture. After all, Jews, unlike Christians, did not promote celibacy as a religious practice. At the same time, however, Jews maintained a gendered hierarchy very similar to that which existed in medieval Christian society. Women were expected to be subservient to their husbands and fathers (unless they were divorced or widowed), and in all cases, they were expected to obey their community's male leadership. They had a specific gendered status both before Jewish courts and as part of Jewish ritual. And they shared with Christian women the experiences of growing restrictions—in divorce and business—starting in the twelfth and thirteenth centuries. Two different communities; two similar gender orders. We will understand both communities better if our future research into the shared worlds of medieval Jews and Christians weighs shared gendered frameworks alongside religious differences.

---

32. Baskin, "Jewish Traditions."

Late Midrashic Literature

"If You Keep Silent in This Crisis" (Esth 4:14): Esther the Medieval Biblical Heroine

Constanza Cordoni

The Scroll of Esther, the name by which the book of Esther is known in the context of Jewish liturgy, is read during the festival of Purim (celebrated on the fourteenth and fifteenth days of the Hebrew month of Adar). The book purports to provide the historical origins of the festival.[1] The narrative as transmitted in the Hebrew Bible may be summed up as follows. Under the reign of Ahasuerus, the Jewish communities of his kingdom faced annihilation because of the malicious plans of the vizier Haman. Haman had been offended by the Jew Mordecai, who refused to bow down before him, so Haman set out to give him a lesson. Haman persuades the king to issue an edict that decrees the extermination of all the Jews of the kingdom. With the help of his niece Esther, who has been chosen among all the beautiful maidens of the kingdom to be queen, Mordecai succeeds in saving their people. He also persuades king Ahasuerus to give the Jews special prerogatives and to punish Haman and all those who are believed to have followed him. The festival that commemorates these events is called Purim, a word said to be derived from the word "Pur." Pur is an expression of uncertain etymology that Scripture explains as "lots" cast by the Persians to determine the day on which the Jews were to be exterminated.[2] On that very day, the book tells us, the Jews killed thousands of gentiles instead without a single Jewish life being lost. The book ends with a description of the festival of Purim as one that commemorates the turning of grief into joy.

---

[1]. See Esth 9:16–19, 20–22, 26–28, 31.

[2]. The festival as its name implies might originally have been a pagan festival. See Carey A. Moore, "Esther, Book of," *ABD* 2:637.

We read near the end of the Esther narrative that Mordecai wrote to the Jews of all the provinces "enjoining them that they should keep the fourteenth day of the month Adar and also the fifteenth day of the same month, year by year, as the days on which the Jews gained relief from their enemies, and as the month that had been turned for them from sorrow into gladness and from mourning into a holiday; that they should make them days of feasting and gladness, days for sending gifts of food to one another and presents to the poor" (Esth 9:21–22).[3] Several precepts concerning this festival were established in talmudic literature to make the holiday a particularly joyous occasion.[4]

1. The Interpretation of the Megillah and the Figure of Esther

An interpretation of the Scroll of Esther can be found as early as the third century BCE in the Septuagint, a Jewish translation of the Hebrew Bible into Koine Greek. This Greek version of Esther adds a religious element to a story utterly devoid of it. God is not present in the Hebrew version of the narrative as transmitted in the Masoretic Text;[5] there are no precepts, no sacrifices, no biblical concepts, no interest in Judean life and institutions.[6] The book's alterity is also evident in that it is not part of the macrostory of the Hebrew Scriptures, which, in Shlomo Goitein's words, is an account of "how the Israelites received the land of Israel, how

---

3. See also Esth 9:1–2. Esther is very much part of this decree. See Esth 9:29, 31.

4. Henry Malter, "Purim," in *The Jewish Encyclopedia* (New York: Ktav, 1965), 10:277, observes: "The jovial character of the feast was forcibly illustrated in the saying of the Talmud (Meg 7b) that one should drink on Purim until he can no longer distinguish "Cursed be Haman" from "Blessed be Mordecai," a saying which was codified in the Shulchan Aruk (ib.), but which was later ingeniously explained as referring to the letters occurring in the sentences ארור המן and ברוך מרדכי in each of which the numerical value of the letters amounts to 502."

5. On the different ancient, medieval, and modern approaches to God's absence from Esther, see Aaron Koller, *Esther in Ancient Jewish Thought* (Cambridge: Cambridge University Press, 2014), 96.

6. See Barry Dov Walfish, *Esther in Medieval Garb: Jewish Interpretation of the Book of Esther in the Middle Ages* (Albany: State University of New York Press, 1993), 75–76; and Carol Meyers, "Esther," in *The Oxford Bible Commentary*, ed. John Barton and John Muddimann (Oxford: Oxford University Press, 2001), 325. For an overview on the Jewish and Christian positions with respect to the contested canonicity of the book, see Moore, "Esther, Book of," 635–36.

"If You Keep Silent in This Crisis" (Esth 4:14)   37

they lost the Land, and how they returned and received the Land again."[7] Several exegetical documents of the rabbinic period of Jewish literature further the Septuagint's attempt at a Judaization of the book of Esther and lay the foundation for the later medieval reception of Esther.[8] This is achieved both by introducing God as a narrative agent and by adapting the depiction of the human characters.

In the following pages, I will focus on the representation of the woman Esther in texts of different medieval literary genres. Each of these texts interprets the scriptural narrative. Some do this in a more explicit manner than others (e.g., quoting the scriptural text and commenting on it). Each text omits part of the Esther story while it focuses on certain other aspects. One crucial choice that both rabbinic and medieval interpreters make is this: Although the Scroll is named after the story's heroine not all exegetical documents place the woman Esther at the center of their interpretive concerns.[9]

In this context a word on how midrash operates is necessary, especially for readers who may be unfamiliar with this chapter of Jewish hermeneutics. Midrash does not interpret episodes of scriptural narra-

---

7. Shlomo Dov Goitein, *Bible Studies* [Hebrew] (Tel Aviv: Yavneh, 1967), 59, as quoted by Koller, *Esther in Ancient Jewish Thought*, 172.

8. For an overview, see Myron Bialik Lerner, "The Works of Aggadic Midrash and the Esther Midrashim," in *The Literature of the Sages, Second Part: Midrash and Targum, Liturgy, Poetry, Mysticism, Contracts, Inscriptions, Ancient Science, and the Languages of Rabbinic Literature*, ed. Shmuel Safrai et al. (Assen: Van Gorcum; Minneapolis: Fortress, 2006), 176–229. The Babylonian Talmud transmits in b. Meg. 10b–17b a running commentary on Esther, a rare genre in this context. See Günter Stemberger, "Midrasch in Babylonien, am Beispiel von Sota 9b–14a," *Henoch* 10 (1988): 183–203. It has been argued that the Babylonian Esther midrash represents a diaspora midrash insofar as it addresses the question of Jewish identity in the diaspora. See Dagmar Börner-Klein, *Eine babylonische Auslegung der Ester-Geschichte* (Frankfurt am Main: Lang, 1991), 271–74; and Gerhard Bodendorfer, "Die Diaspora, die Juden und die 'Anderen'," in *"Eine Grenze hast Du gesetzt": Edna Brocke zum 60. Geburtstag*, ed. Ekkehard W. Stegemann and Klaus Wengst (Stuttgart: Kohlhammer, 2003), 194. The Palestinian collections comprise small midrashim such as Abba Gurion and Panim Acherim A and B as well as the more comprehensive Esther Rabbah.

9. For example, the tenth-century midrash Abba Gurion focuses on Haman's plan and turns Esther into a minor character. On Abba Gurion, see Günter Stemberger, *Einleitung in Talmud und Midrash* (Munich: Beck, 2011), 314; Dagmar Börner-Klein and Elisabeth Hollender, eds., *Die Midraschim zu Ester* (Leiden: Brill, 2000), 23–24.

tives but rather focuses on the wording of the scriptural verse.[10] Verses are segmented, and the resulting segments are interpreted in anonymous statements or in statements attributed to rabbinic authorities.[11] Rabbis are said to read in an atomistic manner.[12] Like hermeneutics in general, rabbinic hermeneutics is a creative enterprise. This manifests itself in the way parts of Scripture are associated with each other; quite often interpretation operates by linking segments of a certain book with completely unrelated scriptural verses. Because of this way of segmenting, of selecting what is to be explained about the scriptural text, and of combining the segment with other scriptural and rabbinic texts, and because of the priority of the rabbinic agenda, a reader of the midrash who is unfamiliar with the book of Esther would find it difficult, if not impossible, to reassemble the base narrative after reading the commentary. Such segmentation and choice of perspective is an ideological focalization that is evident in midrash but also operates in other forms of hermeneutics. Each new narrative of the book of Esther, each staging of a Purim play, focuses on certain aspects of the original story while it leaves out motifs or questions that other interpreters in the past and present might consider to be of interest. This is also the case with the medieval reception of Esther in Jewish literature. An extreme example of segmentation and focalization may be seen in the case of the late midrash Seder Eliyahu (ninth century).[13] To explain *wa-yaʿabor* in Exod 34:6, the anonymous voice of the midrashist claims

---

10. Arnon Atzmon, "Old Wine in New Flasks: The Story of Late Neoclassical Midrash," *European Journal of Jewish Studies* 3 (2009): 183–203, argues that, whereas classical rabbinic midrash is verse-centered, late midrashim *do* interpret biblical stories. He describes the second part of Esther Rabbah as a neoclassical midrash that returns to the verse-centered focus.

11. For this aspect of rabbinic hermeneutics, see chapter 2 of Alexander Samely, *Rabbinic Interpretation of Scripture in the Mishnah* (Oxford: Oxford University Press, 2002); chapter 4 of Samely, *Forms of Rabbinic Literature and Thought* (Oxford: Oxford University Press, 2007); and Gerhard Langer, *Midrasch* (Tübingen: Mohr Siebeck, 2016), 62.

12. This is contested with respect to the rabbinic readings on the book of Esther by Koller, *Esther in Ancient Jewish Thought*, 170–71, who claims that rabbis did not read only atomistically but that "much of the rabbinic attention will be directed to the broad themes of Esther as a whole" and "that the Rabbis were attuned to broader issues, as well."

13. On Seder Eliyahu, see Constanza Cordoni, *Seder Eliyahu: A Narratological Reading* (Berlin: de Gruyter, 2018).

that *wa-yaʿabor* in Esth 4:17 means that Mordecai forgot Esther's first hesitant reaction to his words in Esth 4:14—"For if you keep silence"—after having succeeded in persuading her to stand for her people. Mordecai's words epitomize the message of the story: no other part of it is mentioned in the rest of the late midrash. We assume the intended audience of this text knew that Mordecai's words in Scripture were a clear warning in Esther's ears,[14] but this is not spelled out in the medieval text. Esther, however, reacts properly, acting as Jews would have expected her to act, which is why Mordecai forgives Esther for her initial lack of initiative (see Seder Eliyahu Rabbah 1:3–4).

2. Esther in Pirqe de Rabbi Eliezer

Pirqe de Rabbi Eliezer is a late rabbinic document apparently composed by a single author. Scholars have agreed to disagree to which literary genre it belongs. In two of its chapters near the end, Pirqe de Rabbi Eliezer retells the Esther narrative. Chapter 49 introduces the story, contextualizing it as a fulfilment of the story of destruction of Amalek and a reenactment of Samuel's defeat of the Amalekite Agag, of whom Haman is thought to be a descendant. The first appearance Esther makes in Pirqe de Rabbi Eliezer is in a prayer:

> *Samuel said to him* [Agag], *As your sword has made women childless, so your mother shall be childless among women.* (1 Sam 15:33) Just as the sword of Amalek your ancestor made the young men of Israel outside the cloud childless, so that their women remained childless women and widows, so shall your mother be childless among women. And by the prayer of Esther and her maidens all the sons of Amalek were slain, and their women remained childless and widowed, for it is said, *Samuel said to him, As your sword has made women childless.* (1 Sam 15:33) (Pirqe R. El. 49)[15]

Esther's prayer, which in this retelling also involves her entourage, is in line with Samuel's dictum regarding the destruction of the descendants of

---

14. The entire verse of Esth 4:14 reads: "For if you keep silence at such a time as this relief and deliverance will rise for the Jews from another quarter, but you and your father's family will perish."

15. My translation is based on Gerald Friedlander, *Pirke de Rabbi Eliezer* (London: Kegan Paul, 1916).

Amalek, Israel's adversaries. This may be seen as a first attempt in Pirqe de Rabbi Eliezer at Judaizing the figure and the book of Esther. Elsewhere in the same chapter, Ahasuerus's compulsive feasting is described in a way that implies that there was no danger of assimilation in view of the fact that "Whoever ate their food in purity had their food provided in purity, and whoever ate their food in impurity, had their food provided in impurity, for it is said, [*for the king had given orders to all the officials of his palace*] *to do as each one desired* (Esth 1:8)."

The first woman, however, to be featured in the book of Esther is the king's first wife, Vashti, as it is after her death that Esther is made queen. Vashti is said to have deserved to die naked and on a Sabbath because she made the daughters of Israel work naked during the Sabbath.[16] Pirqe de Rabbi Eliezer then argues that Esther became queen of Persia for two reasons: because the courtier Daniel, who in Scripture goes by the name Memuchan, consoles the remorseful Ahasuerus, encouraging him to marry again; and because God invests Esther with "grace and love in the eyes of all who see her."

3. Esther in Yosippon: Esther in Prayer

The ninth chapter of Yosippon, a Hebrew chronicle allegedly based on a Latin translation of Josephus's *Jewish Antiquities* and composed in southern Italy in the last decade of the tenth century, transmits a shortened version of the story of Esther as we know it from the Hebrew Bible.[17] However, one of the most conspicuous aspects of the Yosippon version is its rich use of material from the Septuagint's additions to Esther.[18] It is with Yosippon that the Hebrew literary tradition appears to have become acquainted with the Septuagint additions. This tendency appears to attest to the fact that a

---

16. This motif is also found in b. Meg. 12b and Leqach Tov ad Esth 2:1.

17. On Yosippon, see Saskia Dönitz, "Sefer Yosippon (Josippon)," in *A Companion to Josephus*, ed. Honora Howell Chapman and Zuleika Rodgers (Malden, MA: Wiley, 2016). For a critical edition, see David Flusser, ed., *The Josippon* [*Josef Gorionides*]: *Edited with Introduction, Commentary and Notes* [Hebrew], 2 vols. (Jerusalem: Bialik Institute, 1980–1981), 1:48–54.

18. Just as his main source is a Latin translation of Josephus's *Jewish Antiquities*, it is likely that, for the additions to Esther, the author of Yosippon used the Latin Vulgate that Jerome appended to his translation after Esth 10:4.

major agenda of the author of Yosippon was the propagation among Jews of unknown material related to the Esther story.

In this medieval rendering Esther comes to the fore as a specifically Jewish heroine in the disproportionately long prayer scene that precedes the account of Esther's audience with the king. The prayer, based on the second part of Septuagint Addition C,[19] makes up approximately a fourth of the entire text of the Esther narrative in Yosippon and reads as follows:

> And Queen Esther fled to the Lord, for she was in fear of the emerging evil. And she removed the royal apparel and her magnificent ornament and put on sackcloth. She loosened the hair of her head and filled it with dust and ashes. And she chastised her soul with fasting. And she fell on her face and prayed and said, "Lord, God of Israel, who have reigned since ancient times and have created the entire world and rule over it, help your lonely handmaid, who has no other helper but You. For lonely have I dwelt and lonely am I in the king's house, without father and mother. Like a poor orphan who goes from house to house begging for charity, so I ask you for mercy from window to window in the house of King Ahasuerus, ever since I was brought hither until this very day. Now, my God, here is my soul, take it from me if it finds favor in your eyes, but if it does not, deliver the flock of your pasture from these lions that have arisen. For my father taught me and told me that you took our fathers from Egypt and killed all the firstborns of Egypt and took your people from their midst and with strong hand and with your stretched arm you caused them to pass through the sea like a horse in the wilderness and you gave them bread from heaven and water from flinty rock. And you also gave them meat to their satisfaction and struck down for them great and mighty kings and you gave them your good land as inheritance."[20]

Esther changes her royal apparel for clothes that express her fear and grief, covers her hair with ashes, and fasts before turning in prayer to God. In her direct address she humbles herself by referring to herself as God's handmaid and insisting on her loneliness, on her actual and metaphorical condition as an orphan, and on the fact that she is at court married to a gentile king against her will, using an image of the everyday life of a woman to depict in most vivid terms what royal lifestyle feels like to her. Her way out of this life of pretense is manifested by her perseverance in her

---

19. On the additions, see Carey A. Moore, "Esther, Additions to," *ABD* 2:626–33.
20. Translated following Flusser, *Josippon*, 51–52.

search for "windows of prayer," a way to live out her piety. She then turns to the history of the salvation of Israel, which is the reason for her trusting that God will once again save the Jews of Ahasuerus's kingdom. She compares the threat to her people to the threat of a lion to a flock.

What Esther asks of God is that he guide the king towards compassion for her and for her people when she approaches him to intercede for the Jews. She must make her husband hate his counsellors because they intrigue against her people, and if God makes use of her beauty to achieve this, it should be his will.

4. Esther in Esther Rabbah

Unlike the texts discussed above, the midrash Esther Rabbah is a running commentary on the book of Esther. It takes a relatively minor amount of scriptural material as a springboard from which to jump into reflections of its present-day agenda.[21] Although many of its traditions go back to late antiquity, the final redaction of Esther Rabbah is assumed to have occurred in Europe by the twelfth century,[22] which is why it can provide us with material on the reception of the biblical Esther in the Middle Ages.

On several occasions the midrash addresses the problem that the book of Esther presents diaspora Jews as assimilated to such an extent to Per-

---

21. For a critical edition, see Joseph Tabory and Arnon Atzmon, eds, *Midrash Esther Rabbah* (Jerusalem: Schechter Institute of Jewish Studies, 2014). Few verses of the scriptural book are explicitly interpreted. The distribution of the interpretation is indeed quite disproportionate: The twelve proems that precede the main body of the commentary interpret the first word of Esth 1:1; the first six chapters of the midrash focus on chapters 1 and 2 of the book of Esther; the remaining four chapters of the midrash *very* selectively interpret verses from chapters 3–9 of the biblical book; finally, chapter 10 of the midrash interprets a few verses from chapters 6–10 of the book of Esther.

22. Scholarship distinguishes two parts of the midrash that have come down to us. Esther Rabbah I, comprising chapters 1–5, is a classical exegetical midrash (i.e., a running commentary), composed in all probability during the sixth century in Palestine. Esther Rabbah II, less classical in character, contains several passages that go back to the Greek Additions in the Septuagint but that found their way into the midrash through Yosippon. This second part of Esther Rabbah could therefore have originated in Europe in the eleventh century and possibly later. See Lerner, "Esther Midrashim," 187; and Arnon Atzmon, "Mordechai's Dream: From Addition to Derashah," *Jewish Studies: An Internet Journal* 6 (2007): 127–40. It is transmitted in only three manuscripts, the *editio princeps*, and Genizah fragments.

sian society that even the interethnic marriage of the Jewess Esther to the Persian king Ahasuerus is not viewed as a scandal. To begin with, Esther Rabbah addresses the problem of the names. The heroine has two names: "Esther," of uncertain though probably Babylonian origin, and the Hebrew name "Hadassah." The two names can be read as two identities, a non-Jewish, Persian one and a Jewish one. In Esth 2:7 we read: "Mordecai had brought up Hadassah, that is Esther, his cousin, for she had neither father nor mother; the girl was fair and beautiful, and when her father and her mother died, Mordecai adopted her as his own daughter."[23] After this verse introducing the heroine, who will from now on be referred to only by her *non*-Jewish name, the midrash interprets *only* the Hebrew name Hadassah. "Hadassah" means "myrtle"; Esther was sweet to Mordecai but bitter to Haman, just as the myrtle smells sweet but tastes bitter (Esth. Rab. 6:5).[24] Apart from this brief focus on Hadassah, only Esther's Persian name is used for the remainder of the story. This can be viewed as evidence of the assimilation of the Jews and is indicative of the cultural setting of this tale,[25] one in which a minority living within a dominant majority culture lives in both cultures at the same time. Assimilation is not recognized as a problem in the biblical book or in Esther Rabbah.[26]

A Babylonian rabbinic tradition focuses on the kinship of Mordecai and Esther, which is alluded to in the second part of Esth 2:7: "Morde-

---

23. Scripture is quoted from the NRSV.

24. Alternative interpretations of Esther's two names are given by Rabbi Meir and Rabbi Judah in b. Meg. 13a. According to the first, her name is Esther, but she is called Hadassah (myrtle) because the righteous are called myrtles in Zech 1:8. According to the latter, her name is Hadassah, but she is called Esther because she concealed (*masteret*) the truth about herself.

25. On the genre of the book of Esther, see Moore, "Esther, Book of," 639; W. Lee Humphreys, "A Life-Style for Diaspora: A Study of the Tales of Esther and Daniel," *JBL* 92 (1973): 211–23; David G. Firth, "The Third Quest for the Historical Mordecai and the Genre of the Book of Esther," *OTE* 16 (2003): 233–43; David J. A. Clines, *The Scroll of Esther: The Story of the Story* (Sheffield: Sheffield Academic, 1984), 9–30.

26. See Meyers, "Esther," 324. Unlike other Second Temple period novels such as Judith and Tobit, where dispersion is understood as having its roots in transgressions of the nation, the book of Esther does not present the diasporic existence of the Jews of Susa as the result of any sins. See Isaiah Gafni, *Land, Center and Diaspora: Jewish Constructs in Late Antiquity* (Sheffield: Sheffield Academic, 1997), 24. In b. Meg. 13a we read the interpretation of Mordecai having left Jerusalem as an exile: "*Who had been exiled from Jerusalem* (Esth 2:6). Rava said: [This language indicates] that he went into exile on his own."

cai adopted her as his own daughter." The rabbinic tradition suggests that Mordecai did not take her as a daughter [*bat*] but as a "house" or wife [*bayt*]: "he took her to himself for a wife" (see b. Meg. 13a). Any problem involved in understanding Esther as being married to Mordecai before she was taken to the king's harem and chosen to be queen, including the emotions that might be involved, are completely suppressed in Esther Rabbah, which is also true for the remainder of the Middle Ages, with the exception of Rashi.[27]

The fact that Esther marries a gentile king because she is able to conceal her Jewishness is not a particular issue in Scripture. In the midrash, Esther chooses not to reveal her ethnic and religious identity. In an interpretation of "Esther had not yet made known her kindred" (Esth 2:20), she is praised as showing the proper behavior of controlling one's emotions: "This teaches that she put a ban of silence on herself like her ancestress Rachel put a ban of silence on herself when she saw her wedding presents in the hand of her sister and said nothing" (Esth. Rab. 6:12).[28] Esther's self-imposed silence is said to have an exemplary precedent in Rachel. Once Esther has been made queen, the midrash addresses the problem of her assimilation by questioning the notion that Esther could be loved by everyone at court, though indicating that this is simply a figure of speech:

> *When the time was fulfilled for Esther ... Now Esther found favor in the eyes of all who saw her* (Esth 2:15). Rabbi Judah said: She was like this statue at which a thousand persons look and equally admire. Rabbi Nehemiah said: They put Median women on this side [of her] and Persian women on this side, and she was more beautiful than all of them. The rabbis, however, explain: *Now Esther found favor in the eyes of all who saw her*, that is to say, in the eyes of heavenly beings and in the eyes of earthly beings, for it is said, *So you will find favor and good repute in the sight of God and of people* (Prov 3:4). (Esth. Rab. 6:9)[29]

---

27. See Barry Dov Walfish. "The Mordecai-Esther-Ahasuerus Triangle in Midrash and Exegesis," *Prooftexts* 22 (2002): 312–15. As Walfish explains, Esth 2:7 does present exegetical problems and does support the reading of daughter (*bat*) as wife (*bayit*).

28. However, Esth 2:10, according to which Esther conceals her Jewishness because Mordecai advises her to, is not explicitly interpreted.

29. The translation of Esther Rabbah follows with modifications that of Maurice Simon, *Midrash Rabbah IX* (London: Soncino, 1939). See Koller, *Esther in Ancient Jewish Thought*, 220–21, on the reading of Esth 2:15 in b. Meg. 13a.

The problem of intermarriage is explicitly in focus when Mordecai justifies to himself his niece's position at court: "He thought to himself: How is it possible that this righteous maiden should be married to an uncircumcised man? It must be because some great calamity is going to befall Israel and they will be delivered through her" (Esth. Rab. 6:6).[30]

After the edict to exterminate all Jews has been sent to all the provinces of Ahasuerus's kingdom, the news eventually reaches Queen Esther. The account in the Hebrew Scripture reads:

> In every province, wherever the king's command and his decree came, there was great mourning among the Jews, with fasting and weeping and lamenting, and most of them lay in sackcloth and ashes. *When Esther's maids and her eunuchs came and told her, the queen was deeply distressed* [*wa-tithalhal*]; she sent garments to clothe Mordecai, so that he might take off his sackcloth; but he would not accept them. (Esth 4:3–4)

What is the cause of Esther's distress? The midrash quotes only the clause emphasized above. Lest the audience suspect that Esther fears her uncle might embarrass her or even harm her in her position at court, the midrash proceeds to provide an alternative to these interpretations. The midrash concludes that the *hapax legomenon wa-tithalhal*, translated above as "deeply distressed," refers to physical pain and indeed to a specific female one: "Our rabbis there [in Babylonia] say that she became menstruous, but our teachers here say that she had a miscarriage and having had a miscarriage never bore again" (Esth. Rab. 8:3).[31]

Further down in a segment concerned with the interpretation of Esth 4:14–15 and 17, Esther is depicted as feeling for her people and participating in the same kind of display of grief as her uncle: wearing

---

30. It is this very midrash which Carey A. Moore quotes when he points out: "If a man can be judged by the friends he keeps, he can also be judged by the enemies he has; and, significantly, everyone had a good impression of Esther (vs. 15). For her to have accomplished this must have involved some 'compromises' in the area of religion: a Judith or a Daniel could never have won the good will of all. In order for Esther to have concealed her ethnic and religious identity (see vs. 10) in the harem, she must have eaten …, dressed, and lived like a Persian rather than an observant Jewess." (*Esther*, AB 7B [Garden City, NY: Doubleday, 1971], 28).

31. The Palestinian tradition is found in Abba Gurion, Panim Acherim B, and Leqach Tov ad Esther 4:4 where a prooftext is adduced: "Therefore my loins are filled with anguish [*halhala*]; pangs have seized me, like the pangs of a woman in labor" (Isa 21:3).

sackcloth, putting ashes on her hair, and fasting. This show of grief is found in a short version of the prayer transmitted in Yosippon and discussed above:

> At that time Esther was greatly frightened at the evil which was threatening Israel, and she took off her royal robes and ornaments and she put on sackcloth and loosened the hair of her head and filled it with dust and ashes and afflicted herself with fasting and fell on her face before the Lord. And she prayed, saying, "O Lord, God of Israel who are ruler of old and created the world, help your handmaid who has been left an orphan without father and mother and is like a poor woman begging from house to house. So I pray for Your mercy from one window to another in the palace of Ahasuerus. And now, O Lord, grant success to your humble handmaid here and deliver the sheep of your pasture from these enemies who have risen against us." (Esth. Rab. 8:6)

Once her private display of grief and prayer is over, Esther changes her mourning clothes for a beautiful dress before approaching Ahasuerus to plead with him for her people. The audience with the king as described in the midrash follows Addition D of the Septuagint and reads:

> *Now it came to pass on the third day, that Esther put on* (Esth 5:1) her most beautiful robes and her richest ornaments, and she took with her two maidens.... She put on a smiling face, concealing the anxiety in her heart. Then she came to the inner court facing the king and she stood before him.... when he lifted up his eyes and saw Esther standing in front of him he was furiously angry because she had broken his law and come before him without being called. Then Esther lifted up her eyes and saw the king's face, and behold his eyes were flashing like fire with the wrath which was in his heart. And when the queen perceived how angry the king was, she was overcome and her heart sank and she placed her head on the maiden who was supporting her right hand. But our God saw and had mercy on His people, and He took note of the distress of the orphan who trusted in Him and He gave her grace in the eyes of the king and invested her with new beauty and new charm. Then the king rose in haste from his throne and ran to Esther and embraced her and kissed her and flung his arm around her neck and said to her, "Esther, my queen, why do you tremble? For this law which we have laid down does not apply to you, since you are my beloved and my companion." He also said to her, "Why when I saw you did you not speak to me?" Esther replied,

"My lord the king, when I beheld you I was overcome by your high dignity." (Esth. Rab. 9:1)[32]

If we look at the Hebrew text of Scripture that describes Esther's audience with the king (Esth 5:1–5), we notice that there is no trace of anger in the king that needs to be assuaged, nor any anxiety in Esther before she sees the king, nor any dread of the king after noticing his fury. For both of the last quoted passages the midrash makes use of Septuagint Additions C and D, probably on the basis of the Yosippon account. The second passage conveys the notion that God manages human emotions and ensures the well-being of his chosen children. This passage also reveals that, according to the rabbis, emotions can be controlled not just by God but also by *some* humans who are capable of manipulating and therefore concealing them.[33] It also suggests that certain physical symptoms associated with the expression of emotions can have more than one reading: Esther's trembling and her speechlessness can be interpreted as a symptom of either fear or extreme admiration.

5. Esther in Midrash Psalm 22

For Christian exegetes, Ps 22 was of major importance. Jesus's last words on the cross, as transmitted in the Gospels of Matthew and Mark (Matt 27:46; Mark 15:34), are an Aramaic version of the psalm's first verse.[34] In Jewish tradition, the rabbis read the psalm in light of the Esther story; thus the poem found its way into the Jewish liturgy of Purim, where it came to be interpreted allegorically as a lament on the anxiety that Haman's planned pogrom brought to the Jews.

Major portions of the commentary on Ps 22 in the medieval Midrash Psalms (Midrash Tehillim) relate the psalm to the Esther story, so that it can be viewed as an Esther midrash in its own right. Her names are interpreted as meaningful not only with respect to her own actions, but also in

---

32. The parallel in Leqach Tov ad Esther 5:1 has three maidens accompany Esther to her audience corresponding to the three angels who appear the moment she faints.

33. See n. 23.

34. See Mitchell Dahood, *Psalms I: 1–50*, AB 16 (Garden City, NY: Doubleday, 1966); Frank-Lothar Hossfeld and Erich Zenger, *Die Psalmen I. Psalm 1–50* (Würzburg: Echter, 1993); Dieter Sänger, ed., *Psalm 22 und die Passionsgeschichten der Evangelien* (Neukirchen-Vluyn: Neukirchener Verlag, 2007).

relation to those of Mordecai, and due to their their implications for the Jews of Ahasuerus's kingdom:

> Esther was called myrtle. Esther, for she was the secret of the secrets. When she had to shine for Israel, she went out. Myrtle, as it is written, *He brought up Hadassah* (Esth 2:7), because of her righteousness. Mordecai is called myrtle, for it is said, *He was standing among the myrtle trees* (Zech 1:8). Like a myrtle tree, whose odor is good and whose taste is bitter, so Mordecai and Esther were a light to Israel and a darkness to the peoples of the earth. (Midr. Ps. 22:3)[35]

The question of how Esther and Mordecai belong together, that is to say, in what kind of relationship they stand to each other, is only briefly touched upon. "You kept me safe on my mother's breast" (Ps 22:10) is explained as referring to the fact that God gave Esther to Mordecai's wife to suckle her and to Mordecai to bring her up (Midr. Ps. 22:23).

The Hebrew expression of uncertain meaning *'ayyelet ha-shaḥar* at the opening of the psalm (Ps 22:1) and which may be translated as "deer of the dawn" is interpreted in Midr. Ps. 22 as a metaphor for the woman Esther and for her role in the history of Israel. As the deer scares snakes, so Esther scared Haman. Moreover, the deer is the most pious of all animals (Midr. Ps. 22:14). Esther is likened to the dawn because the miracle her actions made manifest was the last of the miracles deemed worthy of entering the Jewish canon (Midr. Ps. 22:10).[36] As to the category of gender, it is worth noting that the three mentions of the expression "my God" in Ps 22:2–11 are explained as being related to the three special commandments of women (*niddah, ḥallah,* and *hadlaqat nerot*) that Esther claims never to have disregarded in spite of her marriage to the gentile king (Midr. Ps. 22:16).

In both Yosippon and Esther Rabbah, Esther's Jewishness comes to the fore in her depiction as a woman in prayer. Even though it is evident that the redactor of Midr. Ps. 22 was also acquainted with the Esther commentary in the Babylonian Talmud, what is most salient about this commentary is its focus on the praying Esther and the effects of her prayer.

---

35. The translation is based on William G. Braude, *Midrash on Psalms* (New Haven: Yale University Press, 1959).

36. In the course of the interpretation of the psalm, several verses of other scriptural books are adduced that are understood as referring to Esther (e.g., the expression "light of Israel" in Isa 10:17).

This is a fundamental notion in Midr. Ps. 22. Esther is said to be the reason why David composed this psalm in the first place! "When David realized that the Holy One, blessed be He, hears the hind, he arranged in her honor the Psalm *To the leader: according to the deer of the dawn* (Ps 22:1)" (Midr. Ps. 22:14).[37] During her prayer, which unlike the prayers found in Yosippon and Esther Rabbah is scattered all over the running commentary on the psalm, she is depicted as quoting the very psalm that her own story is assumed to have inspired (Midr. Ps. 22:7, 19, 24, 25).

Esther is not only familiar with the psalm she quotes as well as with the notion that the Jews have two Torahs—the Oral and the Written—and with the commandments that are observed by women, but she is also familiar with the exodus story as a foundational moment in the history of the salvation of Israel (Midr. Ps. 22:6). She compares the danger she incurs in approaching the king unsummoned to her forefathers' crossing of the Red Sea (Midr. Ps. 22:27). An interesting aspect of the depiction of Esther in Midr. Ps. 22, which is in contrast to Scripture and her afterlife in rabbinic literature, is the insistence that Esther is acting of her own volition rather than in reaction to Mordecai's words of warning (Midr. Ps. 22:7 and 24).

6. Esther in Leqach Tov

In the late eleventh century in the Byzantine city of Kastoria (present-day western Macedonia), a certain Tobia ben Rabbi Eliezer composed an anthology of interpretations to the five books of the Torah and the five scrolls, which came to be known as Leqach Tov ("Good teaching"). The title is based on scriptural wording (Prov 4:2) and at the same time alludes to the first name of the author.[38] In the case of the Scroll of Esther, Leqach Tov is the first Jewish exegetical document that not only quotes every single verse of the Hebrew text of Esther but also provides an interpretation for almost every verse.[39]

---

37. Similarly in Midr. Ps. 22:7: "When David foresaw by [the help of] the Holy Spirit that the expression with which she would call upon the Holy One, blessed be He, was *my strength* [*'eyaluti*] (Ps 22:20) he arranged this psalm in her [Esther's] honor: *To the leader: according to the deer of the dawn* [*'ayyelet*] (Ps 22:1)."

38. See Stemberger, *Einleitung*, 395.

39. Leqach Tov on Esther was published by Salomon Buber in his *Aggadic Commentaries on the Book of Esther (Sifre de-Aggadata al megillat Esther)* (Vilna: Romm, 1886), 83–112.

The art of the medieval collectors of traditions does not reside in their original exegesis, but rather rests on the fact that they composed a document with materials from diverse provenances as a running commentary, including some of the earlier materials while rejecting others and explicitly revealing the origin of some sources (e.g., Seder Olam, Yosippon, Genesis Rabbah, b. Rosh Hashanah, and Megillah) while quoting other sources without acknowledging them as such (e.g., Midrash Abba Gurion, Panim Acherim B). Tobia replaces Greek loanwords and most of the Aramaic wording of his sources for Hebrew, revealing a continuing movement towards the Hebraicization of Jewish literature that had already begun in in the early Middle Ages.[40]

What does Leqach Tov make of the figure of Esther found in earlier traditions? Esther, although she is in the diaspora and married to a Persian king, is tacitly imagined as speaking a language other than Aramaic, which after all is the language of Queen Vashti (LeqT ad Esth 1:20). Whatever language Esther is thought to have spoken is not spelled out, but it is probable that hand in hand with her Judaization, it was thought that she spoke Hebrew, the principal language of Leqach Tov itself.

Her Hebrew name is interpreted as allusion to Abraham and his origins outside of the land of Israel. For both figures, the number seventy-five marked an important event in the life of Israel: "The Holy One, blessed be He, said to Abraham, You went out of your father's house when you were seventy-five years old. For your life, I will also cause your children's deliverer (*goel*) to stand in Media (and) he will not be but seventy-five years old. Hadassah's numerical value is seventy-five minus one. Add the value of Esther and there you have seventy-five" (LeqT ad Esth 2:7).[41] Esther is masculinized in that she is referred to as deliverer with a masculine participle.

On several occasions Tobia insists on Esther's attitude towards *food* as her way of asserting her Jewishness.[42] The interpretation of Esth 2:9-11 suggests that Esther did not *say* anything about her lineage, for Mordecai is supposed to have explained to her that revealing prematurely that she is

---

40. See Constanza Cordoni, "'For They Did Not Change Their Language' (MekhY Pischa 5): On Early Medieval Literary Rehebraicisation of Jewish Culture," *Medieval Worlds* 11 (2020): 165–86.

41. My translation.

42. See n. 28.

Jewish could have brought her humiliation before the king.[43] An apparently less straightforward manner of asserting her Jewishness was for Esther to eat Jewish food with her maids instead of the food of the kingdom.[44] Mordecai is understood as having stood outside of the women's court precisely to see to it that Esther did not incur any dietary transgression. Surprisingly, those around Esther fail to realize that she is Jewish, even though, as Haman argues before the king, in eating differently and marrying only within the group, Jews not only follow their own laws but, by doing so, they draw a boundary between themselves and others (see LeqT ad Esth 3:8 // b. Meg. 13b). During the first banquet with Haman and Ahasuerus, both men eat while Esther sits as if in mourning (LeqT ad Esth 5:6; Esth 7:1).[45] Apart from this, Esther is characterized as standing out in comparison with the rest of the girls brought in before the king, in that she wears no special apparel or jewelry (see LeqT ad Esth 2:15), but she does wear royal apparel for the first day of Pesach (see LeqT ad Esth 5:1). In obeying Mordecai, Esther is also said to have had one God and, more generally, to follow the customs of the Jews (see LeqT ad Esth 2:20). The one moment of the Esther narrative which suggests that Esther needs Mordecai's prompt in order to intercede for their people is the one moment in which Leqach Tov suggests that Mordecai criticized her:

> [*For if you keep silence at such a time as this,*] *relief and deliverance will rise for the Jews from another quarter* [ממקום]. (Esth 4:14) Why is God's name not mentioned in the Scroll of Esther? Because it was written among kings of Media and Persia and they did not want to put the honored and fearsome name in it, this is the reason why they wrote *from another quarter*. (LeqT ad Esth 4:14)[46]

Without Mordecai's prompting, Esther hints verbally at her ethnicity and faith when questioned by the king about her ancestors (LeqT ad Esth 2:19).

---

43. Cf. LeqT ad Esth 4:8, where Mordecai is said to have permitted Esther to say that she is Jewish.

44. In this Esther is exemplary, for later on in LeqT ad Est 4:1 the midrash has the prophet Elijah explain that the annihilation of Israel is the consequence of their having eaten from Ahasuerus's banquet. See also LeqT ad Esth 4:17 ("she did not eat until he asked her").

45. LeqT ad Esth 5:6: "they ate and she sat as if in mourning"; Esth 7:1: "Esther ate nothing." However, in LeqT ad Est 6:1 Ahasuerus is told that they have all eaten and drunk the same.

46. See also LeqT ad Esth 5:9 for the name of God.

Answering that she is of royal descent, she leads him to talk about his own royal ancestry. Esther then proceeds to reprimand the king because he has failed to consult, as kings are wont to do, with the sages of Israel, and she identifies Mordecai sitting at the palace gate as a sage of Israel (see also LeqT ad Esth 2:21). However, the midrash judges Esther for not having been more explicit at this point. Elsewhere Esther is rabbinized in that she is praised for having taken the words of Tannaim and Amoraim into her heart and for acting accordingly, that is to say, for acting according to the Oral Torah (see LeqT ad Esth 5:4).

On another note, the figure of Esther, whether acting on her own accord or receiving prompts from her uncle, is so exemplary that Leqach Tov advises that the Scroll of Esther should be read by priests, Levites, Israelites, and also by women, for women were involved in the events of Purim; they actively contributed to the wonder of Purim (see LeqT ad Esth 9:28 // b. ʿArak. 3a).

The aspects described above, part of Tobia's selection of earlier rabbinic materials of multiple provenance, inform us as to how Esther and her story were retold for an intended audience of Byzantine Jews. While the explanation of Esther's deeds of valor remains motivated by Mordecai urging her to act, in several passages Esther is depicted as acknowledging her Jewish identity by acting without prompting. More explicit than earlier rabbinic works on Esther, Leqach Tov emphasizes, both in a lengthy introduction and in the body of the commentary (see LeqT ad Esth 1:14, 3:1, 4:1), the context of the Esther narrative as one of exile. This is why Esther's eating of Jewish food may be understood as addressing the possibility that diaspora settings represented in the eyes of rabbinic-minded authors a danger for the maintenance of Jewish identity.

7. Being Esther in the Middle Ages

Esther, the main female literary persona in the eponymous scriptural narrative, fascinated ancient and medieval exegetes. Early modern Jewish literature would witness how the Esther story would continue to fascinate and entertain with the popular dramatic form of the Yiddish *Purim shpil*.[47]

---

47. See Evi Michels, "Purimspiel," in *Enzyklopädie jüdischer Geschichte und Kultur*, ed. Dan Diner (Stuttgart: Metzler, 2014), 5:53–58.

The reception of the biblical character in the documents discussed above had Esther develop in several directions. Her having *two names*, as the multiple interpretations suggest, needed to be explained, especially when one of the names—the one most commonly used—may be understood as hinting at assimilation and at an endangered Jewish identity in the diaspora. To be properly Judaized, Esther had to be depicted in *prayer*; she had to be imagined as being concerned not only with her own well-being but also as expressing *solidarity and compassion* toward her people, to whom she is related by their common history and a common language. In order to be empowered into acting as a major agent in the history of Israel's salvation, so much so that a scroll was named after her and not after her uncle, Esther, her words, and her story had to be linked to the words and stories of *male* major agents such as Abraham, Moses, and David. Just as biblical men went through a process of rabbinization, biblical women, including Esther, were also *rabbinized* and therefore masculinized. Esther follows at times her uncle's advice, not unlike a rabbinic disciple who follows his master's advice, but she is also capable of acting of her own accord and rightly so, for her actions halakhically conform to and prefigure the statements of sages living hundreds of years after her.

Judith in the Hebrew Literature of the Middle Ages

Dagmar Börner Klein

1. The Figure of Judith in the Biblical Tradition

The heroine of the book of Judith is a young, beautiful widow who lives in the city of Bethulia, which is being besieged by Nebuchadnezzar's troops.[1] The troops of the Assyrian king are led by Holofernes, who wants to capture Bethulia so that he can press forward to Jerusalem.[2] When the drinking water in besieged Bethulia begins to run short and the city elders consider capitulation, Judith plans her own single-handed rescue operation. She puts on her most beautiful clothing and, together with her maidservant, goes into the enemy camp and succeeds in calling upon Holofernes. Holofernes is so impressed with Judith's beauty that he organizes a banquet for her. Judith remains alone with the intoxicated general in his sleeping quarters after the banquet. As soon as he has fallen asleep in his bed, Judith cuts off Holofernes's head with his own sword and returns to Bethulia with the severed head of the general. There the head of Holofernes is identified by Achior,[3] an Amorite military commander. Achior, once allied with the Assyrians, has been cast aside by Holofernes because he had warned Holofernes about the strength of the Jews and the power of their god. Achior is so overwhelmed by Judith and her deed that he converts to Judaism. The inhabitants of Bethulia, for their part, become

---

1. On historicity and geography, see Benedikt Otzen, *Tobit und Judith* (London: Sheffield Academic, 2002), 81–93.

2. On the content and structure of the story in detail, see Gerald West, "Judith," in *Eerdmans Commentary to the Hebrew Bible*, ed. James D. G. Dunn and John W. Rogerson (Grand Rapids: Eerdmans, 2003), 748–62.

3. See Barbara Schmitz, "Zwischen Achikar und Demaratos—die Bedeutung Achiors in der Juditherzählung," *BZ* 48 (2004): 19–38.

convinced by Judith's counsel to mount a surprise attack on the Assyrians, which also succeeds. They utterly destroy the Assyrians.[4]

The oldest attestation of this story about Judith, told in a considerably more detailed form, is found in the Greek Bible, known as the Septuagint.[5] From here it was taken up into the canon of Catholic biblical texts via a Latin translation. It is lacking, however, in Protestant editions of the Bible because it does not appear in the Hebrew Bible. Nor does the story of Judith appear in Josephus, Philo, or rabbinic literature.

Scholars believe that the story of Judith stems from the Hellenistic period, probably composed in either Alexandria or Palestine.[6] For a long time it was a matter of debate whether there was a Hebrew original of the Judith story. Since the story of Judith in the Septuagint uses terms derived from Hebrew, some scholars believed that a lost Hebrew original had exist-

---

4. Mathias Delcor, "Le livre de Judith et l'époque grecque," *Klio* 49 (1967): 151–79. Hans Yohanan Priebatsch, "Das Buch Judith und seine hellenistischen Quellen," *ZDPV* 90 (1974): 50–60.

5. Cameron Boyd-Taylor, trans., "Ioudith," in *A New English Translation of the Septuagint*, ed. Albert Pietersma and Benjamin G. Wright (New York: Oxford University Press, 2007), 441–55. See also Robert Hanhart, ed., *Judith*, SVTG 8.4 (Göttingen: Vandenhoeck & Ruprecht, 1979), 7–12.

6. A date during the Persian period is substantiated by Jehoshua M. Grintz, *The Book of Judith: A Reconstruction of the Original Hebrew Text with Introduction, Commentary, Appendices and Indices* [Hebrew] (Jerusalem: Mossad Bialik, 1957), 18–28. André LaCocque argues for a time of origin after Ezra and Nehemiah in *The Feminine Unconventional: Four Subversive Figures in Israel's Tradition* (Eugene, OR: Wipf & Stock, 1990), 1–6. On a date after the fall of Jerusalem in 70 CE, see Émile Mireaux, *La reine Bérénice* (Paris: Albin Michel, 1951), 167–78. On the location, see Carey A. Moore, *Judith: A New Translation with Introduction and Commentary*, AB 40 (Garden City, NY: Doubleday, 1985), 67–71; Tal Ilan, "And Who Knows Whether You Have Not Come to Domination for a Time Like This? (Esther 4:14): Esther, Judith and Susanna as Propaganda for Shelamzion's Queenship," in *Integrating Women into Second Temple History*, ed. Tal Ilan (repr. Peabody, MA: Hendrickson, 2002), 127–53. On page 135 Ilan dates the book of Judith in temporal proximity to the coronation of Salome Alexandra (Shelamzion) as queen of Judea in 79 BCE. See also Jan Willem van Henten, "Judith as Alternative Leader: A Rereading of Judith 7–13," in *A Feminist Companion to Esther, Judith and Susanna*, ed. Athalya Brenner (Sheffield: Sheffield Academic, 1995), 224–52. On similar motifs in Greek literature, see Mark Caponigro, "Judith, Holding the Tale of Herodotus," in *"No One Spoke Ill of Her": Essays on Judith*, ed. James C. VanderKam, EJL 2 (Atlanta: Scholars Press, 1992), 47–59. See also Barbara Schmitz, "Holofernes's Canopy," in *The Sword of Judith: Judith Studies across the Disciplines*, ed. Kevin R. Brine, Elena Ciletti, and Henrike Lähnemann (Cambridge: Open Book, 2010), 71–80.

ed.⁷ But the fact that all the biblical citations appearing in the Greek Judith story come from the Septuagint support the conclusion that the Greek book of Judith contains the original Judith story, and that the Hebraisms in it were used to adapt the story to the style of the Hebrew Bible.⁸

Jerome (350–420 CE) undertook a translation of the Judith story into Latin. Since various versions of it already existed, he integrated them into a story that, for him, was coherent.⁹ It is for this reason that the Latin Judith story is quite a bit shorter than the Greek story in the Septuagint. In addition, he gives the figure of Judith a different appearance from that in the Greek Bible. He tames Judith's beauty by dressing her modestly.¹⁰ Jerome also explains in detail how God employs Judith's beauty in conquering Holofernes. In the Latin story of Judith, she does not act of her own will but is rather God's instrument in defeating Holofernes and his men. God magnifies her beauty and makes it possible for the divine plan to be carried out successfully by Judith. She is thereby an instrument of God in Jerome's view. With this reinterpretation of the figure of Judith, Jerome, on the one hand, can shift God into the center of the story as the real savior of Israel. On the other hand, he ensures that Judith is not misunderstood to be a soldier's harlot but rather is depicted as a pious Jewish woman who, with

---

7. See Jan Joosten, "The Original Language and Historical Milieu of the Book of Judith," in *Meghillot: Studies in the Dead Sea Scrolls V–VI: A Festschrift for Devorah Dimant*, ed. Moshe Bar-Asher and Emanuel Tov (Jerusalem: Bialik Institute; Haifa: University of Haifa, 2007), 159–76; and Claudia Rakel, *Judit—Über Schönheit, Macht, und Widerstand im Krieg* (Berlin: de Gruyter, 2003), 33–40.

8. See Robert Hanhart, *Text und Textgeschichte des Buches Judit* (Göttingen: Vandenhoeck & Ruprecht, 1979), 7–23; Erich Zenger, *Das Buch Judit: Historische und legendarische Erzählungen*, JSHRZ 1.6 (Gütersloh: Gütersloher Verlagshaus, 1981), 429; André-Marie Dubarle, *Judith: Formes et sens des diverses traditions*, 2 vols. (Rome: Pontifical Biblical Institute, 1966), 1:1–15; Helmut Engel, "Der HERR ist ein Gott, der Kriege erschlägt: Zur Frage der griechischen Originalsprache und der Struktur des Buches Judith," in *Goldene Äpfel in silbernen Schalen*, ed. Klaus-Dieter Schnuck and Matthias Augustin (Frankfurt am Main: Lang, 1992), 155–68.

9. See Barbara Schmitz, "Ιουδιθ and Iudith: Überlegungungen zum Verhältnis der Judit-Erzählungen in der LXX und der Vulgata," in *Text Critical and Hermeneutical Studies in the Septuagint*, ed. Johann Cook and Hermann-Josef Stipp (Leiden: Brill, 2012), 358–80; Dubarle, *Judith*, 1:15–19 and 1:44–47; Zenger, *Das Buch Judit*, 429–30. Note Jerome's statement in "Epistulae S. Hieronymi," in PL 22:960: "Multorum codicum varietatem vitiosissimam amputavi."

10. See Jdt 8:1: "erat autem eleganti aspectu"; 10:3: "inposuit mitram super caput suum."

the help of God, saves the population of her city. The Judith of Jerome is, in contrast to the Judith of the Septuagint, a passive figure who is led by God.

Jerome's version of the Judith story was translated in the Middle Ages several times into Hebrew.[11] In 1966, André-Marie Dubarle published three of these Hebrew translations, which he designated as Versions B, C, and D of the story. Version B designates the text of two manuscripts in the Bodleian Library in Oxford.[12] Version C, another manuscript from Oxford, was printed in 1651 in Venice.[13] The first edition of Version D appeared in 1731 or 1732.[14]

In Version C, Judith becomes the daughter of Beeri; in the Greek story, Judith is the daughter of Merari and the widow of Manasseh (Jdt 8:7–8). A comparison of the Hebrew translations of Jdt 10:3 shows that the descriptions of Judith in these different versions do not agree. This indicates that the figure of Judith continued to be adapted according to the period, so that Judith in her external appearance always corresponds to a woman of the then-current audience. Thus Jerome lets Judith wear a mitra on her head, a headdress that women tied up underneath the chin.[15] In the Hebrew Version C, Judith wears a crown in order to signal that she is on a par with the enemy king. In Version B, Judith wears a veil, which covers her beauty.[16]

---

11. For a substantiation of why the Hebrew translations trace back to Jerome's Latin text, see Dagmar Börner-Klein, *Gefährdete Braut und schöne Witwe: Hebräische Judit-Geschichten* (Wiesbaden: Marixverlag, 2007), 240–46.

12. See Dubarle, *Judith*, 1:20–27 and 2:8–96. MS B^1 = MS Heb. D. 11. fol. 259–265 (twelfth century), B^2 = Oppenheimer 716, fol. 164–176 (sixteenth century).

13. Bodleian Library, Oxford Opp. 8.1105, Number 1211 in *Catalogue of Hebrew Manuscripts of the Collection of Elkan Nathan Adler*, ed. Elkan Nathan Adler (Cambridge: Cambridge University Press, 1921), 79.

14. Adolf Jellinek, *Bet ha-Midrasch: Sammlung kleiner Midraschim und vermischter Abhandlungen aus der älteren jüdischen Literatur*, 6 vols. (repr. Jerusalem: Wahrmann, 1967), 2:12–22; Jehuda Dov Eisenstein, *Ozar Midrashim: A Library of Two Hundred Minor Midrashim. Edited with Introductions and Notes*, 2 vols. (New York: Noble Offset, 1915), 1:203–9. See also Dubarle, *Judith*, 1:33–37; Jellinek, *Bet ha-Midrasch*, 1:xxiii and 2:xi; August Wünsche, *Aus Israels Lehrhallen: Kleine Midraschim zur späteren legendarischen Literatur des Alten Testaments*, 5 vols. (repr. Hildesheim: Olms, 1967), 2:2, 164–81; Börner-Klein, *Gefährdete Braut*, 19–239.

15. Karl Ernst Georges, *Ausführliches lateinisch-deutsches Handwörterbuch*, 2 vols. (Darmstadt: Wissenschaftliche Buchgesellschaft, 1985), 2:951: "a headband with cheek pieces that was tied up under the chin" and was worn by women.

16. For further Judith versions, see Deborah Levine Gera, "The Jewish Textual Traditions," in Brine, Ciletti, and Lähnemann, *The Sword of Judith*, 23–40.

The historicity of the Judith story has been called into question, given that many motifs from other biblical stories are repeated in the Judith story.[17] Tal Ilan has emphasized that the story of Joseph serves as "an intertext for the book of Judith."[18] Van Henten sees in the figure of Judith the embodiment of a female Moses figure.[19] Allusions to Cleopatra, Antiochus IV Epiphanes, and the Seleucid general Nicanor also have been seen in the Judith story.[20]

2. The Hebrew Short Stories in Which Judith Is Anonymous

The first Hebrew version of a Judith story is from Jacob ben Nissim ibn Shahin (ca. 990–1062).[21] Rabbi Nissim locates the story in Jerusalem without indicating in which period it occurs or who the persons are who are involved. The heroine, a young daughter of a prophet, remains anonymous, just like the king that the heroine decapitates. In contrast to the stories in the Greek and Latin Bibles, the anonymous prophet's daughter must pass by the guards at the city gate of Jerusalem; they suspect her of wanting to leave the city because she wants to betray it to the enemy. The young woman, thus, must first convince the guards to trust in her intention to save the city. When she succeeds, she goes to the enemy army's camp before the gates of the city. There, she asks the king to save her and her family when he captures Jerusalem. She vows to the king that her father, who is a prophet, has foreseen his victory. The king believes the young woman and

---

17. See on this Gera, "Jewish Textual Traditions," 25.
18. Ilan, "Esther, Judith and Susanna," 147–48.
19. See Jan Willem van Henten, "Judith as a Female Moses: Judith 7–13 in the Light of Exodus 17, Numbers 20, and Deuteronomy 33:8–11," in *Reflections on Theology and Gender*, ed. Fokkelien van Dijk-Hemmes and Athalya Brenner (Kampen: Kok Pharos, 1994), 33–48.
20. See Peter W. Haider, "Judith—eine zeitgenössische Antwort auf Kleopatra III als Beschützerin der Juden?," *Grazer Beiträge* 22 (1998): 117–28; Solomon Zeitlin, "The Books of Esther and Judith: A Parallel," in *The Book of Judith: Greek Text with English Translation, Commentary and Critical Notes*, ed. Morton Scott Enslin (Leiden: Brill, 1972), 29–30; Gera, "Jewish Textual Traditions," 26–38.
21. See Dubarle, *Judith*, 1:82–84 and 2:104–9; Jellinek, *Bet ha-Midrasch*, 1:130–31; Richard Adelbert Lipsius, "Jüdische Quellen zur Judithsage," *Zeitschrift für wissenschaftliche Theologie* 10 (1867): 348; Wünsche, *Aus Israels Lehrhallen*, 2:183–85; Deborah Levine Gera, "Shorter Medieval Tales of Judith," in Brine, Ciletti, and Lähnemann, *The Sword of Judith*, 81–95; Börner-Klein, *Gefährdete Braut*, 247–57.

promises to grant her request if she will marry him. She agrees, and the king celebrates with a great feast, at which he gets drunk. After the king has fallen asleep, "the young woman turns her heart toward heaven," cuts off the king's head, wraps it in her outer garment, and goes through the camp unscathed until she stands once again before the guards on the city wall of Jerusalem. The guards again think that she is lying when she calls out to them: "Open the gate. For the Holy One, may He be praised, helped me so that I could slay the enemy."[22] A prince of the enemy king, similar to Achior in the biblical story, comes to her aid:

> But the king had a prince among his princes who was in the habit of saying to the king: "Turn away from this people, *do not be hostile toward them and do not fight against them* [cf. Deut 2:19], for their god loves them and will not deliver them into your hands. See what he has done to them (who) were kings and princes before you, which was their end. And he had rebuked the king until the king had become wrathful and commanded that he be bound and hung up alive at the city gate [see Deut 21:22–23].
> And when the young woman saw that they did not believe her words, she said: "If you do not believe me, then see, the prince who is hanging at the gate will recognize the head of the king."
> Then they believed her words and opened the gate. And she showed the head to the prince hanging there. And he recognized it and said: "Praised be YHWH who delivers him into your hands [cf. 2 Sam 18:28] and has saved you from his hands" [cf. 1 Sam 12:11].[23]

The inhabitants of Jerusalem thereupon fight successfully against the enemy army, which they pursue as far as Antiochia. In Jerusalem, the city fathers praise God with a recitation from Lev 26:42: "I will remember my covenant with Jacob."

This story of an anonymous Judith reduces the biblical Judith story to its essentials: a woman employs her beauty and intelligence in order to cut off the head of an enemy king. New in this version of the story is the motif of the danger the heroine faces in defending her actions to the guards of the city. New, in addition, is the motif of the victory of the enemy king which was supposedly foretold by the father of the young woman; the alleged prophecy makes it plausible for the king to believe that this woman

---

22. Börner-Klein, *Gefährdete Braut*, 254.
23. Börner-Klein, *Gefährdete Braut*, 254.

wants to be saved by him. This increases the narrative tension and offers plausible explanations for the heroine's actions.

The anonymous Hebrew story handed down by Rabbi Nissim is expanded further in the Ma'ase Yehudit, which weaves elements of narrative content into the story.[24] In the Ma'ase Yehudit, the Judith figure, who likewise is the daughter of a prophet in Jerusalem, at first remains anonymous.[25] But when she presents herself to the enemy leader, she mentions her name:

> Then they opened[26] *the gate of the city to her, and she went out with her maidservant.*
>
> *She came to the camp. And it happened that, as the army troop that was on guard saw her, they asked her:* "Who are you, from where do you come, and where are you going?"
>
> *And the young woman answered and said to them:* "I am Judith, from the people [in] Jerusalem. When I saw the obstinacy of the people of Jerusalem, that they do not want to bow down to the king, our lord, Oliforni, and to save themselves from death, I fled from them by means of a ruse. I have something to tell the king, our lord, a good plan for how he can take the city. My own life, though, may be booty."[27]
>
> *And her words were good in their eyes, and she found favor in the eyes of all who saw her* [cf. Esth 2:15], *and they delighted greatly in her* [cf. 1 Kgs 1:40] *and went with her.*
>
> *And they brought her before the king.*
>
> *And when the king saw her, she found favor in his eyes* [cf. Esth 5:2].

The essential difference between Ma'ase Yehudit and the Nissim narrative lies in the fact that, in Rabbi Nissim's version, the severed head of the king that is shown in Jerusalem motivates the men of Jerusalem to go to battle against the enemy. In the Nissim narrative, they are not advised in matters of war by Judith, a woman.

---

24. On the development of the text, see Börner-Klein, *Gefährdete Braut*, 260–75.

25. See Dubarle, *Judith*, 1:94–98 and 2:152–63; Börner-Klein, *Gefährdete Braut*, 258–75.

26. Börner-Klein, *Gefährdete Braut*, 262. The elements of the narrative that also appear in Rabbi Nissim's version are in italics.

27. Jer 21:9: "He who dwells in this city will die by the sword and by famine and by pestilence; but he who goes out and goes over to the Chaldeans who are besieging you will live, and he will have his own life as booty."

A third version of the Judith story is found in Moses Gaster's *Exempla of the Rabbis*.[28] In this narrative, Judith is the daughter of Achitob and comes from one of the most respected families in Jerusalem. She is a pious and beautiful woman of royal and priestly origins. The enemy king bears the name of Seleukos[29] and the incident is dated as taking place on the eighteenth of Adar, "on which day Seleukos went up [to Jerusalem]." This addendum signals that the story is to be accepted as an historical event. In this story Judith does not act at her own discretion; God puts into her heart that God will cause a miracle to occur through her. The motif of the danger posed by the gatekeepers is made as brief as possible. Having arrived at the army of Seleukos, Judith announces to the king's servants that she has a secret matter to communicate to the king. When she enters into the presence of the king, he asks her rank, and she answers that she comes from a family of kings and high priests. Thus Judith has the rank of the enemy king, but her additional high priestly origins place her above someone with merely royal origins. When the king organizes a big banquet for Judith and "asks her to do a sinful thing," the motif of original purity is taken over from the biblical Judith story. Judith pretends to be impure for the king and asks for permission to go to the spring in the night so that she can purify herself. Thereafter, so she promises the king, whatever might be good in his eyes may happen to her. The king agrees, organizes the banquet, gets drunk, and Judith cuts off his head. She can move unscathed through the enemy camp in the direction of Jerusalem because the king gave her permission to visit the spring in the night. The guards let themselves be persuaded that Judith is not an enemy when they see the severed head of the king. The narrative ends abruptly with the remark that this day has been declared a feast day. In this narrative, Judith's beauty plays an important role, but still more important is her status: she is of royal and high priestly origins. It is only this that makes her access to the king possible.

---

28. See Dubarle, *Judith*, 1:80–81 and 2:100–103; Börner-Klein, *Gefährdete Braut*, 276–83; Moses Gaster, *The Exempla of the Rabbis, Being a Collection of Exempla, Apologues and Tales* (London: Ktav, 1924), 166.

29. See Elias J. Bickerman, *The Jews in the Greek Age* (Cambridge: Harvard University Press, 1988), 6–7.

3. The Figure of Judith: Between the Biblical and Roman Period

A fourth Hebrew story, Megillat Yehudit,[30] draws from the Esther story and depicts Judith as the daughter of Mordechai. The beginning of the story of Megillat Yehudit, which comprises eight chapters, mentions a conflict between Nebuchadnezzar and Arfachshad and thereby dates the narrative to the Median-Persian period. Then, in Megillat Yehudit 1:10, men from the army of Alexander the Macedonian are brought into the story, and Judith takes herself to the camp of the Greeks. Oliforni is the commander-in-chief of the army of Nebuchadnezzar and Achior is his governor (*hēgemon*). Achior, however, first warns Oliforni about the God of the Jews after the leaders of Moab and Ammon already have done this. By this device, a doubling of the motif of warning about the danger of an attack on the Jews is achieved, and the narrative tension is increased. Striking is the fact that Judith does not go to Holofernes, but rather to "a king." This and the fact that Megillat Yehudit comprises eight chapters suggest that one of the short anonymous narratives and one of the Hebrew Judith stories that built upon a translation of the Latin Judith story of the Bible were combined with each other to form a single narrative without resolving all the discrepancies. In Megillat Yehudit 8:1, the figure of Judith is traced back in a genealogical series to the tribe of Reuben. She is, as in the biblical Judith stories, a widow; the name of her deceased husband is Manasseh. Judith proceeds to the act of salvation only after she has seen that the Israelites keep the commandments (8:7), for only then does God prove to be the savior. This motif of legal piety appears here for the first time while, in the biblical stories, Judith's piety is emphasized through her lengthy prayer and fasting. The enemy in Megillat Yehudit is characterized as the "uncircumcised and impure one" (8:7). Judith does not have royal rank in Megillat Yehudit. She merely tells the king about her brothers, who are prophets (8:7). In the morning, after Judith reaches the city with the severed head of the king, the Israelites move out against the army of the Greeks with the words of the Shema "Hear, O Israel" (Deut 6:4) on their lips. An addendum to this story mentions the fact that the Israelites had killed innumerable Greeks, as well as Gaskalga, whose ordinances they annulled.

---

30. See Text "E" and Midr. Num. 7 in Dubarle, *Judith*, 2:126–37 and 1:90–92; Börner-Klein, *Gefährdete Braut*, 296–325; Susan Weingarten, "Food, Sex, and Redemption in *Megillat Yehudit*," in Brine, Ciletti, and Lähnemann, *The Sword of Judith*, 110–25; and Gera, "Shorter Medieval Hebrew Tales of Judith," 81–95.

It is assumed that "Gaskalga" is Gaius Caligula,[31] since the text of Megillat Taanit mentions that, on 22 Shevat, the temple was purified of the image of the "Gasqelges," and Tacitus reports that Caligula, who was murdered in 41 CE, had an image of himself erected in the temple at Jerusalem.[32] The story of Megillat Yehudit thus ends in Roman times.

4. Judith: The Daughter of Mattathias

By means of a second addendum to Megillat Yehudit, which reports on the Maccabees' discovery of the flacon of oil sealed by the high priest, the Judith story is also connected with the Maccabean period and with the rededication of the temple. A third addendum compares Israel's strength with the sun at the solstice. But from the Megillat Taanit for 17 Elul, there emerges the fact that, in this period, Israel's women were considered to be in danger because enemy soldiers were stationed in Jerusalem.[33] In the entry for this date, it is reported that the Romans were driven out of Jerusalem, and a later addendum states the following in explanation of this:[34]

> The Greek kings let war camps be established in the cities, so that the soldiers could rape the brides [before the wedding], and [only] afterwards were they married to their men. And [in this way] they kept Israel from having pleasure with their women, in order to confirm what is said: *You shall betroth a wife, but another man will lay with her.* (Deut 28:30)
> And no man wanted to marry a woman, because those [from the] war camp repeatedly brought them secretly [into the camp], for it is written: *And I will take from them the voice of joy and the voice of gladness, the voice of the bridegroom and the voice of the bride, the sound of the millstones and the light of the lamps.* (Jer 25:10) And when they heard the sound of the millstones in Burni, they said: "Oath of the son, oath of the son." And when they saw the light of the lamps in Beror Chajil: "there is a feast, there is a feast."
> And Mattathias, whose son was the high priest Yohanan, had a daughter. When the sign for a marriage was given to him, [a group from] the war camp came in order to defile her and they did not leave him

---

31. Börner-Klein, *Gefährdete Braut*, 323–25.

32. See Charles Dennis Fisher, *Cornelii Tacii Historiarum libri* (repr. Oxford: Clarendon, 1990), 5, 9.

33. See Vered Noam, *Megillat Taanit: Versions, Interpretations, History; With a Critical Edition* [Hebrew] (Jerusalem: Yad Ben-Zvi Press, 2003), 90–92, 229–31.

34. Quoted from Börner-Klein, *Gefährdete Braut*, 324–25.

in peace. Then Matthathias and his sons were ready for battle, and the Greeks were delivered into their hands, and they killed them.

And the day on which they were annihilated they made into a feast day.

Thus the statement that the Romans were driven out of Jerusalem is corrected. According to this explanation, it was the Greeks who were driven out of the city because they applied the *ius primae noctis* to all the brides, which means that the sovereign in a district exercised his right to deflower a bride. In order to prevent this, according to the *Megillat Taanit* for 17 Elul, the Israelites had married secretly and had agreed on secret signals for making each other aware of an imminent wedding.

According to the Megillat Taanit for 17 Elul, problems arose when the daughter of Mattathias, the son of the high priest Yohanan, wanted to marry. A royal wedding could not be concealed because it was celebrated as a public event. When soldiers intrude upon the wedding celebration in order to have the *ius primae noctis* carried out upon the bride, Mattathias's men thwart them.

The motif of the endangered bride mentioned in the Megillat Taanit for 17 Elul is intriguingly interwoven with the Judith story in further Hebrew narratives.[35] In each of these stories,[36] a surrogate of the king who claims the right of *ius primae noctis* upon a bride is killed. As a reaction to this, the king whose surrogate was killed besieges Jerusalem, and Judith, the beautiful daughter of Mattathias, makes plans to kill the king.[37] She conceals a dagger on her person to ensure that she has an instrument at hand with which to kill the king at the right moment. In these Judith stories, the king likewise stages a feast for Judith, but he does not drink exorbitantly. He kisses Judith in plain view of all his guests. A quotation from Judg 16:19 ("and she made him sleep in her lap") suggests that more than just kisses were exchanged between Judith and the king. As soon as the king has fallen asleep, Judith draws her dagger and decapitates the king. Thereupon, Mattathias and his men defeat the enemy in devastating fashion.

---

35. Börner-Klein, *Gefährdete Braut*, 326; Gera, "Shorter Medieval Hebrew Tales of Judith," 81–95.

36. Bibl. Nat. de France, Hebr. 1459.2 (fol. 83v–84rv), printed in Dubarle, *Judith*, 1:100–101 and 2:170–77.

37. See Börner-Klein, *Gefährdete Braut*, 326–37.

5. Hannah, Daughter of the Hasmonean, Daughter of the High Priest Yohanan

In a manner similar to that in the Megillat Taanit for 17 Elul, the motif of danger to brides is incorporated into further Hebrew narratives in the Greco-Roman period but through the focus upon a specific woman. This woman is designated either as a "daughter of the Hasmonean" or as a "daughter of the high priest Yohanan," or she bears the name "Hannah."[38] She lives in a time in which the Greeks have decreed strict ordinances against Israel in order to hinder Jews from carrying out the commandments. Circumcision and ritual baths are prohibited, and the *ius primae noctis* is mandated. The situation escalates further when the daughter of the high priest, or the daughter of the Hasmonean, marries. The king sends his governor to the wedding party who demands the surrender of the bride. The bride refuses, however, to be handed over to the governor. Instead, she accuses the wedding party of being complicit in the ordinances imposed by the Greeks but the wedding party does nothing to save her. Those who think themselves pious just look on idly as she is delivered up. Finally, it is the brother of the bride who is ready to step in against the governor. The brother's name is "Judah." The figure of Judah replaces the figure of Judith who, by means of her beauty, can bring about the death of the enemy. Instead, Judah plans an ambush for the purpose of killing the governor. He brings his sister to the governor, wins his trust through his flattery, and is successful in having the guards sent away. When Judah is alone with his sister and the governor, he draws his sword and cuts off the head of the governor. But, since the danger is not yet averted with the death of the governor (because the king still lives), the biblical Judith story is attached to this narrative tradition so as to let Judith, who appears here as a widow, to proceed to her own act of decapitating the king. Narrative elements from the short Judith stories, though, are woven into the text.[39]

Finally, in a further narrative stage, the story of Hannah is attached in the form of an exegesis of Ps 37:15 ("the word comes into their own heart"). Hannah is saved from imminent rape at the hands of a Greek in the temple by her husband Eleazar, who is the son-in-law of the high priest Yohanan. Eleazar kills his wife's attacker. Attached to this story is a com-

---

38. See Dubarle, *Judith*, 1:84–85, 2:110–17 and 1:86–88 (as well as 2:118–25); Börner-Klein, *Gefährdete Braut*, 338–94.

39. See Börner-Klein, *Gefährdete Braut*, 340–42.

ment by a Rabbi Isaac that states that Galisko waged war against the house of the Hasmoneans. The Hasmoneans were victorious against his army with the aid of the heavenly help of the angels. However, this text, too, assumes that Galisko's army consists of Greeks. The narrative concludes with the story of the miracle of the oil at Hanukkah.[40]

6. From Judith to Judah

The Judith story turns up again in Jewish literature in the Middle Ages, around the year 1000, in the form of an anonymous heroine mentioned first by Rabbi Nissim. Rashi (Rabbi Solomon ben Isaac, 1040–1105) does not mention the figure of Judith when, in his commentary on b. Shabb. 23a, he points out that women also are obligated to light the Hanukkah lamp because it was through a woman that a miracle happened to stop the Greeks from obeying a court official's order to copulate with all virgin women before their husbands did so. Rashi gives no information about the nature of the miracle.[41] According to Rashbam (Rabbi Samuel ben Meir, 1085–1174), the grandson of Rashi, the miracle of Hanukkah was brought about by Judith, as the commentary on the Tosafot to b. Meg. 4a emphasizes.

The anonymous Judith figure of the short Hebrew Judith narratives must prove herself before the guards of the besieged city. Before the enemy king, she declares that her brothers are prophets or that her father is a prophet. Thus the beauty motif of the biblical Judith story is vastly diminished. The beauty of the woman is no longer decisive for the king in his decision to entrust himself to her, but rather it is the secret information that she promises to communicate to him. It is this that makes the woman attractive for the king. Judith's beauty is thus removed from the focus of the narrative; it is only superficially the means used in approaching the king. The Judith who then decapitates the king is described, as in the biblical Judith stories, as a woman who trusts in God. But, in the Hebrew Judith stories, she is a less interesting figure than in the biblical narratives because she has less to say in them. The Judith in the Hebrew narrative tradition

---

40. It is interesting that there are further Hebrew narratives about the salvation of women in the Hasmonean/Maccabean period that are handed down without the interweaving of a Judith narrative. See Börner-Klein, *Gefährdete Braut*, 395–436.

41. See Regina Grundmann, "Judit, Hanna und Chanukka," in *Gefährdete Braut*, 471–82.

does not pray to God as in the Latin and Greek Judith stories. In addition, the figure of the beautiful widow is blended into the Hebrew narrative tradition with the figure of the endangered bride, as becomes clear in Kol Bo, the last text that I shall discuss.[42]

In the Kol Bo, which probably comes from the thirteenth or fourteenth century, the anonymous author at first addresses the narrative discrepancy in the Judith story; that is, the king gets drunk during the banquet, although he intends to spend the night with Judith. Thus, in the explanation in the Kol Bo of b. Shab. 23a, it says:[43]

> And the women, too, are obligated in regard to the lamp of Hanukkah, for they, too, are included in this miracle.
>
> Explanation: The enemies had come to destroy all men, women, and children. Then it happened that, through the hand of a woman, a great miracle was done for them. And her name was Judith, as it is stated in the haggadah.[44] She was the daughter of the high priest Yohanan and she was of a very beautiful form. And the Greek king had said that he wanted to sleep with her. But she let him eat a cheese dish so that he might become thirsty from it and drink a lot, so that he might become intoxicated, lay himself down, and fall asleep. And he became drunk, laid himself down, and fell asleep. And she was there when he had fallen asleep. Then she took his sword and cut off his head and brought it to Jerusalem. But, when the army saw that its hero was dead, it fled.
>
> And for this reason, it is the habit to prepare a cheese dish for Hanukkah.
>
> [...] as we read in the Mishnah:[45] Yohanan's daughter gave the leader of the enemies cheese to eat, so that he would intoxicate himself. And she cut off his head so that all [enemies] fled.
>
> For this reason, it is the custom to eat cheese at the Feast of Dedication.[46]

It is clear here in Kol Bo that the different figures of women that appear in the Hebrew Judith stories, the endangered bride and the beautiful widow,

---

42. For the text of the Kol Bo, see http://sammlungen.ub.uni-frankfurt.de/inchebr/content/titleinfo/5307135.

43. Quoted from Lipsius, "Jüdische Quellen zur Judithsage," 357.

44. The literal meaning is "tale." The haggadah comprises the area of rabbinic literature that is not legal.

45. The texts in rabbinic literature that refer to the exegesis of the Bible.

46. The feast of Hanukkah is meant.

blend together in the medieval Hebrew narrative tradition. Buried in the Jewish collective memory is the miracle that, according to b. Shab. 23a, was brought about by women in the Greek period. That miracle is the action of a heroine who is either like the biblical Judith who decapitates the enemy or like the bride endangered by the *ius primae noctis* who rebels against being delivered over to sexual intercourse with the sovereign. As an endangered bride, though, she loses Judith's power to strike back. It is her brother Judah who kills the enemy king. Against this background, it is astonishing that in Kol Bo the daughter of Yohanan, who is an embodiment of the endangered bride, regains the power of Judith to strike back.

Commentary

The Tradition of Eve in the Commentaries of Rashi and Ramban

Gerhard Langer

Biblical and parabiblical themes appear in diverse forms in the Middle Ages. Judith, for example, who for a long time played hardly any role in the Jewish tradition, emerges from obscurity.[1] Along with genres already known from late antiquity, such as midrash, *piyyut*, or parabiblical narratives, there appear now, among others, the commentary, the sermon, and the mystical treatment of the tradition. The halakic pervasion of the commandments is further developed; rules of faith are established. In the liturgy, standards that are valid to the present day are set, but the narrative also is given greater space. The idea of the multiple senses of Scripture is much more fully developed than in antiquity. The word *pardes* becomes known as an acronym for the senses of Scripture: *peshat* (generally recognized exegesis, also the literal meaning), *remez* (allegory), *derash* (rabbinic midrashic[2] exegesis), and *sod* (mystical exegesis). These senses can branch out into various additional senses of Scripture. Separate articles in this volume will go into the kabbalist interpretation.

The medieval tradition undoubtedly does not operate in a vacuum. In the European context (Ashkenaz), the confrontation with Christianity becomes perceptible in religious practice and theory. One example is the significance of blood in the Middle Ages. The twelfth-century French scholar Rabbi Joseph Bechor Shor equated the menstrual blood of women with the covenantal blood of circumcision in reaction to the charge by Christians that Jews did not include women in the process of salvation.

---

1. See Kevin R. Brine, Elena Ciletti, and Henrike Lähnemann, eds., *The Sword of Judith: Judith Studies across the Disciplines* (Cambridge: Open Book, 2010).

2. On the theme of midrash, see Gerhard Langer, *Midrasch* (Tübingen: Mohr Siebeck, 2016).

While Christians baptized men as well as women, there was and is no circumcision of women in Judaism. For Bechor Shor, a process comparable to circumcision was performed through the blood of menstruation within the framework of the correct observance of the rules of purity and impurity; in circumcision, the focus is upon the covenantal blood.[3]

Few stories in the Bible have exerted as much of an impact upon the relationship between the sexes and have experienced such a reception as that of Eve and Adam. The Jewish tradition, too, intensively interpreted it, commented upon it, and developed it further. As a result, I concentrate here upon two exegeses in the form of commentary.

1. Rashi

The important medieval commentator Rabbi Shlomo ben Yitzhak (known as Rashi) from Troyes (ca. 1040–1105) is one of the most influential voices of the Jewish tradition. He forms the bridge between medieval exegesis and the rabbinic exegesis of late antiquity. His commentary on the five books of Torah (the Pentateuch) incorporates numerous traditions and combines them into its own synthesis.

In regard to Rashi's approach to the theme of women and sexuality, Tal Ilan's discussion of Rashi's commentary on the Talmud is deeply rewarding.[4] She concludes that Rashi depicts women as being governed powerfully by their sexual drive, but in so doing Rashi perverts or takes a one-sided view of the original intention of rabbinic texts. In the context of Torah study, in Rashi's interpretation of m. Sotah 3:4 (in his commentary on b. Sotah 21b), he equates the concept of *tiflut* with sexual excess:[5]

> Rabbi Eliezer says: Whoever teaches his daughter Torah teaches her *tiflut*.
> Rabbi Joshua says: a woman prefers one kav *tiflut* to nine kav *perishut*.

Rashi comments:

---

3. See Shaye J. D. Cohen, *Why Aren't Jewish Women Circumcised? Gender and Covenant in Judaism* (Berkeley: University of California Press, 2005), 93–108.

4. Tal Ilan, "Folgenreiche Lektüren: Gender in Raschis Kommentar zum babylonischen Talmud," in *Der Differenz auf der Spur: Frauen und Gender in Aschkenas*, ed. Christiane E. Müller and Andrea Schatz (Berlin: Metropol, 2004), 21–49.

5. Tal Ilan understands *perishut*, on the other hand, as Pharisaic teaching and interprets the text as a preference for the study of the Torah by women as opposed to, as wrongly understood, the Pharisaic interpretation.

She prefers rather to nourish herself with little food and, in sexual relations, to have her *tiflut* rather than nine measures with *perishut*—[that is,] rather than to forego the *tiflut*.

In a commentary on b. ʿAbod. Zar. 18b, Rashi disparages the learned Beruria by pointing out that when her husband, Rabbi Meir, tested her by means of a student, she failed to withstand the student, who eventually seduced her. Thereupon, she strangled herself, and her husband fled out of shame. According to Tal Ilan, "she became the decisive text for what the rabbis really wanted to tell us about a possible female scholar— that such a creature neither has existed nor can exist, since it would be impossible for her to overcome her natural feminine sexual instincts."[6] Naomi Cohen has convincingly shown that the text is almost certainly a late addition (fourteenth century) and therefore cannot be attributed to Rashi.[7]

This essay examines Rashi's views with reference to the creation of the first woman. He speaks indirectly about the creation of woman in his commentary on Gen 2:8. Rashi explains, with the aid of a hermeneutic deduction, that in Gen 1:27 a general statement about the creation of humans is made and that this statement is subsequently concretized in Gen 2:8. Thus, in the first account of the creation only the general plan is presented, but the second creation account presents the effective execution of the plan.

In Gen 2:8, the creation of woman finally occurs. Here Rashi draws upon the midrash Pirqe R. El. 12, which says:

> And (Adam) was at his leisure in the garden of Eden, like one of the ministering angels. The Holy One, blessed be He, said: I am alone in My world and this one (Adam) also is alone in his world. There is no propagation before Me and this one (Adam) has no propagation in his life, hereafter all the creatures will say, Since there was no propagation in his life, it is he who has created us. It is not good for man to be alone, as it is said, "And the Lord God said: It is not good for man to be alone; I will make him a help mate opposite him …" [Gen 2:18].[8]

---

6. Ilan, "Folgenreiche Lektüren," 48.

7. See Naomi Cohen, "Bruria in the Bavli and in Rashi Avodah Zarah 18b," *Tradition* 48.2–3 (2015): 29–40.

8. English translation (slightly adapted) from Gerald Friedlander, ed. and trans., *Pirkê de Rabbi Eliezer* (London: Kegan Paul, 1916), 85–86.

Rashi states:

> "It is not good,[9] etc.": Lest they [people] say, "There are two dominions: the Holy One, blessed be He, is alone among the heavenly beings, and He has no mate, and this one [man] among the earthly creatures, has no mate."
>
> "A helpmate opposite him": If he is worthy, she will be a helpmate. If he is not worthy, she will be against him, to fight him [see b. Yebam. 63a].[10]

The creation of woman, thus, took place not least of all to disabuse humans from the erroneous assumption that humans possess divine authority.

The term ʿ*ezer* (help) has provoked much discussion. In the Bible, it never designates a subordinate person but rather one who is at least coequal. The exegesis is based also on the meaning of *kenegdo*, which can be translated best as "appropriate to him." But since it also can have the meaning "opposite to him," the term is applied by the rabbis to the particular behavior of women.

Rashi continues in regard to Gen 2:20:

> Gen 2:20: "And the Lord God caused a deep sleep to fall": When He brought them [the animals], He brought before him of every species,

---

9. Interesting here are, for example, the exegeses in Gen. Rab. 17:2, where it says: "Not good [the adam being alone]" [Gen 2:18]. Rabbi Yaakov taught: Anyone (man) that has no woman lives without good, without help, without happiness, without blessing, without atonement. Without good: 'Not good for the human to be alone.' Without help: 'I'll make him a helpmate' [Gen 2:18]. Without happiness: 'And you and your house will be happy' [Deut 14:26]. Without atonement: 'And he will atone for himself and for his house' [Lev 16:11]. Without blessing: 'To attach blessing to your house' [Ezek 44:30]. Rabbi Simon in the name of R. Yehoshua ben Levi said: Even without peace, as it is written 'And for you peace, and for your house, peace' [1 Sam 25:6]. Rabbi Yehoshua of Sichnin in the name of R. Levi said: Even without life, as it is written 'See life with the woman you love' [Eccl 9:9]. R. Chiya bar Gamdi said: He is not even a whole human [*'adam shalem*], for it says: 'And He blessed them and called their name Adam.' [Gen 5:2]—the two together are called Adam. And there are those who say: he even diminishes the Image, as it is written 'Because in the Image of Elohim, He made Adam' [Gen 9:6], what is written afterwards? 'And you, be fruitful and multiply' [Gen 9:7]" (translation from Sefaria website).

10. An English translation is found on the Sefaria website or also on "The Complete Jewish Bible with Rashi Commentary" (https://tinyurl.com/SBLPress6014a). The latter one is used here.

male and female. He (Adam) said, "Everyone has a mate, but I have no mate." Immediately, "And God caused to fall" [Gen. Rab. 17:4].
Gen 2:21: "Of his sides": Of his sides, like Exod 26:20: "And for the side of the tabernacle." This coincides with what they [the rabbis] said: They were created with two faces [see b. ʿEruv. 18a; b. Ber. 61a].[11]

At this point, Rashi falls back on the conception of the creation of an androgynous primeval human as described in Gen. Rab. 8:1 or more precisely in b. ʿEruvin:

> Said Rabbi Shmuel bar Nachman: In the hour when the Holy One created the first human, He created [for] him a double face [*di-prosopon/du-partsufin*] and sawed him and made him backs. They objected to him: "But it says, 'He took one of his ribs [*tselaʿot*] …'" [Gen 2:21]! He said to them: [It means] "[one] of his sides," just as you would say, "And for the side [*tselaʿ*] of the tabernacle" [Exod 26:20].[12]

Instead of "rib," the term "side" is to be preferred, which resonates linguistically with an echo of the side parts of the tabernacle.

> Gen 2:22: "And He closed": the place of the incision [see b. Ber. 61a].
> "And he slept, and He took": So that he should not see the piece of flesh from which she was created, lest she be repulsive to him [see b. Sanh. 39a].
> "[And He] built": [He made her] like a building, broad at the bottom and narrow at the top, so that she can carry a fetus, like a storehouse of wheat, which is broad at the bottom and narrow on top, so that its burden should not weigh on its walls.
> "[And He] built the side … into a woman": lit. to a woman, to become a woman.
> "Gideon made it into an ephod": lit. to an ephod, to become an ephod.

For these passages, Rashi again uses other models. In b. Sanh. 39a, the narrative of the creation of woman from the sleeping Adam is used for an instruction of the (non-Jewish) emperor on the Creation. When anyone

---

11. The image of the double face still plays a great role in Jewish mysticism. There, it expresses, among other things, the union of two divine "parts:" the masculine *tiferet* and the feminine *malkhut*. On the conception of *du-partsufin*, see Moshe Idel, "Panim: Faces and Re-Presentations in Jewish Thought," in *Representing God*, ed. Hava Tirosh-Samuelson and Aaron W. Hughes (Leiden: Brill, 2004), 71–102.

12. Cf. also Lev. Rab. 14:1 as well as the sections of Ber. 34b–35a and Shem. 55a, 231a in the mystical book Zohar.

sees raw meat, he will not eat it when roasted since he is disgusted by it. In analogy, Adam would have had the same experience had he realized that Eve was created from his own raw flesh. This is the reason why God anesthetized him to a certain extent.

The model taken from b. Ber. 61a speaks in detail about the creation of the woman:

> It can be explained in accordance with Rabbi Yirmeya ben Elazar, as Rabbi Yirmeya ben Elazar said: The Holy One, Blessed be He, created two faces [*du partsufin*] on Adam the first man, as it is stated: "You have formed me [*tsartani*] behind and before" [Ps 139:5].
> "And God built the side [*tsela'*]" [Gen 2:22]. Rav and Shmuel [disagree over the meaning of the word *tsela'*]: One said: [It means] face. And one said: [It means] tail.

After the citation already known from Genesis Rabbah about the original androgyny of the human, there follows here a discussion of Ps 139:5 between the heads of the two great rabbinic schools in Babylonia, Rav and Shmuel. According to Rav, God formed woman from the face of the man. Shmuel, on the other hand, asserts that she was formed from a rear part of the man, a tail, which leaves a negative aftertaste. Both positions lack the element in Gen. Rab. 8, represented positively by Shmuel bar Nachman, of the androgynous primal human and of the brutal separation that seeks a renewed unification. Further along in b. Ber. 61a, several conclusions are drawn from the "operation." Thus, from the term "build" (*bana*), which is applied in Gen 2:22 to the woman, it is concluded that this means "braided plaits" (because in maritime cities they are called *binyata*, "buildings"). Thus Eve's physique resembles a storehouse: narrow at the top and broad below in order to store fruits. So, in analogy with the body of the woman, she is built in this way to allow the fetus to grow into a baby.[13] Rashi's commentary takes over only one part of the discussion in a selection that avoids denigration of women:

> Gen 2:23: "This time": This teaches us that Adam came to all the animals and the beasts [in search of a mate], but he was not satisfied until he found Eve.

---

13. On the construction of the body of the woman as a building, se Charlotte E. Fonrobert, *Menstrual Purity: Rabbinic and Christian Reconstruction of Biblical Gender* (Stanford, CA: Stanford University Press, 2000), 40–67.

This exegesis is known from b. Yebam. 63a. The sexuality of the union of man and woman is made explicit; union between man and woman is not restricted to procreation.

> "This one shall be called woman [*'ishah*] because, from man [*'ish*]: One expression coincides with the other [i.e., the two words have the same root]. From here is derived that the world was created with the Holy Tongue [from Gen. Rab. 18:4].
> "Therefore, a man shall leave": The Divine Spirit says this to prohibit forbidden unions to the Noahides [see b. Sanh. 57b].
> "One flesh": The fetus is formed by them both, and there [in the child] their flesh becomes one [from b. Sanh. 57b].

If one examines the model in b. Sanh. 57b more closely, one sees that the argument there runs somewhat differently. The rabbis seek scriptural evidence that refers to the children of Noah, that is, non-Jews, who comply with certain basic rules. According to this, the issue is whether the wife of a non-Jew, as with the man, can be punished for sexual infidelity. The rabbis look in the final analysis to the phrase "to become one flesh." They understand the expression as an indication of a bond that demands faithfulness. Rashi takes over the style of the exegesis but explains the phrase "to become one flesh" as applying to the procreation of children and concludes that the baby has portions from both parents.[14]

> Gen 2:25: "But they were not ashamed": for they did not know the way of modesty [*tseni'ut*], to distinguish between good and evil, and even though knowledge was granted him to call [all the creatures] names, he was not imbued with the evil inclination until he ate of the tree, and the evil inclination entered into him, and he knew the difference between good and evil.
> Gen 3:1: "Now the serpent was cunning": What is the connection of this matter here? Scripture should have juxtaposed [Gen 3:21]: "And He made for Adam and for his wife shirts of skin, and He dressed them." But it teaches you as a result of what plan the serpent thrust himself upon them. He saw them naked and engaging in intercourse before everyone's eyes, and he desired her.

---

14. See b. Nid. 31a, where the woman contributes all "red portions" through her "seed." From these arise the skin, the flesh, the hair, blood, and the "black" of the eye. The man, on the other hand, contributes the white portions, from which the sinews, the nails, the brain, the head, and the "white" of the eye are formed.

Sexuality in and of itself does not have a negative significance here. It is rather that, by means of the catchword of the evil inclination, on the one hand, and the conduct of the snake on the other, it can be pointed out that sexuality should ensue within a certain framework under the aspect of modesty (*tseniʿut*). Prudishness is an abbreviated translation here, since other aspects are meant as well. With the word *tseniʿut*, a code of conduct is meant that should distinguish the human being influenced by rabbinic learning. To this also belongs, naturally, not performing sexual intercourse in public. The evil drive frequently is interpreted rabbinically as misinterpreted sexual conduct.[15]

> Gen 3:6: "And the woman saw": She understood the words of the serpent and they appealed to her; so she believed him [Gen. Rab. 19:4].
> "That the tree was good": to [cause them to] be like angels.
> "And that it was a delight to the eyes": As he had said to her, "and your eyes will be opened."
> "And that the tree was desirable to make one wise": As he said to her, "knowing good and evil."
> "And she gave also to her husband": lest she die and he live and marry someone else. [from Pirqe R. El. 13]
> "Also" [*gam*]: to include the cattle and beasts [from Gen. Rab. 19:5].

Rashi here does not deviate from the guideline in Genesis Rabbah. What is interesting is that Eve gives Adam of the fruits[16] because she is jealous of a possible later union entered into by Adam after her own death, a death that she expects as punishment for eating when she was forbidden to eat. It is said that Eve also gave all the animals something to eat. This is derived from a hermeneutical deduction, for in the rabbinical tradition a so-called *ribbui* (inclusion or amplification) is connected with the particle *gam* (also), according to which the word denotes that other further elements also are meant in the statement. In this case, the *gam* refers to the animals that, herewith, are excluded as possible sexual partners for Adam.

---

15. See Ishay Rosen-Zvi, *Demonic Desires: "Yetzer Hara" and the Problem of Evil in Late Antiquity* (Philadelphia: University of Pennsylvania Press, 2011).

16. Which fruits are meant here is controversial. Rashi later assumes dates, but in Genesis Rabbah these fruits are identified as grapes. See also Gerhard Langer, "Die Bibel und die Rabbinen. Exegese und Aktualisierung und noch etwas anderes!," in *Gottes Name(n). Zum Gedenken an Erich Zenger*, ed. Ilse Müllner, Ludger Schwienhorst-Schönberger, and Ruth Scoralick, HBS 71 (Freiburg: Herder, 2012), 37–51.

> "Who told you": From where do you know what shame there is in standing naked?...
> Gen 3:14: Our rabbis established this midrash in b. Bekh. 8a to teach that the gestation period of a serpent is seven years.
> "You shall walk on your belly": It had legs, but they were cut off [from Gen. Rab. 20:5]
> Gen 3:15: "And I shall place hatred": You intended that the man should die when he would eat first, and you would marry Eve, and you came to Eve first only because women are easily enticed, and they know how to entice their husbands. Therefore, "I shall place hatred."

This text takes aim at an established "gender specific" characteristic. Women are said to be more easily influenced than men, but they also understand how to persuade men easily. In principle, this characterization does not denigrate women any more than men since men give into the enticement. Rashi aligns himself here with a long tradition of attributions of personality traits found scattered frequently throughout Jewish tradition, already present in Genesis Rabbah among other texts. Genesis Rabbah 17:8, for example, identifies negative characteristics of woman that derive from her creation from a bone and are contrasted with the creation of man from the earth:

A woman must put on perfume	Earth smells good	Bones begin to stink
A woman is louder than a man	Meat does not make a sound while being cooked	Bones make a sound
A woman is hard to mollify	Earth dissolves in water	Bones do not dissolve in water

But Genesis Rabbah also has an exegesis that upgrades women. In the interpretation of build (*bana*) in 18:1, it says: "Rabbi Elazar said in the name of Rabbi Jose ben Simra: God gave her more intelligence than to the man." Here, *bana* is interpreted as *bina* (intelligence).

> Gen 3:16: "Your sorrow": This refers to the pain of child rearing [see b. 'Eruv. 100b].
> "And your pregnancy": This refers to the pain of pregnancy [see above source].
> "In pain you shall bear children": This refers to the pain of childbirth [see Gen. Rab. 20:6]

"And to your husband will be your desire": for intimacy, but, nevertheless, you will not have the audacity to demand it of him with your mouth, but he will rule over you. Everything is from him and not from you.
"Your desire": Your desire, like: [Isa 29:8]: "a yearning soul" [after Targum Onqelos].

Here, sexual desire, among other things, once again is made the theme. The model in b. ʿEruv. 100b is taken over here but only in part. Along with b. ʿEruv. 100b, ʾAbot R. Nat. B9, 42 and Pirqe R. El. 14 list the negative consequences for Eve as a result of the fall.[17] Among these negative consequences listed in the variant ʾAbot R. Nat. B42 are: menstruation; complaints in regard to pregnancy, birth, and the first years of the life of the children; the rule of man over woman; male jealousy; early aging; and the end of fertility with menopause. In addition, a woman must stay in the house and must cover her head when she goes out. Finally, she must bury her husband. The observance of the *niddah* regulations, the lighting of the Sabbath lamps, and the separation of the dough are means of atonement. If they are not observed, so the rabbis explain, then a woman will die in childbirth.[18] The passage in b. ʿEruv. 100b lists menstruation, painful loss of virginity, pain in the rearing of children, pregnancy, birth, desire for the man, rule of the man, the command to cover the head, staying in the house, prohibition of polygamy or long hair (which she, like the demoness Lilith, wears), sitting while urinating, and the position taken during sexual intercourse (under the man) as the negative consequences of the fall. Rashi takes over this list only selectively and avoids the passages that are especially hostile to women. Nevertheless, he quite assuredly emphasizes the sexual desire that women feel. In b. ʿEruv. 100b, the following is said about this:

"And yet your desire shall be to your husband" teaches that the woman desires her husband, when he sets out on the road.

---

17. Cf. ʾAbot R. Nat. A1 and y. Shab. 2:6 (8b). See Judith R. Baskin, "'She Extinguished the Light of the World': Justifications for Women's Disabilities in *Abot de-Rabbi Nathan B*," in *Current Trends in the Study of Midrash*, ed. Carol Bakhos, JSJSup 106 (Leiden: Brill, 2006), 277–98; Natalie C. Polzer, "Misogyny Revisited: The Eve Traditions in Avot de Rabbi Natan, Versions A and B," *AJSR* 36 (2012): 207–55.

18. So already m. Sabb. 2:6, without mention of the fall: "Women die in the hour of their giving birth because of three transgressions: because they are not attentive in regard to menstruation, the lifting up of the dough, and the lighting of the (Sabbath) light."

"And he shall rule over you" teaches that the woman demands in her heart, but the man demands verbally. This is a good trait in women.

Rashi takes up only the first part of the exegesis and emphasizes the sexual lust of women as established by Tal Ilan. For Rashi, Eve's punishment consists in the impossibility to demand sex from men verbally. We will see that Ramban will contradict him with the reference to the second part of the citation from the Talmud.

The following exegeses need no closer explanation but refer back to what already has been said:

> Gen 3:20: "And the man named": Scripture returns to its previous topic [Gen 2:20]: "And the man named," and it interrupted only to teach you that through the giving of names, Eve was mated to him, as it is written [2:20]: "But for man, he did not find a helpmate opposite him": Therefore, [2:21]: "And He caused a deep sleep to fall," and since Scripture wrote [2:25]: "And they were naked," it juxtaposed the section of the serpent, to let you know that because he saw her naked and saw them engaging in intercourse, he desired her and came upon them with a design and with guile.
> "Eve [*Hawa*]": This coincides with the expression of living [*haya*], because she gives life to her offspring, as you say, [Eccl 2:22]: "For what does a man have [*howe*]?" with the expression "being" [i.e., the *vav* and the *yod* are interchangeable].
> Gen 3:21: "Shirts of skin": Some haggadic works say that they were as smooth as fingernails, fastened over their skin [Gen. Rab. 20:12], and others say that they were a material that comes from the skin, like the wool of rabbits, which is soft and warm, and He made them shirts from it [Gen. Rab. ad loc.; b. Sotah 14a].
> Gen 3:22: "Has become like one of us, having the ability": He is unique among the earthly beings, just as I am unique among the heavenly beings, and what is his uniqueness? To know good and evil, unlike the cattle and the beasts. [from Targum Jonathan; Gen. Rab. 21:5]
> "And now, lest he stretch forth his hand, etc.": And if he were to live forever, he would be likely to mislead people to follow him and to say that he too is a deity [Gen. Rab. 9:5]. There are also haggadic midrashim, but they cannot be reconciled with the simple meaning.

Rashi takes up traditional rabbinical material almost exclusively; above all he borrows from Genesis Rabbah but also from the Talmud. As we have seen, he proceeds in this selectively. Rashi avoids misogynous tones. This definitely does not make him a feminist, as we also know from a series of other exegeses, but in no case can a fundamental degradation of woman on the basis of her creation be discerned in Rashi's commentary, unlike many a rabbinic text found in the Middle Ages, such as in the work of David Kimchi (1160–1235), Levi ben Gershon (Gersonides) (1288–1344), or Isaac Abravanel (1437–1508).[19]

One point is to be emphasized here in any case: although woman is presented by Rashi (in connection with rabbinical texts and occasionally beyond these) as sexually seductive and as provided with desires, he does not fundamentally devalue sexuality either with or without reference to Eve. Women have a right to sexuality in marriage and their need should be taken seriously, even if Rashi's tendency is to emphasize masculine dominance. One might also mention in this context the earlier Iggeret ha-Qodesh from the twelfth century, an anonymous work that discusses sexuality as a holy act; from the description of foreplay to the proper diet, the work gives many recommendations. This text was often incorrectly ascribed to Nachmanides, who will be discussed in the second part of this article.

2. Ramban (1194–1270)

Like so many scholars in the Middle Ages, Moses ben Nachman (also known as Nachmanides or Ramban), who was born in Gerona in Spain, was a multitalented person: doctor, philosopher, mystic, poet, counselor of the king, and representative of Judaism in the Disputation of Barcelona. He spent the last years of his life in the Holy Land, first in a desolate Jerusalem and then in Acre, where he was active as the spiritual leader of the congregation.

In his Bible commentary, he repeatedly criticizes Rashi's positions. Ramban's approach can be illustrated in his exegesis on Eve.[20]

> Gen 2:18: "It is not good that the man should be alone." It does not appear likely that man was created to be alone in the world and not beget children since all created beings—male and female of all flesh—were created

---

19. Cf. Julia Schwartzmann, "The Medieval Philosophical Interpretation of the Creation of Woman" [Hebrew], *Da'at* 39 (1997): 69–87.

20. The Hebrew text can be found, for example, in the database of the Bar Ilan Responsa Project, or at Sefaria. An English translation is offered by Charles B. Chavel, *RAMBAN: Commentary on the Torah* (New York: Shilo, 1999). This translation (adapted slightly) is used here.

to raise seed. The herbs and trees also have their seed in them. But it is possible to say that it was in accordance with the opinion of the Rabbi who says: Adam was created with two faces [i.e., male and female persons combined], and they were so made that there should be in them an impulse causing the organs of generation to produce a generative force from male to female, or you may say "seed," in accordance with the known controversy concerning pregnancy, and the second face was a help to the first in the procreative process. And the Holy One, blessed be He, saw that it is good that "the help" stand facing him, and that he should see and be separated from it or joined to it at his will. This is the meaning of what He said in the verse, "I will make him a helper opposite him." The meaning of the expression, "It is not good," is that it cannot be said of man that "it is good" when he is alone for he will be able to so exist. In the work of creation, "the good" means existence, as I have explained on the text, "And G-d saw that it was good."

This passage requires explanation. One sees here clearly that Ramban deals with the text on a more strong reflective level than does Rashi, who in most cases cites selectively from the traditional literature. Ramban works here above all with the image of the first human, known from Genesis Rabbah and b. Yebam. 61a, among others, as consisting of two parts in a single body. He interprets the two faces as a masculine and a feminine part of humankind, above all in regard to their procreation. The one human being, thus, is divided in order to create a counterpart to man, with which he, as required, can unite sexually and beget descendants.

> Gen 2:19: "And whatsoever the man would call every living creature": [...] Now when the Holy One, blessed be He, wanted to make "the help" for Adam He brought all species before him since He had to bring them before him in pairs so that he should also give a name to the females of the species: for in some [species, both male and female] are called by one name, and in others they differ, such as bull and cow, *tayish* [he-goat] and *'ez* [she-goat], sheep and ewe, and others. When Adam saw them mating with each other he had a desire for them, but as he found among them no help himself, he was saddened and fell asleep. G-d then caused a deep sleep to fall upon him so that he should not feel the removal of a rib from his body. In my opinion, however, "the calling of the names" is identical with "the help" [as I explained in the above verse], and the purport thereof is as follows: the Holy One, blessed be He, brought before Adam all the beasts of the field and all the fowl of the heavens, and he, recognizing their nature, called them names, that is, names appropriate to them. By the names it was made clear who is fit to be the help for

another, meaning, fit to procreate with one another. Even if we are to believe that names are merely a matter of consensus and not of nature, [i.e., that they do not reflect the essence of the object bearing the name], we can say that "the calling of the names" means the division of the species as male and female as they passed before Adam and he contemplated their name as to which of them would be a help to each other in procreation so that they should beget offspring. Thus he called the large creatures by one name and the beasts by another so they would not beget offspring from one another, and so on for all species. And among them all he did not find a natural help for himself so that it could be called by his name, for "the calling of the names" signifies the division of the species and the separation of their powers from each other, as I have explained above. Now it does not mean that it was in Adam's power to find a help for himself among them since they were all created with natures [different from that of man]. But it means that if Adam was to find satisfaction with one of the species and he would choose it for his help, the Holy One, blessed be He, would adapt its nature to him, as He did with the rib, and He would not have found it necessary to build "a new structure." Thus the meaning of the verse, "And whatsoever the man would call every living creature, that was its name"; that is to say, that was to be its name, for the Holy One, blessed be He, would so preserve it along the lines which I have explained. In my opinion it is correct to say that it was His will, blessed be He, not to take Adam's rib from him to make him a wife until he himself would know that among the created beings there is no help suitable for him and until he would crave to have a help suitable for him like her. This was why it was necessary to take one of his ribs from him. This is the meaning of the verse, "But for Adam there was not found a help meet for him"; that is to say, but for the name *Adam* (man), he found no help suited to be opposite him and to be called his name so that he should beget children from that "help." We need not resort here, therefore, to the words of the commentators who say that the name "Adam" comes here in place of the reflexive pronoun ["himself." The verse should thus be read; "But for himself] he found no help meet for him," just as, "You wives of Lemech" [Gen 4:23] [which should read, "my wives"]; "And Jephthah, and Samuel" [1 Sam 12:11], [which should read, "And Jephthah and myself"]. This is the meaning of Adam's saying: "This is now bone of my bones"; that is to say, "This time I have found a help for me which I did not find till now among the other species, for she is 'bone of my bones,' and 'flesh of my flesh,' and is fit to be actually called by my name for we shall propagate together." …

"Therefore shall a man leave his father and his mother, and shall cleave to his wife." The Divine Spirit says this, thus prohibiting immoral relationship to "the sons of Noah." "And they shall be one flesh:" The child is created by both parents, and there in the child, their flesh is united into one. Thus are the words of Rashi. But there is no point to this since in the beast and cattle too, their flesh is united into one in their offspring. The correct interpretation appears to me that to be in cattle and beast the males have no attachment to their females. Rather, the male mates with any female he finds, and then they go their separate ways. It is for this reason that Scripture states that because the female of man was bone of his bones and flesh of his flesh, he therefore cleaves to her and she nestles in the bosom as his own flesh, and he desires to be with her always. And just as it was with Adam, so was his nature transmitted to his offspring, that the males among them should cleave to their women, leaving their fathers and their mothers, and considering their wives as if they are one flesh with them. A similar sense is found in the verse: For he is our brother, our flesh; to any that is near of his flesh [Gen 37:27]. Those who are close members of the family are called *she'er bazar* (near of flesh). Thus man will leave "the flesh" of his father and his mother and their kin and will see that his wife is nearer to him than they are.

Ramban interprets the word "help" in the sense of the essence, the being of a creature. Accordingly, one could translate ʿezer also as "similar in nature." Therewith, the equality of woman becomes clear. The creation of woman, in the last analysis, hearkens back to a request of the first human. The union between man and woman is because, according to Ramban, man constantly yearns for his own substance, for the flesh belonging to him. This is a special variant of the notion of the androgynous primal human being as it appears in Genesis Rabbah and in the Talmud. Eve is thus, to be sure, a secondary creation from out of the primal human, but she is in no way inferior or subordinate to him. The sexual union also has the goal in Ramban of producing children, but the relationship between man and woman goes far beyond this. It is, precisely in contrast to the union among animals, a permanent bond and an "adherence" in a positive sense. Accordingly, to be one flesh means, in distinction to Rashi, not only to "unite" in a child, but rather to return to an original and natural intrinsic unity. The relationship to the woman, in the last analysis, carries more weight than the relationship to blood relations, even though the close cohesiveness of the family is emphasized previously.

In the subsequent exegesis too Ramban gives no signs of misogyny of any kind and does not cite any of the well-known explanations from Genesis Rabbah or the Talmud. Interesting above all, however, is his commentary on Gen 3:12–16, which is reproduced here.

> Gen 3:12: "The woman whom you gave to be with me." The sense of it is to say: "The woman whom Your Honor Himself gave me for a help," "she gave me of the tree," and I thought that whatever she says to me is a help and benefit to me. This is why He said when meting out his punishment, "Because you have hearkened unto the voice of your wife" [3:17], meaning "You should have transgressed My commandment on account of her advice." Our rabbis have called Adam ungrateful for this remark. By this they mean to explain that the sense of his answer was: "You caused me this stumbling for you gave me a woman as a help, and she counselled me to do evil."
> Gen 3:13: "What is this you have done" to transgress My commandment? For the woman was included in the admonition given to Adam since at that time she was yet bone of his bones, and similarly she was included in his punishment. The reason why G-d did not say to the woman, "and you have eaten of the tree," is that she was punished for the advice. This is why she said, "The serpent beguiled me, and I did eat," as the punishment for the beguiling was greater than that for the eating. [Hence as soon as she mentioned that the serpent beguiled her, G-d meted out his punishment immediately, as is stated in the following two verses.] Thus we may derive from here the principle of punishment for those that cause people to sin in any matter, just as our Rabbis [b. Pesaḥ. 22b] have derived it from the verse, "Thou shalt not put a stumbling-block before the blind" [Lev 19:14].

Here, Eve's conduct is reproached, to be sure, but there is no fundamental depreciation of women. Rather, Eve's punishment serves to inculcate the general principle—for men as well as for women—that the inducement to commit a crime is considered worse than the deed itself. Adam, on the other hand, is presented virtually as a blasphemer since he reproaches God with having given him a woman who got him into trouble.

> Gen 3:16: "*Teshuqatek* (And your desire) shall be to your husband," meaning for cohabitation. Yet you will not have the boldness to demand it by word, rather "he shall rule over you." It will all be from him and not from you. Thus are the words of Rashi. But this is not correct, for modesty is praiseworthy in a woman, just as the Rabbis have said [in b. ʿEruv. 100b]. This is a good quality in woman.
> Rabbi Abraham ibn Ezra said: "And your desire shall be to your husband," meaning your obedience. This means you will obey whatever he commands you for you are under his authority to do his desire. However, I have found the expression *teshuqa* used only in connection with desire and lust. The correct interpretation appears to me that He punished her,

that her desire for her husband be exceedingly great, and that she should be deterred by the pain of pregnancy and birth or that he keeps her as a maidservant. Now it is not customary for a servant to desire to acquire a master over himself, rather his desire is to flee from him. Thus her punishment is measure for measure; she gave [the fruit of the tree of knowledge] also to her husband and he ate at her command, and He punished her that she should no longer command him, but instead he should command her entirely at his will.

At this point it becomes clear that Ramban sets himself apart from his predecessors. He accepts neither Rashi's opinion nor that of Ibn Ezra. Rashi, as was shown above, had portrayed women as sexually greedy and referred to the tradition which prohibited women from demanding sex verbally. He had understood this as punishment. In b. ʿEruvin, to which he refers, the biblical citation from Genesis quite definitely plays a role in making legitimate the need for sexuality, which in principle is not disputed in this text. However, women should verbally articulate their desire only seldomly or not at all and instead should make their desire clear "via indirect ways," for example by making themselves attractive for their men. But this behavior is not seen as punishment, but rather fundamentally as a proper character trait in women. Ramban too accordingly does not see in this any kind of punishment deriving from Eve's biblical transgression, but rather generally praiseworthy female conduct, that is, an expression of modesty (tseniʿut). He also does not share in Ibn Ezra's approach, according to which the woman is obligated fundamentally in all things to be obedient. Strictly speaking, he says, desire always applies to sexuality, but that is no reason for the subordination of women in general. According to Ramban, the punishment consists much more in the fact that a woman cannot prescribe anything to her husband in sexual matters, although her desire for him is overpowering.

Sarah and Hagar in Medieval Jewish Commentaries

Carol Bakhos

Much like classical rabbinic literature, medieval commentaries attempt to fill in several gaps in the story of Sarah and Hagar and to address many potentially unsettling implications with respect to the moral character of Abraham and Sarah. And, much like their exegetical predecessors, Jewish medieval commentators were not of one mind in their characterization of these biblical figures. They scrutinize biblical passages for what is said and what is intended to be said, for not only the meaning on the surface but also the meaning in the interstices of any given verse or phrase. This is especially the case with respect to the story of Sarah and Hagar, which raises moral questions that continue to trouble contemporary readers attuned to the power dynamics at play between the matriarch and her Egyptian maidservant.

As is well known, classical rabbinic works fill in scriptural lacunae, ever so tersely and playfully, whereas in the hands of medieval Jewish sages the biblical story is more explicitly a moral code and guidebook for proper behavior. Even if the Jewish forefathers and foremothers do not behave in an exemplary manner, we learn from their shortcomings. This is a clear shift from the tendency in classical rabbinical texts to embellish their actions and whitewash their character.

Abraham's wives Sarah and Hagar have historically received far less attention than their husband and sons, and Keturah, whom Abraham married after Sarah's death in Genesis, receives even less. Exegetes nonetheless have recognized the need to interpret specific verses and storylines as well as to define the role they played in broader theological and moral narratives.[1] How are these women depicted? What role do Sarah and Hagar

---

1. There is a great deal of literature on the subject. Here I provide a brief selection of works: Elizabeth Castelli, "Allegories of Hagar: Reading Galatians 4:21–31 with

play as matriarchs in the founding family of Abraham? How does their depiction impinge on our characterization of Abraham? What insights do medieval readers provide?

1. Biblical Background

God announces to Abraham that he will be a father of many nations. However, his wife Sarah (at this point in the narrative, her name is still Sarai) does not passively trust in God's promise of progeny. She approaches her husband with the idea that he should have a son with her Egyptian maidservant, Hagar, so that through her she can obtain children:

> Sarai, Abram's wife, had borne him no children. She had an Egyptian maidservant whose name was Hagar. And Sarai said to Abram, 'Look, the Lord has kept me from bearing. Consort with my maid; perhaps I shall have a son through her.' And Abram heeded Sarai's request. So Sarai, Abram's wife, took her maid, Hagar the Egyptian—after Abram had dwelt in the land of Canaan for ten years—and gave her to her husband Abram as concubine. (Gen 16:1–3)[2]

Hagar conceives, but the everlasting covenant promised to Abraham's offspring is through Isaac, his son with Sarah, not through Ishmael, his son with Hagar, or the sons he has with Keturah (Gen 25:1–2):

Postmodern Feminist Eyes," in *The New Literary Criticism and the New Testament*, ed. Elizabeth Struthers Malbon and Edgar McKnight (Sheffield: Sheffield Academic, 1994), 228–50; Phyllis Trible, ed., *Texts of Terror: Literary-Feminist Readings of Biblical Narrative* (Philadelphia: Fortress, 1984), 9–36; Jo Ann Hackett, "Rehabilitating Hagar: Fragments of an Epic Pattern," in *Gender and Difference in Ancient Israel*, ed. Peggy L. Day (Philadelphia: Fortress, 1989), 12–27; J. Cheryl Exum, *Fragmented Women: Feminist (Sub)versions of Biblical Narratives* (London: T&T Clark, 2016), 69–86; John L. Thompson, *Writing the Wrongs: Women of the Old Testament among Biblical Commentators from Philo through the Reformation* (Oxford: Oxford University Press, 2001), 17–99; Phyllis Trible and Letty M. Russell, eds., *Hagar, Sarah, and Their Children: Jewish, Christian and Muslim Perspectives* (Louisville: Westminster John Knox, 2006); and Carol Bakhos, *The Family of Abraham: Jewish, Christian and Muslim Interpretations* (Cambridge: Harvard University Press, 2014), 106–37.

2. Unless otherwise noted, all translations of the Hebrew Bible, except citations appearing in the New Testament, are from *Tanakh: The Holy Scriptures* (Philadelphia: Jewish Publication Society, 1985). For a discussion of Jewish, Christian, and Muslim interpretations of the Abrahamic narrative, see Bakhos, *Family of Abraham*.

> And God said, "Sarah your wife shall bear you a son, and you shall call his name Isaac, and I will establish my covenant with him for an everlasting covenant with his offspring to come. And as for Ishmael, I have heard you. Behold, I have blessed him, and I will make him fruitful, and exceedingly numerous; twelve princes he shall beget, and I will make him a great nation. But I will establish my covenant with Isaac." (Gen 17:19–21)

The chosen status of Isaac and his descendants as heirs of the covenant is quite explicit and plays a role in framing the relationship not only between Isaac and Ishmael but also between their mothers.

That the covenant is maintained through Isaac is crucial to understanding the way in which Sarah and Hagar are depicted throughout history, not just in the medieval period. It is also important for understanding the liminal standing of Hagar and the theological implications that Isaac's election poses. The power discrepancy between the women parallels that between the sons. Even though as firstborn Ishmael is the rightful heir to Abraham, it is Isaac's status as the chosen son through whom the covenant is maintained that privileges one son over the other, and hence one mother over the other.

The practice of having children through a surrogate was not unusual in Near Eastern societies. We find a similar prescription to a wife's barrenness in an ancient contract from Nuzi (Mesopotamia, fourteenth century BCE). Sarah gave her slave Hagar to Abraham as a concubine (Gen 16:14); according to the Nuzi marriage contract the childless wife was obligated to provide her husband with a substitute. Should a son be born of that union, it was forbidden to expel the slave wife and her child: "Kelim-ninu [a woman] has been given in marriage to Shennima [a man].... If Kelim-ninu bears (children), Shennima shall not take another wife; but if Kelim-ninu does not bear, Kelim-ninu shall acquire a woman of the land of Lillu as wife for Shennima, and Kelim-ninu may not send the offspring away."[3] This perhaps in part explains Abraham's reluctance to send Hagar and Ishmael away. And again, as we shall see, the status of Hagar as Abraham's second wife is taken up by the medieval commentators. Whereas classical rabbinic literature explicitly avoids regarding Hagar as his wife, medieval commentators by and large accept that she is his wife, but also

---

[3]. James B. Pritchard, ed., *The Ancient Near East: An Anthology of Texts and Pictures* (Princeton: Princeton University Press, 2010), 188.

maintain that she is Sarah's maidservant. That Hagar is both at the same time contextualizes and legitimizes their attitude toward her.

Abraham complies with his wife's request; Hagar conceives, and Ishmael is born. However, when Hagar conceives, "her mistress was lowered in her esteem" (Gen 16:4). Sarah complains to Abraham, who tells her that she should do as she wishes with Hagar. When Sarah deals harshly with her, Hagar flees into the wilderness, where the messenger of God finds her. He informs her that God will multiply her seed exceedingly, that she is with child, and that she shall call him Ishmael, which means "God hears," because the Lord "has paid heed to your suffering and heard your affliction" (Gen 16:11).

When Abraham hears that Sarah will conceive and that it is through Isaac and his descendants that the covenant will be maintained, he voices concerns about his older son, Ishmael. God also blesses Ishmael and makes him a great nation. Although Ishmael is circumcised along with Abraham and the male members of Abraham's household, he is not part of the covenant. In short, the younger sibling is chosen over the older.

Sarah gives birth to Isaac, and on the day he is weaned Abraham makes a banquet, but one mother's joy is another's sorrow. Genesis 21 ushers in the son of the covenant and ushers out the son of the maidservant, for we read: "Sarah saw the son whom Hagar the Egyptian had borne to Abraham playing [*meṣaḥeq*, from the Hebrew root *ṣḥq*]. She said to Abraham, 'Cast out that slave-woman and her son, for the son of that slave shall not share in the inheritance with my son Isaac'" (Gen 21:9–10). The matter greatly distresses Abraham, who does not readily acquiesce to Sarah's request. In fact, God intervenes and tells him to listen to Sarah. He allays Abraham's concerns about Ishmael's fate. Abraham sends Hagar and her son into the wilderness of Beer-sheba. Putting his trust in God, Abraham gets up "early in the morning,"[4] takes some bread and a skin of water, and gives them to Hagar. He places them on her shoulder, "together with the child,"[5] and sends her away, sacrificing them to the wilderness of Beer-sheba, where their water runs dry. Unable to watch her son die, Hagar leaves him under

---

4. "And Abraham rose early in the morning," also in Gen 21:14, is one of the many literary parallels between both sacrificial stories.

5. For a philological discussion of Gen 21:14, and of the theological and moral issues raised when it is understood in the broader narrative structure, see Larry Lyke, "Where Does the Boy Belong? Compositional Strategy in Genesis 21:14," *CBQ* 56 (1994): 637–48.

one of the bushes, sits away from him, and bursts into tears. God hears the cry of the boy, and an angel of God calls to her from heaven and informs her that God has heard his cry and will make a great nation of him. God opens her eyes, and she sees a well of water. The child is saved and grows up to be a father of twelve nations. We learn that Ishmael buries his father along with Isaac but of Hagar we learn nothing more.

The expulsion of Hagar and Ishmael in Gen 21 is in many respects unprecedented.[6] Ancient, medieval and modern commentators alike have grappled with the verse in which Sarah changes her mind about her maid-servant's place in the family. Why does Sarah, who provided Abraham with Hagar for the purposes of procreating, now want her and her son "cast out"? What does it mean that Sarah was lowered in Hagar's eyes? Does it justify Sarah's maltreatment of Hagar?

2. Medieval Commentators

Premodern Christian and Jewish exegetes, for the most part, reiterate Hagar's lowly status and advocate overwhelmingly on Sarah's behalf. As the wife of Abraham and the mother of Isaac, Sarah is often seen as above reproach in her behavior, although we see some portrayals that question her attitude toward Hagar, and indeed she is taken to task for her insensitivity and unjust actions.

Take, for example, the comments of the well-known grammarian and exegete Rabbi David Kimchi (Radak), who lived in Provence from about 1160 until 1235:[7]

---

6. For an illuminating comparison of Ishmael's expulsion from the promised land, on the one hand, and of Cain's expulsion from Eden, on the other, see Jon D. Levenson, *Death and Resurrection of the Beloved Son: The Transformation of Child Sacrifice in Judaism and Christianity* (New Haven: Yale University Press, 1993), 91–92, and also 102, where he writes, "The terse narrative of Gen 21:9-13 looks, Janus-like, both back to the story of the primal family and forward to the next generation of Patriarchs." Furthermore, Levenson astutely draws our attention to the "intertextual connection between the supernatural deliverance of Ishmael in Gen 21 and another story of a first-born son whose life is spared, the story of Joseph" (108).

7. Kimchi was born in Narbonne in 1160 and died there in 1235. See discussion in Adele Reinhartz and Miriam-Simma Walfish, "Conflict and Coexistence in Jewish Interpretation," in *Hagar, Sarah and Their Children: Jewish, Christian and Muslim Perspectives*, ed. Phyllis Trible and Letty M. Russell (Louisville: Westminster John Knox, 2006), 101–26.

> She [Sarah] tormented her and worked her harder than necessary. It is possible that she also struck and verbally abused her [literally "cursed"] until she could no longer bear it and fled. In this respect, Sarah did not act ethically or charitably. Not ethically, for even though Abraham said, "Deal with her as you might think right," for his sake she should have restrained herself and not punished her. Not charitably, for a good person, even if permitted to act harshly would not do so. God did not approve of her behavior, as evidenced from what the angel told Hagar, "For the Lord has paid heed to your suffering" (Gen 16:11), and blessed her for her forbearance. Abraham did not prevent Sarah from inflicting Hagar even though he thought it was wrong in order to keep the peace between him and his wife (*shalom bayit*). The story is written in the Torah in order for us to learn how to behave and to avoid bad behavior. (Kimchi on Gen 16:6)[8]

Although Abraham had given Sarah a free hand when he said "deal with her as you might think right," from a moral point of view she should have treated Hagar in a manner befitting her status as a wife or legal companion to Abraham. From the point of view of practicing human kindness (*ḥassidut*), she should have treated a subordinate with all possible consideration. Instead, Kimchi tells us that Sarah worked Hagar ruthlessly and possibly hit her and cursed her until she could no longer endure the suffering and degradation. Moreover, Kimchi comments that for the sake of Abraham's honor, Sarah should have treated Hagar with greater compassion. Sarah's behavior toward Hagar was also displeasing to God, so much so that he rewarded Hagar with a blessing. This is evidenced in verse 11: "For the Lord has heard your suffering" (*ki shamaʿ Adonai ʾel-ʿonyekh*).

Kimchi's sharp criticism of Sarah is striking in light of classical rabbinic literature that goes to great lengths to preserve the positive character of the Jewish patriarchs and matriarchs.[9] Without equivocation Kimchi excoriates Sarah for her mistreatment of Hagar. Noteworthy is his attempt to justify Abraham's silence. Is marital harmony more important than

---

8. Unless stated otherwise, all translations are my own.

9. There are of course exceptions to this general rabbinic attempt to whitewash them. Take for example Gen. Rab. 45:6 suggesting that Sarah cast an evil eye on Hagar, thus making her lose her baby. This is the explanation given for the angel's annunciation to Hagar, "Behold, you are with child" (Gen 16:11). The angel informs Hagar that she is pregnant (again) because Sarah's evil eye caused her to miscarry. Rashi also states this. Gen. Rab. 45:6 in general attributes unflattering characteristics to the matriarchs.

speaking out against injustice? Kimchi skirts the question and gives Abraham a pass. In fact, he consistently depicts Abraham as a paragon of virtue. Had Abraham known firsthand that Hagar was insolent toward Sarah (Gen 16:5, "I was lowered in her eyes"), he would not have tolerated that kind of behavior from Hagar, even though Hagar "had been raised in status to his wife instead of being merely Sarai's slave." Moreover, when Sarah requests the expulsion of Ishmael and his mother, the matter is disturbing in Abraham's eyes. For Kimchi, it is not only grievous on account of Ishmael but also Hagar: "God knew that Abraham was not only displeased about Sarah's request to expel Ishmael, but he was also distressed because he was asked to expel Hagar." The Torah, notes Kimchi, only mentions Ishmael because that was Abraham's principal concern, but God knew how Abraham really felt about Hagar.

Indeed, when Abraham sends Hagar and Ishmael into the wilderness, he gives Hagar provisions to last only a day or two because that was all she could carry. In addition, he gave her silver and gold in order for her to replenish her supplies, although Kimchi notes, "The Torah does not explicitly mention this" (Kimchi on Gen 21:14). According to Kimchi, Abraham was an outstanding husband and father.[10]

In fact, Sarah's superior status should have led her to behave more benevolently toward her maidservant, first and foremost out of human decency but also out of respect for her husband. Even though Abraham gives her permission—"Do to her as appears fit in your eyes"—Sarah should have restrained herself out of respect to her husband and should not have mistreated Hagar. Sarah should have treated her in a manner befitting her position as the wife or legal companion of Abraham. Moreover, Kimchi notes that even though Abraham disapproved of Sarah's mistreatment of Hagar, he did nothing to prevent it on account of *shalom bayit* (domestic harmony).

According to Kimchi, the story is preserved in the Torah in order to teach ethical lessons, lessons derived from Sarah's behavior and not from Abraham's. While Kimchi does not implicate Abraham in the unjust treatment of Hagar, Nachmanides (Ramban), who lived in Spain from 1194

---

10. On Gen 21:11, Kimchi emphasizes that even though Ishmael was a son of a slave-woman, he was nevertheless Abraham's firstborn, and Abraham loved him as a father loves one's son. He was merciful toward him, like a father is merciful toward all his children. Abraham taught Ishmael how to behave and instructed him in the ways of the Lord.

until 1271, certainly does.[11] He, however, emphasizes that Abraham was acting like a dutiful husband. Commenting on "Abraham heeded Sarah's request" (Gen 16:2), Nachmanides writes: "Scripture does not say, 'And he did thus,' but rather that he listened to Sarah's voice to hint that even though Abraham wanted children, he would not do anything without Sarah's consent. And now, he had no intention to have a family with Hagar, only to comply with Sarah's wishes in order for her to gain peace of mind and be fulfilled through her (Hagar)."

At the same time, Nachmanides explicitly states that Sarah sinned on account of her treatment of Hagar, as did Abraham for allowing her to do so. And how does Nachmanides arrive at this conclusion? From Gen 16:11–12: the angel brings Hagar good tidings, "Behold, you are with child and you shall bear a son, and you shall call his name Ishmael; because the Lord has heard your suffering. And he will be a wild man." According to Nachmanides, God gave Hagar a "son who would be a wild man to torture the seed of Abraham and Sarah with all sorts of mistreatment." The persecution that the Jews face under the rule of the children of Ishmael is explained as punishment for the suffering Abraham and Sarah caused Hagar. He does, by the way, go on to mention the superiority of the children of Sarah over Hagar. That is, the angel commands her to go back to Sarah and thus accept her authority. "This alludes," comments Nachmanides, "to the fact that she would not be freed of Sarah, and that the children of Sarah would rule over her children forever" (Nachmanides on Gen 16:6–11). As we will see shortly, Ovadiah Seforno interprets the story similarly, that is, as a prognostication of future events.

Whereas Kimchi and Nachmanides seem to be troubled by the morally improper, if not outright reprehensible, behavior of Sarah and, in Nachmanides's case, the actions of Sarah and Abraham, Rabbi Levi ben Gershom (also known as Gersonides or Ralbag), who lived in France from 1288 until 1344, shifts the blame away from Sarah to Hagar. For this known talmudist, philosopher, and mathematician, Sarah tortured Hagar in order to rid her of her bad trait, namely, her refusal to admit her lowly status vis-à-vis Sarah. Sarah's intent was for Hagar's own good, "not to

---

11. See Barry D. Walfish, "An Introduction to Medieval Jewish Biblical Interpretation," in *With Reverence for the Word: Medieval Scriptural Exegesis in Judaism, Christianity and Islam*, ed. Jane Dammen McAuliffe, Barry Walfish, and Joseph Ward Goering (New York: Oxford University Press, 2010).

extract revenge from her," but rather to make her a better person (Ralbag on Gen 16).

Let us consider another medieval commentator, Rabbi Ovadiah Seforno, who was born in 1470 in Cesena near the town of Bartinura in Romagna (central Italy) and died around 1550. Seforno explains Sarah's maltreatment of Hagar—"and Sarah dealt harshly with her" (Gen 16:6)—as an attempt to remind Hagar that she remained Sarah's slave and thus was not to insult her mistress. He goes on to contend: "She meant to make clear that any gentile who insults Israelites will experience similar harsh treatment. Compare Isa 60:14, 'Bowing before you, shall come the children of those who tormented you; prostrate at the soles of our feet shall be all those who reviled you.'" For Seforno, not only was Hagar deserving of Sarah's severe treatment, but the story serves as a warning for gentiles who dare to condemn Israel. They, like Hagar, will be put in their place, that is, in a subordinate status. Like Nachmanides, Serforno reads the story prophetically as a forewarning to gentiles should they misbehave toward Jews.

His negative attitude toward Hagar is furthermore expressed in his comment on Gen 21:9: "Sarah saw the son whom Hagar the Egyptian had borne to Abraham playing." Ishmael spoke disparagingly about Isaac, claiming that Abimelech was Isaac's father and thus calling into question his legitimacy as heir to Abraham. Seforno maintains that Ishmael learned this from his mother. At the banquet Abraham had given to mark the weaning of Isaac, Ishmael claimed that surely Sarah must have become pregnant from Abimelech. Lest one question why Ishmael did not make these comments sooner, when, for example, Sarah was pregnant or when Isaac was born as opposed to the weaning ceremony, Seforno has a response: Ishmael overheard the wicked gossip at a later stage, after Isaac was born, and was only now repeating what he had heard. Sarah wanted him cast out for what he did at the instigation of his mother. That is, Ishmael spread lies about Isaac's legitimacy in order to establish a claim to Abraham's inheritance.

3. Conclusion

Let us now step back and make a few observations. The survey of medieval Jewish commentaries on the Sarah and Hagar episodes reflects a variety of attitudes toward these women and their husband Abraham. Far be it for ancient exegetes to regard Hagar as having experienced what many modern commentators describe as "use, abuse and rejection." Some medieval sources, such as Kimchi, however, show sympathy for Hagar. That being said, they do not employ a strategy of reading against the grain such that they would take issue with Hagar's relegation to the margins or find her banishment into the wilderness with little provisions exceedingly troubling as to call into question God's command. Reading with the Jewish metanarrative in mind, or within a Christian theological framework, some scriptural exegetes of old whitewashed Sarah's and Abraham's behavior and, by and large, perpetuated Hagar's marginality, but others, even as early as the medieval period, were prepared to question Hagar's and her son's expulsion from Abraham's household. They do so not in order to indict the matriarch and patriarch, but rather to draw attention to their imperfections; they use their behavior to teach moral lessons. While some commentators go to great lengths to whitewash their behavior, especially Abraham's, even those who are more freely critical do not portray the forebears of the Jewish tradition in a way that undermines their importance.

Rabbinic literature strips the biblical story of its complexity in order to justify the matriarch's behavior toward her handmaiden, and the patriarch's treatment of his surrogate wife.[12] But medieval Jewish commentators in comparison draw distinctions between Sarah's relationship to Hagar (mistress-to-servant), and Abraham's to Hagar (husband-to-second wife). They do not uniformly justify Sarah's treatment of Hagar, and Nachmanides is critical of Abraham's willingness to let Sarah do as she will with Hagar. According to Nachmanides, Abraham should have protected Hagar, whereas Kimchi claims Abraham would have rebuked Hagar himself if he had known firsthand how she treated Sarah.

Taken as a whole, medieval commentators on the Hagar-Sarah relationship speak to the complexity of that relationship. It is true that Sarah wielded power over Hagar, yet Hagar, fertile and pregnant, had power over the barren Sarah. To varying degrees depending on the commentator, the fraught dynamic between the women, as well as the broader story's emotional depth and potency, are made palpable.

As a point of comparison, medieval Muslim qur'anic commentators also give voice to the tension between Sarah and Hagar, who are both recognized as matriarchs in the Islamic tradition. Al-Tha'labi transmits

---

12. For a discussion of the views of several medieval Jewish commentators on Sarah's treatment of Hagar, see Reinhartz and Walfish, "Conflict and Coexistence in Jewish Interpretation."

accounts claiming that Sarah became pregnant with Isaac after Hagar was already pregnant but that the women gave birth at the same time. Sarah's envy and her fear that Ishmael might physically threaten her son, as well as her fear that he would inherit over Isaac are given as the reasons for Hagar's expulsion. Sarah's jealousy was so fierce and overwhelming that "she swore to cut off a piece of Hagar's flesh and deface her appearance," but she thinks twice about it and settles on piercing her ears. Al-Tabari's history also mentions that the boys fought. Sarah becomes angry and jealous toward Hagar, who is sent away and brought back only to be sent away again and brought back yet again. In this rendition, however, Sarah does more than pierce Hagar's ears: "She said to herself, 'I shall cut off her nose, I shall cut off her ear—but no, that would deform her. I will circumcise her instead.' So she did that, and Hagar took a piece of cloth to wipe the blood away. For that reason women have been circumcised and have taken pieces of cloth down to today."[13]

Ibn Kathir's rendition of the birth of Ishmael in his *Al-Bidāyah wa-al-nihāyah fi al-ta'rīkh* most closely parallels the biblical story and like other renditions does not simply note Sarah's jealousy. Rather it places some blame on Hagar for Sarah's jealousy: "When she (Hagar) became pregnant her soul was exalted and she became proud and arrogant to her mistress, so Sarah became jealous of her."[14]

As the mother of Ishmael, Hagar plays a more important role in the Islamic tradition, but Sarah is also the wife of Abraham and mother of the prophet Isaac. Medieval Muslim and Jewish commentators alike, however, note Sarah's jealousy as the cause of the rivalry but also complicate the situation. Some place the blame squarely on Sarah, whereas others point to Hagar's insensitivity to Sarah's situation. In other words, both women are treated as praiseworthy but are also subject to criticism.

Modern readers regard Hagar as a victim of patriarchy, of a class and race-conscious culture, as a pawn in the family dynamics of Sarah and Abraham, and at the same time as a victor who, on her own initiative and with the help of God, transforms her oppressive situation into a form of liberation. The biblical story of Hagar attests to God's concern for those who are marginalized yet attests also to the centrality of the Abrahamic

---

13. *Prophets and Patriarchs*, vol. 2 of *The History of al-Tabari*, trans. William Brinner (Albany: State University of New York Press, 1987), 72.
14. Ibn Kathir, *Al-Bidāyah wa-al-nihāyah fi al-ta'rīkh*, 7 vols. (Cairo: Maṭba'at al-sa'ādah, 1932–1939), 1:153.

covenant. Indeed, it is not difficult to understand the empowering effect of the story of Hagar for those who are oppressed and have been denied their share of power. At the same time, however, while God comforts Hagar, she and Ishmael, along with his progeny, are nonetheless relegated to the periphery of the main narrative. When Hagar first flees from Sarah's harsh treatment, God gives her assurances and consoles her with the promise of the birth of Ishmael. But then she and her son are cast out of Abraham's household and sent into the wilderness, where she endures the pain of watching Ishmael nearly die of thirst.

Contemporary readers are also interested in how the story of Sarah and Hagar speaks to political and social issues; how it might illumine power dynamics, the clash of classes, the power of victimhood; how it might reveal the anxieties of mothers-in-waiting. They are moved by the desire for the children of Sarah and Hagar—Arabs and Jews, Israeli Jews and Palestinians, Jews and Christians and Muslims—to live in peaceful coexistence. What those who use the story politically seem to ignore is that the narrative's framework does not support their desiderata. The very paradigm of rivalry between the women, as well as the power dynamic undergirding the biblical storyline, does not support a reading whereby the two women live together happily ever after. If, however, one adopts an alternative reading of the story that allows one to appreciate the personal struggles each woman faces in her particular station, a reading that does not focus on the enmity between them but rather on the emotions that led to fear and loathing, a reading that highlights the common challenge and individual sacrifices each mother faces in order to secure her son's survival, and if one understands the story of Ishmael and Isaac as one of reconciliation, then perhaps everyone can begin to move beyond the ideological strictures imposed on the story's past and present interpreters and begin to appreciate the myriad ways the story speaks to women, mothers, daughters, husbands, and sons.

The Voice of the Woman: Narrating the Song of Songs in Twelfth-Century Rabbinic Exegesis

Robert A. Harris

1. Introduction

From the period of canonization through the premodern era, the Song of Songs has been almost universally interpreted as an allegorical work. This holds true for Christianity as well as Judaism. Rabbinic masters such as Rabbi Akiva championed the book as celebrating God's love for the people of Israel and narrating (among other things) the exodus from Egypt and the revelation of the Torah on Mount Sinai.[1] While exegesis of

---

This essay has had a long gestation. It originated in a lecture I gave at the International Medieval Congress in Leeds in 2007 ("To Ignore the Allegory: Preliminary Thoughts on Twelfth Century Contextual Commentaries of the Song of Songs"). I revisited the subject in a talk I gave in Ravenna at the European Association of Jewish Studies Conference in 2010 ("Ignoring the Allegory/Encompassing the Allegory: Twelfth Century Contextual Commentaries of the Song of Songs"). Under the present title, I was due to present it at the conference in Vienna (in 2014) represented by the essays in this volume, but in the end I could not attend. Between 2014 and the present publication, many additional studies on the subject of northern French rabbinic exegesis on the Song have been published, particularly by Sara Japhet. Coincidentally, Barry Walfish published an article in 2018 ("Song of Songs: The Emergence of Peshat Interpretation." TheTorah.com, https://tinyurl.com/SBL6014b) with observations remarkably similar to my own. To truly encompass all of this scholarship would have required a complete rewriting of my essay. In lieu of that, I have endeavored to note additional bibliographic information throughout while still retaining the original citations for scholarship upon which I had relied.

1. Rabbi Akiva's famous dictum concerning the sanctity of the Song is found in m. Yad. 3:5: "the whole world was never as worthy as it was when the Song of Songs

the Song is found throughout ancient rabbinic literature (both talmudim and midrashim), the most centralized location for rabbinic interpretation eventually found its expression in the midrash on the Song of Songs, which was edited in the medieval period.² The rabbinic allegorization of the Song had its concomitant in patristic literature. Beginning with Origen in the third century CE, Christianity espoused the belief that the book detailed God's or Christ's love for the church.³ In the high Middle Ages, Christianity furthered the allegorical approach to the Song of Songs in developing Marian exegesis.⁴

However, among rabbinic exegetes in the late eleventh and early twelfth centuries, Rashi began to articulate a vision of the book that, while maintaining the rabbinic allegorical approach (which he called *dugma'* and culled from various midrashim), stressed at the same time the sense of the allegory in its own literary context.⁵ This initiated what ought to

---

was given to Israel; for all of the Writings are holy, but the Song of Songs is the holy of holies."

2. This is sometimes called Midrash Hazit or Midrash Hazita, since (in the standard editions) the first interpretation offered begins with a citation of Prov 22:29, where the word חזית is contained. See Günter Stemberger, *Einleitung in Talmud und Midrasch* (Munich: Beck, 1992), 342–44; see also Joseph Chaim Wertheimer, *Midrash Shir Ha-Shirim: Printed from a Geniza Manuscript* [Hebrew] (Jerusalem: Ketav-Yad va-Sefer Institute, 1981), 11–23. A popular modern version of the standard edition is Samson Dunsky, *Midrash Rabah Shir Ha-Shirim: Midrash Hazit* (Jerusalem: Devir, 1980). For a brilliant discussion of Song of Songs interpretation in ancient and medieval Jewish culture, see Gerson Cohen, "The Song of Songs and the Jewish Religious Mentality," in *Studies in the Variety of Rabbinic Cultures* (Philadelphia: Jewish Publication Society, 1991), 3–17.

3. On the ancient zeitgeist and possible mutual influences of ancient rabbinic midrash and Christian allegory, see Marc Hirshman, *A Rivalry of Genius: Jewish and Christian Biblical Interpretation in Late Antiquity* (Albany: State University of New York Press, 1996), 84–95; and Reuven Kimmelman, "Rabbi Yokhanan and Origen on the Song of Songs: A Third-Century Jewish-Christian Disputation," *HTR* 73 (1980): 567–95.

4. See E. Ann Matter, *The Voice of My Beloved: The Song of Songs in Western Medieval Christianity* (Philadelphia: University of Pennsylvania Press, 1990); and Ann W. Astell, *The Song of Songs in the Middle Ages* (Ithaca, NY: Cornell University Press, 1990).

5. Among modern scholars investigating the history of contextual interpretation of the Song, Sarah Kamin stands as a brilliant innovator and pioneer. See Sarah Kamin, "Rashi's Commentary on the Song of Songs and Jewish-Christian Polemic" [Hebrew], *Shnaton Lemikra Uleheker Hamizrah Hakadum* 7–8 (1983): 218–48; Kamin, "דוגמא in

be considered a revolution in exegesis of the Song. We may see in this stance a reflection of Rashi's moderation of the transition between ancient rabbinic exegesis (*midrash*, from the Hebrew verb "to seek") to the plain-sense exegesis (*peshat*, from the Hebrew "to strip away" or "to lay bare")[6] that is more typical of the northern French rabbinic exegetes of the Bible during the twelfth-century renaissance.

While Rashi may be credited with initiating the movement from midrash to plain-sense interpretation among rabbinic exegetes, it was Rabbi Samuel ben Meir (Rashbam), Rashi's grandson, who two generations later boldly departed from Rashi in his exposition of the Song, much as he did in his other biblical commentaries.[7] While it is true, as Sara Japhet

---

Rashi's Commentary on the Song of Songs." *Tarbiz* 52 (1983): 41–58. Both essays are reprinted in *Jews and Christians Interpret the Bible* (Jerusalem: Magnes, 2008), 22–57 and 69–88. See also Sara Japhet, "Rashi's Commentary on the Song of Songs: The Revolution of the Peshat and Its Aftermath," in *Mein Haus wird ein Bethaus für alle Völker genannt werden (Jes 56,7): Judentum seit der Zeit des Zweiten Tempels in Geschichte, Literatur und Kult. Festschrift für Thomas Willi zum 65. Geburtstag*, ed. Julia Mannchen and Torsten Reiprich (Neukirchen-Vluyn: Neukirchener Verlag, 2007), 199–219. The trajectory of this essay closely approximates my own, and I am grateful to Japhet for having been in close correspondence with me over the years over questions relating to the history of contextual exegesis of the Song. Indeed, I wish to acknowledge her many contributions to my understanding of the rabbinic exegesis of the Bible.

6. Rashi himself more typically employed the related term, *peshuto*, the noun *peshat* not really coming into vogue until after Rashi's death. See Sarah Kamin, *Rashi's Exegetical Categorization in Respect to the Distinction between Peshat and Derash* [Hebrew] (Jerusalem: Magnes, 1986). On the transition from *derash* to *peshat* in rabbinic exegesis, see Robert A. Harris, "Jewish Biblical Exegesis in the Middle Ages: From Its Beginnings through the Twelfth Century," in *The New Cambridge History of the Bible*, ed. Richard Marsden and Ann Matter (Cambridge: Cambridge University Press, 2012), 596–615.

7. In this essay, I will not take up the question of the authenticity of Rashbam's commentary on the Song of Songs; I have already explained my own take on the issues and support Japhet's attribution of the commentary to Rashbam. See Robert A. Harris, "The Rashbam Authorship Controversy Redux: On Sara Japhet's *The Commentary of Rabbi Samuel Ben Meir (Rashbam) on the Book of Job*," *JQR* 95 (2005): 163–81 (see 169 n. 23 there). However, with the publication of Sara Japhet's edition of the commentary and the introduction, perhaps we can, at last, let the matter rest: Sara Japhet, *The Commentary of Rabbi Samuel Ben Meir (Rashbam) on the Song of Songs* [Hebrew] (Jerusalem: World Union of Jewish Studies, 2008). The commentary has also been included as Rashbam's in Menachem Cohen, *Mikra'ot Gedolot 'Haketer': A Revised and Augmented Scientific Edition of 'Mikraot Gedolot' Based on the Aleppo Codex and Early*

has shown,[8] that Rashbam claims that a figurative level of understanding inheres in the surface meaning of the book, a far greater percentage of his commentary engages the Song by means of a literary-contextual interpretation. Thus, while he recognizes a figurative level (which he calls *dimyon*, "metaphorical" or "figurative" interpretation), which he considers to operate primarily in the realm of Jewish-Christian polemics, Rashbam emphasizes—as always—what modern readers would call an "actual" or "contextual exegesis" (*peshat*) in the broad contours of his commentary. He interprets the book as a sustained dialogue between a young woman and her female friends, in which she reports conversations and actions between herself and her lover. As we shall see, Rashbam ultimately draws a comparison between the genre of the Song as erotic love poetry and contemporary jongleurs who sang of love in popular fashion in twelfth-century France.[9]

Medieval Mss: The Five Scrolls (Ramat Gan: Bar Ilan University Press, 2012). Japhet has stated her case with erudition and authority, as she has done previously with regard to the commentaries on Qoheleth and Job. In any case, the commentary speaks for itself, whether or not its attribution to Rashbam is correct. All English translations (of these and other rabbinic texts) are my own. For studies of Rashbam's exegesis on other biblical books, see Elazar Touitou, *Exegesis in Perpetual Motion: Studies in the Pentateuchal Commentary of Rabbi Samuel Ben Meir* [Hebrew] (Ramat Gan: Bar Ilan University Press, 2003); Sara Japhet and Robert Salters, *The Commentary of R. Samuel Ben Meir (Rashbam) on Qoheleth* (Jerusalem: Magnes; Leiden: Brill, 1985), 11–68 (English section); Avraham Grossman, *The Early Sages of France: Their Lives, Leadership and Works* [Hebrew] (Jerusalem: Magnes, 1995), 168–70, 251–52, 260–61, 304–6, 467–70, 475–81, 531–33. Martin Lockshin has translated and critically annotated Rashbam's Pentateuch commentary; see his *Rabbi Samuel Ben Meir's Commentary on Genesis: An Annotated Translation* (Lewiston, NY: Mellen, 1989), 391–424 for conclusion and appendices; Lockshin, *Rashbam's Commentary on Exodus: An Annotated Translation* (Atlanta: Scholars Press, 1997); Lockshin, *Rashbam's Commentary on Leviticus and Numbers: An Annotated Translation* (Providence, RI: Brown Judaic Studies, 2001); Lockshin, *Rashbam's Commentary on Deuteronomy: An Annotated Translation* (Providence, RI: Brown Judaic Studies, 2004). See also Lockshin, "Rashbam as a 'Literary' Exegete," in *With Reverence for the Word: Medieval Scriptural Exegesis in Judaism, Christianity and Islam*, ed. Jane Dammen McAuliffe, Barry D. Walfish, and Joseph W. Goering (Oxford: Oxford University Press, 2003), 83–91.

8. Japhet, *Song of Songs*, esp. 82–85 and 165–95.

9. Sara Japhet has written extensively about this commentary and other matters related to the history of *peshat* interpretation of the Song of Songs. In addition to the preceding, see Sara Japhet, "Exegesis and Polemic in Rashbam's Commentary on the Song of Songs," in *Jewish Biblical Interpretation and Cultural Exchange: Comparative*

Finally, there are several important anonymous commentaries that carried forward Rashi's and Rashbam's pioneering efforts. A critical edition of one of these (that had formerly been published in the so-called "Eiger Pentateuch") has been recently published by Japhet in a volume of essays she edited with Eran Viezel.[10] Another anonymous commentary was published by H. J. Mathews in 1896.[11] Japhet and Barry Walfish have published a critical edition and translation of this, thus superseding the earlier publication.[12] These anonymous commentaries ignore altogether the allegorical interpretation of the Song and exclusively expound the book in its own

---

Exegesis in Context, ed. Natalie B. Dohrmann and David Stern (Philadelphia: University of Pennsylvania Press, 2008), 182–95; 304; Japhet, "Two Introductions by Rabbi Samuel Ben Meir (Rashbam): To the Song of Songs and Lamentations," in *Transforming Relations: Essays on Jews and Christians throughout History*, ed. Franklin T. Harkins (Notre Dame: University of Notre Dame Press, 2010), 205–23; Japhet, "'Lebanon' in the Transition From Derash to Peshat: Sources, Etymology and Meaning (With Special Attention to the Song of Songs)," in *Emanuel: Studies in Hebrew Bible, Septuagint and Dead Seas Scrolls in Honor of Emanuel Tov*, ed. Shalom M. Paul et al. (Leiden: Brill, 2003), 707–24. For additional essays (in Hebrew), consult Sara Japhet, *Collected Studies in Biblical Exegesis (Dor Dor Ufarshanav: Asufat Mehqarim be-Farshanut Hamiqra)* [Hebrew] (Jerusalem: Bialik Institute, 2008), 55–102, 135–56, 275–309. For a contrary perspective, see Hanna Liss, "The Commentary on the Song of Songs Attributed to R. Samuel Ben Meir (Rashbam)," *Medieval Jewish Studies-Online* 1 (2007): 1–27.

10. See Sara Japhet, "The Anonymous Commentary on the Song of Songs in Ms. Prague: A Critical Edition and Introduction" [Hebrew], in *"To Settle the Plain Meaning of the Verse": Studies in Biblical Exegesis*, ed. Sara Japhet and Eran Viezel (Jerusalem: Bialik Institute, 2011), 206–47. The *editio princeps* of this commentary was Adolf Hüsch, *Die fünf Megilloth nebst dem syrischen Thargum genannt "Peschito"* (Prague: Senders & Brandeis, 1866); see Japhet, "Anonymous Commentary," 206 n. 2.

11. H. J. Mathews, "Anonymous Commentary on the Song of Songs: Edited from a Unique Manuscript in the Bodleian Library Oxford" [Hebrew], in *Festschrift zum achtzigsten geburtstage Moritz Steinschneider's* (Leipzig: Harassowitz, 1896), 164–85. For critical essays concerning this commentary and its original publication, see Sara Japhet, *Collected Studies*, 313–27; and Japhet, "The Lovers' Way: Cultural Symbiosis in a Medieval Commentary on the Song of Songs," in *Birkat Shalom: Studies in the Bible, Ancient Near Eastern Literature, and Postbiblical Judaism Presented to Shalom M. Paul on the Occasion of His Seventieth Birthday*, ed. Avi Hurvitz, vol. 2 (Winona Lake, IN: Eisenbrauns, 2008), 863–80.

12. Sara Japhet and Barry Dov Walfish, *The Way of Lovers: The Oxford Anonymous Commentary on the Song of Songs (Bodleian Library, Ms Opp. 625): An Edition of the Hebrew Text, with English Translation and Introduction*, Commentaria 8 (Leiden: Brill, 2017).

literary context.[13] The present essay examines this *peshat* tradition of interpretation and attempts to account both for its rise and its eclipse.[14]

2. Ancient Rabbinic Midrash

In order to be able to truly appreciate the work of the medieval exegetes in working toward a contextual exegesis of the Song of Songs, let us first consider one brief example of the ancient pure allegory, as this played itself out in rabbinic midrashic texts. To recall, the rabbis typically understood the Song allegorically as referencing God's love for "the gathering of Israel" (*knesset yisra'el*) particularly during the period of the exodus.[15] Thus in a gloss on Song 4:5—"Your breasts are like two fawns, twins of a gazelle, browsing among the lilies"—we should not be surprised to find this understood as an allusion to Moses and Aaron:

> *Your two breasts*: These are Moses and Aaron: Just as breasts[16] are the glory and the splendor of a woman, so Moses and Aaron are the glory and the splendor of Israel. Just as breasts are the beauty of a woman, so, too, are Moses and Aaron the beauty of Israel. Just as breasts are the honor and the praise of a woman, so, too, are Moses and Aaron the honor and praise of Israel. Just as breasts are full of milk, so, too, do Moses and Aaron fill Israel from the Torah. And just as breasts—everything that the woman eats, the baby eats and suckles from them, so, too, the entire Torah that Moses our Rabbi learned, he taught to Aaron, as it

---

13. Again, see Japhet, *Collected Studies*, esp. 306 n. 9. Baruch Alster discusses yet another anonymous medieval Song commentary that mixes *peshat*/plain-sense exegesis with a type of rabbinic allegory; see Alster, "Human Love and Its Relationship to Spiritual Love in Jewish Exegesis on the Song of Songs" [Hebrew] (PhD diss., Bar Ilan University, 2006). He calls this commentary "Pseudo-Rashi"; see 14–17 for a description.

14. For a point of view that differs in a significant number of ways, see Michael Fishbane, *The JPS Bible Commentary: Song of Songs* (Philadelphia: Jewish Publication Society, 2015), 245–55. Curiously, Fishbane states that Rashi studied in Spain (245), a certain mistake; moreover, the essay contains a number of other problematic statements about the northern French rabbinic exegetes in what is otherwise an insightful volume.

15. Again, for a discussion of how rabbinic Judaism built its allegorical understanding of the Song within the broader contours of biblical literature, see Cohen, "Song of Songs."

16. Lit. "these breasts," and so throughout.

is written: *And Moses told Aaron all the words of the Lord* (Exod 4:28). (Midr. Song 4:5)[17]

Note that midway through the pericope (at "just as breasts are the honor and the praise of a woman"), the midrash departs slightly from the formula it has established. Having built up a pattern ("just as ... so, too, ..."), the reader would have expected "so, too, are Moses and Aaron filled with Torah" instead of the actual formulation of the midrash, "so, too, do Moses and Aaron fill Israel from the Torah." Similarly, the *casus pendens* with which the midrash concludes further disrupts its formulaic opening. But structural observations aside, the reader may be struck by the overt feminization of two of the exodus narrative's two central male characters. This interpretive move is made all the more remarkable by the complete absence of any awareness of irony at associating male characters with feminine qualities. While it is not the purpose of this essay to explore gender shifts in midrashic readings of biblical narratives or to make any claim about its prevalence in the ancient rabbinic interpretation of the Song, the movement is nonetheless noteworthy and perhaps points a way forward to the medieval northern French interpretive postures that center the narrative in a female perspective. In any case, to whatever degree gender shifts of this nature might be present in the midrashic tradition, they would be built on a solid foundation of biblical figurations of ancient Israel as a female character—in particular, the wife of God.[18]

2. Rashi and Rashbam: Grandfather and Grandson Comment on the Song

Turning from ancient midrash to medieval commentary, let us first consider Rashi's commentary. Rashi's exegesis of the Song of Songs draws on the midrashic tradition in its many and varied iterations. But unlike the midrashic sources, Rashi follows a distinct exegetical program and correlates the midrashic interpretations with the order and structure of the biblical composition. His introduction to the Song revisits the method-

---

17. See Wertheimer, *Midrash Shir Ha-Shirim*, 83.
18. See, e.g., Num 15:39; Isa 50:1; Jer 3:1–13; Ezek 16; Hos 1–3. For analysis of these and other biblical passages, see Nelly Stienstra, *Yhwh Is the Husband of His People: Analysis of a Biblical Metaphor with Special Reference to Translation* (Kampen: Kok Pharos, 1993).

ological statement he made towards the beginning of his commentary on the Pentateuch and additionally sketches out his specific understanding of the setting of the Song:[19]

> *One thing has God spoken; two have we heard* (after Ps 62:12). One scriptural verse yields many meanings, and the end of the matter is that no scriptural verse ever escapes the hold of its sense.[20] And even though the prophets spoke their words in allegory [דוגמא] one must reconcile the allegory according to its characteristics and its order, just as the verses of Scripture are ordered one after the other. I have seen for this book [Song of Songs] many homiletical midrashim, for some of which the entire book is arranged in one midrash, whereas others are scattered in many books of midrash, on individual verses. But these are not reconciled according to the language of Scripture or the order of the verses. I have intended to capture the sense of the scriptural verses, to reconcile their explanations according to the order. And as for the midrashim—the rabbis have fixed them, each midrash in its place.
>
> I state that Solomon saw, through the agency of the Holy Spirit, that in the future [the Israelites] would be exiled in exile following exile, destruction following destruction; and would mourn in this exile over their former glory; and would remember the first love when they were treasured above all peoples; and would say: *I will go and return to my first husband, for it was better for me then than now* (Hos 2:9); and would call to mind God's loving acts, and their betrayal with which they betrayed [God], and the bounties that He said He would give them in the End of Days.
>
> And he [Solomon] composed this book through the agency of the Holy Spirit in the language of a woman bound in living widowhood, yearning for her husband, longing for her beloved, calling to mind the love of her youth for him. Even so her beloved is troubled by her trouble, and makes mention of the loving acts of her youth, and the splendor of

---

19. See his celebrated methodological statement in his comment on Gen 3:8, cited below. The version of Rashi's Song of Songs commentary that I reference in this essay is based on JTS MS L778, as transcribed in Sarah Kamin and Avrom Saltman, *Secundum Salomonem: A Thirteenth Century Latin Commentary on the Song of Songs* (Ramat Gan: Bar-Ilan University Press, 1989).

20. The word משמע Rashi uses here stands in the place of the more enigmatic word פשוטו he employs in the famous programmatic statement he presents in his comment on Gen 3:8; both are roughly the equivalent to the term *sensus literalis*, the so-called literal sense, used by contemporary Christian exegetes. For more, see below in this section.

her beauty, and the fitness of her actions wherein he was attracted to her in a fierce love (see Song 8:6); and he informs her that it is not his intention that she be afflicted, nor is there a true separation between them,[21] for she is yet his wife and he her husband.[22]

Rashi's commentary on the Song has been fully explored by such scholars as Sarah Kamin and Sara Japhet.[23] For now let us discuss several features of this introduction. First, Rashi is forthright in his intention to present both allegorical (דוגמא) and "plain sense" levels of interpretation (generally what he calls פשוטו, *peshuto*, but here he uses משמעו, *mashmaʿo*, sense). The questions surrounding the precise meaning of Rashi's technical terminology are a subject in their own right, as he never precisely defines his understanding of the terms he employs. Therefore, before proceeding, it behooves us at the very least to offer a working definition of these terms.

As Kamin states, Rashi references the rabbinic allegorical interpretation through use of the term דוגמא. Moreover, Kamin points out that the way in which Rashi employs the term is itself an innovation, as is the increased use he makes of it.[24] As he does with plain-sense methodology, Rashi adopts ancient rabbinic terms and reinvests them with new exegetical significance, and he does so against the backdrop of contemporary Christian hermeneutic.[25]

With respect to the plain-sense level of interpretation, in lieu of his typical favored term (פשוטו), Rashi employs the synonym משמעו "sense"

---

21. Literally, "nor are her castings-off, castings-off."
22. I published a transcription and a similar translation in Robert A. Harris, "Rashi's Introductions to His Biblical Commentaries," in *Shai Le-Sara Japhet: Studies in the Bible, Its Exegesis and Its Language*, ed. Moshe Bar-Asher et al. (Jerusalem: Bialik Institute, 2007), 219*–41*. For a different translation of this programmatic introduction, cf. Michael A. Signer, "God's Love for Israel: Apologetic and Hermeneutical Strategies in Twelfth-Century Biblical Exegesis," in *Jews and Christians in Twelfth Century Europe*, ed. Michael A Signer and John Van Engen (Notre Dame: University of Notre Dame Press, 2001), 123–49.
23. See in particular Kamin, "דוגמא in Rashi's Commentary" and "Jewish-Christian Polemic"; Japhet, "Rashi's Commentary on the Song of Songs."
24. Kamin, *Jews and Christians Interpret the Bible*, 70–74.
25. This is not the place to make this argument, which I have done in "From 'Religious Truth-Seeking' to Reading: The Twelfth Century Renaissance and the Emergence of Peshat and Ad Litteram as Methods of Accessing the Bible," in *The Oral and the Textual in Jewish Tradition and Jewish Education*, ed. Jonathan Cohen, Matt Goldish, and Barry Holtz (Jerusalem: Magnes, 2019), 54–89.

here. In any case, both terms appear to be a rough approximation of the Christian hermeneutic term *sensus literalis*; Rashi, however, as I stated above, does not provide a definition of the term. Kamin's definition of plain-sense (*peshat*) methodology has become accepted in the modern academy: "[*Peshat* is] an explanation (of a biblical passage) according to its language; its syntactic structure; its (immediate) literary context; its literary type, within a dynamic interaction among all of these components. Put differently, an interpretation according to *peshat* is an interpretation that considers all of the linguistic foundations in its literary composition, and assigns to each of them an understanding within a complete reading."[26] Rashi's rabbinic allegory aside, the question remains as to what degree we may consider Rashi's *peshuto/mashmaʿo* comments on the Song to truly be contextual in the way this definition indicates. Nonetheless, there is no doubt that Rashi's formulation of his exegetical program paved the way to what developed later as a truly contextual methodology among the rabbinic exegetes of twelfth-century northern France.

Let us return to our analysis of Rashi's introduction to the Song. Following his methodological statement, Rashi writes that Solomon had composed the Song through prophetic-like inspiration as a prediction of Israel's future exilic sufferings. He thus provides for his immediate Jewish readership a significance for the Song that not only describes an analysis of events in biblical Israel's history, but also enables a reading of the book as a source of comfort to contemporary Jews. Finally, Rashi presents the image of the woman in the Song as that of a widow, thus describing her as a mature woman reminiscing about a love affair of long ago. While an exegetical innovation on its own, it is strikingly different, as we shall see, from later twelfth-century Jewish exegetes.

Rashbam, for his part, two generations removed from Rashi, takes a dramatically different approach to the Song. As Sara Japhet has persuasively argued, Rashbam only considers the Song according to its *peshat* and considers the דמיון (*dimyon*) or figurative level as part of the contextual fabric.[27] As we shall see, this figuration is not exactly analogous to Rashi's דוגמא and operates on a more contemporary, polemical level with

---

26. Kamin, *Rashi's Exegetical Categorization*, 14.

27. We might consider this as an appreciation of the literal-contextual continuum, and George Orwell's *Animal Farm* can stand in as a familiar example: whereas on a literal level, Orwell's narrative is in fact a barnyard fable featuring pigs and horses as characters, no one would doubt that its actual meaning is rooted in Orwell's disillusionment over

regard to the interaction between Christians and Jews. In his introduction, however, Rashbam gives no inkling of any figuration or allegory and boldly presents the Song—even if authored by a male—as one composed in a woman's voice:

> Let the one who would understand be clever and let him set his heart to understand the mellifluous language of the book which teaches and relates its context according to its mode and expression, as one would expect according to its setting, in its language. For Agur[28] gathered up the wisdom of all the "sons of the East"[29] [and] wrote his book and composed his song before his speech.[30] Moreover, his wisdom is praiseworthy and wondrous in the ways of the world, as a young woman[31] pining and yearning for her lover, who had separated from her and went to far-off places. She makes mention of him when he loved her with an everlasting love, and sings and says: "My beloved showed me such a passionate love when he was still with me!" And she speaks and relates to her friends and maidens: such and such said my beloved to me, and so did I respond to him.

The differences between Rashi's and Rashbam's approaches are striking: Rashi, as in his programmatic statement found first in his commentary on Gen 3:8,[32] sets out to present those aspects of the classical rabbinic

---

the Molotov-Ribbentrop pact in the summer of 1939. Thus, *Animal Farm* authentically yields both literal and figurative interpretations.

28. Rashbam's choice of name for Solomon; see Prov 30:1. For a discussion, see Japhet, *Commentary of Rabbi Samuel Ben Meir*, 131, see also 233 n. 3.

29. Or "ancient ones." See Mayer I. Gruber, *Rashi's Commentary on Psalms* (Leiden: Brill, 2004), 401 n. 30 (at Rashi on Ps 55:20).

30. As Japhet presents it, Rashbam thus agrees with the midrash that states that Solomon wrote Proverbs ("his book") and Song of Songs ("his song") before Qoheleth ("his speech"); see Japhet, *Commentary of Rabbi Samuel Ben Meir (Rashbam) on the Song of Songs*, 131.

31. My translation of בתולה as "young woman" throughout and not as "virgin" is warranted on philological grounds as well as appropriate to the context as Rashbam understands it.

32. "There are many narrative midrashim, and our rabbis have already ordered them in their places, in Bereshit Rabbah and other midrashim. Whereas I have only come for the plain sense of Scripture and the Aggadah that settles a word of Scripture and its sense." This translation incorporates a slight conjectural emendation I have advocated (adding a prefixed *mem*), reading Rashi's last word as "ומשמ[מ]ו," "and its sense." It should be noted that the authoritative Leipzig manuscript (Universitätsbibliothek

allegory that he can reconcile within the order and structure of the biblical book. Thus, his commentary in fact includes a great deal of midrash, although artfully presented in Rashi's own inimitable and brilliant style. On the other hand, Rashbam—at least here, in this programmatic introduction—presents an exclusively contextual approach to the book and does not include even a whiff of classic rabbinic (or newly minted, individually-generated) allegory. Again, he can do that precisely because he considers that the Song operates on both an immediate, plain-sense level as well as on a figurative level; both of these he interprets as part of the "authentic," contextual meaning of the book.

Moreover, Rashbam offers here a conceptual understanding for what he takes as a narrative frame for the book: the Song of Songs presents a continuous, integral story of a young girl in love. While Rashbam of course references Solomon as the author of the Song—he had no choice in the matter, as the Song's biblical superscription makes that point abundantly clear, at least for rabbinic authorities—he by no means foregrounds this biblical persona, and in fact he mentions Solomon on only a handful of occasions. Rather, taking a page out of Rashi's book, so to speak, Rashbam presents the book almost exclusively from the perspective of a woman and through a woman's voice and experience. Put plainly, by diminishing any significant narrative role for King Solomon, Rashbam functionally (and remarkably) turns the female protagonist of the story into the Song's narrator, who creates this role as she relates her experience in speeches she makes to her girlfriends. It is important to make this point clear: for Rashbam, all speech in the book is reported speech. The female lover relates her own feelings; she describes the love-making of her (male) beloved and the love speeches through which he wooed her, and she tells the story of their falling-out and other events—all within the conceit of conversations she has with her girlfriends.

To further clarify the distinction between Rashi's and Rashbam's approach to the book, let us examine Rashi's comment on the first verse of Song of Songs:

Leipzig, B.H.1) presents a slightly different version of this crucial sentence: "Whereas I have only come to explain Scripture according to its plain meaning [*peshuto*], and according to the aggadah that settles matters of Scriptures and [both] its plain meaning and its sense (will be) a matter understood according to its character [lit. "a word fitly spoken"; see Prov 25:11]" (ואני לא באתי אלא לפשוטו של מקרא, ו[ל]אגדה המיישבת דברי המקרא, ופשוטו ושמועתו, דבר דבור על אפניו). This version, as well, defies precise translation, and the variants deserve their own study.

The Song of Songs, by Solomon: Our rabbis have taught: Every [instance of the name] "Solomon" found in the Song of Songs is "holy" [i.e., it is a reference to God] [see, e.g., b. Shabb. 35b]: the King to whom belongs peace.[33]
Song: One that is superior than all other songs sung to the Holy[34] One, by his congregation and people, the gathering of Israel. Said Rabbi Akiva: the world was never worthier than the day on[35] which the Song of Songs was given to Israel, for all of the Writings are holy, but the Song of Songs is the holy of holies. Rabbi Eleazar ben Azariah said: To what may this be compared? To a king who took a *se'ah*[36] of wheat and gave it to a baker. He said to him: take out of this for me such and such amount of semolina, such and such an amount of bran, such and such an amount of coarse bran. Prepare for me out of this one fine and superior loaf. So, too, all of the writings are holy, but the Song of Songs is the holy of holies, since it is entirely about the awe of God and the reception of God's kingship.

Where Rashi's comment is replete with midrashic references and theological orientation towards the book as a whole, Rashbam's first and third comments pertain only to the contextual understanding of the superscription with which the Song opens (שיר השירים, אשר לשלמה):

The Song of Songs, by Solomon: A song that is the most praiseworthy of all songs. This is like [the expression]: *He is the God of Gods and Lord of Lords* (Deut 10:17), [which means], "a God who is greater and more awesome than all divinities" and "a Lord greater than all lords."
By Solomon: King Solomon composed it through the agency of Holy Spirit. For he saw that in the future Israel would mourn in their exile over the Holy One, blessed be He, who would remove himself from them

---

33. Some printed versions of Rashi's commentary on the Song of Songs contain what appears to be a gloss (not found in L778): "[Rashi asks this question] since he found it difficult that the book did not relate to Solomon according to his father's name, as was done in the case of Proverbs and Qoheleth." Contrast the opening verses of the other biblical books ascribed to Solomon: "The proverbs of Solomon son of David, king of Israel" (משלי שלמה בן־דוד מלך ישראל; Prov 1:1); "The words of Qoheleth son of David, king in Jerusalem" (דברי קהלת בן־דוד מלך בירושלם; Eccl 1:1).

34. MS L778 has the abbreviation 'ק here; in this essay I expand abbreviations for the benefit of the reader. Where the abbreviation might yield more than one interpretation, I will make reference to this in a footnote.

35. MS L778 has ביום.

36. The *se'ah* is a biblical unit of dry measure (see, e.g., Gen 18:6; 2 Kgs 7:1). Although any number of proposals have been put forth to determine its precise measure, none has achieved universal agreement.

as a bridegroom who had become separated from his beloved, and who began to sing his song in the place of the gathering of Israel, who is like a bride before him.

By Solomon is just like: *A prayer, by Moses* (Ps 90:1); *A praise-song, by David* (Ps 145:1).

Rashbam's second comment bears an uncanny resemblance to the second paragraph of Rashi's introduction to the Song of Songs. However, even here there is a notable distinction between the two. Whereas, as we have noted, Rashi presents the character of the woman in the Song as an older woman looking back on a love relationship of her youth, Rashbam understands the character of the woman as an unmarried young woman and the man as one who had only recently been separated, in what would typically be construed as a more youthful image than Rashi's. And even according to the figurative level of understanding that he presents (*dimyon*), Rashbam's image of the woman is more youthful than Rashi's.

To solidify our understanding, let us contrast Rashi's and Rashbam's gloss to one final verse, Song 1:2: "Let him kiss me with the kisses of his mouth; for your love-acts are better than wine" (ישקני מנשיקות פיהו כי טובים דדיך מיין). Note that commentators of all ages have needed to contend with the change from third person in the first stich of the line ("Let him kiss me …") to a direct address in the second stich ("for your love-acts are better …"). Our exegetes are no different. Moreover, as we saw earlier, both Rashi and Rashbam incorporate a degree of figurative interpretation in their comments. Rashi first addresses what he considers to be the plain meaning of the verse and afterwards interprets according to its rabbinic allegory:

> *Let him kiss me with the kisses of his mouth*: She recites this song with her mouth, in her exile and in her widowhood: "If only King Solomon would kiss me with the kisses of his mouth as of old," because in some places they kiss on the back of the hand or on the shoulder,[37] but I desire and wish that he behave toward me as he behaved toward me originally, like a bridegroom with a bride, mouth to mouth.
> *For they are better* to me, *your love-acts* (are better), more than any banquet of *wine*, more than any pleasure and joy. In the Hebrew language,

---

37. I have often wondered whether the reference to "shoulder kissing" here is the medieval analogy of contemporary "la bise," or French "double-cheek kissing," in which the upper arms are gently grasped.

every feast of pleasure and joy is called (so) on account of wine, as the context in which it is stated: *to the house of the banquet of wine* (Esth 7:8); *In song they shall not drink wine* (Isa 24:9); *And there were harp and lute, tambourine and flute, and wine at their drinking feasts* (Isa 5:12). This is the explanation of its sense.

The figurative interpretation that is stated is on account of (the fact that God) had given them His Torah and had spoken to them face to face, and those love-acts are still sweeter to them than any delight, and they are assured by Him that He will yet appear to them to clarify to them the secret of its meanings and its hidden mysteries, and they entreat Him to fulfill His word. This is (the meaning of) *Let him kiss me with the kisses of his mouth.*

In contrast with Rashi's approach, Rashbam sets the tone for his interpretation in his comment on the initial verse of the Song (1:2):

Let him kiss me: Oh, would that it would be possible for my beloved to come and kiss me the kisses of his mouth, out of his great love—just like he used to! For better and delightful and sweeter for me are his love words—more than any drink or sweet thing!... *Of his mouth ... for your kisses...*: Sometimes the bride sings as though she were speaking with her lover, and sometimes she recounts to her girlfriends about he that is no longer with her.... *than wine*: Any sweet drink is called [here] wine. Figuratively, this is a reference to the Torah, in which it is said to Israel, by the mouth of the Holy One: *mouth to mouth [will I speak with them]* (Num 12:8).

Note how Rashbam attempts to keep within the rubric of his understanding of the book's frame. The narrative is essentially about the love between two young people; the language shifts back and forth between the second and third person as befits the flow of reported speech. It is somewhat puzzling that Rashbam does not attempt to justify his figurative comment or otherwise work it into some sustained narrative flow. Ironically, this cited verse in its own context actually represents a speech of God to Miriam and Aaron in an angry, not loving, moment. Nonetheless, that did not apparently seem an impediment to the commentator.

3. Rashbam's Song Commentary

Let us leave our comparative/contrastive analysis for now and consider some representative contextual interpretations given by Rashbam, since these mark a significant departure from earlier interpretations (both Jewish and Christian) and point toward a more truly contextual understanding of the Song in its erotic, "profane" setting.

For Rashbam, Song 1:6 ("Don't stare at me because I am swarthy, because the sun has gazed upon me. My mother's sons quarreled with me, they made me guard the vineyards; my own vineyard I did not guard," אל־תראוני שאני שחרחרת ששזפתני השמש בני אמי נחרו־בי שמני נטרה את־ הכרמים כרמי שלי לא נטרתי) reflects a key plot element: the disdain exhibited toward the female lover by her brothers:

> *Don't stare at me*: She is yet speaking to her young friends and saying to them: *Do not stare at me* to ridicule me. For I am not black from my mother's belly, but white and fair I left the womb of my mother, and now I am darkened and blackened from the tanning of the heat of the sun, and the toil and labor which happened to me and came my way from the day that my lover, my beloved separated from me. For my brothers, the sons of my mother, were angry at me, and I became cheapened in their eyes, on account of my beloved who removed himself from me, and they made me stand watch guarding the vineyards in the heat of the sun. Whereas I did not want [to do this work] nor was I able to guard, but they made me do it against my will, guarding it in the heat of the day. Therefore I became black. Yet from a little blackness like this I can quickly again become white, when my beloved returns to me. This figuration concerns the nations who despise the gathering [of Israel] in this exile. Whereas she responds to them: do not despise me on account of you all making me do the work of slaves, for suddenly my lover will return to me, and the God of my salvation will never (again) abandon me.

Note how in this comment there is a natural interrelationship between the plain interpretation and the figuration; both assume "darkness" or "blackness" to connote something negative, as it indeed appears to do in the biblical text itself.

In his approach to Song 1:15–2:3, Rashbam begins by altering the biblical metaphors to similes but sets the erotic circumstances of the biblical scene in startling clarity:

> *Behold you are beautiful, my love*: And he responds to her, indeed, *you are beautiful, my love, and your eyes are doves* of love, like the eyes of doves. *And you are fair, my beloved*: She responds to him: *Behold you are fair* and also *pleasant*. Moreover *our bed is refreshing* and seemly; *the beams of our house*, that we lay in the midst of them, are built and made from

excellent cedars. And *our rafters are cypresses*.³⁸ And I am perfumed and resplendent with good fragrance like *the lily* that grows in the flat valley and like a *rose of the valley*. And therefore you must expand your mind in considering me [only?] as a fine woman with a fine dwelling and fine belongings.

As we see, the point of his comment goes far beyond merely reinterpreting the precise nature of the Bible's figurative language. Rather, he unabashedly presents the woman as highlighting features of the house in which she and her lover engage in lovemaking. He follows this up with an even bolder description, at Song 2:5–6:

> *Sustain me with raisin cakes*: Thus she bemoans to her young girlfriends to get her the things she needs in her lovesickness. And she says: *sustain me with raisin cakes* to sustain and feed my heart, and refresh the refreshments of my bed with apples. Perhaps I shall eat to feed my heart from the fruits. For indeed I am sick with love, from the love of my beloved, my lover, and for the measure of love in which he engaged with love with me. For we would lie together, I and he, on our bed, my beloved would stretch forth and place his left hand under my head, and with his right he would hold me that he might pull my mouth and body towards him—it is for such a love that I have become sick with lovesickness!

Even when considering that Rashbam frequently offers figurative interpretations (דמיונות) that orient the reader toward contemporary polemical concerns,³⁹ there is no mistaking the fact that on the *peshat* level, Rashbam clearly interprets the Song as one of a young woman intimately relating the circumstances of her love affair. Moreover, considering Rashbam's explicit presentation of the young woman's description of her lovemaking, we

---

38. From his subsequent gloss on the words some moderns translate as "cypresses, our rafters" (see e.g., NJPS, RSV), Rashbam interprets the biblical *hapax legomenon* as best he can "according to its context" (פתרונו לפי עניינו) as "one of the buildings of the house." Perhaps Rashbam, thinking of the biblical Solomon, has in mind the larger manor houses of contemporary royalty.

39. For example, he continues this comment with a figurative gloss: "The figure is of the gathering of Israel who are sorrowful in exile, since the Holy One has removed himself from [being] with her. She sighs to the nations to make her burden lighter, for it is enough [suffering] for her that the Holy One has removed himself from her [i.e., that the nations should not add to that]" (דימיון לכנסת ישר' המצטערת בגלות על שנתרחק הק' מאצלה. ומתאוננת לאומות להקל מעליה את שיעבודה כי דיי לה בצרותיה (שנתרחק הק' ממנה).

ought to address the issue of the social circumstances of the young couple in his understanding of the Song, specifically whether the lovers were a married couple. Comments such as the one on Song 2:9–13 make it clear that at least in this instance[40] Rashbam is not thinking of marital love only, or even particularly:

> *My beloved is like a gazelle* and a stag in the swiftness of his feet, in which he speeds to come down to the house of my father, to take me out of there. And when he comes there, he stands outside the house of my father, and he spies, and glances and peers at me through the windows and the latticework of the house, in order to look at me—only he can't see me that well. And he is ashamed to enter the house to speak with me and to see me, on account of it is my father's house! And so my beloved responds and makes his voice heard to me to go to him and to escape with him: "For indeed, the days of winter and rains have passed, and the blossoms and the flowers have appeared in the land, in the trees. And the time of pruning, the harvesting of the vineyards, has arrived, and the voice of the turtledove and the birds is heard in our land. [This is] on account of the summer days which have arrived. And the fig trees have brought forth green figs and the vines have sent forth their blossoms and have given off their fragrance. And therefore I (m., i.e., the beloved) have said to you: come, arise and escape with me!" This is the context of a lover who waits until the days of summer, so that his beloved may go with him. And when the days of Nisan have arrived, when the flowers are in the trees and all of creation is in love! He returns to her that she might go with him.

Consider how Rashbam teases out details from the laconic biblical narrative. Again, with startling clarity, Rashbam lays bare the circumstances of the couple's erotic encounter. Rashbam understands the context as speaking about premarital love, in which the male lover needs to sneak around, as it were, outside the home of his beloved's father! For after all her description of "our house" (in Rashbam's comment on 1:15–2:3) or "our bed" (see at 2:5–6), it becomes clear that she still lives in her father's house, and it is due to that fact that the young couple must be circumspect about their encounters. Indeed, as Rashbam presents the narrative, it is for that very reason that she reports her lover's entreaty for her to escape with him to the countryside. Moreover, as Rashbam makes clear, the season itself bespeaks the occasion for the proposed "love-flight": the

---

40. Cf., e.g., Rashbam's comment on Song 3:9–11.

rains of spring have ceased, so a couple inclined to make their love bed in nature's midst could expect to do so not only without soaking themselves in a wet pasture but could meet "when the flowers are in the trees and all of creation is in love," a beautiful and romantic turn of phrase that apparently is Rashbam's own.

In considering the contextual orientation of Rashbam's exegesis, perhaps the most spectacular comment of all is his comment on Song 3:5 ("I adjure you, O maidens of Jerusalem, by gazelles or by hinds of the field: Do not wake or arouse love until it please!"; השבעתי אתכם בנות ירושלם (בצבאות, או, באילות השדה: אם-תעירו ואם-תעוררו את-האהבה, עד שתחפץ):

> And this is the way this song works: that she sings and sighs with them all about the love of her beloved. And following several recountings with her girlfriends of her lover's words, in which she said: with this [act of] love did my beloved love me, and with this [act of] love did I show him love, they would rebuke her and say to her: remove his love from your heart, for he has spurned you, nor will he return to you ever again! Rather, cling to our lovers. At this point does she adjure them that they should not continue to speak to her thus.[41] For she will not ever forget his love. And this the text demonstrates: that she relates everything—her words and the words of the lover. "Thus my [m.] beloved responded and said to me" and it did not say "thus did my [f.] lover respond and say to her." And thus "I am asleep [f. verb] and my heart is awake … the voice of my [m.] beloved." And so *I adjure you* the oaths that she makes her young girlfriends swear. And even today the way of the jongleurs[42] is to sing a song which relates a deed of love of two lovers with songs of love, in the way of the world.

---

41. The text reads שלא תוסיפו here (i.e., a second-person plural address). Since that does not make sense here, I have translated as though the Rashbam had written either שלא תוספנה (or even שלא יוסיפו). In fact, it seems that Rashbam here adumbrates (or even cites) his comment at Song 7:12–8:4, where it is more appropriate given his understanding of the Song's narrative: by that point, the couple has (temporarily) broken up, and the young woman's girlfriends are attempting to entice her with the prospects of a new boyfriend. Rashbam understands the young woman's adjuration (8:4) as a plea to her girlfriends to stop trying to dissuade her from waiting for her lover to return. Moreover, for Rashbam this works on the contextual as well as the figurative level of interpretation.

42. Literally "singers." It is more likely that Rashbam would have seen jongleurs, or at least heard of them performing, than any other type of performer in his contemporary world. See the following footnote.

Here Rashbam boldly draws a comparison between the text he is reading and the social setting in which he lives. For Rashbam, the genre of the Song fits perfectly with the type of entertainment provided by the jongleurs, who would pass through French towns and sing of love (courtly or otherwise).[43]

Let us consider another excerpt from Rashbam's commentary. According to the narrative plot that Rashbam understands, how can one account for the couple's separation? Thus, whether one considers the "plain sense" of the Song or the figuration concerning the contemporary interaction of Jews and Christians that Rashbam understands as part of the book's fabric, why did the couple "break up"? Rashbam's comment on Song 5:2–7 provides his answer:

> *I am asleep, but my heart is awake*: Now she sighs over her deeds and because her beloved has removed himself from her. *I am asleep*, slumbering sorrowfully (lazily?)[44] on my bed, yet my heart is awake. And here is the voice of my beloved as he knocks on the door and calls to me, saying, "Open up, my sister, my beloved, my perfect dove, for my head is filled with dew and my locks are filled with tiny droplets of dew that fall at night: Indeed, all this night have I speedily ridden to come to you!" And I responded, "I have already pulled off my night shirt, so that I might lay naked. And I am lazy! How shall I wear it again and rise when it is so cold?! And I washed my feet at the time of my laying down—how shall I now go barefoot and dirty my feet to open the door for you?" When he heard my words, he sent forth his hand and returned it to himself, from the hole in the door upon which he was knocking, with the great strength of his hand, on account of the cold that seized him. And my innards stirred within me with compassion for him. And I arose to open for him, my hands dripping with oil of myrrh with which I anointed at night, after bathing, on the bar at the doorpost, on the lock of the door— and I opened the door for him. But he was already hidden from me, and had passed off and gone away. And when I realized that he had gone away, my soul practically left and escaped from me, since he had spoken to me that I should open the door for him, and I had not answered him

---

43. See L. M. Wright, "Misconceptions concerning the Troubadours, Trouvères and Minstrels," *Music & Letters* 48 (1967): 35–39; John W. Baldwin, "The Image of the Jongleur in Northern France around 1200," *Speculum* 72 (1997): 635–63.

44. Japhet's text is עצבה "troubled, sorrowful" here; however, she notes a manuscript variant that reads ודומה לעצלה "this is like being lazy," and this latter reading makes more sense to me here. See further on in this comment.

rightfully nor had I opened the door for him. I should have, when I heard him knocking, hurried to open the door for him. And I sought him but did not find him, and I called [to him] in a loud voice but he did not answer me. I went wandering in the city to search for him, and the city guards found me and struck me and injured me. For they suspected me: "for the purpose of depravity and theft you are walking and going about at night!" And when I was saved from them, the guards of the tower ramparts and forts injured me and stripped me of my jewels.

Rashbam thus interprets the pericope as providing the circumstances for the couple's separation: as the young woman reports, she was lazily lying in bed, "dripping with oil of myrrh with which [she] anointed at night." Despite the entreaties of her beloved outside, she hesitates to arise from her bed and let him in. Only belatedly does she consider his perspective: at that hour of the night or early morning, he presumes she is in bed; from outside, he can perhaps hear her voice, and sense her aroma. The only thing he knows for certain is that, despite the increased intensity of his knocking at her door … she delays! Horrified, "on account of the cold that seized him" (Rashbam does not make a comment only on the temperature here), he thinks the worst: she is with someone else! The moment of realization comes to her as well—"my innards stirred within me with compassion for him"—only she is too late! She arises quickly to let him in, at last, but he is gone. She is immediately beside herself with sorrow and anguish: "when I realized that he had gone away, my soul practically left and escaped from me." She runs outside to catch up with him and rectify his misunderstanding, but she does not find him. Walking alone at night, and calling aloud for him while dressed in her bedclothes only, the city guards mistake her purpose and abuse her. What a terrible turn of events, especially given the intensity of their love as prior to this she has reported. Neither party is guilty of betrayal; if they could only communicate with one another they would discover that their love is alive and well. Only, as is too often the case in young love, their mutual misunderstanding and immaturity in love has caused them to separate. At this point in the narrative, there is scant hope that they will find one another again and renew their love.

Rashbam's understanding of the narrative context also informs his figurative interpretation:

> The figuration is of the gathering of Israel that despaired of [God's] commandments. The Holy One sent prophets and visionaries to them and

> rebukers to rebuke them so they would return to him to keep his commandments and laws. Instead, they spurned them and did not listen to them. And therefore they became enslaved in the yoke of their exile. And they cried out to the Lord when they were in trouble, yet [God] did not incline his ear to listen to their pleas, because he had appointed a time for them [to be punished], since they had refused to listen to his prophets and visionaries.

Thus Rashbam interprets this passage to indicate a heart-wrenching breakup rooted in a tragic misunderstanding between the young woman and her lover. According to Rashbam's schema, neither the young woman nor her figure, Israel, was steeped in wickedness, nor was her separation from her lover/God due to any permanent rejection. Rather, the breakup was due in part to her laziness and in part to his misunderstanding about why she had tarried in bed. One can easily construe, on the purely contextual level, that the young man had imagined the very worst when he wished to enter to make love to her, and she came up with surely the lamest excuses! And even on the figurative level, one does not see the type of "rejection of Israel" that was so typically imagined by Christian persecutors—and perhaps feared by the Jewish audience whom Rashbam addressed. Rather, while there is a temporary interruption in the young people's love affair (and a concomitant disruption in the relationship between God and the Jewish people), this is circumstantial only and not substantive. The parties are still in love, and, given time and a certain amount of reflection, they will be restored to one another in that love.

Rashbam understands subsequent pericopes of the Song as continuing this narrative. He sees the section immediately following (Song 5:8–6:3) as featuring the young woman's entreaties to her girlfriends to reassure her lover, if they happen upon him, that she still loves him:

> Now she sighs and adjures her friends: "If you find my lover, tell him that lovesick for him am I.... If you see him, say to him that I became sick with the sickness of love for him." And they respond to her: In what manner is your love greater and more significant than other loves, that you have become sick for him with lovesickness, that you should adjure us to tell him of your (love) sickness? And she responds to them, "Therefore am I sick about him, for he is more beautiful and grand in all of his limbs, from his head down to his feet, than all men upon the face of the earth, as I will relate to you now from top to bottom.... Despite all, even insofar as my lover has distanced himself from me, I am still his beloved. And he, who shepherds his flock among the lilies, is still my beloved, and in the end of days he will nonetheless return to me."

While the couple does not meet again in the book, Rashbam does understand that they find ways of communicating. Indeed, he understands Song 6:4–7:11 as a kind of "love letter" that the young man sends his lover: as he proclaims his love for her ("now he relates the praise of his lover"; עכשיו הוא מספר בשבח אהובתו), Rashbam sees in this section an occasion for the (male) lover to tell his (female) lover that he still misses her ("I can't live without you"; גם לא יכולתי להתאפק ממך).[45] Moreover, as Rashbam continues to expound the Song, he makes no pretense about knowing the end of the story; given the continuing circumstances of the couple's separation, his narrator—the young woman herself—can only await a reunion. Thus, he interprets the book's final section (7:12–8:14) as her plea for him to restore their love in an active way:

> Now she appeases her lover that he should come and stroll and be affectionate with her: "Come, my beloved, let us go, I and you, from the city to the field and tonight let us lie among the villages.[46] And in the morning we will arise early and stroll in the vineyards, and we shall see whether the time of love has arrived."

Rashbam concludes his commentary (Song 8:13–14) on a note of hope, even confidence:

> *O you who sit in the garden*: Thus she relates about her lover, thus did my lover say: my sister, my love, you who sit and move about and stroll in the gardens and vineyards. Friends and companions who have come with me are listening and are desirous of your voice, for it is sweet [see Song 2:14]. Let me hear your voice and the pleasantness of your song, and let my friends also hear. And she responds: flee, my beloved, resemble a deer or ram, and run to the mountains of fragrances and the hills of frankincense. And also I will surely go with you, and we will make love[47] there, I and you.

Thus Rashbam remains true to his scheme, and while he cannot bring the couple back together again, he can and does interpret that the love that had sustained them before the breakup may still be expressed. Moreover, his

---

45. Literally "I cannot restrain myself from you."
46. Or "henna shrubs." It is not clear how Rashbam understands the term here. On a possible "double-valanced" understanding, see Fishbane, *Song of Songs*, 195.
47. Or "act affectionately."

approach works well within the figurative dimension as well; here it is God who addresses Israel, expressing his wish (and that of the "friendly angelic host") to hear Israel's sweet prayers and worship. In turn, Israel responds as did the female lover with the wish to be returned from her exile and restored to the pure, intimate worship of God. Rashbam concludes with his own prayer, "May the one who waits merit and behold this sweetness."

4. Epilogue: Two Anonymous *Peshat* Commentaries

Let us turn now to the two anonymous, purely contextual commentaries on the Song that I mentioned at the beginning. Again, Sara Japhet has written comprehensive studies that analyze each of these commentaries; I will but briefly introduce them here.[48] One of the first striking things about the Prague Anonymous commentary (the erstwhile "Eiger Pentateuch" Song of Songs commentary) is its author's attribution of the Song's superscription to an anonymous redactor:

> *The Song of Songs that is Solomon's*: The redactor tells us that Solomon sang this song, but they are not (themselves) the words of Solomon. Rather, the beginning of the book is *Let him kiss me* (Song 1:2). So, too, (with regard to) *The words of Qoheleth* (Eccl 1:1), they are the words of the redactor. So, too (with regard to) *The proverbs of Solomon son of David* (Prov 1:1), they are the words of the redactor, who relates that the proverbs of this book are Solomon's, and the beginning of the book he makes explicit below.

That a northern French exegete should attribute the frame of a biblical book to an anonymous redactor is not in and of itself surprising. Rashbam, Rabbi Eliezer of Beaugency, and other exegetes regularly commented in similar fashion using a variety of technical terms (הסופר, סדרן מסדר, etc.).[49] Still, to the best of my belief it is the only example we

---

48. See Japhet, "Anonymous Commentary"; Japhet, "Lovers' Way"; Japhet and Walfish, *Way of Lovers*.

49. See e.g., Rashbam's comment on Eccl 1:1 and 12:8 and Rabbi Eliezer's comment on Ezek 1:4. See my "Awareness of Biblical Redaction among Rabbinic Exegetes of Northern France" [Hebrew], *Shnaton* 13 (2000): 289–310; also Gershon Brin, "Problems of Composition and Redaction in the Bible according to R. Abraham Ibn Ezra" [Hebrew], in *Te'uda 8: Studies in the Composition of Abraham Ibn Ezra*, ed. Israel Levin (Tel Aviv: Tel Aviv University Press, 1992), 121–35; Richard C. Steiner, "A

know of such an attribution in a Song of Songs commentary. Nonetheless, despite this role of the redactor, the commentary's author presents the Song as but one of the many songs that the Bible attributes to King Solomon.[50] Moreover, this author features the biblical Solomon as the male protagonist of the Song, and as the female lead he casts one of the many of King Solomon's wives, albeit his favorite wife. But even more important for our purposes than these details, however interesting they may be, is our author's determination to present the contents of the Song in a purely contextual way, admitting neither to midrashic allegory nor to any figuration whatsoever. For this author, the Song of Songs is, in this sense, a purely secular poem. A single example, the commentary to Song 1:2, should help to clarify this claim:

> *Let him kiss me of the kisses of his mouth*: According to its contextual meaning, one of Solomon's wives was beloved more than all his wives, and she loved him, and about her he stated this song, and about the abundance of her love and about all that transpired below. And there are verses below that help [us frame this perspective] that there was one [wife] beloved more than any other, as it says, *There are sixty queens, And eighty concubines*—all of whom he married, but *Only one is my dove* (Song 6:8–9), beloved to me more than them all. She is the one who states and requests that [he][51] grants her request. And what is her request? *Let him kiss me of the kisses of* the king, my husband, *of the kisses of his mouth*, for that is a proper kiss, inasmuch as there are those who kiss on his hand or her hand. *For better is your loving than wine*: its

---

Jewish Theory of Biblical Redaction from Byzantium: Its Rabbinic Roots, Its Diffusion and Its Encounter with the Muslim Doctrine of Falsification," *Jewish Studies Internet Journal* 2 (2003): 123–67; Aharon Mondschein, "Additional Comments on Hasadran and Hamesader" [Hebrew], *Leshonenu* 67 (2005): 331–46. For an approach that differs with the evidence adduced in these articles and sees instead further instances of authorial and not redactional composition, see Eran Viezel, "Medieval Commentators on the Question of the Composition of the Bible: Research and Methodological Aspects" [Hebrew], *Tarbiz* 84 (2016): 103–58.

50. See 1 Kgs 5:12 (4:32 in Christian tradition): "Solomon composed three thousand proverbs, and his songs numbered one thousand and five." See Japhet, "Anonymous Commentary," 210.

51. The commentary reads שתעשה, either that "she" makes (i.e., grants) the request or that "you" (m.) make; neither one makes particular sense, and I have translated as though it read שיעשה (i.e., the female protagonist requests that he, the king, grant her request).

explanation is that far *better* and sweeter are your loving and lovemaking. From drinking wine I long for *the kisses of his mouth*.

This amazing passage sets the tone for the rest of the commentary, which, despite its brevity, manages to achieve an unprecedented and striking, utterly plain-sense interpretation.

By way of conclusion, let us turn to the anonymous commentary originally published by H. J. Mathews and now republished with an extensive introduction by Japhet and Walfish in *The Way of Lovers*.[52] As Japhet had already concluded,[53] this commentary is truly one that interprets the Song entirely על דרך חושקים, a Song interpreted entirely as a human, erotic love poem. The author makes this much clear not only by the eschewal of allegory or overtly religious interpretation, but as well by the consistent and detailed presentation of the Song in clearly "profane," earthy descriptions of love. For example, let us once again examine the interpretation given to the poem's very first verse (Song 1:2):[54]

> *With the kisses of his mouth*: Mouth kisses are the way of lovemaking and affection, more than those when they kiss the hands of their lover or their shoulder, for that kind of kiss is not really an affectionate kiss. *With the kisses*: many kisses, for I was not satisfied with one kiss or two, only with many kisses. *For your lovemaking is better than wine*: Therefore did she compare his kisses to wine since with regard to all other beverages in the world, although a person is satisfied with them once but eventually hates them (if he continues to drink them) a long time; but with regard to wine, any time he drinks it he craves it all the more, since it warms the body and enraptures him (literally "ignites him").[55]

One immediately senses the commonality of this commentary with the Prague Anonymous commentary.[56] Whether in observing the difference

---

52. See notes 11 and 12 above.
53. Japhet, "Lovers' 'Way.'"
54. Alas, the manuscript appears to be damaged and the commentary lacks what likely would have contained a methodological introduction of some type. See Japhet and Walfish, *Way of Lovers*, 4.
55. See again the observation of the Prague Anonymous (i.e., "Eiger Pentateuch") commentary: מתוך שתיית היין אני משתוקקה לנשיקות פיהו "out of drinking wine I yearn for the kisses of his mouth." One may note that some things never change!
56. Indeed, as Japhet points out ("Lovers' Way," 865 n. 13) there is some degree of overlap between the two anonymous commentaries.

between romantic and courteous kisses or in noting the age-old association between alcohol and lovemaking, our author spares no effort in clarifying the human dimensions of the Song of Songs as a profane love song and does not move in the direction of religious instructions to any degree whatsoever. To choose but one, final example, we may consider this second commentary's comment on Song 2:6:

> His left hand is under my head and his right hand caresses me: This is the "bed of lovers"[57] and of those who desire, for out of his great love he places her heart (directly) on his heart, and that is what is stated below, *place me as a seal upon your heart, as a seal upon your arm* (Song 8:6).

As Sara Japhet has written, this entire commentary explicates the Song as directed toward "those who desire." Indeed, the root חשק in its various formulations occurs multiple times throughout the commentary and explicitly indicates various love acts, as the author sees these described in the Song. Japhet accurately portrays the view of the commentary's author that "the essence of love, its focus and climax, is the consummation of the act of love."[58]

In reflecting about the two anonymous, completely contextual commentaries, what is striking is that, despite their exclusive devotion to the *peshat*, one misses the riveting narrative—the power, the passion, the pathos—that Rashbam finds in the Song, even given his occasional foray into figurative exegesis. For what he describes is not only the exquisite pleasure and coming together that expressed love features, but also the stunning suffering and pain that lovers experience when love is lost.

5. Conclusion

I have offered a broad overview of the development of twelfth-century exegesis of the Song of Songs, as commentators sought either to relate somehow to the ancient rabbinic midrashic allegory or to dispense with it altogether. This development from midrash to *peshat*, from the authority of the ancient rabbinic interpretive community to the independence of the contextual exegete who combined reasoned, grammatically based readings with intuitive leaps of literary imagination, is one that characterizes the

---

57. The commentator cites the language of Ezek 23:17 to indicate sexual intercourse.
58. Japhet, "Lovers' Way," 872.

entire enterprise of the twelfth-century northern French rabbinic school. Whether addressing the conflicts between *peshat* exegesis and the halakhic-midrashic exegesis on biblical law, or the disparity between literary context and rabbinic allegory in the Song of Songs, the northern French rabbinic exegetes ultimately championed the search for contextual truth as having a place at the exegetical table at least as deserved as any earlier authoritative approach: אין מקרא יוצא מידי פשוטו (Scripture never escapes the clutches of its context), whatever else Scripture might come to have meant to the rabbinic community, its plain sense was never and would never be lost, and it continued to be a legitimate source of investigation.

Early in this essay I alluded to an argument that I have been making that the development of plain-sense exegesis among the twelfth-century rabbinic commentators is best understood against the backdrop of the renaissance in reading that took place among Christian clergy in northern France.[59] In brief, this argument states that, as Christian scholars from the Carolingian period into the twelfth-century renaissance increased their awareness of rhetoric (and the trivium, in general), they increased their attention to rhetorical and literary concerns in their biblical exegesis. This accounts for the heightened role of *ad literam* interpretation among the Christian schoolmen who were the contemporaries of the northern French rabbinic interpreters, in particular those at the Parisian school of Saint Victor. I see an analogous development among rabbinic exegetes, beginning with Rashi and continuing until the eclipse of *peshat* exegesis following the Christian destruction of the Jewish community in northwest Europe during the thirteenth and fourteenth centuries.

In the specific case of Song of Song exegesis, the northern French rabbinic exegetes seem to have far outstripped their Christian colleagues in their willingness to apply the norms of contextual exegesis to the interpretation of this biblical book. Whereas Christian exegetes on the Song remained exclusively in the realm of allegory (from ancient Christian

---

59. Again, the fullest argument I have made to date is the essay entitled "From 'Religious Truth-Seeking' to Reading," referenced above. See also Robert A. Harris, "What's in a Blessing? Rashi and the Priestly Benediction of Numbers 6:22–27," in *Birkat Kohanim: The Priestly Benediction in Jewish Tradition*, ed. Martin S. Cohen and David Birnbaum (New York: New Paradigm Matrix, 2015). See also Harris, "The Book of Leviticus Interpreted as Jewish Community," *Studies in Christian-Jewish Relations* 6 (2011): 1–15; as well as my "On the Origins of Peshat Commentary," TheTorah.com, https://tinyurl.com/SBL6014c.

allegorical interpretation through Marianic exegesis in the thirteenth century),[60] Jewish exegetes, as we have seen, boldly followed the programmatic trends of *peshat* into Song of Songs interpretation.

Finally, particularly with respect to Rashbam, we see, perhaps for the very first time in the history of biblical interpretation, an exegete who hears an authentic woman's narrative voice emerging above the din of male-centered perspectives, albeit an imaginary woman's voice nonetheless.[61] Moreover, it goes without saying that he accomplishes this without a feminist agenda, as though it is even possible to imagine such a thing in the world of medieval rabbinic culture. He does so with nary a forced interpretation and only considering his understanding of what *peshat* exegesis demands, namely, the fullest possible accounting for the contours of biblical language and literary composition. Among Rashbam's many innovations in biblical interpretation (e.g., the attribution of the Torah to Moses's authorship within human history, the identification of prolepsis as a technique in biblical composition), the willingness to essentially ascribe a biblical book's narration to a female character is, perhaps, the most idiosyncratic.

---

60. Again, see Matter, *Voice of My Beloved* and Astell, *Song of Songs*. Tellingly, whereas Marianic exegesis has no reverberations in northern French rabbinic *peshat* exegesis, it does appear to have influenced the mystical rabbinic exegesis of the Song in kabbalistic circles. See e.g. Arthur Green, "Shekhinah, the Virgin Mary, and the Song of Songs: Reflections on a Kabbalistic Symbol in Its Historical Context," *AJS Review* 26.1 (2002): 1–52.

61. One could make the claim that this is Rashi's innovation, of course, although I have proposed that much to most of what Rashi attributes to his female character's voice is midrashic allegory and does not appear to fit the literary context of the Song.

The Irony of the *Eshet Hayil*: Proverbs 31:10–31 in Jewish Medieval Exegesis

Sheila Tuller Keiter

The book of Proverbs, along with Ecclesiastes and the book of Job, constitutes a major portion of the Jewish Bible's wisdom literature. Like Song of Songs and Ecclesiastes, Proverbs attributes its authorship to King Solomon. Following the lead of the rabbis of the Talmud and midrash, the rabbinic commentators of the Middle Ages took the Solomonic authorship of these books for granted. However, the rabbis of the Middle Ages made little effort to read into Proverbs content specific to the Solomon narrative beyond that which was already contained in midrash. This includes their treatment of the final twenty-two verses of Proverbs, a self-contained poem in praise of the ideal wife, the *Eshet Hayil*.[1] Given the problems that Solomon encounters in the book of Kings as a result of his numerous foreign wives, it is surprising that the medieval commentators fail to note the irony of such a poem being authored by a king whose wives led him to ruin. In examining the female figure presented in Prov 31:10–31, we will discuss the poem's function in Proverbs, the nature and identity of the woman described, and midrashic and medieval treatments of the poem as well as speculate as to why the medieval exegetes neglected to read the *Eshet Hayil* in terms of Solomon's narrative.

---

1. Since there is no consensus on how to translate the sobriquet *'eshet hayil*, this essay will refer to the poem as *Eshet Hayil* (capitalized) and to the woman described in the poem as the *'eshet hayil*.

1. *Eshet Hayil* in Proverbs

Since scholarly consensus sees the book of Proverbs as a compilation of multiple works, dating the work is fairly tricky.[2] Michael Fox understands chapters 10–29 to contain four separate collections that date to the monarchy around the eighth or seventh centuries.[3] To this corpus were added chapters 1–9 as a prologue, perhaps in the postexilic period. Chapters 30 and 31 were the final additions. However, even within those sections, it is impossible to date the antiquity of any given proverb or to isolate later additions. Regardless of the antiquity of the material within, Proverbs as a whole may not have been edited until the postexilic period. We can determine with precision that it cannot date to any later than 200 BCE, given its inclusion in the Septuagint.[4]

The *Eshet Hayil* poem itself is similarly difficult to date. Its description of the woman's activities is more consonant with urban life during the Second Temple period than with the agrarian lifestyle of the First Temple period.[5] Christine Yoder has dated it to the Persian period, somewhere in the early to mid-fifth century BCE, based on the language of chapter 31. However, its depiction of women and their roles outside the home is not only consistent with the Achaemenid, or Persian, period but also with the freedoms enjoyed later by women during the Hellenistic period in the Greco-Roman Mediterranean.[6]

Chapters 30 and 31 operate as appendices to the greater book with chapter 31 containing two such appendices: the teaching of Lemuel's

---

2. James L. Crenshaw, "The Sage in Proverbs," in *The Sage in Israel and the Ancient Near East*, ed. John G. Gammie and Leo G. Perdue (Winona Lake, IND: Eisenbrauns, 1990), 205–16; see esp. 205, 214, 216; Katharine J. Dell, *The Book of Proverbs in Social and Theological Context* (Cambridge: Cambridge University Press, 2006), 4; R. N. Whybray, *The Composition of the Book of Proverbs* (Sheffield: Sheffield Academic, 1994), 157.

3. Michael V. Fox, *Proverbs 10–31: A New Translation with Introduction and Commentary*, AB 18B (New Haven: Yale University Press, 2009), 499.

4. Fox, *Proverbs 10–31*, 499, 504, 915–16; Mark P. Sneed, *The Social World of the Sages: An Introduction to Israelite and Jewish Wisdom Literature* (Minneapolis: Fortress, 2015), 181; Al Wolters, *The Song of the Valiant Woman: Studies in the Interpretation of Proverbs 31:10–31* (Carlisle: Paternoster, 2001), 40 and n. 45.

5. Avigdor Hurovits, *Mishle: 'im Mavo U-ferush: Kerech 2, Perakim 10–31* (Tel Aviv: Am Oved, 2012), 598.

6. Fox, *Proverbs 10–31*, 899–901; Sneed concurs with this dating, although he acknowledges the challenges to any accurate dating of Proverbs. See Sneed, *Social World of Sages*, 302.

mother (Prov 31:1–9), and the *Eshet Hayil* (Prov 31:10–31). The first nine verses of chapter 31, the only known wisdom text of the ancient Near East to be attributed to a woman, are linked to the *Eshet Hayil* by the theme of the wise woman and mother. At the same time, the *Eshet Hayil* makes reference to material found elsewhere in Proverbs.[7] The quest to find the ideal wife echoes material found earlier in Proverbs that emphasizes the importance of finding a supportive wife.[8] More specifically, the *Eshet Hayil* makes several literary references to material in chapters 1–9. Chapters 1–9 and the *Eshet Hayil* act together as a frame for Proverbs. With its references to Lady Wisdom in chapters 1–9, the *Eshet Hayil* reminds the reader of the role of the female as provider and mediator of Wisdom.[9] Some see the poem as a culmination and recapitulation of the entire book of Proverbs through one figure: her virtues, strength, preciousness, diligence, skill, generosity, self-confidence, and wisdom all culminate in the fear of God.[10]

2. Who Is the 'Eshet Hayil?

2.1. In Terms of the Poem Itself

One point of contention is whether such a woman exists. The opening line asks, "Who can find her?" (Prov 31:10). Most read this not as a declaration of her nonexistence but rather as an expression of her rarity. Rendering

---

7. Dell, *Social and Theological Context*, 85; Fox, *Proverbs 10–31*, 849, 883; Hurovits, *Mishle*, 585; Whybray, *Composition*, 153.

8. Megan K. DeFranza, "The Proverbs 31 'Woman of Strength': An Argument for a Primary-Sense Translation," *Priscilla Papers* 25.1 (2011): 22. See, e.g., Prov 18:22: "He who finds a wife has found happiness and has won the favor of the Lord." This verse must imply that the wife in question is a good wife, for 21:19 warns: "It is better to live in the desert than with a contentious, vexatious wife."

9. Christopher B. Ansberry, *Be Wise, My Son, and Make My Heart Glad: An Exploration of the Courtly Nature of the Book of Proverbs* (Berlin: de Gruyter, 2011), 177–78; Dell, *Social and Theological Context*, 87; Fox, *Proverbs 10–31*, 916; Hurovits, *Mishle*, 583–84; Sneed, *Social World of Sages*, 298–99; Whybray, *Composition*, 159, 161–62, 165; Wolters, *Song*, 153; Yair Zakovitch, "A Woman of Valor, 'eshet hayil (Proverbs 31.10–31): A Conservative Response to the Song of Songs," in *A Critical Engagement: Essays on the Hebrew Bible in Honour of J. Cheryl Exum*, ed. David J. A. Clines and Ellen van Wolde (Sheffield: Sheffield Phoenix, 2011), 401–2.

10. Ansberry, *Be Wise*, 162; Fox, *Proverbs 10–31*, 916. See Whybray, *Composition*, 156: Wisdom is synonymous with the fear of God.

her existence an impossibility might deter young men from even making the effort to find such a wife. Rather, her rarity makes her exceedingly precious. She exists as a real type of woman but also as an ideal and a paradigm. Thus, many see her as the ideal wife for a young man to seek.[11] Despite the fact that the *Eshet Hayil* revolves around a female figure, the intended reader is male, and it is his concern that is primary. The poem acts as instruction to a young man on what to seek in a potential wife. However, the *Eshet Hayil* can also operate as a primer for young women on what virtues to emulate.[12]

An interesting feature of the poem's description of the ideal woman is its use of terms more commonly associated with physical strength and military valor. The female figure is immediately introduced as an *'eshet hayil* (Prov 31:10), a woman of *hayil*. The word *hayil* normally means strength or power and is normally employed with reference to males or in a military context. *Hayil* can also connote wealth as well as general competence or strength of character. Its association with a female figure in verse 10 has prompted a number of alternative translations for the word *hayil*, including valor, industriousness, worth, and virtue. The use of the term *hayil* echoes Lemuel's mother's exhortation (Prov 31:3) that he not give his *hayil* to women. In the latter context, *hayil* implies sexual strength.[13]

In addition to *hayil*, we also see the use of other overtly masculine or martial terms. Verse 11 tells us that the *'eshet hayil*'s husband will have no lack of *shalal*. Typically translated as "gain," *shalal* normally refers to booty or plunder gained in military conquest. In verse 19, she is described as sending or stretching out her hand. Although the context here is her charitable reaching out to the poor and needy, the idiomatic phrase to send out one's hand is more commonly seen as an act of aggression. Verse 15 uses the word *teref* to mean food, when its literal meaning is prey, that is, food that is torn to pieces by a predator. Hence, she is likened to a lioness providing food for her young. Verse 17 attributes to the woman *'oz*, strength, and describes her as girding her loins. This is the

---

11. Ansberry, *Be Wise*, 181–82; Dell, *Social and Theological Context*, 86; Fox, *Proverbs 10–31*, 891, 912; Hurovits, *Mishle*, 590, 591, 596; Sneed, *Social World of Sages*, 295; Whybray, *Composition*, 154.

12. Dell, *Social and Theological Context*, 86; Fox, *Proverbs 10–31*, 889–90, 905; Hurovits, *Mishle*, 590; Whybray, *Composition*, 154.

13. DeFranza, "Woman of Strength," 21–22; Fox, *Proverbs 10–31*, 885–86, 891; Wolters, *Song*, 9–10.

only occurrence in Tanakh in which girding one's loins is discussed with reference to a woman.[14] Some scholars have noted that the use of military imagery renders the *Eshet Hayil* a heroic panegyric, albeit one that has been modified to replace male military exploits with female domestic and communal accomplishments.[15]

Many see the *'eshet hayil* as Lady Wisdom personified.[16] There are certainly linguistic and thematic parallels between the two. However, the *'eshet hayil* is a rare commodity, whereas Lady Wisdom is available to all who seek her. Furthermore, the material on Lady Wisdom is clearly allegorical, whereas the *Eshet Hayil* may be read literally.[17] There is also a tendency to read the *'eshet hayil* as a metaphor for wisdom itself. However, this would render wisdom exceedingly rare and nearly unobtainable, which is certainly not the intended message of the book of Proverbs. Rather, Lady Wisdom personifies Wisdom, while the *'eshet hayil* typifies wisdom.[18]

2.2. Is the Poem Feminist or Misogynist?

As we will see, it is extremely difficult to characterize the *Eshet Hayil* as exhibiting either feminist or misogynist tendencies. The intent of the poem is certainly to praise its subject. Since the poem enumerates the *'eshet hayil*'s praises, whether one views the poem as feminist or misogynist depends on how one values the virtues for which she is praised. Furthermore, one must be cautious of anachronistically imposing modern values on ancient societies. The Jewish Bible reflects the patriarchal society from which it emerged.[19] The Bible does not portray women as equals, but not all of its

---

14. DeFranza, "Woman of Strength," 22–23; Fox, *Proverbs 10–31*, 891, 893–94; Wolters, *Song*, 9–10.

15. Ansberry, *Be Wise*, 179; Wolters, *Song*, 12–13.

16. Ansberry, *Be Wise*, 181; DeFranza, "Woman of Strength," 21; Whybray, *Compostion*, 154; Wolters, *Song*, 142–43.

17. Fox, *Proverbs 10–31*, 908–9. In fact, Fox argues that nothing in the *Eshet Hayil* signals the need for an allegorical reading, since the *'eshet hayil*, while an ideal, is well within reason (909). Of course, the very fact that so many throughout history have read the poem allegorically may be a sufficient refutation of Fox's position.

18. Dell, *Social and Theological Context*, 86; Fox, *Proverbs 10–31*, 891, 907–10; Hurovits, *Mishle*, 590.

19. Tikva Frymer-Kensky, *Reading the Women of the Bible* (New York: Schocken Books, 2002), xiii–xv. Depending on how one defines *patriarchal*, one can argue that

portrayals of women are positive. They are often depicted only in relationship to men, as mothers and wives, and not as independent humans.[20] However, many stories in the Bible revolve around women. While the book of Proverbs was written for a male audience, it is arguably the most gender-concerned book of the Bible.[21] Its female figures include good wives, contentious wives, a queen mother, mothers as teachers, Lady Wisdom, Lady Folly, prostitutes, and adulteresses. These women are seen primarily through the effects they have on men. While the book is androcentric, men are often seen as weak and vulnerable in the face of female actors.[22]

The description of the 'eshet hayil flies in the face of many stereotypes of women in ancient Near East society. While the home is her hub, this woman enjoys broad independence beyond its confines. She can buy real estate and may even engage in international trade.[23] Her husband's prestige is attributable to her. Furthermore, the wife is depicted as active and a protector, while the husband is passive and protected. Still, the emphasis of the poem is on the production of food and clothing, her wisdom seemingly limited to craftsmanship and home management. Meanwhile, the husband retains his superior status.[24] Many feminist scholars embrace the 'eshet hayil's independence and economic contribution. However, while admiring the female figure of the poem, feminists are critical of the *Eshet Hayil*'s patriarchal perspective. The husband and wife occupy separate spheres, with the husband in the public sphere, while the wife is relegated to the domestic sphere. Furthermore, while the husband has the leisure to go out, the wife's work never ceases. However, Fox dismisses this complaint, arguing that it is a product of the world in which the poem was composed. Yet

---

ancient Israel was never a pure patriarchy. However, there is little controversy with regard to the proposition that ancient Israel conveyed higher social status to men than to women.

20. Frederick E. Greenspahn, "A Typology of Biblical Women," *Judaism* 32.1 (1983): 45.

21. Fox, *Proverbs 10–31*, 889; Frymer-Kensky, *Women of the Bible*, xv; Hurovits, *Mishle*, 590; Julia Schwartzmann, "Gender Concepts of Medieval Jewish Thinkers and the Book of Proverbs," *JSQ* 7.3 (2000): 183; Sneed, *Social World of Sages*, 293.

22. Greenspahn, "Biblical Women," 45–46, 50; Whybray, *Composition*, 158.

23. Fox, *Proverbs 10–31*, 890; Sneed, *Social World of Sages*, 317; Shulamit Valler, "Who Is the ēšet hayil in Rabbinic Literature?," in *A Feminist Companion to Wisdom Literature*, ed. Athalya Brenner (Sheffield: Sheffield Academic, 1995), 85.

24. Fox, *Proverbs 10–31*, 896; Sneed, *Social World of Sages*, 316–17; Valler, "Rabbinic Literature," 85.

despite being written in a man's world, the *Eshet Hayil* extols the female figure for her ambition and independence and not for being a slave-like minion of her husband. Some go so far as to argue that the *'eshet hayil* supplants her husband as the true master of the home.[25]

Tikva Frymer-Kensky argues that, while the Bible portrays women as subordinate to men, it does not portray them as other, nor does it view them as different or inherently inferior. In other words, they display the same human goals, desires, strategies, methods, personality traits, and psychological characteristics as men. In this sense, the Bible views humanity as gender neutral.[26] The book of Proverbs fits this model in the sense that it has nothing negative to say about women in general. It is critical of foolish, bad, or unpleasant women, but it is equally critical of foolish, bad, or unpleasant men. This is equally true for those whom the book praises. The book of Proverbs is ready to praise men for embodying the same virtues exemplified by the *'eshet hayil*.[27]

A stronger feminist critique is the inequitable status of women and men with regard to the ownership of wealth and property. Yet even this can be construed as effecting praise of the woman. A man who earns money does so only for his own personal enrichment, but the *'eshet hayil*'s efforts to enrich her household are made selflessly. The final verse urges husbands to render to their wives *from* the fruit of the wife's labors, not just to praise her, but to give her a share in her earnings.[28]

Verse 30's moralistic warning against valuing physical beauty seems to act as a fulcrum in the debate over whether the *Eshet Hayil* is feminist or misogynistic. One can read the absence of praise for the *'eshet hayil*'s physical beauty as either positive or negative, as celebrating women for their true selves or denying them their sensuality. The use of military, specifically masculine, terminology accentuates the lack of praise for her physical beauty. This use of military terminology in the *Eshet Hayil* suggests a parallel between this female figure and the *'anshe hayil*, men of strength or military heroes of ancient Israel. The poem uses masculine metaphors to praise her financial, physical, moral, and mental strength.[29]

---

25. Fox, *Proverbs 10–31*, 912–13; Greenspahn, "Biblical Women," 46; Sneed, *Social World of Sages*, 317–18; Wolters, *Song*, 141–42.
26. Frymer-Kensky, *Women of the Bible*, xv–xvi.
27. Fox, *Proverbs 10–31*, 908, 914, 916.
28. Fox, *Proverbs 10–31*, 899, 914.
29. DeFranza, "Woman of Strength," 24.

The use of military imagery may act as a polemic against the ancient Near Eastern practice of praising women solely for their physical appearance or sex appeal, recasting military prowess as moral strength.[30] This line of argument sees the absence of praise for the *'eshet hayil*'s beauty as positive, celebrating her many strengths.

In contrast, Yair Zakovitch sees the *Eshet Hayil* as a polemic against the sensualized female figure depicted in the Song of Songs. The Song of Songs casts the female as the lead character, celebrates her femininity and sexuality, depicts equality between the sexes, and extols romantic love. The *Eshet Hayil* responds by transforming the depictions of physical beauty into depictions of industriousness and competence. Rather than admire the use of masculine or martial terms, Zakovitch sees them as a concerted effort to rob the female figure of her femininity and sensuality.[31] Of course, the flip side of this argument is that Song of Songs ignores the female figure's human qualities and objectifies her solely as a sexual object. Once again, one's evaluation of the poem has less to do with its actual content and more to do with how one values womanly virtues, in this case the importance of female sexuality in evaluating feminine worth. Ultimately, physical beauty and grace are gifts from God, and, as such, they are transitory and can fail.[32] The poet further warns that beauty and grace can be misleading, whereas fear of God is what is truly praiseworthy.[33]

3. Rabbinic Treatment of the *Eshet Hayil*

3.1. Midrashic Interpretation

While our focus is on medieval interpretation, many of the Jewish commentators of the Middle Ages took their cue from the midrashic treatment of the *Eshet Hayil*. Several of the sections of Proverbs are attributed to Solomon, either independently or through the scribal efforts of the men of Hezekiah. For the most part, the rabbis of late antiquity took these ascrip-

---

30. Wolters, *Song*, 13.
31. Zakovitch, "Conservative Response," 401–7; See also Wolters, *Song*, 141.
32. Fox, *Proverbs 10–31*, 898; Greenspahn, "Biblical Women," 46.
33. Fox, *Proverbs 10–31*, 898. Whybray rejects the contention that the mention of fear of God was a later addition to the poem. The Septuagint also features fear of God, which acts as a natural climax to the poem summing up her virtues. See Whybray, *Compostion*, 154–55.

tions to Solomon at face value, believing him to have authored the entire book.[34] Modern scholars, on the other hand, generally see the Solomonic ascriptions as pseudepigraphic. These ascriptions may serve less to attribute actual authorship than to create a sense of association with Solomon. Solomon, of course, was best known for his wisdom. However, the material within the book of Proverbs does not resemble anything Solomon was known to have said, rendering Solomonic authorship highly unlikely. Rather, since God granted Solomon his celebrated wisdom, Solomonic attribution may have served to imply divine inspiration behind Proverb's composition.[35]

In keeping with the belief that Solomon was the author of all of Proverbs, rabbinic midrash identifies both Agur of chapter 30 and Lemuel of chapter 31 as Solomon.[36] Modern scholarship prefers to identify both Agur and Lemuel as Massaites, foreign figures from the northern Arabian tribe of Massa.[37] However, Agur clearly advocates Israelite faith. Thus, *massa'* in 30:1 and 31:1 may refer to prophetic experience rather than a geographic location.[38] This is not to say that Agur and Lemuel are necessarily pseudonyms for Solomon. However, the rabbinic tradition presumes they are, finding Solomonic themes in the words attributed to them.

With regard to the *'eshet hayil*, rabbinic tradition tended to approach it allegorically from the start. The Babylonian Talmud likens her to the Torah.[39] Similarly, Midrash Mishle (Midrash on Proverbs) identifies her allegorically with the Torah. In other places, the Talmud, as well as in other midrashic sources such as Midrash Eshet Hayil, identify the *'eshet hayil* with historical figures.[40] According to the Yalqut Shimoni and Midrash Tanhuma, she is the matriarch Sarah. Other sources, such as Midrash

---

34. See, e.g., Song Rab. 1:5; Qoh. Rab. 1:1; S. Olam Rab. 15.

35. Crenshaw, "Sage in Proverbs," 213; Dell, *Social and Theological Context*, 3–4; Sneed, *Social World of Sages*, 194, 254–55.

36. Fox, *Proverbs 10–31*, 884; Wolters, *Song*, 62–63. See b. Sanh. 70b; Exod. Rab. 6:1; Num. Rab. 10:4.

37. Ansberry, *Be Wise*, 168; Crenshaw, "Sage in Proverbs," 207; Dell, *Social and Theological Context*, 82; Fox, *Proverbs 10–31*, 884; Hurovits, *Mishle*, 553; Whybray, *Composition*, 148.

38. Fox, *Proverbs 10–31*, 852; Sneed, *Social World of Sages*, 313. See, e.g., Zach 12:1.

39. Wolters, *Song*, 60–61. See b. B. Metz. 84b; b. Sukkah 49b.

40. Fox, *Proverbs 10–31*, 905–6; Hurovits, *Mishle*, 591; Valler, "Rabbinic Literature," 86; Wolters, *Song*, 62. See b. Sanh. 20a; b. Ber. 10a.

Mishle, identify her with male figures such as Noah, Adam, and Moses.[41] However, other rabbinic material deals with the poem more literally.[42] Thus, while the rabbis leaned toward the metaphorical, they did not categorically reject reading the poem as literal praise of the ideal woman.

Furthermore, the midrashic tendency toward allegorical treatment does not necessarily represent an unwillingness to portray women positively. In dealing with those midrashim that relate the *Eshet Hayil* to historical women, Shulamit Valler focuses on how the midrash views those women. She finds material in Midrash Mishle as well as in other midrashic sources that portray Sarah as the spiritual equal to Abraham. Valler sees the repetition of this idea in multiple sources as evidence that Sarah's spiritual equality with Abraham was fairly universally accepted, indicating rabbinic readiness to see past conventional gender roles and attribute so-called male attributes to female figures. The willingness of the midrash to identify more proactive, courageous, and clever women, such as Miriam, Jael, Rahav, Michal, and the wise woman of Abel Beth Maachah with the *'eshet hayil* indicates the willingness of some sages to adopt more liberal concepts of women and womanhood.[43]

3.2. Medieval Rabbinic Treatment

More controversial is how the *'eshet hayil* and, by extension, women faired in medieval commentary. By the Middle Ages, the Jewish commentators tended to adopt the allegorical approach of the midrash to the *Eshet Hayil*.[44] For example, based upon the midrashic identification of Lemuel as Solomon, Saadia Gaon reads 31:1–9 as Bathsheba's castigation of Solomon.[45] As for the *Eshet Hayil*, Saadia first interprets the poem according to its plain meaning, or *peshat*, then treats the poem metaphorically. Ignoring gender, he identifies the *'eshet hayil* as the wise man.[46] Several commentators follow this lead, reading the *'eshet hayil* as a figurative representation of more abstract concepts. Maimonides, for example, refers to the poem

---

41. Fox, *Proverbs 10–31*, 906–7; Valler, "Rabbinic Literature," 86.
42. Wolters, *Song*, 63. See b. Pesaḥ. 50b; b. Taʿan. 26b.
43. Valler, "Rabbinic Literature," 87–97.
44. Wolters, *Song*, 80.
45. Fox, *Proverbs 10–31*, 885. This essentially follows the haggadic account in b. Sanh. 70b.
46. Fox, *Proverbs 10–31*, 907; Hurovits, *Mishle*, 591–92.

in his *Guide to the Perplexed*, calling it a figurative expression in which the woman represents the healthy body in service of the human equilibrium. Rashi and Ibn Nachmiash treat the *peshat* of the *Eshet Hayil* and then, following the midrash, separately address the metaphoric meaning of the poem as representing the Torah. Rabbi Levi ben Gershon (Ralbag) renders the *'eshet hayil* as the physical body or baser soul that serves her husband, who represents the intellect, so that it can attain perfection.[47] Similarly, Rabbi Zerachiah ben Isaac ben Shaltiel Chen identifies matter with the female, so that women come to represent sexuality and all that is antithetical to the soul, which hates matter and loves intellect. He reads *Eshet Hayil* as an exhortation to avoid bodily pleasures by depicting an ideal woman who is not physically attractive. Rabbi Menachem Hameiri renders the *'eshet hayil* as good matter that is ready to accept appropriate form. Thus, Hameiri sees the ideal woman as obedient and ignores her other qualities. Isaac Aramah, like Rashi, distinguishes between the real woman of the poem and its allegorical representation of reason or Torah. But he relates these two approaches to the two creation narratives in Gen 1–3. The spiritual co-creation of man and woman and the real creation of physical woman represent woman's dual roles in tending to man's spiritual and physical needs, both being necessary.[48]

3.3. Medieval Views of Women

Julia Schwartzmann presumes the misogyny of the medieval exegetes and is not disappointed. Schwartzmann argues that most of the medieval commentators ignore Wisdom's identification with woman. Rather, they viewed Wisdom as a divine attribute or genderless abstract entity. In addition, Schwartzmann sees this effort to ignore Wisdom's female gender as a deliberate and unanimous move on the part of the medieval exegetes. So with regard to Lady Wisdom, these commentators tend to depersonify her and defeminize her, identifying her with men or as broader concepts, such as Torah learning. While some commentators allow that a wise woman can exist, they usually equate female wisdom with modesty and silence.[49]

---

47. Fox, *Proverbs 10-31*, 906; Hurovits, *Mishle*, 591–92; Schwartzmann, "Gender Concepts," 197; Wolters, *Song*, 80.

48. Schwartzmann, "Gender Concepts," 198–200.

49. Schwartzmann, "Gender Concepts," 183–86, 192–95.

The medieval tendency to interpret the *Eshet Hayil* metaphorically seems to defy the spirit of the poem itself, which does not obviously beg for metaphoric treatment.[50] According to Schwartzmann, medieval presumptions about gender often forced the commentators into awkward allegorical interpretations that fly in the face of scriptural intent. She argues, for example, that Ralbag's woman as body/soul subservient to the intellect is often forced, failing to adhere to the details of the poem. The *'eshet hayil*, in contrast, is independent and in command of the household. Because medieval Jewish women were deemed intellectually inferior, they were associated with the base and material, the very antithesis to wisdom. Therefore, argues Schwartzmann, the medieval exegetes had no choice but to deny Wisdom her feminine identity and to reconstruct the meaning of the poem to confirm woman's social and intellectual inferiority.[51]

No doubt there is truth to Schwartzmann's assessment. However, it is incomplete. A number of medieval commentators read the *'eshet hayil* as a real woman. Although Saadia Gaon offers an allegorical interpretation, he also sees the *'eshet hayil* as a real female ideal, one that can exist in the real world, because if she were an unachievable ideal, then the details of the poem would be rendered pointless.[52] Abraham ibn Ezra offers a modest commentary to the poem that consists only of interpretation of the *peshat*. He offers no allegorical alternative, indicating that he read the poem at face value. Similarly, Joseph Kimchi offers a strictly *peshat*-based explication of the poem. Joseph's son, Moses, follows suit, restricting his interpretation of the poem to its more literal sense. Both Joseph and Moses Kimchi presume Solomonic authorship, yet neither feels compelled to render the poem metaphorically.[53]

Furthermore, allegorical interpretation does not necessarily reflect an inability to attribute positive virtues to women. Fox views the rabbinic

---

50. Hurovits, *Mishle*, 593.
51. Schwartzmann, "Gender Concepts," 197–201.
52. Fox, *Proverbs 10–31*, 891.
53. Joseph Kimchi, *Introduction to Proverbs*; Moses Kimchi, *Introduction to Proverbs* 31. Interestingly, David Kimchi does not expressly credit Solomon with authorship of Proverbs. Rather, in his introduction to Proverbs, he sees the attribution to Solomon as the author's hinting that the book contains high concepts and wisdom on a par with Solomon's famed wisdom. David Kimchi is more willing to read the book metaphorically than his father or brother. Unfortunately, his commentary to Proverbs extends only into chapter 21, leaving his thoughts on the *Eshet Hayil* unknown.

willingness to identify the *'eshet hayil* as a man as a sign that they did not view her virtues as gender specific. Thus, they had no hesitation in applying these attributes to men. Fox impliedly views the medieval male's coopting of the *'eshet hayil* as a sign of gender neutrality and not misogyny. In addition, sometimes the metaphor is complimentary to women. For example, Moshe Alshich flips Ralbag's conceit, casting the *'eshet hayil* as the soul and her husband as the body, both being wed together to produce good deeds. This conceit reverses the stereotype that women are associated with the physical, the base, and the material. The kabbalists associated the *'eshet hayil* with the *Shekhinah* or God's divine presence. Because the kabbalists would recite the *Eshet Hayil* on Friday nights to greet the Shekhinah at the beginning of Sabbath, the popular custom of singing the *Eshet Hayil* at home on Friday nights emerged.[54] Subsequently this practice took on its current meaning of praising of the woman of the house, bringing it back to its more literal intent.

Admittedly, Moshe Alshich and the kabbalists postdate most of the medieval commentators we have discussed. Perhaps there was a perceptible shift in rabbinic attitudes toward women in the sixteenth century, when they lived and wrote. Shaul Regev examines the use of the *Eshet Hayil* in sermons given by select rabbis in the Ottoman Empire during the same century. These sermons, typically given at weddings and funerals, incorporated biblical interpretation. Rabbi Moshe ben Baruch Almosnino used the *Eshet Hayil* to address the question of how women, who did not receive formal education and who did not systematically learn Torah, could achieve perfection. They could do so by motivating their husbands and sons to learn Torah. Furthermore, Almosnino, in contrast to Maimonides, saw the practice of Torah values as of greater value than learning, thus granting women a spiritual advantage. Regev emphasizes the significance of Almosnino's as well as a number of his contemporaries' literal approach to the *Eshet Hayil*.[55] While one might reasonably construe these attitudes as condescending, they do represent a real attempt to construe the *Eshet Hayil* as praise for women who are valued by their rabbinic contemporaries.

---

54. Fox, *Proverbs 10–31*, 905–7; Hurovits, *Mishle*, 592.

55. Shaul Regev, "'Woman of Valor' אשת חיל: The Character and Status of Women in Jewish Philosophy of the Sixteenth Century," *European Journal of Jewish Studies* 4 (2010): 243–46, 248, 254.

4. The *Eshet Hayil* and Solomon

4.1. Connection to Bathsheba

As discussed above, since the rabbis of late antiquity and of the Middle Ages took for granted that Solomon was the author of Proverbs, the rabbinic lens reads chapters 30 and 31 together, identifying both Agur and Lemuel as Solomon.[56] In 31:2–9, Lemuel's mother chastises him, warning him to avoid women and wine. Since the rabbis identified Lemuel as Solomon, Lemuel's mother became equated with Bathsheba. In discussing these verses, the Talmud envisions Bathsheba leaning Solomon over a post to flog him and berate him for his excesses. The Talmud then has Solomon recant and admit his wrongdoing, with Prov 30:2 representing his confession of foolishness (b. Sanh. 70b).[57] Because of this identification of Lemuel's mother with Bathsheba, some of the medieval commentators read the *Eshet Hayil* as Solomon's praise for his mother and her wisdom (Joseph Kimchi, Commentary on Prov 31:1; Moses Kimchi, introduction to Proverbs 31).[58] However, that is the entire extent to which the medieval exegetes try to connect the *Eshet Hayil* to Solomon. Oddly, they do not seek any further connections between the poem and Solomon.

This omission is made all the more puzzling given the substance of Lemuel's mother's rebuke. Specifically, in Prov 31:3 she exhorts Lemuel: "Do not give your strength to women." While Solomon may not have had a recorded drinking problem, his excesses with women are well documented. Solomon had seven hundred wives and three hundred concubines (1 Kgs 11:3). It is precisely these foreign wives who lead Solomon to his downfall, swaying his heart from God to idolatry (1 Kgs 11:4). Furthermore, literary connections between the *Eshet Hayil* and Prov 31:1–9 indicate deliberate thematic connections. The text links Prov 31:3 with the *Eshet Hayil*, the former of which depicts Lemuel's mother rebuking him by using the word *hayil* to mean strength: "Do not give your *hayil* to women." The word *hayil* appears only five times throughout the thirty-one chapters of Proverbs. Three of those five occurrences appear in its final chapter:

---

56. Hurovits, *Mishle*, 559, 585.
57. Fox, *Proverbs 10–31*, 885.
58. Abraham ibn Ezra may make the same argument, but he can also be understood to be arguing that the *Eshet Hayil* is a tribute to wise women in general. See Abraham ibn Ezra, Commentary on Prov 31:1.

once in verse 3 and twice in the *Eshet Hayil*. Thus, there is a deliberate literary attempt to link the rebuke of Lemuel's mother regarding women with the depiction of the ideal woman. Since Lemuel's mother is certainly not advocating his celibacy, her rebuke relates to wasting sexual strength on the wrong women. Lemuel's mother warns him not to squander his strength on unworthy women who stand in sharp contrast to the worthy woman described in the *Eshet Hayil*.[59] Yet none of the medieval commentators read *Eshet Hayil* as a response to Solomon's sexual excesses.

4.2. Critique of Solomon

While midrashic literature has little difficulty criticizing Solomon, and the medieval Jewish commentators are willing to draw upon that material, there is also a countervailing current within rabbinic exegesis that is hesitant to castigate him. Defense of Solomon is somewhat surprising, given how often Scripture criticizes him. Solomon is an oppressive king.[60] He imposes forced labor on the populace in order to build both the temple and his personal palace (1 Kgs 5:27–30). He spends nearly twice as much time constructing his palace than building the temple (6:38–7:1). Furthermore, the book of Kings makes explicit that Solomon systematically violates the kingly prohibitions enunciated in Deut 17:16–17. Solomon amasses horses and chariots (1 Kgs 5:6; 10:26), extraordinary wealth (10:23, 27), and many foreign women, collecting the aforementioned seven hundred wives and three hundred concubines (11:1–3). It is this final violation of the kingly precepts that causes Solomon to sin most gravely, as his foreign wives turn his heart to foreign gods, and he commits idolatry (11:4–8).

It is specifically Solomon's issues with women that are of the greatest interest to us. Much of Solomon's life is punctuated by his relationships with women, including his mother, Bathsheba, the Queen of Sheba, and his foreign wives. They operate as foils for his wisdom.[61] It is Bathsheba, not Solomon, who secures his ascendancy to the throne through guile and shrewd court politics (1 Kgs 1:11–31). Solomon's most famous decision, in which he must decide who is the true mother of a disputed baby, is rendered in a dispute brought by two women (3:16–28). The queen of Sheba

---

59. Hurovits, *Mishle*, 586.
60. Crenshaw, "Sage in Proverbs," 213; Hurovits, *Mishle*, 561.
61. Greenspahn, "Biblical Women," 50.

tests Solomon's wisdom (10:1–9). Finally, his foreign wives lead him to his downfall despite his wisdom (11:4–8).

The extent of Solomon's wisdom may explain a hesitance to criticize him. King Solomon is granted unparalleled wisdom (1 Kgs 3:9, 12) and is described as the wisest of all men (3:12; 5:9–14; 10:23). Yet this wisest of all men is so easily led to sin. By implication, Solomon's narrative reveals a more practical problem: If the wisest human in the world could not avoid sin, what hope is there for the rest of humanity? One answer to that question is that there are limits to human wisdom. Agur's confession of his foolishness in Prov 30:1–4 describes precisely such limits. Rather, God is the sole possessor of wisdom. Thus, human wisdom cannot achieve comprehensive knowledge but must rely on divine revelation as preserved in the covenantal tradition. This conclusion parallels that of Eccl 12:13, that, given humanity's limited understanding, the best one can do is obey God's commands. [62] Hence the midrash can identify Agur with Solomon and cast Agur's confession of foolishness as Solomon's effort to repent of his sins, admitting the limits of human wisdom and the need to heed God's commandments (b. Sanh. 70b; Num. Rab. 10:4).

In addition, Solomon is the builder of God's temple. Even King David was not allowed to do this (2 Sam 7:5–16).[63] God specifically chooses David's son to build his temple (2 Sam 7:12–13).[64] Given rabbinic reverence for the temple, perhaps the rabbinic instinct to defend Solomon stems from the cognitive dissonance rendered by the builder of the holy temple also building altars for foreign gods. Finally, the defense of Solomon may also reflect a general exegetical desire to defend the honor of Israel's forebears and kings. Thus, the rabbis of late antiquity and of the Middle Ages are willing to criticize Solomon but only to a point. There seems to be a deliberate effort to find a happy medium, one that allows

---

62. Ansberry, *Be Wise*, 167–68; Dell, *Social and Theological Context*, 83; Hurovits, *Mishle*, 558 and 564.

63. The book of Samuel offers no specific reason why David cannot build God's temple. Rather the book of Samuel implies that God is content to remain in the more mobile tabernacle. In the book of Kings, Solomon explains David's failure to build the temple as one of lack of opportunity, since David was kept too preoccupied with war (1 Kgs 5:17). Only Chronicles, a much later text, suggests that David was disqualified from building the temple because he had shed too much blood (1 Chr 22:7–10).

64. Solomon is not specified by name, but as the ultimate builder of the temple the text impliedly refers to him.

criticism of biblical cherished figures in a way that still seeks to defend their dignity and historical status.[65]

While the extent of Solomon's wisdom or his status as builder of the temple may explain the tendency to minimize the severity of Solomon's sins, it does not explain why the rabbis of the midrash and the rabbis of the Middle Ages failed to read the *Eshet Hayil* in light of those sins. If anything, midrashic literature seems more comfortable critiquing Solomon than the medieval exegetes. The medieval commentators are content to recall the midrashim, but they are unwilling to extend the criticism beyond that which has already been set out in the midrashim. Thus, they do not read *Eshet Hayil* as a rebuke of Solomon's indiscriminate conduct with women, despite the fact that it is precisely his failing with women that leads him to sin. It seems logical that they would read a poem about the ideal woman who embodies virtues inspired by fear of God as a polemic against Solomon's poor marital choices. Yet they demur.

This tendency to minimize or at least mitigate the severity of Solomon's sins is more directly seen in commentary on the book of Kings. Many of the commentators are hesitant to allow the possibility that Solomon himself actively participated in idolatry. Thus, Rashi informs us that the text ascribes idolatry to Solomon not because he personally committed idolatry, but because he allowed his wives to do so (Rashi, Commentary on 1 Kings 11:7). David Kimchi and Ralbag follow suit (David Kimchi, Commentary on 1 Kings 11:1, 4–8; Ralbag, Commentary on 1 Kings 11:4). This mitigation should not be mistaken for excuse. Ralbag concedes that facilitating or even countenancing a sin is tantamount to personally committing that sin (Ralbag, Commentary on 1 Kings 11:4). This exegetical move made by Rashi, David Kimchi, and Ralbag is not an attempt to absolve Solomon of guilt. However, it does reflect significant discomfort at the thought of Solomon's direct participation in idolatry.

Ralbag articulates a reason for this discomfort: he notes that Solomon "understood the Blessed Name more than any other person, as those books which he composed through divine inspiration already attest to this, and additionally, the Blessed Name appeared to him twice. And thusly it does not make sense that a man like this would commit idol worship" (Ralbag, Commentary on 1 Kings 11:4). Note that Ralbag does not focus

---

65. Amos Frisch, "The Sins of the Patriarchs as Viewed by Traditional Jewish Exegesis," *JSQ* 10.3 (2003): 259 and 273.

on Solomon's famed wisdom per se but rather on his relationship with God. Not only is Solomon's wisdom divinely granted (1 Kgs 3:5–12),[66] but the nature of Solomon's wisdom that separated him from other people was his knowledge of the divine. Thus, Solomon's direct relationship with God, his prophetic experience of the divine, makes idol worship unthinkable.

Presuming Ralbag speaks for other medieval exegetes, perhaps we can understand their hesitancy to add to Solomon's castigation. They concede that Solomon's wives lead him to sin. Thus, they read Prov 31:1–9 as Bathsheba's approbation. However, they also read Prov 30:1–4 as Solomon's admission of guilt and foolishness. Thus, following the midrashic tradition, the medieval exegetes see Solomon repenting his sins and doing *teshuvah*. This being the case, Solomon has atoned for his sins, and there is no need for further castigation. Instead of reading the *Eshet Hayil* as an opportunity to criticize Solomon's sexual excesses, perhaps the rabbis understood the *Eshet Hayil* as evidence of his repentance. Again, since the rabbis of late antiquity and the medieval commentators presumed that Solomon authored the poem, the description of a single, ideal, hard-working, God-fearing woman serves as his repudiation of his multitudinous, sinful, idle, idolatrous wives. In this sense, the *Eshet Hayil* functions as Solomon's acknowledgment of sin and his recognition of the source of that sin. Perhaps the rabbis refrain from criticizing Solomon through the *Eshet Hayil* because he has already done it for them.

---

66. Of course, Solomon must have already had fair amounts of wisdom to have requested wisdom when God asked him what he should grant him.

Hasidei Ashkenaz

Representations of Biblical Women in the Writings of the *Hasidei Ashkenaz*

Judith R. Baskin

In this essay I examine representations and personifications of biblical women in some of the writings of the medieval *Hasidei Ashkenaz* (German-Jewish pietists) who were connected with Rabbi Judah he-Hasid (the Pious). I begin by discussing the context of this group of writers, their major ethical work, Sefer Hasidim (Book of the Pious), and their attitudes toward women found in this text and related writings. In the second part of the essay, I explicate the ways in which the authors of Sefer Hasidim signify specific biblical women and female personifications. The final section discusses the extensive exegesis of the "woman of valor" poem of Prov 31:10–31 by Rabbi Eleazar ben Judah of Worms.

1. The *Hasidei Ashkenaz*

The term *Hasidei Ashkenaz* refers to several discrete circles of pietists and mystics who were active mainly in the Rhineland from the mid-twelfth through the thirteenth centuries. Despite their small numbers, the introspective and penitential religious outlook of the *Hasidei Ashkenaz* had a significant and lasting impact on European Jewry. The most influential branch of the *Hasidei Ashkenaz*, and the group that is the focus of this essay, was descended from the prominent Kalonymus rabbinic family, which had settled pre-Crusade Mainz. The founder of the movement, Rabbi Samuel ben Kalonymus of Speyer (b. ca. 1115), was distinguished by the epithets *he-hasid* (the Pious), *ha-qadosh* (the Holy), and *ha-navi'* (the Prophet). Samuel's leadership passed to his son, Rabbi Judah he-Hasid (1140–1217), and Judah in turn was succeeded by his disciple and relative Rabbi Eleazar ben Judah (ben Kalonymus) of Worms (ca. 1165–1238; also known as the Rokeah). Rabbi Eleazar, the most prolific writer of this circle, was the author of a halakic work, Sefer Rokeah (Book of the Perfumer), as well as a number of esoteric texts.[1]

Sefer Hasidim has traditionally been attributed to Rabbi Judah, but it is likely that its authors also included Rabbi Samuel ben Kalonymus he-Hasid and Rabbi Eleazar, who was probably the volume's editor as well. Consisting of more than a thousand pericopes on a range of subjects, Sefer Hasidim reflects the troubled spiritual atmosphere that followed the ravages suffered by Rhineland Jewish communities during the 1096 First Crusade. Indeed, it can be said that Sefer Hasidim exhibits a post-traumatic covenantal theology that understands the violent actions of the crusaders as a form of merited divine chastisement. Afflicted with a sense of crushing guilt, the *Hasidei Ashkenaz* sought forgiveness for sins whose commission was certain, even if their actual substance was mysterious. This consciousness of culpability underlies the emphasis in Sefer Hasidim on avoiding transgressions of both the mind and the body and its interest in appropriate acts of atonement when temptation overtook prudence. Beyond the insights it offers into its authors' ethical preoccupations, Sefer Hasidim is an important witness to many aspects of Jewish daily life in medieval Ashkenaz. Moreover, its contents also reveal various influences from contemporary Christian formal and popular religion, including penitential practices.

---

1. On this circle of the *Hasidei Ashkenaz*, see Joseph Dan, *Jewish Mysticism and Jewish Ethics* (Seattle: University of Washington Press, 1986); Ephraim Kanarfogel, "R. Judah he-Hasid and the Rabbinic Scholars of Regensburg: Interactions, Influences and Implications," *JQR* 96 (2006): 17–37; Ivan G. Marcus, *Piety and Society: The Jewish Pietists of Medieval Germany* (Leiden: Brill, 1981); Haym Soloveitchik, "Three Themes in the *Sefer Hasidim*," *AJSR* 1 (1976): 311–57; and Kenneth R. Stow, *Alienated Minority: The Jews of Medieval Latin Europe* (Cambridge: Harvard University Press, 1992), 121–34. On the composition and literary context of the Sefer Hasidim, see Ivan G. Marcus, "*Sefer Hasidim*" *and the Ashkenazic Book in Medieval Europe* (Philadelphia: University of Pennsylvania Press, 2018). Citations of the Sefer Hasidim in this essay are from *Sefer Hasidim*, ed. Judah Wistinetzki, with an introduction by Jacob Freimann (Frankfurt am Main: Vahrmann, 1924), based on an Ashkenazic manuscript ca. 1300, now in Parma (henceforth SHP); and *Sefer Hasidim*, ed. Reuven Margaliot (Jerusalem: Mossad Ha-Rav Kook, 1957), an edition of the second printed version (1580) of a manuscript now in Bologna (henceforth SHB). The Princeton University Sefer Hasidim Database (PUSHD) includes all known manuscript and printed versions of this work (https://etc.princeton.edu/sefer_hasidim/index.php).

Sefer Hasidim, which was written by men and intended for a male audience, reveals a profound ambivalence toward women. This pronounced discomfort is also evident in its representations of female biblical characters, a topic discussed below. Such attitudes are emblematic in many ways of its authors' profound alienation from what they perceived as a world of carnal temptations and human hypocrisies in which the pious were scorned and persecuted and martyrdom was more desirable than a quiet death (SHB §222).[2] It is not surprising that the authors of a work so focused on the ubiquity of incitements to male sexual desire would construct a vision of women in general as flawed beings and as amenable potential partners in a range of imagined indiscretions, even while praising the treasured and irreproachable women of their own family circles. Indeed, some women of the pietist circle are represented in Sefer Hasidim and related documents as surpassing their husbands in righteousness. An exemplary woman of this milieu, like Dolce, the wife of Rabbi Eleazar, not only played religious roles such as leading women's prayers in the synagogue but also supported her household economically so that her husband could devote himself to study and teaching.[3] Thus the authors of Sefer Hasidim are ambivalent; they are caught in the contradiction that women, even the most pious and God-fearing of them, simply by virtue of their gender have the potential, however unwittingly, to tempt a man to sin or sinful thoughts and to distract him from his focus on serving God. For this reason Sefer Hasidim recommends extremely limited social converse with all women, including one's own wife, advising that, "Each one who wishes to return in repentance and achieve a status of piety ... let him forsake ... converse with his wife except while making love ... and let this not be a burden upon him because of his love for his Creator" (SHB §29; also SHP §§984 and 989).[4]

However, maintaining too great a distance from one's wife could also lead to sin. For the pietist, happy marital relations in themselves became an essential fence against the possibility of sexual temptation elsewhere.

---

2. For more on this topic, see Judith R. Baskin, "From Separation to Displacement: The Problem of Women in Sefer Hasidim," *AJSR* 19 (1994): 1–18; and Baskin, "Women and Sexual Ambivalence in Sefer Hasidim," *JQR* 96 (2006): 1–8.

3. On women who exceed their husbands in giving charity, see SHP §§669, 670, and 1715; SHB §§872–73. On Dolce of Worms, see below.

4. The precept that one should refrain as much as possible from converse with one's wife except during sexual intercourse is based on b. Hag. 5b.

As Rabbi Eleazar advised, "One should avoid looking at other women and have sexual relations with one's wife with the greatest passion because she guards him from sin"; and "since she is his intimate partner he should display affection and love toward her."[5] Similarly, Sefer Hasidim counsels that time and effort should be devoted to building a positive and creative sexual relationship within marriage so that the husband's thoughts will not stray to other women.[6]

However, even marriage as a licit location for sexual expression had its limits. Although Sefer Hasidim places great importance on happy spousal relations as a barrier against the appeal of other potential sexual partners, for the *Hasidei Ashkenaz* a man's affection for his wife always had to be secondary to his mystical yearning for the divine. Since avoiding marriage was usually not possible for a Jewish male, the pietist attempted to spiritualize his sexual desire by channeling it to a divine purpose.[7] This displacement of women from an equal partnership in spousal relations was furthered by pietistic traditions that sought to transform human sexuality into erotic theology. This dichotomy as to the true purpose of marital sexuality is exemplified in the following passage:

> The root of loving God is to love God with all your heart (Deut 6:5). Our Creator commanded us to serve Him with reverence, that the love of our soul be bound up with His soul in joy and in His love and with a good heart. And the joy of this love is of such intensity and so overpowers the heart of those who love God, that even after many days of not being with his wife and having a great desire for her, in the hour that a man ejaculates he does not find it as satisfying as the intensity and power of loving God and finding joy in his Creator. (SHB §14)[8]

---

5. Eleazar ben Judah of Worms, *Sefer ha-Rokeach ha-Gadol* (Jerusalem, 1968) see *Hilkhot Teshuvah* no. 20, p. 30, and no. 14, p. 27; both translated in David Biale, *Eros and the Jews: From Biblical Israel to Contemporary America* (New York: Basic Books, 1992), 78.

6. SHB §509 advocates a male-superior position for sexual intercourse when conception is desired, since this is most pleasurable for the woman (should she achieve orgasm first, she is likely to conceive a son), but states that at other times the husband may conduct their sex life as he wishes in order to prevent fantasies about other women.

7. As Yitzhak Baer wrote, the "Jewish mystic-ascetic may never go beyond a certain point in self-denial because of legal prohibitions." See Yitzhak Baer, "The Religious and Social Tendency of *Sefer Hasidim*" [Hebrew], *Zion* 3 (1937–1938): 12.

8. All biblical translations are from the *JPS Hebrew-English Tanakh* (Philadelphia: Jewish Publication Society, 2000).

Certainly, from the perspective of rabbinic Judaism, with its acute consciousness of human sexuality's potential for causing societal disorder if strict controls are lacking, there is nothing unusual in these admonitions to avoid contact with women. In the rabbinic patriarchal system women as a group are represented as fundamentally other than men, constituting a separate category of human creature, and their activities are ideally confined to the private sphere of husband, children, and family economic endeavors where the possibilities of falling into unsanctioned sexual liaisons are less likely.[9] The *Hasidei Ashkenaz* continued in this tradition, painstakingly erecting as many obstacles as possible against encounters between men and women, encounters that were far more common in their constricted urban milieu, in which women played active and independent economic roles beyond the domestic domain than in the late ancient environments reflected in rabbinic literature.[10]

However, if there is little novel in Sefer Hasidim's representation of women as potential snares to the righteous, the *Hasidei Ashkenaz* are distinguished by the nature of their commitment to the divine. As Joseph Dan has written, "God expects the *hasid* to break the laws of nature, of the human body and soul, and of human history and society" in the almost impossible effort to achieve the miracle of full adherence to divine wishes. Through this intense mystical love, which is presented in erotic terms, the righteous may hope to achieve a closer relationship with the revealed divine glory.[11] The pietist's desire for separation from the corruption of the material world, and his wish to displace the pleasures of human sexuality through his devotion to God, is built, in part, upon the displacement and objectification of women. Moreover, in the larger Christian environment of medieval Ashkenaz, this pietistic attraction toward separation from women and all the dilemmas that contact with them entails became intensified. There can be little doubt that medieval Christian convictions of the

---

9. On representations of women in rabbinic Judaism, see Judith R. Baskin, *Midrashic Women: Formations of the Feminine in Rabbinic Literature* (Hanover, NH: Brandeis University Press, 2002).

10. On Jewish women in medieval Ashkenaz, see Avraham Grossman, *Pious and Rebellious: Jewish Women in Medieval Europe* (Waltham, MA: Brandeis University Press, 2004); Elisheva Baumgarten, *Mothers and Children: Jewish Family Life in Medieval Europe* (Princeton: Princeton University Press, 2004); and Baumgarten, *Practicing Piety in Medieval Ashkenaz: Men, Women, and Everyday Religious Observance* (Philadelphia: University of Pennsylvania Press, 2014).

11. Dan, *Jewish Mysticism and Jewish Ethics*, 75.

inherently carnal nature of human beings, the negative role of woman in man's fall, and the preferable option of celibacy for those who were spiritually capable of it also played a significant role in the heightened uneasiness of the *Hasidei Ashkenaz* regarding the potential perils occasioned by the opposite sex.[12]

2. Representations of Biblical Women

Sefer Hasidim is an ethical manual that advises men how to pursue piety in a world replete with temptations. Its moral advice is copiously supported by biblical prooftexts and references to rabbinic literature. Rather surprisingly, however, its authors only occasionally invoke biblical figures, female or male, as exemplars of desirable or undesirable conduct. While the patriarchs—Abraham, Isaac, and Jacob—are always represented as idealized exemplars of piety, other male biblical characters are presented as more fallible, especially in instances where the biblical evidence is explicit that specific men gave way to sexual temptations despite their other admirable qualities. Thus, a didactic passage in Sefer Hasidim recounts that Samson was the strongest of all men, David the most pious, and Solomon the most wise, yet each stumbled because of a woman. Scripture is said to have recorded these events in order to warn of the overwhelming force that love for women can exert, even on the best of men. Thus:

> the story of David and Bathsheba comes to inform us that the most pious of men, even though all of his actions were for the sake of Heaven, nevertheless stumbled when he saw a woman. [He did so] when he was approaching old age; therefore, how much more so must a young man be careful not to look at a woman and to distance himself from women. (SHB §619)

The story of Samson is said to teach the additional lesson that a man should not reveal secrets to a woman, since had Samson, "the most valiant of valiant men not told [the secret of his strength] to Delilah, he would not have stumbled" (SHB §619). The pericope also voices a polemic

---

12. On Christian ritual and spiritual influences on the Jews of Ashkenaz, see Robert Chazan, *European Jewry and the First Crusade* (Berkeley: University of California Press, 1987), 195–96; Ivan G. Marcus, *Rituals of Childhood: Jewish Acculturation in Medieval Europe* (New Haven: Yale University Press, 1998); and Stow, *Alienated Minority*, 129–31.

against intermarriage, a frequent source of apprehension in *Hasidei Ashkenaz* literature, attributing the downfalls of Samson and Solomon to their involvement with foreign women. The prooftext cited is, "You shall not intermarry with them: do not give your daughters to their sons or take their daughters for your sons" (Deut 7:3),[13] and the passage goes on to say, "If a king [Solomon], the wisest of all the wise, stumbled because of them and foreign women overcame his heart," how much more so are ordinary people at risk. So too the Samson narrative is said to support Solomon's warnings to beware of foreign women (e.g., Prov 2:16; 5:20; 6:24, etc.).

Another pericope in Sefer Hasidim that also deals with David's weakness for women reads as follows: "Even if you withstood a great test, you still cannot be confident in yourself until the day of your death.... Behold David did not sin with Abigail but he did sin with Bathsheba" (SHB §161). In fact, the biblical account (1 Sam 25) and rabbinic interpretations, including b. Meg. 14b, make clear that David's sexual interest in Abigail preceded her husband's death. From the point of view of the *Hasidei Ashkenaz* he would seem culpable since he allowed himself to have converse with a married woman. According to b. Meg. 14b Abigail advised David to restrain his desire for a later occasion; this was her meaning when she said, "Do not let this be a cause of stumbling ... to my lord" (1 Sam 25:31). The rabbis explain: "The word 'this' implies that something else would be [a stumbling-block], and what was that? The incident of Bathsheba; and so it was eventually." It is for this prescience that the rabbis consider Abigail among the seven female prophets (b. Meg. 14a).

While SHB §161 absolves David of fault in the case of Abigail since he did not have illicit sexual relations with her but waited until after their marriage to consummate his desire, he is blamed for subsequently committing adultery with Bathsheba and for causing the death of her husband (2 Sam 11). Although the relevant biblical passages are clear that Abigail

---

13. This biblical prooftext does not refer directly to Solomon and Pharaoh's daughter (who is among those women blamed for establishing worship of foreign deities in 1 Kgs 11:1–10) but to Solomon's descendants who were brought to catastrophe by another foreign woman: Athaliah, the widow of Jehoram, king of Judah; and the daughter of Ahab, king of Israel (and according to tradition, of his wife Jezebel). Following the death of her son Ahaziah, Athaliah seized power and reigned over Judah for six years, during which time she is said to have established the worship of Baal. According to b. Sanh. 21b, God punished Solomon's marriage to Pharaoh's daughter by enabling the founding of Rome.

was acting to preserve her household when she conversed with David and that Bathsheba did not set out to entice the king, both women are constructed as objects of desire and potential occasions of sin, even if the sin was not fulfilled in the case of Abigail.[14] Moreover, the focus of attention as far as transgression and atonement is on David. This willful blindness to the possibility that women are also moral and spiritual beings who are capable of expressing both agency and repentance is found throughout Sefer Hasidim.

Strangely, SHB §619, which was discussed above, began by stating that the missteps of Samson, David, and Solomon were caused by women and concludes with the positive representation of a female biblical character:

> The story of Ruth is recorded because she was extremely modest, and acted with great kindness to Naomi by leaving Naomi at home so that she would not be shamed and she gleaned to fulfill Naomi's needs ... and kings and prophets issued from her" (SHB §619)

This representation of Ruth is in complete concord with a trend in rabbinic exegesis to emphasize Ruth's positive qualities and to gloss over and justify more troubling aspects of her story, such as her Moabite origins and her nocturnal approach to Boaz on the threshing room floor. Since Ruth was an ancestress of King David and ultimately the messiah, this focus on qualities perceived as self-effacing and nonthreatening to men make sense. As Tamar Meir points out, rabbinic traditions speak of Ruth's modesty and explain that her visit to Boaz was in compliance with "Naomi's instructions and her concern for her mother-in-law." Meir writes that "Ruth's modesty, coupled with her great beauty, are qualities frequently mentioned by the rabbis in their portrayals of exemplary biblical women (Sarah, Rebekah, Tamar)," as is her uprightness (Ruth Rab. 4:9) and her acts of kindness toward Naomi (Ruth Rab. 2:14). Meir goes on to say that numerous midrashic traditions about Ruth focus on her descendants from the Davidic line: "In the words of *Ruth Zuta* 1:1, Ruth is 'the mother of royalty.'"[15] It is evident that the *Hasidei Ashkenaz* are fol-

---

14. References to women who importune men to sin appear in SHP §15 and in Eleazar of Worms, *Sefer ha-Rokeach*, see *Hilkhot Teshuvah* no. 1. See also Marcus, *Piety and Society*, 26 and 42.

15. Tamar Meir, "Ruth: Midrash and Aggadah," *Jewish Women's Archive Encyclopedia*, https://tinyurl.com/SBL6014e.

lowing in a long tradition in their wholly positive representation of Ruth in this passage. But why mention her at all in the context of women who lead men into sexual impropriety? It is possible that this segment represents a response to criticisms of Ruth's apparent sexual forwardness that some were equating with the behavior of biblical figures such as Samson, David, and Solomon. It could also be that there is a polemical response here to Christian teachings that portrayed the gentile Rachel as a typological representation of the church and its openness to converts of all backgrounds as well as an ancestress of Jesus Christ. The genealogy of Jesus in Matt 1:1–17, as has often been noted, includes four women with problematic pasts, including Tamar (Gen 38), Rahab (Josh 2; 6:25), Ruth, and Bathsheba as well as their descendants David and Solomon. Perhaps adding this representation of Ruth, whose every action was motivated by modesty, kindness, and virtuous intentions, is in response to such traditions as well as an expression of a preferred vision of a pious woman as compliant and self-effacing. Sefer Hasidim also alludes to Bathsheba in a paragraph in which David expresses his guilt for his adultery and the death of Bathsheba's husband Uriah:

> When Shimei cursed David, he responded, "Let him go on hurling abuse, for the Lord has told him to" (2 Sam 16:11). [David's meaning was] "My sin is the cause. If I had not transgressed, Amnon would not have lain with Tamar [2 Sam 13] and Absalom would not have rebelled against his father and slept with his father's wives [2 Sam 16:22]." (SHB §183)

In this instance, the rape of Tamar and the despoliation of David's wives are constructed as divine chastisements directed at David. Convinced of God's justice, the *Hasidei Ashkenaz* believed that the pietist must seek atonement for the sins that had brought deserved divine chastisements on himself and his community. This assumption of moral responsibility for the tragedies of others is a common theme in Sefer Hasidim and in other writings of the *Hasidei Ashkenaz*. In the conclusion of Eleazar ben Judah's second poetic elegy for his murdered wife and daughters, he laments, "Over and over my sins have found me out.... The judge who judges me is faithful to me; He has crushed me on account of my transgressions and my crimes."[16] It is important to note that the women who figure in these narra-

---

16. See below and Baskin, "'Dolce of Worms': The Lives and Deaths of an Exemplary Medieval Jewish Woman and her Daughters," in *Judaism in Practice: From the*

tives are not considered morally responsible agents of their own destinies but as objects through which men may be punished.

Sefer Hasidim sometimes represents specific biblical women as flawed in order to make ethical and didactic points about the dire consequences of even small transgressions, as in this instance concerning Sarah:

> From this we derive that the Holy One, blessed be He, deals strictly with the righteous, even to a hair's breadth. An example is Sarah, who lied on account of Isaac [Sarah laughed when she heard she would bear a child at the age of ninety but when she was challenged as to her laughter]: "Sarah lied, saying 'I did not laugh,' for she was frightened" (Gen 18:15). Accordingly, the reason for her death was on account of Isaac: when she heard the report of the Akedah [the binding of Isaac] her soul fled and she died on account of Isaac. (SHB §102)

The tradition that Sarah died of grief when she heard that Abraham had taken their son Isaac to Mount Moriah to bind him and offer him as a sacrifice to God appears in rabbinic literature (Gen. Rab. 58:5) as well as in the commentary of Rabbi Solomon ben Isaac (Rashi) on Gen 23:2. The textual basis for this midrash is that although Sarah is not mentioned in Gen 22 (the narrative about the Akedah), Gen 23 begins with the announcement of her death. This juxtaposition led to a number of related traditions, including the elaboration in Pirqe R. El. 32 that Samael brought about Sarah's death by telling her that Isaac had been sacrificed.[17] However, I am not aware of any rabbinic passages that draw a cause-and-effect relationship between Sarah's embarrassed mendacity in Gen 18 and her death as a result of learning about Isaac's ordeal. Rather, this statement in Sefer Hasidim conforms to the penitential certainty of the *Hasidei Ashkenaz* that every misfortune can be understood as a divine punishment for transgression, even in the case of such an indubitably righteous person as Sarah.

Another passage in which biblical women are represented begins with the premise that women are responsible for men's descent into sin, a common theme in Sefer Hasidim. However, in this instance its author

---

Middle Ages through the Early Modern Period, ed. Lawrence Fine (Princeton: Princeton University Press, 2001), 429–37, esp. 437.

17. In rabbinic writings Samael is a member of the divine retinue who often serves as a tempter or adversary. In the course of the Middle Ages, and in works like Pirqe Rabbi Eliezer, Samael is portrayed as a demonic force of evil.

comes up against the rabbinic contention that women may also be responsible for male righteousness. The following passage uses representations of two biblical women, Jezebel and Sarah, in order to explore the extent and domains of female vice and virtue:

> It is common[ly] accepted that a man is influenced by his wife, as we read about Ahab, "Indeed, there was never anyone like Ahab, who committed himself to doing what was displeasing to the Lord at the instigation of his wife Jezebel" (1 Kgs 21:25). It happened that a certain pious man married a pious woman but in time he divorced her. He then went and married a wicked woman, a daughter of iniquity [Belial], and his former wife married a completely evil man. The pious man abandoned his former ways and became transformed through the advice of his evil wife and the wicked man turned from his wickedness and became a completely pious man on account of his wife." (SHB §135)

This anecdote derives from Gen. Rab. 17:7, where it refers to a pious infertile couple who divorced after ten years of marriage because of their apparent inability to have children. The story, which is part of a haggadic thread that is uncomfortable with obligatory divorce because of childlessness, relates that the pious man then married a wicked woman and became wicked himself, while the pious woman married a wicked man and he became righteous.[18] The anecdote ends with an implied warning against the dissolution of happy albeit infertile unions and offers a paean to feminine virtues: "So [we learn that] all depends upon the woman."

The larger frame of the Sefer Hasidim passage comes from b. B. Metz. 59a, a *sugya* that discusses the importance of not shaming another person. The relevant portion begins: "Rab also said: 'He who follows his wife's counsel will fall into Gehenna,' for it is written, 'Indeed, there was never anyone like Ahab, who committed himself to doing what was displeasing to the Lord at the instigation of his wife Jezebel' (1 Kgs 21:25)." The passage in b. Baba Metz'ia does not cite the anecdote from Genesis Rabbah. Instead, it turns directly to the question of whether Rab's statement is correct or whether a woman's advice to her husband can, in fact, be valuable: "R. Papa objected, ... 'But people say, if your wife is short, bend down and hear her whisper!'" The rabbis then agree that there is no contradiction between these statements: Rab is referring to public matters, while Rabbi Papa is talking about domestic affairs. Or, in another version, the second

---

18. On rabbinic responses to infertility, see Baskin, *Midrashic Women*, 119–40.

half of which appears in this Sefer Hasidim passage, "the one refers to religious matters [*mitzvot*], the other to worldly things [*divre ha-'olam*]." This is the conclusion of the rabbinic discussion on this issue.

SHB §135 repeats this teaching and then continues with a midrash about Sarah:

> When it comes to the performance of a commandment [*mitzvah*], a God-fearing man should not take advice from his wife because she tends not to be generous, even if she is God-fearing. Is there anyone more God-fearing than Sarah, our mother? Yet, in spite of it all when Abraham said to her, "Quick, three measures of choice flour"[19] (Gen 18:6), she prepared to use coarse flour until he told her to use the finest flour. And from this our scholars explained that a woman looks with a more grudging eye on guests than a man. But in worldly things, if your wife is short, bend down and let her whisper in your ear. (SHB §135)

This tradition about Sarah is found in b. B. Metz. 87a and, as the talmudic text explains, it originates in a textual problem: "Scripture writes, [*ordinary*] *flour*, and [it is then written], *fine flour*! Thus, Abraham had to give her clear and specific instructions to use fine flour. R. Isaac said: 'This shows that a woman looks with a more grudging eye upon guests than a man.'" Sefer Hasidim incorporates this midrash and then concludes the paragraph with the sentence from b. B. Metz. 59a that a man may consult his wife about "worldly things" but not when it comes to fulfilling commandments. This midrash, in which Sarah is represented to disadvantage, does not appear in the b. B. Metz. 59a discussion about the value of a wife's counsel. The conflation of these two traditions in Sefer Hasidim is an indication of the conviction that even the most righteous of women are ultimately unreliable, particularly when they attempt to make decisions on their own concerning divine commandments.

Sefer Hasidim refers to the matriarch Rebekah, although without naming her, in a didactic passage about a woman's right to consent to her marriage:

> It is written, "If you don't agree, say so, and I will go to the right or the left" (Gen 24:49) [these are the words of Eliezer, Abraham's servant, when he negotiated with Rebekah's brother and father about the possibility of her

---

19. Literally, this verse appears to read: "quickly, three measures of coarse flour (*kemah*)—fine flour (*solet*)—knead it and make cakes." The midrash explains that Abraham has to specify "fine flour" since Sarah is not liberal in her hospitality.

marriage to Isaac]. This teaches us that if someone is courting a woman and she does not want to marry him and they [her family or representatives] say to him, "We do not want [the match]," he should immediately turn his addresses to another woman." (SHB §514)[20]

The matriarch Rachel appears in an interesting passage in which the moon is personified as both the mourning of Rachel of Jer 31:14 and as the female condition in general:

> When Jews are forced to convert by those who hate Israel, the moon is eclipsed like Rachel weeping for her children (Jer 31:14). Why is a woman compared to the moon? Just as the moon waxes for half a month and wanes for half a month, so a woman has a strong attachment to her husband for half a month and she is isolated from him for half a month during her *niddah*. And what can be compared to the pleasantness of the moon at night? This is like a woman in the evening when she is coming [home from the ritual bath]. (SHB §1148)

A similar discussion of the meaning of eclipses occurs in b. Sukkah 29a: "When the sun is in eclipse, it is a bad omen for the whole world.... but when the moon is in eclipse, it is a bad omen for Israel, since Israel reckons by the moon and idolaters by the sun." The connection in this pericope between the moon in eclipse and the mourning Rachel of Jer 31:14 may also have its origins in a subsequent passage in the same biblical chapter: "Thus said the Lord, who established the sun for light by day, the laws of the moon and stars for light by night, who stirs up the sea into roaring waves, whose name is Lord of Hosts. If these laws should ever by annulled by Me—declares the Lord—only then would the offspring of Israel cease to be a nation before me forever" (Jer 31:35–36). These biblical verses could be read to mean that an eclipse is an indication of cosmic disorder and the dissolution of the covenant between God and Israel. Thus, when Jews are forced to leave the community, it is an abrogation of Israel's pact with God: it is as if the moon is in eclipse and Rachel is weeping for her children who will never be born.

---

20. Rebekah indicates her acceptance of the match with Isaac later in the biblical chapter: "They called Rebekah and said to her, 'Will you go with this man?' And she said, 'I will'" (Gen 24:58). Rebekah is also invoked in SHB §336 in a discussion about maintaining harmony between parents based on Rebekah's words, "Let any curse be on me, my son" (Gen 27:3).

The comparison of a woman to the moon in SHB §1148 is a trope common to many cultures, since women's menstrual cycles and the phases of the moon generally follow a twenty-eight-day sequence. In some medieval Jewish communities women abstained from work on *Rosh Hodesh*, the day marking the new moon, which was also the beginning of the new Hebrew month. According to Pirqe R. El. 45, because the Israelite women refused to contribute their jewelry to the forging of the golden calf, God rewarded them by granting special privileges for women on *Rosh Hodesh*. And in the world to come, the passage goes on to say, "women are destined to be renewed like the new moons."

Sefer Hasidim (SHB §1148) also invokes Rachel and the eclipsed moon in discussing the portion of the month when husbands and wives must maintain physical separation due to the wife's state of *niddah*. Rabbinic Judaism understood female observance of the *hilkhot niddah* (laws pertaining to the ritually impure woman) as essential to enable men to fulfill their obligation to avoid any contact with a woman in a state of ritual impurity.[21] Correct observance of *hilkhot niddah* was a major concern of the *Hasidei Ashkenaz*, and therefore they emphasized the importance of teaching women to observe these commandments scrupulously. However, maintaining domestic harmony between husband and wife was also crucial. Documents connected with the *Hasidei Ashkenaz* also articulate that any delay on the part of the wife in immersing in the *mikveh* as soon as legally possible could increase her husband's sexual frustration, leading perhaps to sinful thoughts and even illicit sexual activities. This concern for a speedy reunion following ritual cleansing is expressed in the final lines of the paragraph. Here again women are essentially constructed as objects that can occasion sin in men, and satisfactory marital sex is presented as the only possible antidote. Thus, this complex passage concludes with the projection of male desires and expectations onto women's bodies.

3. The Woman of Valor

A long passage in Sefer Hasidim discusses diverse forms of "fearing God." These are variously said to correspond to the eighteen defects that render

---

21. On this topic, see Judith R. Baskin, "Women and Ritual Immersion in Medieval Ashkenaz: The Sexual Politics of Piety," in *Judaism in Practice: From the Middle Ages through the Early Modern Period*, ed. Lawrence Fine (Princeton: Princeton University Press, 2001), 131–42; and Baskin, "Male Piety, Female Bodies: Men, Women, and Ritual Immersion in Medieval Ashkenaz," *Journal of Jewish Law* 17 (2007): 11–30.

cattle unfit (*trefa*), listed in b. Hul. 42a, to "the eighteen forms of the body upon which life depends" and to the eighteen benedictions of the silent prayer. The passage begins by listing fifteen biblical verses in which the term "the fear of the Lord appears." The final verse cited in this listing is Prov 30:30: "Grace is deceitful and beauty is vain; but a woman who fears the Lord, she shall be praised" (SHB §158).

Proverbs 31:10–31 describes the *'eshet hayil*, frequently translated as "woman of valor." This poetic passage portrays a wife who manages all of her family's domestic, parental, economic, and philanthropic affairs. Her excellent management abilities allow her husband "to be prominent in the gates; As he sits among the elders of the land" (Prov 31:23). Her husband trusts in her completely and she is to be extolled "for the fruit of her hands; And let her works praise her in the gates" (v. 31). The *'eshet hayil* is often represented in medieval Jewish literature as the exemplar of the ideal wife, and this biblical passage forms the basis of an extraordinary document composed by Eleazar ben Judah of Worms some time after the 1197 murders of his wife Dolce and their two daughters, Bellette and Hannah. These writings comprise a prose account of the attack on the family and two poetic elegies. Eleazar's description of the range of endeavors of "the saintly Mistress Dolce, who supported her family through her lending activities," are important sources for knowledge of the activities of medieval Jewish women.[22] The epithets Eleazar uses in these documents to describe his wife, which include "pious" or "saintly" (*hasidah*), "God-fearing" (*yirat shamayim*), and "righteous" (*tzadeqet*), tell us a great deal about the qualities for which women in his pietistic circle were esteemed. Eleazar also uses the Hebrew *ne'imah* ("pleasant") four times in the first elegy, a play on the meaning of Dolce's name.[23]

The first of the two poetic laments is an exegesis of the biblical *'eshet hayil*, who is invoked to represent Dolce's various virtues and accomplishments. This document is written in two line couplets and it possesses a

---

22. On Dolce's life and death and for Eleazar's prose and poetic accounts, see Baskin, "Dolce of Worms"; and Baskin, "Women Saints in Judaism: Dolce of Worms," in *Women Saints in World Religions*, ed. Arvind Sharma (Albany: State University of New York Press, 2000), 39–69. See also the essay by Elisheva Baumgarten in this volume and Ivan G. Marcus, "Mothers, Martyrs, and Moneymakers: Some Jewish Women in Medieval Europe," *Conservative Judaism* 38.3 (1986): 34–45.

23. "Dolce," also transliterated Dulcia, Dulcea, Dulzia, and Dulcie, is of Latinate origin, based on the adjective *dulcis*, "agreeable, pleasant, charming, kind, or dear."

complexity of form that is impossible to transmit in translation. Proverbs 31:10–31 is an alphabetic acrostic; the first word of each verse begins with a successive letter of the Hebrew alphabet. In Eleazar's elegy, many of the first lines of his poetic couplets begin with the first few words of the corresponding verse in Proverbs that is being interpreted, and even when they do not, the first letter of the first word of each couplet begins with the appropriate letter of the alphabet. Thus, his poem retains the alphabetic pattern of the original in addition to elaborating on its contents. However, Eleazar also introduces an additional acrostic element: the first letter of the first word of the second line of each couplet spells out *'Eleʿazar, ha-qatan, he-ʿaluv, veha-'evyon*, "Eleazar the small, the lowly, and the bereft," the author's epithet for himself.

Eleazar's first elegy proceeds through Prov 31:10–31, although it does not explicate every verse. It begins as follows (biblical text in italics):

> *What a rare find is an 'eshet hayil* (v. 10): Such a one was my saintly wife, Mistress Dolce. *A capable wife* (v. 10): the crown of her husband, the daughter of community benefactors. A woman who feared God, she was renowned for her good deeds. *Her husband put his confidence in her* (v. 11): She fed him and dressed him in honor to sit with *the elders of the land* (v. 23) and involve himself in Torah study and good deeds.[24]

His representation of Dolce as the *'eshet hayil* concludes with these words:

> *Her mouth is full of wisdom* (v. 26): she knew what was forbidden and what was permitted. On the Sabbath she sat and listened to her husband's preaching. Outstanding in her modesty, she was wise and well-spoken. Whoever was close to her was blessed. She was eager, pious, and amiable in fulfilling all the commandments. She purchased milk for the students and hired teachers from her exertions. Knowledgeable and wise, she served her Creator in joy. Her legs ran to visit the sick and to fulfill her Creator's commandments. She fed her sons and urged them to study, and she served the Holy One in reverence. She was happy to do the will of her husband and never angered him. Her actions were "pleasant." May the Eternal Rock remember her. May her soul be enveloped in the wrappings of eternal life. *Extol her for the fruit of her hands* (v. 31) in Paradise.[25]

---

24. Baskin, "Dolce of Worms," 435.
25. Baskin, "Dolce of Worms," 436.

It is only in this final segment of the exegetical poem that Eleazar moves beyond the exemplar of the biblical 'eshet hayil to stress both the religious convictions and the female qualities that were most important to his circle of the *Hasidei Ashkenaz*. These are evident in his emphasis on Dolce's fear and reverence for God, as well as her modesty, amiability, and eagerness to fulfill her husband's will. The statement that his wife never angered him is telling as well. Eleazar's evocation of the afterlife is a departure from Prov 31 and an indication of the firm belief of the *Hasidei Ashkenaz* in appropriate reward and punishment in the world to come.

4. Conclusion

The interpreter tends to find references to her or his own beliefs, concerns, and dilemmas in the text being expounded. This is certainly the case in the representations of biblical women in Sefer Hasidim and in Rabbi Eleazar ben Judah's exegesis of Prov 31:10–31. The *Hasidei Ashkenaz* were convinced of their own sinfulness and of the culpable carnality of those around them. One significant cause of transgression, in their view, was men's sexual desire for women, whether manifested in sinful thoughts or actual physical action. Regardless of the nature of these sins, the *Hasidei Ashkenaz* believed that they were instigated by women—by their bodies, their voices, and their very presence in the world. The only recourse for the pious man was to limit contact with women, even the women of his own family, as much as possible. Some biblical women such as Jezebel, Delilah, and Bathsheba provided vivid models of women who led men into sin, but even the matriarch Sarah was shown to be capable of transgressions that brought reproof and death. Although representations of any biblical women are rare in Sefer Hasidim, it is worth noting that some of the Hebrew Bible's more influential and assertive females—such as the judge Deborah, the prophet Huldah, and the courageous Esther—go unmentioned.[26] The only praiseworthy female traits for this circle of

---

26. The rabbis of the Babylonian Talmud presented Deborah and Huldah in a negative light because these women assumed roles usually constructed as male; thus their attitude toward Esther was decidedly ambiguous. See Judith R. Baskin, "Female Prophets in the Babylonian Talmud Megillah 14a–15a," in *Rabbinic Literature*, ed. Tal Ilan, Lorena Miralles-Maciá, and Ronit Nikolsky, BW 4.1 (Atlanta: SBL Press, 2022), 263–80.

pietists were modesty, kindliness, and respectful obedience to both male and divine authority.

The challenge for the *Hasidei Ashkenaz* was that some women of their circle met these criteria. This is why the '*eshet hayil* of Proverbs provided an essential biblical model of the God-fearing, enabling wife. Rabbi Eleazar's encomium to the departed Dolce is seamlessly woven into his interpretation of the words of Prov 31:10–31. This biblical personification of female virtues provided him with the language and the template with which to praise his beloved partner beyond the confines of his cultural parameters.

Poetry and *Piyyut*

Biblical Women in the Hebrew Poetry of Al-Andalus

Aurora Salvatierra Ossorio

1. By Way of Introduction: The New Hebrew Poetry of Al-Andalus

During the tenth through fifteenth centuries, first in al-Andalus[1] and later in Christian Spain, medieval Iberia became the stage for one of the most fascinating expressions of Jewish culture throughout its history. Particularly from the time of the Caliphate of Córdoba, the Jews of al-Andalus were a people who prided themselves on living exclusively in accordance with the religious values that served as their sign of identity, zealously protecting themselves from outside influences and yet feeling attracted by the intellectual and artistic climate of the era. Arab culture was thus added to the Jewish tradition as part of the education transmitted from parents to children. Jewish courtiers took on the values of their environment and became experts in Arabic language and literature and patrons of poets and scholars. This process, however, does not in any way suppose a loss of their own identity: the Jewish communities of al-Andalus combined a program of traditional religious study with the study of scientific knowledge and literary creation, both in secular poetry and in the liturgy that was destined for the synagogue. These intellectuals brought together codes of religious law and at the same time investigated grammar and lexicography, composed verses in the style of al-Andalus, and dedicated themselves to philosophy and theology as well.[2]

---

1. This is the name given to the Iberian Peninsula while under Muslim power in the Middle Ages.
2. On this new model of the Jewish intellectual, see Raymond Scheindlin, "La situación social y el mundo de valores de los poetas hebreos," in *La sociedad medieval a través de la literatura hispanojudía: VI Curso de cultura hispano-judía y sefardí de la Universidad de Castilla-La Mancha*, ed. Ricardo Izquierdo Benito and Ángel Sáenz-

Within this process of acculturation led by the Jewish elite in the Arab-Islamic cultural context, poetry became the means of expression par excellence for the Hebrew aristocracy. Their verses combine the best of their own tradition (the Bible, the Hebrew language) with the best of Arabic literary tradition. On the one hand, Arabic poetry was adopted and imitated in all of its characteristics: its meter, genres, and images became part of this new poetry.[3] But together with this system, which was accepted without much debate, the Hebrew language and the Bible act as identifying elements among this select Jewish minority and its literary creations. In these poems, the biblical text becomes a linguistic paradigm and stylistic reference, and Hebrew is the means through which the new ideals of the court society are expressed. In an effort to create their own culture, the Jews of al-Andalus saw their biblical language as an element that would symbolize and unite the community to which they belonged, a community that was conscious of forming a distinct group within the sphere of al-Andalus.

2. The Bible: A Linguistic and Literary Universe

It is within the caliphate of Córdoba where the process of revitalizing Hebrew as a vehicle for poetic expression begins, a phenomenon that is inseparable from the flourishing of grammatical studies of the Bible. In al-Andalus, Hebrew was seen as a gift that God gave humans to express themselves, and this certainty caused authors to worry about the purity and correctness of its use.[4] These poets made biblical language a model that they tried to faithfully follow, avoiding any change or innovation. Whether this was achieved in practice is another question. The Bible did not only provide these poets a language for poetry: it was also a creative and aesthetic resource. The myriad figures, images, and expressions that fill its

---

Badillos (Cuenca: Universidad Castilla-La Mancha, 1998), 53–70; Ross Brann, "La poesía en la cultura literaria hebrea de al-Andalus," in *Poesía hebrea en al-Andalus*, ed. Judit Targarona-Borrás and Ángel Sáenz-Badillos (Granada: Universidad de Granada, 2003), 9–25.

3. On Hebrew poetic themes and motifs shared with Arabic poetry, see Arie Schippers, *Spanish Hebrew Poetry and the Arabic Literary Tradition: Themes in Hebrew Andalusian Poetry* (Leiden: Brill, 1994).

4. Ángel Sáenz-Badillos, "Philologians and Poets in Search of the Hebrew Language," in *Languages of Power in Islamic Spain*, ed. Ross Brann (Bethesda, MD: CDL, 1997), 49–75.

pages formed part of the poets' literary strategy. We must keep in mind that their audiences had a good knowledge of the sacred text through their education and through readings in the synagogue. They were thus capable of understanding changes in the nuance of verses as compared to what was written in the Torah. This allowed the poets to play with biblical references by inserting them into a totally different and nonreligious context: secular poetry. With their audience's complicity, these poets constructed a literary universe in which quotes, characters, and situations from the Bible were moved into a different textual framework in which they acquired other meanings and values that had to be deciphered by the audience.[5]

Thus Hebrew, the *holy language*, becomes in al-Andalus the vehicle for writing secular poetry that included themes absent until then from the Jewish tradition.[6] The Bible, its motifs, and topics were used without objection to discuss amorous relationships (with both female and male characters) and to compose poems about wine that have nothing to do with religion and were recited in courtly parties far removed from the synagogue's sphere.

It is worth questioning whether this introduction of the biblical text into a profane sociocultural setting far removed from the Jewish tradition could be considered a desacralization of the Scriptures. It is not unreasonable to think that, among more orthodox communities, this practice would have indeed merited a negative judgment. In fact, we have some early testimonials that reflect a certain discomfort around this literary convention, and we know that, later Maimonides himself was in disagreement with such use of the Bible.[7] Except for a few instances, though, we

---

5. This use of biblical references, called *shibbutz* (insertions) is one of the most used conventions in the Hebrew poetry of al-Andalus. A poem can eventually be composed of a mosaic of quotes taken from the Bible which link to one another in order to deal with profane ideas (love, wine, praise, etc.). For a presentation on this process, see Shari Lowin, *Arabic and Hebrew Love Poems in al-Andalus* (New York: Routledge, 2014), 11–13.

6. On the other hand, Arabic, which was the language of communication for the Jews of al-Andalus, was employed in the rest of the texts these scholars composed on secular subjects (philosophy, medicine, science). In this vein, an interesting analysis of the role that the Hebrew language played in the process of constructing the identity of the medieval Jewish society from the tenth century onward can be found in Esperanza Alfonso, *Islamic Culture through Jewish Eyes: Al-Andalus from the Tenth to Twelfth Century* (New York: Routledge, 2008), 9–33.

7. Yosef Tobi, "Maimonides' Attitude towards Secular Poetry, Secular Arab and Hebrew Literature, Liturgical Poetry and towards their Cultural Environment," in

do not have proof that Jewish Andalusian society understood this use of Scripture to be scandalously irreligious. Although the poets themselves express on occasion certain reservations, one thing is certain: medieval Hebrew poetry was defined by the way Jewish poets reclaimed their culture through their use of the Bible.

3. Biblical Women in Courtly Poetry

This phenomenon of fusing Arabic stylistic conventions with the world of the Bible allows for the appearance of numerous Biblical characters. However, in secular poetry, which was the great innovation of medieval Jewish literature, very few female figures from the books of the Bible appear, and those who do appear are highly stereotyped. This contrasts with the much more extensive gallery of male characters who appear in the verses. These include both negative features (Agag, Haman, Amalek, etc.) as well as positive characters (Noah, Joseph, David, etc.). Even though these male characters often reflect stereotypical patterns, their use in a large number of poetic modalities also allows for richer and more innovative literature.

When examining the role of biblical male and female figures in medieval Jewish poetry, however, it is necessary to keep in mind that the poems written in al-Andalus respond to a predetermined literary system to which the authors had to adhere. The true challenge for the poet was to make something new and original by combining forms, characters, voices, and spaces that were predetermined and required by convention. Poetry in this context was not a vehicle for expressing personal experiences or for narrating biographical anecdotes. The poet did not try to reflect real episodes but rather sought to embellish a known reality until it became almost unrecognizable while working within the established canon. In this sense, it was common for poets to regularly resort to the same models.

In the case of female characters, this challenge was accentuated, since there were so few genres that allowed for their presence (and those that did were counted among the most conventional). Songs of love and wine and wedding poems gave female figures the most textual representation,[8]

Between Hebrew and Arabic Poetry: Studies in Spanish Medieval Poetry (Leiden: Brill, 2010), 422–66.

8. On these genres, one may consult, among others, Raymond P. Scheindlin, *Wine, Women and Death: Medieval Hebrew Poetry on the Good Life* (Philadelphia: Jewish Publication Society, 1986); Aurora Salvatierra Ossorio, *Cantos de boda hispano-*

but we cannot forget that we are dealing with a literature that was created by men and destined fundamentally for a male audience. The verses reflect their ideas and tastes, and the female representations fit their accepted cultural and literary framework. Their fundamental goal was to show their mastery of the language and their capacity for achieving complex metaphors or interweaving biblical verses in ways that their audience would admire. And these assumptions conditioned the selection and treatment of women of the Bible in this poetry, blurring the qualities that individualized them.[9]

In fact, poetic fiction is constructed on a dramatic monologue that functions around the absence of an ideal love; she makes her lover suffer from a distance, often to the point of death. These depictions of women thus represent more of an "idea" of the loved one rather than a detailed description of the "love" herself within the structure of this poetic game. This explains why we do not find real or individualized women who are invoked through their biblical ancestors. The female characters who populate these poems are the gazelle or the doe or the dove—terms frequently used to refer to beloved maidens without giving their actual names. Even though many of the images that describe these women originate in the Torah, these characters all respond to the same model built upon common ideas linked to the poetic genre.

The biblical women used by the poets are, with few exceptions, those whom the Jewish community identified with stereotypes of the beloved or the faithful spouse. In general, from the catalog of female characters in the Bible those who tend to be considered "bad women" are excluded (Eve, Lot's wife, Potiphar's wife, etc.), though there is little mention of the many who are considered good women either, especially if they are also strong, heroines, or prophetesses (Deborah,[10] Miriam, Rahab). The female

---

hebreos: Antología (Córdoba: El Almendro, 1998). For this work, Shari Lowin's book, *Arabic and Hebrew Love Poems in al-Andalus* (New York: Routledge, 2014), is of special interest.

9. The poets certainly make an effort to convince us that their loved one is unique and that no one is comparable to her. But all of the women look alike, and thus they represent a single stereotype. On the conventional traits used to describe a love, see Schippers, *Spanish Hebrew Poetry*, 168–212.

10. The war poems of Shmuel ibn Nagrella (Shmuel ha-Nagid) are an exception to this general rule, where on occasion he refers to Deborah, as in the following verse: "Do to them as to Sisera and for me as you did for Baraq and Deborah." See Leon J. Weinberger, *Jewish Prince in Moslem Spain: Selected Poems of Samuel ibn Nagrela* (Alabama:

characters that are of most interest are those that the public could easily associate with love, with being a good wife, and, above all, with beauty. Despite the fact that the majority of women who appear in the Bible are, in one moment or another, described as beautiful (Sarah in Gen 12:11, Rebecca in Gen 24:16, Bathsheba in 2 Sam 11:2, Abishag in 1 Kgs 1:3–4, etc.), only a few of them are used, and only on a few occasions, to sing of amorous passion or marriage. The same use is made of male characters like Joseph or David to describe the beauty of the male lover.[11] In both cases, we are dealing with an attempt to take advantage of the resonance that a simple name can produce in a reader/listener who is familiar with the biblical text by assigning to the character the same role in the medieval poem that he or she played in the Bible.

Among the few women who appear in these love poems is Abigail, Nabal's wife and later David's (1 Sam 25:14–42). Shlomo ibn Gabirol, a poet from Málaga in the eleventh century, mentions her to highlight the attractiveness of the young woman who takes her lover prisoner and then abandons him:

> What is the matter with Abigail that first she took
> my soul with her eyes and then forsook it?
> All her suitors told her that I hate her
> With a most enduring hatred.
> Yet despite this slander, and though she has forgotten my affection
> I shall keep love's pact, I shall not forget.
> The son of Jesse sent messengers to Abigail's house (1 Sam 25:39)
> But I shall go to her in person, not by proxy.
> In time of exile no sacrifices can be offered to God;
> Then I shall slaughter whole offerings and sacrifice to this woman.[12]

The University of Alabama Press, 1973), 25. Hebrew text and Spanish translation in Ángel Sáenz-Badillos and Judit Targarona-Borrás, *Semuel ha-Nagid: Poemas I; Desde el campo de batalla; Granada 1038–1056; Edición del texto hebreo, introducción, traducción y notas* (Córdoba: El Almendro, 1988), 10.

11. See for example the well-known poem of Yishaq ibn Mar Shaul in which the male lover is described as follows: "Like Joseph in appearance, with Adonijah's hair / his eyes like Ben Yishai's, kill me like Uriah." English translation in Peter Cole, *The Dream of the Poem: Hebrew Poetry from Muslim and Christian Spain 950–1492* (Princeton: Princeton University Press, 2007), 28–29. Hebrew text and Spanish translation in Federico Pérez Castro, *Poesía secular hispano-hebrea* (Madrid: CSIC, 1989), 23.

12. See T. Carmi, *The Penguin Book of Hebrew Verse* (New York: Penguin, 1981), 312. Hebrew text in Hayyim Brody and Jaim Schirmann, eds., *Solomon ibn Gabirol:*

Of the woman characterized as "intelligent and beautiful" in 1 Sam 25:3, it is this last trait (her beauty) which is used to describe the beloved. What stands out about her in this context is her power to subdue her lover with just a glance. Thus, the function of the female character is to cause pain to whomever desires her and to even take away life through the force of her passion. And if, as we see in the following poem, other virtues are alluded to, it is to lament their loss since the "fair" Abigail has turned into a Jezebel (1 Kgs 16:31):

> In form you're like a stately palm,
> Your beauty's like the sun.
> You fancied yourself a righteous girl
> Fair like Abigail.
> Now I know you want to kill me,
> You're evil like Jezebel.
> All splendor and beauty,
> I've grown sick from your love.
> So release my soul from Hades,
> In front of you I will not die.[13]

Although infrequent, we find some poems that feature a female from the Bible whose role is completely transformed with respect to the original text. In this way the author shows his ability to create unexpected associations with well-known themes. A very interesting case is, again, that of Shlomo ibn Gabirol:

> Like Amnon sick am I, so call Tamar
> And tell her one who loves her is snared by death.
> Quick, friends, companions, bring her here to me.
> The only thing I ask of you is this:
> Adorn her head with jewels, bedeck her well,
> And send along with her a cup of wine.
> If she would pour for me she might put out
> The burning pain wasting my throbbing flesh.[14]

Secular Poems [Hebrew] (Jerusalem: Schocken Institute, 1974), 27. For a discussion of Ibn Gabirol's poetry, see the essay by Meret Gutmann-Grün in this volume.

    13. My own translation. Hebrew text in Brody and Schirmann, *Solomon ibn Gabirol*, 159.

    14. See Scheindlin, *Wine, Women and Death*, 111.

The poet from Málaga makes use of the dramatic and violent biblical story narrated in 2 Sam 13. Its protagonists are Amnon, David's son, and his sister Tamar, a beautiful virgin according to the text. The Andalusian author projects this episode within the framework of a love poem and rereads it in light of the conventions of this genre in al-Andalus (beauty, the sickness of love, wine, etc.). The Jewish reader knows what happened to the Tamar of the Bible, and Ibn Gabirol knows what effect he will produce when transforming this tale of rape and incest into an idyllic scene between two people in love. An episode of tragic consequences in the sacred text appears here as courtly entertainment. In both cases, however, Tamar continues to be beautiful and to awaken a sick passion in Amnon.[15]

More common is the allusion to certain biblical women in wedding poems, secular compositions where Jewish marriage is celebrated. There is an attempt in these poems to create an association between the anonymous bride and biblical women who are examples of virtue. The wife is frequently compared to Rachel, Leah, or Anna, and there is an emphasis on her value as a future mother or her dedication to marriage. We can see this in the following verses taken from two nuptial poems by Yishaq ibn Gayyat (eleventh century). The first reads, "May your wife be like a fruitful vine within your secret house (Ps 128:3) / May God make the woman who enters / your home be like Rachel and Leah." The second poem declares, "Beautiful gazelle, loved by young men, / be blessed among the most beautiful of women / be visited as Anna by a male son / and may your son live for many years!"[16] In these and other similar verses, it is the ability to be a mother that is the most important attribute for these women.

The mention of these biblical characters in the poem does not indicate that this is the wife's real name—her identity is not revealed. In fact, the female protagonists in these songs often have the same name: Esther, perhaps the biblical bride par excellence. Most often, the poet uses the Hebrew name that the queen receives in the Bible: *Hadassah* (Esth 2:7, 15). This term is quite similar to the Hebrew word *hadas* ("myrtle"), a bush associated with fertility in the Jewish tradition and, because of its good smell and the shade it provides, is used to adorn the nuptial *huppah*. The

---

15. For the interpretation of this poem, see Scheindlin, *Wine, Women and Death*, 111–13; Lowin, *Arabic and Hebrew Love Poems*, 179–203.

16. Spanish translation in Salvatierra Ossorio, *Cantos de boda hispanohebreos*, 31 and 33; English translation by Anna Deckert; Hebrew text in Yonah David, *The Poems of Rabbi Isaac ibn Gayyat* (Jerusalem: Ahshav, 1987), 374 and 389.

similar sounding *Hadassah-hadas* (Esther-myrtle) is part of the wordplay seen in this fragment of a poem from Yehudah ha-Levi (eleventh-twelfth centuries):

> From the myrtle blows over Hadassah a wind of love,
> which cures he who is sick from love.
> It passes through the garden beds of balsam trees (Song 5:13)
> Looking anxiously at the fawns with a present
> and persuades them with tenderness.
> The hand of love has written on them:
> the moment of the union comes closer.[17]

The use of this homophonic convention is retained when the wife is presented in some of these songs as "the daughter of Abihail" (Esth 9:29), in his own turn a model for a fair man:

> Why risest thou, O sun, why shinest thou?
> The turn of Abihail's daughter hath come
> She shameth the face of the sun
> with the splendor of her form,
> She hindereth the host of heaven from their work.
> She chooseth not to dwell in the heavens above,
> But maketh her heaven of the myrtle tree.[18]

In these verses the bride's beauty makes the sun and stars useless since she shines brighter than they do, and yet she has renounced living in the heavens to inhabit the nuptial room adorned with myrtle.

The presence of Rachel, Esther, and other women from the Bible responds, above all, to the desire to create beauty with language. As a result, the poets selectively read from the entire corpus of female characters within the Torah, limiting both their number and their characterizing traits.

---

17. Spanish translation in Salvatierra Ossorio, *Cantos de boda hispanohebreos*, 74; English translation by Anna Deckert; Hebrew text in Hayyim Brody, ed., *Dîwân des Abû -l-Hasân Jehuda ha-Levi* [Hebrew], 3 vols. (Berlin: Schriften des Vereins Mekize Nirdamin, 1894–1930), 2:55–56.

18. English translation in Nina Salaman, *Selected Poems of Jehudah Halevi* (Philadelphia: Jewish Publication Society, 1924), 54; Hebrew text and Spanish translation in Ángel Sáenz-Badillos and Judit Targarona-Borrás, *Yehudah ha-Levi: Poemas* (Madrid: Editorial Alfaguara, 1994), 115; see also 149.

4. The Beloved in the Song of Songs: The Court and the Synagogue

Outside of these and other similar examples, the presence of women from the Bible is not very meaningful in secular Hebrew poetry because of the characteristics of the genre itself. But this literature does give space to a woman who is, without a doubt, the most celebrated female biblical protagonist in this genre: the beloved of the Song of Songs. As was previously mentioned, when Jewish authors started to compose poetry in Hebrew using the Andalusian style, the authors judaize the Arabic literature by using the Torah as a reference. The Song became a key text when adapting and bringing the Jewish public toward the Arab style of love poetry because of the numerous literary traditions that the two share. In both traditions the gardens, aromas, and sounds that make up the amorous setting, and the comparisons and metaphors that describe the lovers or their emotions, have a great deal in common. Conscious of these similarities, the Hebrew poets brought together Arab motifs and biblical allusions, and in this way they created a singular lyrical landscape where there is a blurring of lines between the profane and the religious.

The fixed elements that describe the idealized woman in Arabic love poetry (pale face, dark hair, thin body, red lips) and the topical situations of which she is the protagonist (a plea to the beloved, the pain of separation) are reelaborated and reread in light of the Hebrew sources. In this way, the lover in secular songs fuses with the Shulamite, the beloved of the Songs. Images such as the hill of frankincense (Song 4:7), the dripping myrrh (5:5), the wine on the lips (1:1), the cheeks like pomegranates (4:3), and the beloved as sister or the spying watchmen are introduced in the poems and allow the Jewish aristocracy to enjoy the erotic poetry of al-Andalus through their own cultural references. The beloved of the Song is thus adapted to the literary model that is recreated in these medieval texts; she becomes, above all, a beautiful woman whose great virtue is her ability to make others fall in love with her.

The Hebrew poets will only very rarely allow us to hear the woman's voice or know her feelings. In appearance, the women are powerful in the poetry of al-Andalus: they are often described with physical characteristics that underline their aggressive nature (curls like serpents, breasts sharp as swords, hearts like rocks). In fact, it is a cliché that their strength is in direct opposition to the apparent weakness of their lovers, the victims of their beauty. When digging into these poems, however, one can see that it is the lover, the male character, who controls his glance, who controls language. It is he who looks at her and thus turns her into an object of desire.[19] The female beloveds, although the lives of their lovers come to depend upon them, generally remain silent. And the Shulamite is not in this way an exception. Unlike what happens in the biblical text, she is also silent in these love poems.

On the other hand, in the wedding songs the female voice is heard again. In this genre, the woman converses frequently with the groom since the ideal of love that is celebrated here is very different: their relationship is now harmonious, mutual, and long-lasting; the community approves of it and God blesses it. The bride, however, still retains some character traits from the love poems. She continues to be the erotic figure from the period before the marriage and continues to be described with images that underline the beauty of her face, her hair, her eyes, or her breasts. And again the Jewish authors find material from the Song of Songs, although any association to Eros that might be deemed inconvenient is accommodated to the new context. It is worth examining an example from a fragment of a *muwashshah*, a strophic poem of Arabic origin, by Yehudah ha-Levi:

> My beloved, turn in to me, (Song 4:16)
> To my porch and my temples,
> To feed in the gardens. (Song 6:2)
>
> Show thyself in my tents,
> Among the beds of mine aloe tress,
> To gather lilies
>
> Behold, for thee, breast of pomegranates
> Given for a gift!
> My beloved is mine and I am his
> When I knock at the habitation of his Temple;
> To feed in the gardens. (Song 6:3)
>
> His banner over me is love,
> And his left hand is under my head;
> To gather lilies. (Song 2:4)[20]

---

19. See Tova Rosen, *Unveiling Eve: Reading Gender in Medieval Hebrew Literature* (Philadelphia: University of Pennsylvania Press, 2003), esp. 30–63.

20. English translation by Salaman, *Selected Poems of Jehudah Halevi*, 64–65; Hebrew text and Spanish translation in Saénz-Badillos and Targarona-Borrás, *Yehudah ha-Levi. Poemas*, 121, vv. 5–13.

The influence of Arabic poetry is not limited to this type of secular composition. Surprisingly, in the synagogue congregants began to recite verses whose style comes from Andalusian culture. Although Jews had used poems (*piyyutim*) in Palestine since the Byzantine era to accompany different parts of the liturgy, in al-Andalus they prayed in Hebrew with texts that imitate love poems. Their audience was no longer a small group of courtesans holding a courtly celebration in a garden. It was the assembly, the entire Jewish community, who listened to the poetry, distant from their own tradition, in a religious setting. Upon hearing it in the synagogue, they would have perceived the fusion of elements of Arabic love poems with other elements from the Song of Songs. Centuries earlier ancient synagogal poetry had taken from the Song of Songs its model to present God and Israel as lovers who, although separated, would finally be united. But here, in medieval Jewish poetry, the verses take on a different light since they take advantage of the similarities between the situations and images from the biblical book and erotic Arab poetry, blurring the lines between the secular and the religious.[21]

These Jewish authors, as we have seen, were conscious of the number of parallels that existed between the love poetry of al-Andalus and the Song. These similarities also allowed them to transmit a religious message in the main Jewish space: the synagogue. For example, "the friends of the lover"—a motif whose function in secular poetry is to observe and censure one's surrender to passion—came to identify themselves with the "daughters of Jerusalem" (Song 1:5, 7, etc.) in the poetry of the synagogue. And within this new framework this collective character ("daughters of Jerusalem"), who in the Song looks jealously at the Shulamite, is transformed in the religious poems into a symbol of Israel's detractors during the exile. In a similar way, the sad and frustrated love typical of Andalusian poems becomes a vehicle to develop key themes of liturgical poetry. Concretely, the problem of exile finds in this convention an effective vehicle to express the pain caused by God's abandonment and the trust in recovering His love.

Thematically, the Jewish poets applied an allegorical procedure to love poetry that is similar to what was used in the traditional interpretation of the Song of Songs. Taking advantage of similarities with Arabic models,

---

21. Raymond P. Scheindlin, *The Gazelle: Medieval Hebrew Poems on God, Israel and the Soul* (Oxford: Oxford University Press, 1991), 18–25 and 36–41.

the Jewish poets carried out a transfer to liturgical poetry. This happens with the gazelle, an image of the beloved in the verses of al-Andalus. This motif is made to equal that of the gazelle of the Bible (for example, in Prov 5:19), which in turn comes to symbolize God and his people. In the following poem, written by Ibn Gabirol, we hear one of these dialogues where Israel, like an abandoned bride, longs for the return of its beloved, the messiah:

> The gate long shut
> Get up and throw it wide;
> The stag long fled
> Send him to my side.
> When one day you come
> To lie between my breasts,
> That day your scent
> Will cling to me like wine.
> How shall I know his face, O lovely bride,
> The lover you are asking me to send?
> A ruddy face, and lovely eyes
> A handsome man to see?
> Aye, that's my love! Aye, that's my friend!
> Anoint that one for me![22]

The beloved of the Song has found a new setting in these poems in which to show off her beauty and the strength of her feelings. With images that secular poetry has made its own, she expresses the sadness of separation or the desire for reuniting. But in the synagogue, the lover is no longer the young woman who awakens her lover's passion and submits him to her will. She now personifies Israel and her partner is none other than the Redeemer for whom the Jewish community waits.

5. Final Reflections

If Hebrew poetry in medieval Spain does indeed offer us a very limited and prescribed use of the women in the Bible, their presence in these verses is an interesting change in respect to how they were represented in prior Jewish literature. The rereading that is offered of the beloved of the Song of

---

22. See Scheindlin, *Gazelle*, 91; Hebrew text in Hayyim Schirmann, ed., *Hebrew Poetry in Spain and Provence*, vol. 1 [Hebrew] (Jerusalem: Bialik Institute, 1954), 240.

Songs is of particular interest as it shows us how her figure is rebuilt and singularized to respond to the tastes and circumstances of Jewish communities in medieval Iberia. Within this new framework the Shulamite also recovers characteristics that had been lost during an earlier period.

There is no better way to see the change that occurred than to think about classic Jewish literature (roughly from the third through the eighth centuries). There, the interest in the Song of Songs and its protagonists was oriented toward religious questions on the interpretation of the sacred texts, both in the Written Law (Bible) as well as in the Oral Law (Mishnah). In works composed during this period, the Song, like the rest of the biblical books, was not of interest for its literary value but only for its theological-religious intention. It is sufficient for this purpose to think about the Midrash Song of Songs. In this work almost all of the verses of the biblical book are meticulously discussed, and each of them is seen as an image of the main acts of liberation from the history of Israel. This is the interpretation, for example, of the verses that start that text:

> "The words of the Torah are **compared** to water, to wine, to oil, to honey and to milk (...) Another explanation: *For thy loved ones are better than wine* refers to the patriarchs. *Than wine* indicates the **princes** (...) Another explanation: *For thy loved ones* indicates the offerings; *Than wine* indicates the drink-offerings (...) Another explanation: *For better are thy loved ones*: This refers to Israel. *Than wine*: This refers to the **Gentiles'** nations.[23]

The beloved in these writings is no longer the passionate woman who looks all night for her lover. The free and happy woman has become an allegory; her emotions and body are diminished. Something similar happens in a passage taken from the Babylonian Talmud in relation to Song 7:3:

> R. Aha Haninah said: Scripture states, *'Thy navel is like a round goblet* [*'aggan ha-sahar*] *wherein no mingled wine is wanting'* (Song 7:3). *'Thy navel'*—that is the Sanhedrin. Why was it called *'navel'*?—Because it sat at the navel-point of the world. [Why] *goblet* [*'aggan*]?—Because it protects [*meggin*] the whole word. [Why] round [*ha-sahar*]?—Because it is moon-shaped. [Why] in which no mingled wine is wanting?—i.e., if

---

23. English translation in Harry Freedman and Maurice Simon, *The Midrash Rabbah: Lamentations, Ruth, Ecclesiastes, Esther, Song of Songs* (London: Soncino, 1977), 33–36.

one of them had to leave, it had to be ascertained if twenty-three, corresponding to the number of the minor Sanhedrin, were left in which case he might go out; if not, he might not depart. Thy belly is like a heap of wheat: Just as all benefit from a heap of wheat, so do all benefit from the deliberations of the Sanhedrin." (b. Sanh. 37a)[24]

In a similar vein, the Targum (the Aramaic translation of the Bible), in another classic interpretation, reads the relationship between the lovers of the Song as an allegory of the relationship of God with Israel from the time of the exodus from Egypt until the end of the exile when the messiah arrives.[25]

However, when the center of Jewish life is moved from the East to the lands of al-Andalus, certain lost traits of the woman in the Song, such as her beauty, will again become important in Hebrew literature. The rich Andalusian culture made it possible for liturgical and secular poetry to recover the passion of the Bible's text and to return the female lover to her place as protagonist. From the tenth century onward, verses that speak of kisses, caresses, and embraces will again be heard. When evoking the Shulamite and some other female figures, the poets embellish their verses but, at the same time, they offer a renewed vision and distinctive reading of the Torah. In their verses, traditional images and themes are updated in order to allow the female lover of the Song to express her longing for messianic times while in the synagogue, but also to celebrate secular love in courtly gatherings while enjoying wine and music in the garden. In both of these spaces, the woman of the Song of Songs takes life and allows us to hear her voice again.

---

24. English translation in Isidore Epstein, ed., *Soncino Babylonian Talmud. Sanhedrin* (London: Soncino, 1935).

25. English translation in Philip Alexander, *The Targum of Canticles: Translated with a Critical Introduction, Apparatus and Notes* (London: T&T Clark, 2003).

The Female Figure Zion in the Liturgical Literature of Al-Andalus

Meret Gutmann-Grün

1. Who Is Speaking Here? Is This Zion? A Literary-Critical Introduction[1]

Alas! Watchers found me—they hit me, they wounded me!
Alas! Princes loved me—in oppressors' hands they left me!
They pampered me, they reared me, they didn't care offending me.
They stilled my thirst, they covered me, in the end they scorned me.
   —Shmuel Hanagid, no. 180, "Alas! Watchers" (אהה שומרים)[2]

Is the female person speaking here Zion? On the basis of the Hebrew forms, it cannot be determined whether the "I" who is speaking here is masculine or feminine. But the voice sounds like an echo from Song 5:7 where the loving woman laments that watchmen beat her. Here though, the voice adds being loved and being spurned to that scene of being beaten, elements that are not found in the Song of Songs. These scenes

---

1. For a more detailed presentation of the feminine figure Zion in which the religious poetry of the classical period (sixth through eighth centuries in Israel) is taken into consideration, see Meret Gutmann-Grün, *Zion als Frau: Das Frauenbild Zions in der Poesie von al-Andalus auf dem Hintergrund des klassischen Piyyuts* (Bern: Lang, 2008). On Shmuel Hanagid and on this specific poem see Yonatan Vardi, "Poems of Salvation by Shemuel Hanagid," *Hispania Judaica Bulletin* 14 (2019): 114 n. 25.

2. Based on the edition of Dov Jarden, *Divan Shemuel Ha-Nagid: Ben Tehillim* (Jerusalem: privately published, 1966). If not explicitly noted, all translations are mine and are found, in part with the original Hebrew text, on the CD to *Zion als Frau*. Shmuel ben Yosef Halevi ibn Nagrila Hanagid (b. 993 in Cordoba; d. 1056 in Granada) was the vizier of King Habbus in the city state of Granada, held the same office under King Badis, and carried out wars at the command of this king against other city states in al-Andalus. He was a recognized presider (*nagid*) of the Jewish congregation. Along with the collection Ben Tehillim, he also wrote Ben Mishle and Ben Kohelet.

possibly allude to the bitter postbiblical experiences of Zion as a mirror image of the Jewish people. If this poem actually does portray the bitter lament of Zion and not that of a different figure, then the reader[3] definitely can identify easily with the feelings of this figure, and that likely was the intention of this poem by Shmuel Hanagid.

The fact that the poet does not reveal the identity of the person speaking fits with the style of the Hebrew poems in al-Andalus, both the secular and the religious ones, which intentionally play ambiguously with the reader and "break down the distinctions between the holy and the profane."[4]

Discerning whether we have before us a secular poem about a flesh-and-blood woman or a religious poem about Zion is not always easy. But there is a clear criterion: in the secular love songs the woman does not speak[5] and is always addressed only as a beloved person. Thus, if a female person speaks in a poem, it must be either a wedding poem[6] or a religious poem. To these religious texts also belong the synagogal poems in poetic form (*piyyutim*), which clearly are defined as such by the specification of their liturgical purpose and genre.[7] In the *piyyutim*, the poet has complete freedom to use erotic words. When Hebrew *secular* poetry emerges in al-Andalus for the first time,[8] the use of erotic words in the mouth of a

---

3. I use the term *reader* here and throughout in a gender-neutral sense.

4. Ross Brann, *The Compunctious Poet: Cultural Ambiguity and Hebrew Poetry in Muslim Spain* (Baltimore: John Hopkins University Press, 1991), 42, writes: "Another sort of literary pleasure involved precisely the breaking down of distinctions between the sacred and the profane." Al-Andalus is the Arabic designation for Islamic Spain from 710 until 1492. See Georg Bossong, *Das Maurische Spanien, Geschichte und Kultur* (Munich: Beck, 2007).

5. On the categories distinguishing the feminine voice and, hence, a *piyyut* from a secular song, see Matti Huss, "Pshat o Alegoria—Shirat haHesheq shel Shmuel Hanagid," *Meḥqare Jerushalayim beSifrut Ivrit* 15 (1995): 34–72.

6. The fact that the bride speaks represents the only exception to the rule of the otherwise mute woman!

7. Cf. the *piyyutim* examples in the text. Almost without exception, a *piyyut*, in contrast to the secular song, is "signed" (*hatima*) by the poet in an acrostic that is composed of the first letters of the verses and that reveals his name (for example, SHLMH). This, too, is a distinctive category.

8. The impulse for the creation of a secular poetry came from Dunash ben Labrat, who, in the style of the Arabs, introduced the quantative meter in Hebrew poetry. Dunash ben Labrat came from Fes, was educated in Baghdad by Saadia Gaon, and came to Cordoba to Hasdai Ibn Shaprut (905–975), the Vizier of Abd al-Rahman III.

feminine speaking figure is, in contrast to the *piyyutim*, offensive. Yehosef, the son of Shmuel Hanagid, as he himself attests, was commissioned by his father in the year 1040 at the age of eight to copy out the collection of the latter's songs.[9] He excuses his father in the introduction in the following manner: "The erotic words in the style of the Arabic *nasīb*[10] are here designations [*kinayah*] for the Knesset Israel and similar things, as found in some of the prophetic books. God will reward his intention. Every person who interprets them in a way different from what he intended will bear his own guilt."[11]

Barely a hundred years after Shmuel Hanagid, Moshe ibn Ezra composed songs of friendship and lust and songs about wine as well as *piyyutim*.[12] Toward the end of his life, he wrote a work on poetics in the Judeo-Arabic language for prospective poets,[13] because he understood himself as a teacher and transmitter of Andalusian Jewish culture. He defended the metaphorical diction in Andalusian poetry against the charge that it was a lie. By using examples from the Koran and the Bible, he attempted to prove that linguistic ornament, and especially the metaphor,

---

Twelve songs by him have been preserved, among them the Sabbath song "Dror Yiqra" (He Proclaims Freedom) that is still sung today.

9. For the text, see Jarden, *Ben Tehillim*. This collection, Ben Tehillim, contains war songs, hymns of praise, friendship songs, wine songs, songs of passion, songs for special occasions, and also *piyyutim*. Whether Shmuel Hanagid himself named this collection "Ben Tehillim" is a matter of controversy in research. On the attested dating of the text to the year 1040 (4800 in the Jewish calendar), see Chaim Schirmann, *The History of Hebrew Poetry in Muslim Spain* [Hebrew], ed. Ezra Fleisher (Jerusalem: Magnes, 1995), 222–23. Yehosef, one of the three sons of Shmuel Hanagid, died in 1066 in the pogrom of Granada.

10. A *nasīb* is an introduction to a *qasīda*, which is a nonstrophic song with continuous rhyme (see also n. 33).

11. Quoted in Arabic phonetic transcription with English translation in Arie Schippers, *Spanish Hebrew Poetry and the Arabic Literary Tradition: Themes in Hebrew Andalusian Poetry* (Leiden: Brill, 1994), 151.

12. Moshe ibn Ezra was born in 1055 to one of the most significant families of Granada. He left the city sometime after its conquest by the Almoravids (1090). To which location in Castile (Christian Spain) he fled is, however, unknown. Up to his death after 1139, he remained the friend and patron of Yehuda Halevi, who had come to Granada no earlier than 1085. He wrote *piyyutim* only after coming to Castile; before that he wrote secular songs.

13. For an edition of this work with Hebrew translation and commentary, see A. S. Halkin, *Kitāb al-muhādara wa'l-mudhākara* (Jerusalem: Mequitze Nirdamim, 1975).

already appear in the Bible and that there are also love songs in the Bible. In the discussion conducted at that time in al-Andalus, about whether the new "ornamented" (*badī'*) style was suitable for *piyyut*, he defended the metaphor because "the idea of the metaphor is that you describe an unknown thing with one that is known."[14] In addition, he said, it is just that which constitutes the beauty of poetry.

Moshe ibn Ezra, like Yehosef Hanagid, could no longer explain the secular song to his readership as a song that was to be understood allegorically, and thus he could no longer identify the woman addressed in it with the Knesset Israel. The public had in the meantime become accustomed to secular love songs in which a beloved person is addressed, and the poets themselves deliberately blurred the boundary between secular poems and *piyyutim* in the imagery of their language.

Before we come to the question about what role the woman's voice plays in the *piyyutim*, it must be made clear that the feminine voice is never identified. The woman is not named but is only described, and this is also true in most cases with the imagery used in the Song of Songs. Thus, the reader understands the voice in accordance with the allegorical exegesis of the Song of Songs as "Knesset Israel,"[15] that is, as the timeless, ideal congregation of Israel. It also can be called, in short, "Zion," just as it is called "Zion" in the Bible, representing a personal union between the city and the people.

The metaphorical names of the female voice from the Song of Songs are numerous (especially in the salutation):[16] my dove (*yonati*; Song 2:14), young gazelle (*'ofrah*, the feminine form of *'ofer*; 2:9, 17 and throughout), gazelle (*tzviyah*), dove from afar (Ps 56:1), noble daughter (*bat nadiv*, Song 7:2). The following dialogue between "him" and "her" shows vividly how descriptions that had become hackneyed in the classical *piyyut* and had ossified into lexicalized metaphors here become once again full of life and point to the beauty of the beloved:[17]

---

14. Halkin, *Kitāb al-muhādara*, 228–29. The *badī'* style means "ornate, original or new style." See Schippers, *Spanish Hebrew Poetry*, 77. On the discussion about acculturation, see Brann, *Compunctious Poet*.

15. *Knesset Israel* is a postbiblical term. The midrash on Lamentations replaces the name "Zion" with Knesset Israel. See Gutmann-Grün, *Zion als Frau*, 27.

16. Gutmann-Grün, *Zion als Frau*, 257.

17. In the classical *piyyut*, "the bright and ruddy" is a synonym for the messiah; "my sister and bride" (Song 4:12) is a synonym for Israel. See Gutmann-Grün, *Zion als Frau*, 82–86.

"Greetings I bear my Friend[18]
   My Friend, so lithe and fair (Song 5:10),
Greetings from her whose brow
   Breathes the fruit-garden's air (Song 4:3).
Come, with thy saving grace,
   Come forth, thy sister (Song 5:1) greet,
Gallant as Jesse's son
   when he his foes did meet"
"My fairest, what is cause
   Passion to stir so fast,
With tinkling voice, like bells
   Heard when robed priests go past? (Exod 28:35)
When love herself shall judge (Song 2:7)
   'Tis time, then, at her cue,
I haste Me to thy side
   Gentle as Hermon's dew."
            —Shlomo ibn Gabirol, no. 96 (a *reshut* for Simhat Torah),
              "Greetings to You, My Friend" (שלום לך דודי)[19]

She and he address one another with descriptions of each other's beauty. He is bright and ruddy (Song 5:10); she woos with pomegranate-like temples (Song 4:3). Her voice alone already arouses his love (Song 2:7); the comparison of her voice with the bells of her robe connects the erotic with the

---

18. Loewe's capital letter here expresses the same sense as my annotation to my capital writing of "Ich" in my German version: when God is meant, I decide to capitalize the personal pronouns, which, of course, removes the ambivalence of the imagery from the text that it has in Hebrew but emphasizes the immanence of the sacred in the profane.

19. English translation from Raphael Loewe, ed., *The Rylands Haggadah: A Medieval Sephardi Masterpiece in Facsimile; An Illuminated Passover Compendium from Mid-Fourteenth-Century Catalonia in the Collections of the John Rylands University Library of Manchester with a Commentary and a Cycle of Poems* (London: Thames & Hudson, 1988), 48. My thanks to Dr. Peter Sh. Lehnardt, senior lecturer in Medieval Hebrew Literature in the Department of Hebrew Literature at Ben-Gurion University of the Negev, who sent me this English translation. The biblical citations, annotated on nearly every line, are Raphael Loewe's annotations. The other annotations are mine. For the Hebrew text, see Dov Jarden, *Shirey haQodesh le-Rabbi Shlomo Ibn Gabirol*, 2 vols. (Jerusalem: American Academy of Jewish Research, 1971–1972). In this essay, I quote exclusively from this edition. The *piyyut* today still belongs to the repertoire of (among others) the Moroccan Jews for the Baqqashot prayers sung, for example, by Joe Amar (1930–2009), who was born in Morocco and emigrated to Israel. The "Rylands Haggadah," which includes this *piyyut*, is proof of the ongoing use of the *piyyut* in Spain.

cultic.[20] She desires of him that he might rescue her like a hero, just like David in his heroic feat in battle against Rabbat Ammon (2 Sam 12:29). She, of course, arouses His love, and He for this reason will bring about the (metaphorically interpreted) release. Read in the literal sense (*peshat*), the *piyyut* climaxes in the last two lines in its highly sensual language in the unification of love: "*'alaikh 'ered ketal ḥermon* (Ps 133:3), literally translated, "I will come down on you like the dew of Hermon." As is usual in the *piyyutim*, Shlomo ibn Gabirol "signs" his *piyyut* with the acrostic ShLMH.

On what occasions was this *piyyut* prayed? The tradition records its purpose as a part of Simhat Torah (the feast of joy in the Torah celebrated in the fall). And, as a liturgical station in prayer, it is recorded that it is a *reshut*, that is, the opening prayer spoken by the prayer leader, who first of all must obtain permission (*reshut*) from the congregation to be allowed to speak the prayer in its name.

1.1. The Role Played by Zion as a Woman in Prayers

When the feminine figure is the speaker, the *piyyut* poets can express everything to God that the woman in the Song of Songs says to her beloved. In a comprehensive sweep of emotions from love for Him to the disappointment over His departure and the yearning for His return, she represents the exile as a continuation of her love story after her wedding with Him on Sinai. She was not able to do this in the classical *piyyut* in the land of Israel (sixth to eighth century) because her speaking role there was limited to the laments (*kinot*) over the destruction of Jerusalem on the Ninth of Av and to the *piyyutim* for the so-called consolatory *shabbatot* after the Ninth of Av.[21] She already had this lamenting role in the Bible in Lamentations (*'Eikah*) as an uncomforted woman or widow (e.g., Lam 1:12–22). As a former queen who now must serve as a laborer (Lam 1:1), she bewails her misfortune and the death of her children (Lam 1:20). In al-Andalus too, she retains her role as the lamenting mother. But, what distinguishes the al-Andalus *piyyut* from classical *piyyut* is, first of all, the new speaking

---

20. That is, the robe of the high priest (Exod 28:35).

21. Gutmann-Grün, *Zion als Frau*, 74. Note El'azar Kallir in part 1 of the Qedushta for the consolatory Shabbat "Ronni Aqarah": "I sit childless, outcast, hard-pressed, a withered leaf; I was pregnant, have borne, have reared, and they are no more." See Shulamit Elizur, *Qedushta waShir, Qedushta'ot leShabbatoth haNechamah leRabbi El'azar berabbi Kallir* (Jerusalem: self published, 1988), 74.

roles assumed by Zion as a loving, yearning, and beautiful woman and, second, the new love motifs that, surprisingly, come not only from the Song of Songs, but also from the secular songs of praise and friendship.[22]

1.2. The Song of Songs and the Song of Praise and Friendship as Contributors of Themes in *Piyyut*

In the golden age of al-Andalus, the higher-placed Jews and Arabs communicated with each other in songs of praise and friendship sent to one another as letters.[23] A song that was an encomium would be recited during a feast at court.[24] To the patron, who ideally is also a friend, one would address a song with erotic rhetoric, praising the friend, asking for protection, bewailing the fact that he has withdrawn himself and his "betrayal of love," indulging in nostalgic remembrance, and expressing one's yearning for him. These same men who wrote these songs of friendship to each other and would also compose love songs addressed to women are, in part, the same men who wrote the prayer poetry sung in the synagogues.[25] As intellectual and social elite, they often occupied important positions at court thanks to their diplomatic skills and their linguistic fluency, although as Jews they had the legally restricted status of a *dhimmi*.[26] We do not need to

---

22. Dan Pagis, *Secular Poetry and Poetic Theory: Moshe Ibn Ezra and His Contemporaries* [Hebrew] (Jerusalem: Bialik Institute, 1970); Schirmann, *Hebrew Poetry in Muslim Spain*.

23. The golden age is from the middle of the tenth century to the twelfth century. The German publishers of the Andalusian poets in the nineteenth century coined the term *golden age*. For more on this, see Gutmann-Grün, *Zion als Frau*, 28 n. 23.

24. These feasts were called *moshav*, *mesibbah*, or *yeshivah*. See Dan Pagis, *Innovation and Tradition in Secular Poetry: Spain and Italy* [Hebrew] (Jerusalem: Keter, 1976), 38.

25. These men included Shmuel Hanagid, Shlomo ibn Gabirol (ca. 1021 Malaga– 1058 Granada), Moshe Ibn Ezra (ca. 1055 Granada–after 1139 Castile), Yehuda Halevi (ca. 1075 Tudela–1141 land of Israel), Abraham ibn Ezra (1089 Tudela–after 1164 exile). For the most important data on the first four named here, see Schippers, *Spanish Hebrew Poetry*, 52–64; Schirmann, *Hebrew Poetry in Muslim Spain*. On Yehuda Halevi, in particular, see Joseph Yahalom, *Yehuda Halevi: Poetry and Pilgrimage* (Jerusalem: Magnes, 2009). According to his own testimony, Moshe ibn Ezra wrote "more than 6,000 lines in quantifying meter…. Many of them are songs of praise that I composed for my brothers and friends." See Halkin, *Kitāb al-muhādara*, 102.

26. That is, they were legally restricted but tolerated and thereby had to pay a head tax. Shmuel Hanagid, up to the time of his death in 1056, and Moshe ibn Ezra

investigate here how serious or playful these poetic letters are meant to be. What we can say is that they play skillfully with a double repertoire of literary motifs, the Arabic and the Hebrew. The Arabic motifs are reminiscent of pre-Islamic Udhri poetry, and the Hebrew motifs come from the Bible, especially from the Song of Songs. What do these two literary forms have to do with each other? The Jews in al-Andalus lived in constant cultural contact with the Arabs in the caliphate that Abd al-Rahman III had refounded in 929 on the Iberian Peninsula.[27] This acculturation resulted, on the one hand, in the adoption of Arab literary models.[28] On the other hand, the Jews emphasized the purity of *their* language, and they revived biblical Hebrew[29] not only for use as a liturgical language but also for use in new secular poetry. Above all, they rediscovered the plain sense of the Song of Songs, that is, they read it as a love song and not as an allegory on the love of Israel and God.

As an example of a poem of friendship, let us examine extracts from the beginning of the sixty-line long poem that Yehuda Halevi wrote to Moshe ibn Ezra:[30]

> [1] Stand still, my brother, stand still a moment more,
> that I may bless you and my spirit[31] a farewell-blessing.
> [3] Do you think it is too little to send to me the fire of your departure [*nedod*]
> that on that very day you took me even as a captive?!
> [7] How did you endure to bring about you the departure
> which quenched my glowing glamour?

---

up to 1090, held high positions at the Muslim court of Granada (see above nn. 2 and 12), until there was a pogrom against the Jews in 1066 in Granada. In 1109, there was a pogrom in Christian Toledo, which Alfonso VI had recaptured from the Muslims in 1086 and where Yehuda Halevi was active as a doctor.

27. Hasdai ibn Shaprut (915–970) is mentioned as the first Jewish scholar who had a crucial position as a diplomat at the cosmopolitan court of Cordoba.

28. Rina Drory, *Models and Contacts: Arabic Literature and Its Impact on Medieval Jewish Culture* (Leiden: Brill, 2000).

29. Instead of Mishnaic Hebrew and the Targumic Aramaic.

30. The Arabic heading of this poem indicates that it is directed to Moshe Ibn Ezra, "the first person to whom he turned when arrived from out of his city." Meant here is his arrival in Granada from the city of his birth, Tudela, sometime after 1090. Granada was the city where Moses ibn Ezra resided until around 1095. See on this subject the short remark by Yahalom, *Yehuda Halevi*, 25 and 58.

31. The spirit of the one speaking is taken along by the one leaving!

¹¹ The night before the separation I didn't wish
the morning light, but it came despite my wish.
¹³ There wouldn't be any soul left in me
if I didn't hope for the day when "the dispersed will be gathered" (Isa 11:12).³²

The motif of separation, called *nedod*, is a conventional motif in the introduction of the Arabic *qasīda*.³³ The specific Arabic term for this separation (*firāq*) is sometimes found in the Judeo-Arabic titles of the Hebrew songs of praise and friendship that often begin with this motif. Responsible for the separation is cruel fate, referred to as "time" (*dahr* in Arabic). The longing felt by the one left behind is expressed metaphorically in the sense that one's own soul or spirit has been taken captive by the one leaving. In the Hebrew love song, this motif becomes a mannered cliché that characterizes the unapproachable, fleeing beloved one. The separation motif sometimes is combined in the *qasīda* with weeping over the "ruins of the places for sleeping and making love," the so-called *atlāl* motif. Below is an example of how Moshe ibn Ezra, in a religious song, transfers the *atlāl* motif to the destroyed Zion:

> Hurry to the lovers' camp,
>   Dispersed³⁴ by Time, a ruin now;
> Once the haunt of love's gazelles,
>   Wolves' and lions' lair today.
> From far away I hear Gazelle,³⁵
>   From Edom's keep and Arab's cell,
> Mourning the lover of her youth,³⁶
>   Sounding lovely,³⁷ ancient words:

---

32. Hayyim Brody, *Diwan des Abu-l-Hasan Yehuda Halevi, Shire haChol*, 3 vols. (repr. Farnsborough: Gregg International, 1971), 2:273 no. 53 (commentary on 3:249).
33. For more on *nedod* (Arabic *firāq*), see Gutmann-Grün, *Zion als Frau*, 190–93 and 415–31. The *qasīda* is an Old Arabic, nonstrophic song form in continuous rhyme and quantifying meter. The literature on it is very large. For a short, good overview, see Renate Jakobi, "The Origins of the Qasida Form," in *Qasida Poetry in Islamic Asia and Africa*, ed. Stefan Sperl and Christopher Shackle (Leiden: Brill, 1996), 21–31.
34. The beloved persons are the dispersed ones mentioned here.
35. Here the word *gazelle* is feminine. The masculine gazelle, the beloved in the Song of Songs, is *tzvi*, whereas the feminine gazelle is *tzviah*.
36. That is, God.
37. An allusion to Song 2:14: "with a sweet voice."

"Fortify me[38] with lovers' flasks,[39]
Strengthen me with sweets of love."[40]
—Moshe ibn Ezra, no. 37 (an *'ahavah*), "Hurry Please" (מהרו נא).[41]

As is the case in the *atlāl* motif, the anonymous speaker summons other people to come to see the destroyed place and to hear his lament. The place once was inhabited by the "beloved," a conventional designation for Israel in the classical *piyyut*. Time rather than God is responsible for the destruction. The ruins, though, are not mute, as in the *atlāl* motif or in the short lament of the dead over the destroyed land of Israel found in Jeremiah (Jer 9:9, 10). Rather, the speaker, the lyrical "I," hears a moaning gazelle. The reader is reminded here of Rachel's lament in Jer 31:15. The female gazelle in the love song is a conventional metaphor for the beloved, but here the metaphor is completely turned around for it is the beloved who moans. As soon as she names her enemies, Edom (Christians) and Arabs, the reader is given the signal that the captive gazelle is the Zion figure. At the conclusion she herself begins to speak, a literary device corresponding to the so-called *kharja* in the songs of passion and love.[42]

---

38. Literally a plural in Hebrew. But, since it was the convention in al-Andalus to speak of the one addressed in the plural, Moshe ibn Ezra here transfers the plural to the address directed to God.

39. This version is according to Abraham ibn Ezra, *Perush leShir HaShirim*. See www.sefaria.org or, in print: *Miqra'ot gedoloth*, 10 vols., Tanakh with Traditional Commentaries (New York: Pardes, 1959). Other translations read "cakes of raisins." It is a variation of the double statement of Song 2:5, "Strengthen me with raisin cakes and succor me with apples." See more on this in the appendix to the text of Gutmann-Grün, *Zion als Frau*.

40. "Sweets of love," actually love in the plural. The delicacies are in Song 7:14 and 4:13, 16. These are the things that *she* gives to him or that *she* has saved up for him. Here, however, it is intended that God gives her these things!

41. Translation Raymond Scheindlin, *The Gazelle: Medieval Poems on God, Israel, and the Soul* (Oxford: Oxford University Press, 1991), 65. Annotations are mine. See also Shimon Bernstein, *Moshe Ibn Ezra: Shire ha-Qodesh* (Tel Aviv: Massada, 1957), no. 37. It is a matter of controversy whether this poem ever had a liturgical purpose, that is, as a *piyyut*. Bernstein takes it up in his edition of religious songs and designates it as *'ahavah*, that is, a *piyyut* for the second Berakhah of the Morning Prayer. For more on this, see Gutmann-Grün, *Zion als Frau*, 235.

42. At the conclusion of the *kharja*, the beloved woman gives her sudden assent to love in popular speech, sometimes in song citations.

1.3. Summary of and Perspective on the Various Roles of Zion in *Piyyut*

Before I cite further examples, it can be said in summary that in the *piyyutim* of al-Andalus Zion assumes the role of the abandoned, beseeching friend and protégé who turns to his patron and friend. In this way, the *piyyutim* echo the subject matter in the songs of praise and friendship (see §2.1).

As we will see (§2.2), when Zion, in the context of the hope of redemption, makes an invitation to the fulfillment of love, her beauty is praised with the attributes of the ideal of beauty that the secular beloved has in the Hebrew songs of passion and in the Song of Songs.[43] However, in contrast to the secular beloved who, to be sure, is beautiful but mute and dismissive, Zion, like the bride in the wedding song, has a euphonious voice just like the woman in the Song of Songs. Indeed, she even sings. Also like the beloved woman in the Hebrew secular songs (see §2.3), Zion also suffers as a loving woman at the hands of her critics and female rivals.

All of these roles are based, on the one hand, on new literary motifs. On the other hand, Zion still has the classical role of the lamenting mother.[44]

2. Shared Motifs in the Song of Songs and Arabic-Jewish Poetry

There are primarily three new motifs that one can locate in both the Song of Songs *and* in the Arabic-Jewish songs of praise and friendship:

1. "I must wander about the streets and seek him whom my soul loves" (Song 3:2). This motif serves in the effort to cope literarily with the exile; it is combined with the Arabic motif of separation, or *firāq*.
2. "May my beloved come into his garden." (Song 4:16); "Let me hear your voice, for your voice is love" (Song 2:14). Both motifs express the hoped-for fulfillment of love, that is, the deliverance from exile. The garden, like other places for love, has an affinity to the *atlāl* motif.
3. "The watchmen who make the rounds in the city found me; they struck me and wounded me" (Song 5:7); "I adjure you, you daughters

---

43. Songs of passion are considered in Arabic poetics as songs of praise directed to the woman. See especially Tova Rosen, *Unveiling Eve: Reading Gender in Medieval Hebrew Literature* (Philadelphia: University of Pennsylvania Press, 2003).

44. See section 3 below.

of Jerusalem, if you find my beloved, what should you say to him? That I am lovesick.... Why is then your beloved so different ... that you adjure us so?" (Song 5:8–9). The enemies of Zion are reinterpreted as the rivals of the lovers who are known in the Hebrew love song but who originated in Arabic love stories.

2.1. Wandering about and the Search for the Beloved

"I must wander about the streets and seek him whom my soul loves" (Song 3:2)
My Dove—wandered through the streets by night
Goes on—to seek out for the One she loved. (Song 3:1)

1 Release her — / so she might voice with weeping
   Because her sickness / grew to the grade of her sin.
   She counted a thousand / time but her yoke did not disappear.
The great / with people (Lam 1:1) sat like a bereaved,
turns around / calculating end after end.

2 I was like / a roving owl of deserts,
   I became / a bird alone on a roof (Ps 102:7–8),
   I wept / because weeping I shall rove.
My tear / on my cheek never dried up (Lam 1:2),
poured / on Your city because it is deserted.

3 Be consoled / O heart broken by sorrow.
   Time to warm up / remembering past times.
   Who shall fight / the ordinance of God so strong.
My hope / is not disappointed by You,
lingers on / and Your covenant did not lie.
—Yehuda Halevi, no. 326 (an 'ahavah or selihah),
"My Dove in the Night" (יונתי לילה)[45]

---

45. Text from Dov Jarden, *Shirey haQodesh le-Rabbi Yehuda Ha-Levi*, 4 vols. (Jerusalem: privately published, 1978–1985). I cite exclusively from this edition. A new edition by Joseph Yahalom is in preparation. English translation by Dr. Peter Sh. Lehnardt, who has shared my love for Hebrew medieval poetry for decades. I thank him wholeheartedly for his contribution. Lehnardt thinks that one strophe of the *piyyut* is missing, since the acrostic YEHUDAH lacks the letter *vav*.

According to form, this *piyyut* has a strophic construction.⁴⁶ Its liturgical placement is not clear: it is either an *'ahavah* or a *selihah*.⁴⁷

There are various speakers: the voice of God, a concealed speaker, and Zion as a female speaker. God speaks in the first two introductory lines that broach the subject and talks tenderly in the metaphors of the Song of Songs about "His dove." In the first strophe, a concealed speaker corrects this statement by God and says that the dove in her wanderings is unhappy to the greatest extent. He enlightens God, so to speak, about the fact that she suffers in exile because of her guilt, and to the misery of exile there is the added disappointment over the incorrect calculation of the end time.⁴⁸ The view of the exile as a punishment is the classical interpretation that Zion herself confirms in her answer in the second strophe: She laments and quotes verses from Ps 102, a threnodic psalm that changes over from a personal to a national lament and beseeches God for the rebuilding of Zion. The female speaker weeps like Zion in Lamentations on the Ninth of Av, the day of the destruction of Jerusalem (Lam 1:2). In the third strophe, though, comes the reversal in the manner of the love songs: With the topos of the burning pain of separation, which actually is a fire of love and in which the tears always flow,⁴⁹ she remembers the way it used to be. Thereby, her heart once again becomes "hot" from love, and she asserts her lasting faith in His fidelity. Thus, the *piyyut* ends with the new, positive interpretation of the exile as a wandering about in search of the beloved. But, in contrast to the Song of Songs, the relationship between the lovers has a past history

---

46. For more on this *piyyut*, see Gutmann-Grün, *Zion als Frau*, 448.

47. For *'ahavah*, see n. 41. This text can be a *piyyut* for the second Berakhah of the morning prayer, called *'ahavah*, per Dov Jarden in the annotation in his edition, *Shirey haQodesh le-Rabbi Yehuda Ha-Levi*, 3:266. Or it can be a *selihah* (a prayer of penitence and contrition), per Leon Weinberger, *Jewish Hymnography: A Literary History* (London: Littman Library of Jewish Civilization, 1998), 93.

48. The year 1068 (one thousand years after the destruction of the temple) heralded omens of of messianic distress, because the Christian *Reconquista* already had reconquered Zaragoza, and Toledo was taken back by Alfonso VI in 1085. Likewise, the year 1040 (= Jewish 4800) was expected as the end time. See Gutmann-Grün, *Zion als Frau*, 353 and 355.

49. The "fire of separation" (*'esh ha-nedod*), for example, appears in the song of friendship by Yehuda Halevi to Moshe ibn Ezra (cited above; see n. 36); see also the "fiery glow" of love in Song 8:6. See more on the fire of love (אש אהבים) and tears in Gutmann-Grün, *Zion als Frau*, 186–93.

upon which the abandoned party looks back—just like the abandoned friend in the songs of friendship.

In the interpretation of the exile as a wandering search,[50] the image of the dove is the obvious symbol for the figure of Zion: Because the dove in the Song of Songs positively connotes the lover's amorous form of address directed to the woman, her wandering about becomes positive through this usage alone. This is shown by another *piyyut* by Yehuda Halevi:

> 1 Far-flown dove[51] wandered[52] to a wood,
>   Stumbled there and lay lame,
> 2 Flitted, flailed, and flustered
>   Storming,[53] circling round her love's head.
> 3 A thousand years she thought would bring her time,
>   But all her calculations failed.
> 4 Her lover hurt[54] her heart by leaving[55] her
>   For years; she might have died.
> 5 She swore she'd never say his name again,
>   But in her heart it burned like fire.
> 6 Why so hostile to her?
>   Her mouth is open always to your rain.
> 7 She keeps her faith, does not despair,
>   Whether in your name her lot is pain or fame.
> 8 Let God come now, and not come quietly,
>   But round him raging storms and wild flame.
>
> —Yehuda Halevi, no. 357 (an *'ahavah*),
> "Far-Flown Dove" (יונת רחוקים)[56]

---

50. For the interpretation of the exile as *nedod*, "wandering about," see Gutmann-Grün, *Zion als Frau*, 409–70 and in Gutmann-Grün, "Schlafend auf den Flügeln des Umherirrens. Exilsmetaphorik bei Yehuda Halevi," *Judaica* 2.3 (2008): 97–117.

51. Cf. Ps 56:1 on the mute dove from afar. The Targum declares on this: "In praise of Knesset Israel, which is compared with a mute dove in the time in which she is apart from her cities" (information from the editor Dov Jarden in regard to this passage).

52. The Hebrew word is *nadedah*, "go away, separate oneself, to wander about." See more about this key word in Arabic and Hebrew Andalusian poetry in Gutmann-Grün, *Zion als Frau*, 457–59.

53. Literally "storm-tossed," Isa 54:11.

54. Torment (*'inah*) belongs to the language of love in the secular songs.

55. The Hebrew *nod* (*nedod*) used here can also mean "wandering about," "going away," or "being far away," and is therefore more comprehensive than the Arabic term *firāq*. See Gutmann-Grün, *Zion als Frau*, 457–59.

56. Translation from Scheindlin, *Gazelle*, 71. Annotations are mine.

The negative images such as "fled," "stumbled," and "storm-tossed" contrast sharply with the positive image that she "hovers about her beloved." Thus, the *piyyut* presents the dialectic or paradox of exile. In the book of Isaiah, Zion is also addressed as "storm-tossed" along with "poor" and "unconsoled." Isaiah 54:11 is the beginning of the *haftarah* (the reading from the Prophets) for the third of the seven consolatory *shabbatot* after the Ninth of Av (Isa 54:11–55:5), and it is for this reason that "storm-tossed" belongs to the vocabulary of grief over Jerusalem. The fourth line, though, brings love once again into the misery of the exile; the term *dod* (beloved) for God and also the mention of His *nedod* (going away) point to the Song of Songs, where the beloved likewise goes away for no reason (Song 5:6). The term nedod used here to describe the wandering of the lover is also used in al-Andalus to describe the departing of friends in the songs of friendship. The friend's or lover's *departing* (*nedod*) causes the other to *wander about* (*nedod*) in search of the friend / the beloved: the same term *nedod* is used. The tonal assonance of *nedod* and *dod* is popular with Yehuda Halevi.[57] The heart blazing like a fire (line 5) also belongs, of course, to the language of love, as we already have seen in the third strophe of *piyyut* 326 by Yehuda Halevi quoted above.

Sometimes, the *piyyutim* give reasons for God's departure and then convey the classic interpretation of the exile, as we saw in *piyyut* 326 by Yehuda Halevi. In other *piyyutim* God's departure is formulated as an incomprehensible question: "Dove in Egypt's trap has left her nest. Why have You in wrath forsaken her after having drawn her to Yourself with the bands of love?"[58]

2.2. Fulfillement of Love—Deliverance from Exile

2.2.1. The Place for Love

"May my beloved come into his garden." (Song of Songs 4:16)

Among the places for love in the *piyyut* of al-Andalus are the room (Song 1:4), a sedan chair (3:9), a wine house (2:4), beds of balsam (6:2), a hill

---

57. The same paronomasia is also used by Yehuda Halevi in *piyyut* 206, "The Dove Was Hurt" (יונה נכאבה).
58. E.g., see Yehuda Halevi, no. 379, "A Dove in Egypt's Trap" (יונה בפח מצרים). See §2.3 below.

of frankincense and mountain of myrrh (4:6), a vineyard (1:6; 7:13, see also Isa 5:7), a tent, and a dove's nest.[59] But above all the garden, because of its feminine connotation, has the greatest affinity to the figure of Zion and represents, because of its double valence as "place" and "person," both of these aspects of Zion. The garden is now God's place of residence for which He yearns in order to unite there once again with the Knesset Israel. At another time the garden is itself the feminine figure. The garden can be destroyed, like Jerusalem, but it also can bloom again,[60] as the following *piyyut* shows:

> [1] "Living on the field,[61] together with Kushan's tents,[62]
> Go up to Carmel-mountain, look out toward Bashan,[63]
> [2] your eyes turn to the garden,[64] which was destroyed, O bride,
> look to your little field how it's filled up with lilies."
> [3] "How could you leave my garden, you with your beautiful eyes,
> to browse in Yokshan's garden, under Dishan's trees?
> [4] Come on, go down to my garden,[65] there eat your choice fruits
> and there in the lap of the girl, charming with beautiful eyes (Song 4:9),
> lie down and there you'll sleep.
> —Shlomo ibn Gabirol, no. 95 (a *reshut* for Simhat Torah),
> "Living on the Field" (שוכנת בשדה)

This *piyyut* represents the liberation from exile as a return to the garden, and it dramatizes this in the manner of Song 4:8–9. The male lover, or bridegroom, grasps the initiative and exhorts the female character, the

---

59. The tent is an element that belongs to the *atlāl* motif, especially the deserted tents of the lovers. For an example of the dove's nest, see Yehuda Halevi, no. 324, "Distant Dove, Sing Well" (יונת רחוקים נגני היטיבי).

60. A blossoming garden is an image that also belongs to the repertoire of the songs of praise. For instance, a man or his works are praised as a blossoming garden. See Gutmann-Grün, *Zion als Frau*, 337.

61. See Mic 4:10.

62. Kushan is seen as an appellative for the Arabs, instead of the otherwise usual term Qedar (Gen 25:13; Song 1:5).

63. For Carmel and Bashan, see Jer 50:19. God will lead Israel back to his pasture.

64. This is an echo of Song 4:8: "[Come] with me from Lebanon, my bride ... look down from the mountain peak of Amana."

65. Cf. Song 4:16: "May my beloved come into his garden, and eat its choice fruits [מגדים]!" Song 7:12–13: "Go, my beloved, let us go out to the fields, spend the night under the pomegranate blooms ... there I will give you my love."

bride, to behold once again a blossoming, lily-filled garden. The key word "lilies" calls to mind the beloved, who, in the Song of Songs, "grazes his flock among the lilies" (6:3). The bride who is addressed is self-assured in that, to be sure, she addresses Him affectionately with the praise of His beautiful eyes, but at the same time she charges him with infidelity due to Him leaving her in order to "graze" elsewhere, because He prefers the Arabs (Yokshan) and the Christians (Dishan).[66] The idea that the enemies of Israel become rivals in love is a thought that originates from love poetry. Her invitation to God to come into her garden is formulated by her in the manner of a *kharja* with the almost identical citation from the Song 4:16.[67]

A similar wooing and accusatory invitation to partake in the enjoyment of love is incorporated by Shlomo ibn Gabirol in his *piyyut* 131:

> O You, asleep on golden couches in my palace spread—
> When, O Lord, will You prepare for the ruddy one my bed?
> Why asleep, my handsome stag, why asleep my dear,
> When dawn has risen like a flag on Hermon and Senir?[68]
> Turn aside from desert-asses,[69] turn to the gazelle;[70]
> I am right for one like you, and your kind suits me well.
> He who comes to visit me my precious stores will find:
> My myrrh, my pomegranates (Song 8:2), my cinnamon, my wine (Song 4:13, 14).
>
> —Shlomo ibn Gabirol, no. 131 (a *reshut*),
> "Lying on Golden Beds" (שוכב עלי מטות)[71]

The scene is a palace with golden beds,[72] which refers metaphorically to the temple, in which God resides or "lies." This image has a pleasant effect,

---

66. The attribute "with the beautiful eyes" is applied to David in 1 Sam 16:12, a reference to the messiah. In Song 4:9 the male says that he is enchanted by the bride's eyes. Yokshan, a son of Abraham and Keturah, is an allusion to the Arabs. Dishan is one of the sons of Seir in the land of Edom (Gen 36:20–21). Edom is a codename for Rome, that is, for the Christians.

67. A *kharja* is the conclusion of a love song. See note 42.

68. For Senir and Hermon, see Song 4:8.

69. "Wild ass" is a code word for the Arabs; according to Gen 16:12, Ishmael will be a wild ass of a man.

70. For the chamois of grace, see Prov 5:19.

71. Translation from Scheindlin, *Gazelle*, 101. Annotations are mine.

72. An allusion to the golden cherubim over which God sits on His throne (Exod 25:18; 1 Sam 4:4).

but the speaking female is not satisfied; she immediately puts forth an impatient question: When will God prepare a bed in this palace for the "ruddy one," that is, the messiah?[73] She does not directly ask the question "When will you bring about redemption?" but speaks rather in the metaphors of love, of "preparing a bed." She is highly impatient for the morning, a metaphor for redemption; already it is beginning to dawn, and God still is sleeping. In other *piyyutim*, she is the one sleeping, in keeping with the midrash on Song 5:2; that is, she is in exile and waits until He wakes her for redemption.[74] But here, with Shlomo ibn Gabirol, *she* "wakes" Him by addressing Him and reproaching Him for sleeping and, in addition, for adhering to the wild asses, the Arabs. In opposition to this image of the wild asses, she describes herself as the "chamois of grace." The chamois of grace not only has all the feminine attributes in accordance with Prov 5:19, but she also resides in the palace like the "respectable woman" in love poetry; this woman is called the "gazelle of the palace" in contrast to the "gazelle of the fields, the ordinary, non-aristocratic woman."[75] For this reason, she is the one suitable for Him, a thought which she, in contrast to the beloved woman in the Song of Songs,[76] expresses quite defiantly. Her invitation to Him to come into her palace sounds almost as though she wants to make Him jealous. He should find the "treasure" before someone else comes.

These doubled semantics whereby the palace is, at the same time, the temple and a place for love, are also found in the following *piyyut*:

> Come to me at dawn, love,
>   Carry me away;
> For in my heart I'm thirsting
>   To see my folk[77] today.
> For you, love, mats of gold
>   Within my halls I'll spread.

---

73. "Ruddy" refers to David (1 Sam 16:12) or to the messiah.

74. Song Rab. 5:2 on p. 127, ed. Shimon Dunski (Dvir Publishing, 1980), 127: "I am sleeping from all the (waiting for the) end—my heart is awake for redemption. I am sleeping from all the (waiting for the) redemption—and the heart of the Holy One, blessed be He, is awake in order to redeem me."

75. On the "gazelle of the palace" and the "gazelles of the field," see Gutmann-Grün, *Zion als Frau*, 248 n. 9.

76. Song 2:16, "My beloved is mine and I am his who grazes among the lilies."

77. Like Jarden, I prefer "my mother" (*'immi*) instead of "my folk" (*'ammi*).

> I'll set my table for you,
>   I'll serve you my own bread.
> A drink from my own vineyards
>   I'll pour to fill your cup—
> Heartily you'll drink, love,
>   Heartily you'll sup.
>   I'll take my pleasure with you
> As once I had such joy
> With Jesse's son, my people's prince,
>   That Bethlehem boy.
>
> —Shlomo ibn Gabirol, no. 133 (a *reshut*),
> "Come to Me at Dawn, Love" (שחר עלה אלי דודי)[78]

Read on the literal level, a woman entertains her beloved in her salon and delights herself in him like the loving woman in the Song of Songs (1:4). As in the Song of Songs, eating and drinking "from the grapes of my vineyard" are metaphors for the enjoyment of love. Setting the table, breaking bread, and offering wine also can be understood on the cultic level as references to the sacrificial worship service in the temple. The "dawn" signals from the very beginning that the *piyyut* is invoking the yearning for liberation from the exile, and the conclusion also clearly names the liberator, the messiah: David, the son of Ishai.[79]

With the phrase "to see my mother," the female speaker, the Knesset Israel, shows that her relationship to Zion is like that of a daughter to her mother (see section 3 below).

2.2.2. Beautiful Voice of the Singing Dove

> "Let me hear your voice, for your voice is lovely." (Song 2:14)
> "The voice of the turtledove is heard in our land." (Song 2:12b)

In accordance with the *midrashim* on the Song of Songs,[80] Knesset Israel sang the Song of Songs in her exodus from Egypt just before or during her passage through the Sea of Reeds. For this reason, the Song of Songs

---

78. Translation by Scheindlin, *Gazelle*, 97; annotations mine.
79. See Gutmann-Grün, *Zion als Frau*, 324–26. The dawn is not a time for love; the evening wind is an invitation to love in Song 4:16.
80. See Gutmann-Grün, *Zion als Frau*, 88–102 on the use of the Song of Songs by Jannai and Kallir.

is the prescribed scroll for the celebration of Passover. The first strophe of a *piyyut* for the morning prayer on Passover is quoted here as a short example. The *piyyut* belongs to the genre *nishmat*, and therefore the word *nishmat* (the soul of) is repeated at the beginning of each strophe in reference to the *nishmat* prayer (e.g., "the soul of every living thing shall bless Your name"):

> The soul / of the most beautiful among women (Song 8:11) shall find its joy in the Friend of her youth (God) and in His pleasant speech.
> She shall / sing day after day the song of my friend about his vineyard (Isa 5:1–7; Song 8:11), the "Song of Songs which is Solomon's" (1:1).
> —Yehuda Halevi, no. 159 (a *nishmat* for Passover),
> "The Soul of the Most Beautiful among Women" (נשמת יפת עלמות)

Her role as the singing woman is additionally amplified by the Arabic-Hebrew love songs in which the singing "dove" sometimes is a mirror image of the lovesick speaker, because the voice of the dove was also regarded as plaintive. On the other hand, a friendship poem sometimes is a song from the mouth of a fictitious beautiful singing woman who is sent to the friend in order to praise him.[81]

While in literature the ideal image of a beautiful female singer is always praised, the female singers in the real world are of a lower social status. This does not have a negative effect, however, on the ideal image, so that the poets can use the female singer as a model for Zion. It is precisely her task of singing and praising God that makes her the ideal mirroring figure both for the poet and also for the praying congregation. With this figure, one can identify oneself:

> Distant dove, sing your song well,
> and give good answer to Him who calls you.[82]
> Your God it is Who calls, so hurry,
> bow low to the ground, and make your offering.
> Back to your nest! Retrace your steps

---

81. Shlomo ibn Gabirol sends a song of praise in this form to his patron Yekutiel; see Gutmann-Grün, *Zion als Frau*, 207.

82. On the dove as a messenger of love, see Silvia Schroer, "Altorientalische Bilder als Schlüssel zu biblischen Metaphern," in *Hebräische Bibel—Altes Testament. Schriften und spätere Weisheitsbücher*, ed. Christl Maier and Nuria Calduch-Benages (Stuttgart: Kohlhammer, 2013), 141.

to Zion, where your tent awaits you;
set clear way-posts along the road.
Your lover turned you out because you sinned—
today He redeems you! Why do you complain?
Arise, return to the Lovely Land.[83]
Ruin the fields of Edomite and Arab!
Destroy the home of your destroyers,
but make your love a wide and loving home. (Isa 54:2)

—Yehuda Halevi, no. 324 (an *'ahavah*),
"Distant Dove, Sing Well" (יונת רחוקים נגני היטיבי)[84]

Like a prophet who has heard God's voice (line two), the speaker immediately proclaims imminent liberation to the Knesset Israel, which is addressed as a "dove from afar"[85] or, respectively, to the Zion figure, and commands her to return quickly to Zion. The "mute dove"[86] shall no longer be mute but rather shall sing to her God and answer Him affectionately. She is no longer banished but rather has been freed from her punishment,[87] and she should fly back to her nest, to Zion, and there open wide the "house of love" to her beloved, an image for the rebuilt temple. The redemption, however, is connected with the removal of oppression; this action is here not delegated to God, but rather the Zion figure herself is to destroy in wrath the fields of her enemies: Edom (Christians) and Arabs. The idea of revenge belongs thematically to the hope for liberation, but it is not very pronounced in the *piyyutim*.[88] Striking and new,

---

83. Lovely Land: *Eretz haTzvi*. In this phrase, the Hebrew word *tzvi* means both lovely and gazelle, stemming from two etymologically different roots. Gazelle is also a metaphor for lover.

84. Translation from Raymond Scheindlin, *The Song of the Distant Dove: Judah Halevi's Pilgrimage* (Oxford: Oxford University Press, 2008), 65. Annotations are mine.

85. See n. 59 above.

86. See Ps 56:1. See n. 51 above and Yehuda Halevi piyyut 357.

87. The exile is the punishment for her past transgressions; see above Yehuda Halevi, *piyyut* 326.

88. The battles between Muslims and Christians in al-Andalus beginning around 1086 and the destruction of the Jewish congregation in Jerusalem in 1099 by the Crusaders intensified the expectations of an end time, see Esperanza Alfonso, *Islamic Culture through Jewish Eyes: Al Andalus from the Tenth to the Twelfth Century* (London: Routledge, 2008), 93. In his edition of the text, *Diwan R. Yehuda Halevi* (Lyck, 1864), 2b, Shmuel David Luzzato declared these verses of revenge as "not worthy of a Jewish poet." Remark mentioned in Yahalom, *Yehuda Halevi, Poetry and Pilgrimage*, 12.

however, in the Andalusian *piyyut* is the strengthened self-consciousness of the Zion figure who is able to rebuild the temple and the land, so to speak, with her own hands. Such a vigorous ideal Zion figure compensates literarily for the political weakness of the Jewish community.

Moshe ibn Ezra, too, who often represents himself as *poeta exul* after his departure from Granada (after 1090), calls upon Zion in a *piyyut*: "Dove, may your songs multiply and your singing, in order to gather your scattered ones within your firm walls!"[89] Zion as an autonomous, active feminine coworker of God in the liberation from the exile belongs, in my opinion, to her properties as a mother who defends her children.

The enemies of Israel, too, are seen in the *piyyutim* of al-Andalus in the context of the drama of the love between Zion and God. They receive the role of the evil rivals in love, a role that the Midrash Mekilta on Songs 5:7–9 already gives them.

2.3. Rivals in Love

> "The watchmen who make the rounds in the city found me; they struck me and wounded me.... They took away my veil." (Song 5:7)
> "I adjure you, you daughters of Jerusalem, if you find my beloved, what should you say to him? That I am lovesick."... "Why is then your beloved different ... that you adjure us so?" (Song 5:8, 9)

The seemingly harmless question directed to the female lover that asks in which way her friend surpasses all the others is understood in the Mekilta exegesis as criticism of Israel by other nations.[90] The "daughters of Jerusalem" are identified as the "nations" who criticize Israel because of her love for God and who want to seduce her to renounce God. They are characterized in *piyyut* 379 by Yehuda Halevi as "traitors and ambushers" because they claim for themselves God's bridal gifts of love to Zion, the "veil and the wrought necklace," and they want to force their way into the relationship. They are worse than the watchmen in Song 5:7 because they not only rob Zion of her veil, but they also adorn themselves with it (here a partial quotation):

---

89. Moshe ibn Ezra, no. 2, "Dove, Your Singing" (יונה זמירך). Text in Bernstein, *Shire ha-Qodesh*. This *piyyut* is for the *'ashmorot* (night watches) in the month before the New Year's feast.

90. See Hayim Shaul Horovitz, ed., *Mekhilta de Rabbi Yishmael* (Jerusalem: Bamberger & Wahrman, 1960), *Beshallaḥ deShiratah*, 3, 127.

Dove in Egypt's trap, / among oppressing foes / has left her nest.
Why angrily did You forsake her / after with loving ties / near you'd drawn her to You?

¹ My heart is pounding (Song 5:4) and ailing / since my lover left [*nod*].
How can put on my veil (Song 5:7) / the oppressing foes?
How do they rob my jewels, / traitors, waiting in ambush?[91]

How does the prudent spouse / stripped of her precious clothes / silent just lie down,
after His left hand (Song 8:3) had / shielded me, and love / over me had been His banner. (Song 2:4)

² The covenant of youth, / my friend and my lover, remember! (Jer 2:2)
How can You abandon to strangers / Your inheritance, left imprisoned.
Or do You want to escape / like a gazelle over the mountains? (Song 2:17; 8:14)

—Yehuda Halevi, no. 379 (an *'ahavah*),
"Dove in Egypt's Trap" (יונה בפח מצרים)

The idea that Israel's enemies become rivals in love comes not only from the exegesis of the Song of Songs, but the idea is also reinforced by the Arabic literature of love. There, it is a topos that the jealous critics of the loving couple[92] slander the beloved in the eyes of the lover because they themselves desire him (or her).

In the *piyyut*, Zion's chief rivals are the "daughters of Edom," that is, the Christians, or "Hagar" or her son "Ishmael," that is, the Arabs. The following examples should suffice to illustrate this point.

Yehuda Halevi writes in a *me'orah* for the Shabbat before the Ninth of Av: "The beautiful daughter of the king has become the handmaiden of the daughter of Molech, who the Eternal has appointed for the pres-

---

91. Traitors and ambushers (בוגדים ואורבים).
92. The medieval handbook "Das Halsband der Taube" (The Necklace of the Dove), written in 1027, devotes a chapter each to various figures. See Léon Bercher, *Ibn Hazm al-Andalusi, Le Collier du Pigeon: Texte arabe et Traduction française* (Alger: Carbonel, 1949); Haviva Ishai, "Patterns in the Secular Literature of Love (Ghazal) in the Cultural Sphere of Medieval Spain. How Arabic Narrative Tales Can Help Us Understand Hebrew Love Poetry in spite of the Difference between the Two Forms of Discourse" (PhD diss., Tel Aviv, 2001), 137–68.

ent generation."[93] This harsh statement, that God Himself could prefer the Christians, is new in al-Andalus in comparison with the classic *piyyut*. In the classic *piyyut*, to be sure, Arabs and Christians are typologized as the enemies of Israel, but only with regard to the secular, worldly power; they are not represented as rivals to Israel for God's love.[94]

In another *me'orah* with the same liturgical purpose, Yehuda Halevi lets Zion lament: "My beloved has abandoned the lovely chamois and remembered the son of Mahalath; every day I cry from heartache while he sings and plays a song."[95]

In allusion to the Arabs, Shlomo ibn Gabirol describes Zion as "a captive, wretched woman, taken in a foreign land to be a handmaiden for the Egyptian handmaiden."[96] Here Hagar, the mother of Ishmael, that is, the mother of the Arabs, is meant. The paradox exists in the fact that the Knesset Israel, sometimes personified as Sarah (which also means "female ruler"), now has become the handmaiden of her own handmaiden Hagar.[97]

Along with these lamenting tones, there are also the triumphal ones too, as we have seen above in *piyyut* 131 by Shlomo ibn Gabirol ("Lying on Golden Beds") in which Zion, as a "chamois of grace," places herself above the "wild asses" (i.e., Arabs).

3. Zion as Mother

In the Bible, the typical mother figure grieving for her children is Rachel.[98] The image of Zion as a lamenting mother is also found in the *piyyut*.[99] Yehuda Halevi writes, for example: "The delightful hind, saddened, waits

---

93. Yehuda Halevi, no. 390 (a *me'orah*), "She Was Sitting Desolate and Deserted" (ישבה שוממה). This poem is the first Berakhah of the morning prayer. Molech, the "Horror of the Ammonites" (1 Kgs 11:7), is a code name for the Christians.

94. Gutmann-Grün, *Zion als Frau*, 368, on the *piyyutim* of Jannai and Kallir (sixth to eighth century, land of Israel).

95. Yehuda Halevi, no. 208 (a *me'orah*), "When to the Mountain of Myrrh" (מתי להר חמור). Mahalath, the daughter of Ishmael, becomes Esau's wife (Gen 28:9). A son is not mentioned.

96. Shlomo ibn Gabirol, no. 163 (a *ge'ulah*), "Captive, Wretched Woman" (שביה עניה). A *piyyut* for the third Berakhah of the morning prayer.

97. Gutmann-Grün, *Zion als Frau*, 353–72.

98. See Jer 31:15: "A voice of lamentation is heard on the hill, the sound of bitter weeping: Rachel weeps for her children and cannot be comforted."

99. See n. 21.

upon the call of help ... on the wings of the wind is heard the voice of Rachel, who mourns."[100]

New in al-Andalus now, though, is Rachel's role as intercessor for her children. In this role she turns to God: "May You once again choose my abode and erect for the sons of Your servants the temple of the Eternal that Your hands have erected," writes Yehuda Halevi in a *piyyut* for the ending of Shabbat.[101]

The view of Zion as a mother is expanded in the first strophe of the following *piyyut* by Yehuda Halevi by adding God as father of the "children of Israel":

> Graceful deer, your voice is sweet, (Song 1:14)
>   while over Horev's laws[102] you reflect.
> ¹ Daughter of My faithful ones, recall in your heart
> ² how you stood on mount Sinai
> ³ and answer all my haters' gang:
> ⁴ "what, oppressors, do you plague My sons?"
> ⁵ "My son, oppressed even if down he lies
> ⁶ The Eternal, high on clouds he rides!" (Isa 19:1)
>   —Yehuda Halevi, no. 181 (an *'ahavah* for Shavuot),
>   "Graceful Deer, Your Voice Is Sweet" (יעלת חן קולך)

Zion, or the Knesset Israel, the daughter of the faithful (the Jews), is reminded by God of the revelation on Sinai, which is celebrated on Shavuot. She is given the commission to rebuke, in the name of God, the enemies who beset the sons of Israel, and to point out the fact of His power to reveal Himself once again at any time, as on Sinai where He "came down in fire on the mountain of Sinai" (Exod 19:18). It remains uncertain whether, in line four, it is God who speaks of His sons, or whether it is Zion who here begins to speak. But, because God speaks in line three about those "who hate Me," it is more likely that He is the one who says "My sons" in line four, and that only in line five does Zion speak of "my son." In my opinion, the ambiguity is intended: the sons of Israel have, as it were, father and mother, God and Zion.

---

100. Yehuda Halevi, no 152, "Call, Your Angels of Heaven" (קראו מלאכי). A *piyyut* for Passover; see lines 3–5.

101. Yehuda Halevi, no. 272, "Friendship of My Soul" (ידידות נפשי). See lines 33–36.

102. Horev is equivalent to Sinai; by the laws of Horev, the Torah is meant.

Zion's search for her beloved (God), through the motif of yearning, also has enriched her depiction as a mother: She is not only the mother who has lost her children, but also the mother for whom, or for whose room, the children yearn.[103] An example of this is the following *piyyut* by Yehuda Halevi for the nights of repentance (*'ashmorot*) before the New Year's feast (two and a half strophes out of five):

> [1] Jerusalem, moan, and Zion, let your tears flow,
> because your children—when they remember you, their eyes can't hold back weeping.
> May my right hand be crippled, if I forget you, city of everlasting glory,
> may my tongue stick to the roof of my mouth, if I don't remember you![104]
> [2] Look, my sins drove me out of the house of my mother,
> And my father had determined a catastrophic end for me because of my sin,
> and my brother together with the son of my handmaiden[105] have taken my birthright for themselves.
> Therefore, pour out, my soul, your supplications to your rock.
> [3] Offer your cheeks to those who scratch them; don't hide your face from spitting (Isa 50:6).
> —Yehuda Halevi, no. 251 (a *selihah* for the *'ashmorot*),
> "Jerusalem, Moan" (ירושלים האנחי)

As in *piyyut* 181, the speaker sees himself as a child of the father/God and the mother/Zion.

4. Conclusion

In prayer poetry, Zion as a female speaker or as the one addressed has the role, on the one hand, of the beloved or the bride of God. On the other, she has the role of the mother of the children of Israel. The praying person can identify herself or himself with the speaking or addressed figure of Zion as an "I," not only as a "we" of the congregation. Even when the praying person addresses her as mother, the person praying speaks in a personal tone of

---

103. See above in *piyyut* 133 by Shlomo ibn Gabirol.
104. The two lines cite Ps 137:5–6 in a slightly varied form.
105. "My brother" refers to Esau (Gen 27:11); "son of my handmaiden" is Ishmael (Gen 21:9).

voice, as a child to a parent, so to speak. This personal tone originated in the fact that, toward the end of the tenth century, the poets of liturgical poetry in al-Andalus also wrote secular songs, a first in Hebrew literature.

Common to both liturgical and secular songs were love motifs such as yearning, disappointment, lament, and the enjoyment of love. In the secular poems, which are not the subject of this article, the Zion figure also could appear: Shmuel Hanagid and Yehuda Halevi are outstanding examples for this, as I note only very briefly here. We see how their lyrical "I" turns with its yearning for liberation from exile to Zion, just as we have found the same theme of redemption in *piyyutim*.

Shmuel Hanagid, for example, began his victory song/song of praise to God, "My Heart Burns,"[106] about a battle that he had to fight in 1041 by order of King Badis (1038–1073) against the prince of the Berbers, Yaddair, with words of wistful longing for the "daughter in the garden of nut trees" (Song 6:11). Like a visionary, he described the return of the "young men of Zion to Zion, the noble daughter whose garden is now occupied by roaring lions."[107] In this and other battles against enemies of the city-state of Granada, he saw himself as a Jew who, like David, Moses, or Mordechai, wages a messianic struggle against the enemies of Israel.[108]

In a completely different style, one rather like that in Ps 137, Yehuda Halevi created a new genre of odes to Zion, which had no liturgical function. One of them, though, the thirty-four line Ode 401, was taken up in the course of time in the Ashkenazi rite into the *kinot* for the Ninth of Av, and it has inspired poets up to the present time.[109] For this reason, the first lines are quoted here:

Jerusalem! Have you no greeting
for your captive hearts, your last remaining flocks,
who send you messages of love?
Here are greetings for you from west and east,
from north and south, from near and far, from every side—

---

106. Shmuel Hanagid, no. 9, "My Heart Burns" (לבבי בקרבי חם).
107. Line eight of the poem.
108. For more on the poem, see Gutmann-Grün, *Zion als Frau*, 238–40.
109. P. Halevi Bamberger, *Die Trauergesänge für Tishah beab (Lamentations for Tisha B'Av)* (Basel: Viktor Goldschmidt, 1983), 256–60. On Yehuda Halevi, no. 401, see Gutmann-Grün, *Zion als Frau*, 240–45. On the history of reception, see Yahalom, *Yehuda Halevi*, 1–7. Naomi Shemer took over the expression "I am your harp" in her song "Jerusalem of Gold" (*Yerushalayim shel Zahav*) in 1967 (before the Six-Day War).

greetings also from a certain man,
a captive of your love,[110]
who pours his tears like dew on Mount Hermon,
and longs to shed them on your slopes.
My voice is like a jackal's when I mourn your suffering,
but when I dream of how your exiles will return,
I turn into a lyre.[111]

—Yehuda Halevi, no. 401,
"Zion, Will You not Ask" (ציון הלא תשאלי)[112]

---

110. Following Zech 9:12, the returnees from the exile are "prisoners of hope."

111. That is, the dreams and the singing of the returnees to Zion. Ps 126:1–2 is spoken on Shabbat and on feast days in the Berakhah after the meals, on workdays, however, Ps 137 is spoken.

112. Translation from Scheindlin, *Song of the Distant Dove*, 173–77. Annotations are mine.

Mysticism

The Development of the Feminine Dimension of God in the Mystic Tradition

Rachel Elior

Unlike other languages, Hebrew has no gender-neutral nouns or any gender-neutral verbs. Each inflection of a verb in all of its tenses, each and every pronoun, every pluralization of a noun and its accompanying adjective, each compound construct (noun or adjective) touching on person, object, or concept—in *all* such cases the speaker or writer must choose between the feminine or masculine form of expression. This iron-clad grammatical requirement has far-reaching consequences concerning the identity of an unseen biblical God, a God who creates and who explains, a giver of laws and dispenser of justice and benevolence, one who makes appearances both in myth and story, finally a God who imparts lawfulness to the unfolding of history itself.

According to Jewish tradition, which extends back to days of antiquity, this God, having no visible form or body, nevertheless possesses the power of clear and lucid speech directly addressing the forefathers and prophets of the Jewish nation who, having heard God's spoken words, set them down in writing. However, this is a God who speaks in the masculine voice, first heard by the entire nation during the Covenant of Sinai and read from the Torah with limpid clarity each and every Shabbat beginning in those days of antiquity and right up to present times.

In all references to the biblical God, that God speaks in the masculine voice—whether elaborating, commanding, assuring, or narrating in both prose and poetry. This God leaves no room for doubt as to the identity of the speaker: a male entity that is eternal, all-powerful, authoritative, wise, all-knowing, source of law and justice—an everlasting and ever-relevant presence. Furthermore, whenever one of the biblical heroes, be they prophet or poet, addresses God, they do so in the masculine form of whatever verbs, pronouns, or adjectives used. Indeed, we can state with complete certainty that, in all descriptions of the biblical God, one cannot find a single instance of an exclusively female entity, both divine and immortal, in possession of her own independent voice—this despite the fact that in the ancient prebiblical writings that have come to light in archeological findings from the eighth century BCE one can find references to Asherah, goddess of fertility and, from our knowledge of the Canaanite pantheon, also wife to God himself. This ancient and godlike female figure completely disappears from the Jewish monotheistic thought of biblical times.

All this begs these questions: When is it that we can discern, for the very first time, the voice of a female entity, unencumbered by the constraints of a mortal earthly body, possessing a name, and endowed with her own life story? And what were the circumstances that first gave rise to this immortal female entity speaking in the first-person voice, whose words are spoken, heard, written, and then read?

The unanticipated answer is to be found in the voice of the Shekhinah, a term never mentioned in biblical texts, whose two-stage evolution as an immortal presence with female attributes occurs first in the sixth century BCE in the aftermath of the destruction of Jerusalem and the first temple at the hands of the Babylonian King Nebuchadnezzar II and his army, and secondly in 70 CE following on the destruction of Jerusalem and the second temple at the hands of Titus, commander of the Roman army. In other words, an immortal female voice first makes its appearance in Judaism as the female personification of Jerusalem, a city in mourning, weeping at the ravages of an unimaginable catastrophe that takes in both the destruction of the first temple, God's place of residence, and of Jerusalem herself, the holy city in which God has chosen to dwell. This female voice emerges against the accepted monotheistic tradition of the biblical world order, which holds no place for her, and over the centuries it develops into a multidimensional presence.

1. The Rabbinic Period

The Shekhinah embodied the divine presence in the Jewish congregation in the new forms of divine worship that emerged in the world of the sages after the destruction of the temple. The priestly service in the sanctuary no longer existed and Jerusalem was no more; a considerable portion of the people had been killed, and a large number had gone into exile. For thousands of years, the Shekhinah had carried within herself in allusions, in explicit forms, in her nature, and in her symbols all those concrete holy things that had been lost: the Holy of Holies and the cherubim; the temple on Mount Zion; the holy cult of the priests and Levites that was bound together with the liturgical-mystical language of the temple; and the Holy Language (Hebrew) of the priestly order. She embodied the presentation of the offering in the temple in seven-year ritual cycles; the cycles of holy hymns; the revelatory teaching of the priesthood and prophecy; Zion and Jerusalem; and the congregation of Israel in its own land. Now, she emerged as a new and many-faceted form of the divine presence in the world of the sages. That world encompassed those who learn Torah, pray, speak benedictions, go into exile and in those places of exile continue to thrive, by combining the Holy Language and Aramaic. The Oral Torah, in turn, was bound together with the Shekhinah and human speech so that the holy place was not limited to a geographic or historic holy place. That physical and geographically located holy complex, the temple on Mount Zion, had been lost. It was replaced by the timeless "world of speech" composed of the letters of the Holy Language established in the Written Torah and a speaking, changing spirit found in a divine and a human dimension at the same time—"voice, spirit, and speech: that is the Holy Spirit," in the words of the Sefer Yetzirah (Book of Creation). The Holy Spirit, an expression that the Sefer Yetzirah coined, is the spirit of God, who creates the world by means of speech, who makes and renews creation every day through the letters of the Holy Language, with whose power the world was created, and who reveals itself in the spirit of the human being who studies these letters and, in them, creates further. The world of speech in the Holy Language is a world that contains study, benedictions and prayer, preaching and exegesis, the administration of justice, halakhah and haggadah, poetry and translation. All of these come together in the figure of the Shekhinah, who is designated as "world of speech" and embodies the weaving together of Oral Torah and the Written Torah. In the same period, the absolute duty to teach this language to all sons was established in Sifre, the halakic midrash on Deut 11:19: "When the infant begins to speak, his father shall speak with him in the Holy Language and shall teach him Torah; and if he does not speak with him in the Holy Language and does not teach him Torah—it will be so counted against him as though he buried him."

The Shekhinah is an immanent divine presence and exists as a feminine reality in the world of those who learn and pray. She was combined after the destruction of the second temple with three new elements that have to do with the world of speech in the Holy Language and were strictly adhered to in the holy Jewish congregation. First, she represents the study of the Oral Torah, which replaced the temple and the holy cult: "Ten who sit with each other and deal with the Torah—the Shekhinah is found between them" (m. 'Avot 3:6). Second, she embodies the prayer that replaced the sacrificial cult in the temple: "Ten who pray—the Shekhinah is with them" (b. Ber. 6a). Finally, she is a diffused divine presence that accompanies the children of Israel at all times in the holy congregations in exile, in which all the sons are taught the Holy Language as their only language: "R. Shim'on bar Yochai says: Come and see how much the Holy One, blessed be He, loves Israel—at everyplace whence they were banned is the Shekhinah with them" (b. Meg. 29a); "everywhere where Israel went into exile, the Shekhinah went with them into exile" (Yalkut Shim'oni on 1 Sam 2:92).

Along with the biblical God, the Creator and Lawgiver, the God of history and the covenant whose speaking and lawgiving masculine memory survived in the Written Torah, in the language of revelation, there emerged in the course of exile in the first Christian millennium a new feminine divine being. This being is bound together with the earthly and heavenly "Assembly of Israel." She creates in the Holy Language and awakens to new life in the new word-creation in the world of the sages. She breaks out of the world of the Bible and finds her expression in the Mishnah and in prayer, in preaching and exegesis, in halakah and jurisprudence, in the benedictions and legends, in the midrashim and *piyyutim* (poetry), in the salvation midrashim and in the hekhalot literature (mysticism of the world of the heavenly throne).

The biblical world before the sages had united the physical holy place that God had chosen in order to let His name dwell there (the temple), with the holy eternal cycles of the holy feasts. These feasts were, in turn, connected with the pilgrimage to the holy city and with the holy cult of sacrificial worship and the holy guardians around the temple in Jerusalem and the holy biblical books. Those books described the particulars of the established, eternal, continual cycles of the holy cult, which were bound together with the Written Torah, holy reading, priesthood, and the masculine figure of God speaking at a single holy place. In contrast, in the world that emerged in the language of the sages after the destruction of the temple, every place, every time, every worship service in the heart, all oral learning, every sermon and every exegesis, every discussion and every legal pronouncement of the halakah in the Holy Language that created a connection between the holy biblical text and the study of it in halakah and haggadah, in midrash and *piyyut*, could become the place of the feminine Shekhinah. She represents the Oral Torah in its various aspects. The Oral Torah is in a constant state of creation simply by virtue of the human speaking of the Holy Language; this language changes in the course of the generations, each generation adding its own creative mix of new ideas to the biblical foundation. Another aspect of the Oral Torah is that it is continually created in the mouth of those who learn and connect with the world of speech, that is, with the Shekhinah, who is found everywhere where learning and praying in the Holy Language occurs.

During the first millennium, the figure of the Shekhinah goes with her children into exile, is found in exile, and expects redemption. The Shekhinah was also identified with the eternal, earthly, and heavenly "Assembly of Israel," which was seen as the Beloved and with whom at the feast of Shavuot, the feast of the giving of the Torah, the covenant on Sinai was concluded. Likewise, the Shekhinah was identified with the Oral Torah, which is created continually in the circle of those learning and praying. Their act of learning the Holy Language renewed the covenant by virtue of the act of learning during speech and by virtue of the act of creation in the continually expanding language of the sages, of the midrash and *piyyut*, of prayer and the *merkabah* (divine chariot) tradition. The Shekhinah was understood as the one present with her holy presence in the group of those learning and praying who everyday pray in the Holy Language for the coming of the messiah and the return to Zion. Everywhere that "three study the Torah, there the Shekhinah is found among them" or "ten who pray—the Shekhinah is among them" (Pirqe Avot 3:6).

The messiah, who, like the Shekhinah, was born on the Ninth of Av, the day of the destruction of the temple, is described in the haggadic and salvation midrashim, which were composed in the second half of the first Christian millennium, as one fettered in a prison in criminal Rome, the city that destroyed Jerusalem, as a leper who binds his wounds or as a bitterly weeping prisoner in a prison. But the messiah, like the Shekhinah, had additional changeable dimensions that expressed the hope of the persecuted exiles: the messiah, it was said, would eventually be freed from prison and would exercise the vengeance of the persecuted who yearn for a just, heavenly judgment in a world in which they experienced no justice from human beings. The Shekhinah was similarly described, on the six days of the week, as a widow, a divorced woman, and, like the messiah, a prisoner. On the Sabbath, the Shekhinah was the beloved, the bride representing salvation. Finally, the Shekhinah was the place of rest for the dead of Israel, who hoped "to find true rest under the wings of the Shekhinah" (Sifre Deut. 355; b. Sotah 13).

The feminine figure of this divine presence was changing and multifaceted. During the workdays, the Shekhinah was the widowed, weeping, exiled Daughter of Zion yearning for redemption. On the Sabbath, the Shekhinah was the Mother of Zion (beginning with the Septuagint translation of Ps 87; 4 Ezra 8; Pesiq. Rab. 26) and was the beloved bride who unites herself on the Sabbaths and feast days as the "Assembly of Israel" with her beloved. The Shekhinah figure embodied the Oral Torah and was the divine presence among those who learn, study, and pray. Finally, the Shekhinah was the last resting place of the dead who, in the garden of Eden, "find true rest under the wings of the Shekhinah."[1]

2. The Early Kabbalists

The kabbalists who were active between the end of the thirteenth century up until the end of the fifteenth century in southern France and northern Spain carried through a radical change in regard to the conceptions of God, the Shekhinah, the Torah and commandments, the halakah, and the human being.[2] In their literature, they depicted the Shekhinah for the first time in relationship to God, instead of just in relationship to the holy city and to the people of Israel. They set her place in the world of the *sefirot*.

Kabbalah commenced in the twelfth century in Provence with the anonymous Sefer Habahir (Book of Illumination) composed in Hebrew and in the style of the midrashim, a book that combined unprecedented ideas with the seemingly well-known framework of exegesis. Kabbalah

---

1. *El Malei Rachamim* is a Jewish prayer for the soul of a person who has died, usually recited at the graveside during the burial service and at memorial services during the year.

2. Gershom Scholem, *On the Kabbakah and Its Symbolism* (New York: Schocken, 1965); Scholem, *On the Mystical Shape of the Godhead: Basic Concepts of the Kabbalah* (New York: Schocken, 1991); Scholem, *Major Trends in Jewish Mysticism* (New York: Schocken, 1946); Rachel Elior, *Jewish Mysticism: The Infinite Expression of Freedom* (Oxford: Littman Library of Jewish Civilization, 2007); Moshe Idel, *Kabbalah: New Perspectives* (New Haven: Yale University Press, 1988); Arthur Green, "Shekhinah, the Virgin Mary, and the Song of Songs: Reflections on a Kabbalistic Symbol in Its Historical Context," *AJSR* 26.1 (2002): 1–52.

researcher Joseph Dan has characterized the uniqueness of this text in this way: "In the Sefer HaBahir, the people of Israel were provided with a position of power, which influences and shapes the form and the status of the divine world."[3]

Sefer Habahir concerns itself with a two-faced God that is divided into an upper and a lower area. The masculine God is construed as the highest emanation source (*maʿazil*), as the origin of light and the creation, and as the origin of the written law. Under it is found the emanated (*neʿezal*) area of the Shekhinah, the daughter of light who is described as a recipient of splendor. The author articulates for the first time an intrinsic identity between the Shekhinah and the halakah and says that the actions carrying out the commandments are the limbs of the Shekhinah and that the Shekhinah is the mystical location of the 248 positive commandments that correspond to the 248 limbs of the human being. Alon Dahan, who has researched Sefer Habahir, describes the innovation:

> The Shekhinah now is identified with the religious act, which is bound with the commandments and the halakhic prescriptions and which is left to human beings. The body of the Shekhinah is equated with the divine being that receives the emanation from the upper level of the divinity, but she is at the same time identical with the acts of the people of Israel and with the Halakhah, which composes her body. The *Sefer Habahir* establishes a clear identity between the Halakhah, inclusive of its practical observance, and the Shekhinah in the following words: "When they [Israel] are good and just, then the Shekhinah dwells among them, and through their works they linger in God's bosom, and he lets them be fruitful and multiply" [Sefer HaBahir, sign 119].[4] The same Shekhinah that is found in the deeds of Israel is hidden in the bosom of the Holy One, blessed be He, and is the emanated area of the "Holy One, blessed be He."[5]

The Sefer Habahir established the distinction between the masculine emanation source and the feminine emanated being in the mystical

---

3. Joseph Dan, "A Re-evaluation of the 'Ashkenazi Kabbalah'" [Hebrew], *Jerusalem Studies in Jewish Thought* 6 (1987): 138–39. See also Joseph Dan, *Early Kabbalistic Circles* [Hebrew], vol. 7 of *History of Jewish Mysticism and Esotericism: The Middle Ages* (Jerusalem: Zalman Shazar, 2012).

4. Following the Hebrew edition by Reuven Margaliot, ed., *Sefer ha-Bahir* (Jerusalem: Kook, 1978), 53.

5. Alon Dahan, "Ashkenazic Motifs in the Halachah of the 'Bahir'" [Hebrew], *Jerusalem Studies in Jewish Thought* 22 (2011): 162–63.

tradition. It also established the identification of the Creator with the Written Torah and the Shekhinah with the halakah and the Oral Torah, whereby both received a new mystical position. The emanated space was enriched with new comparisons and symbols that stood in relationship to the halakah as well as with mysticism; these symbols lent a new content to the world of religious practice, which was bound together with the Shekhinah. The Shekhinah proves in the Sefer Habahir to be a many-faceted being who can don and cast off interchangeable forms. Sometimes she is the recipient of splendor and sometimes the Daughter of Light; sometimes she is the thirty-two wonderful pathways of truth of the Sefer Yetzirah, which consist of "twenty-two basic letters and ten bodiless [infinite] *sefirot* (numbers)." Sometimes she is called blessing, wisdom, Torah, and beginning; sometimes she is the tree of knowledge of good and evil or a tree that grows from two sides; sometimes she is the "Eternal Living One," and sometimes she is the halakah and the commandments; sometimes she is the king's daughter, the kingdom, and the splendor. It is said about her that her bridegroom is the "Holy One, Blessed be He." The author of the Sefer Habahir says about this emanated being: "And in his great love for her, he sometimes calls her 'my sister,' for they come from one place, sometimes he calls her 'my daughter,' for she is [of course] his daughter, and sometimes he calls her 'my mother'" (Sefer Habahir, sign 63).[6] There is no hierarchy among the daughter, the sister, the bride, and the mother. The subject here is a single, emanated being. The Shekhinah is designated by names that change according to the theme of the allegory treated. The innovation of Sefer Habahir is that the intimate and familial relationships between God and the Shekhinah, or between the King and the bride, are dependent exclusively upon the people of Israel and upon its mystically motivated observance of the commandments. The people of Israel are bound together with the body of the Shekhinah and upon the observance of the halakah. This relationship is identical with the union of the Shekhinah with her beloved, or with her distance from him, because of Israel and through Israel (Sefer Habahir, sign 76).[7] The school of Ramban (Nachmanides) has this description of the Shekhinah:

---

6. Margaliot, *Sefer ha-Bahir*, 29; Aryeh Kaplan, trans., *The Bahir: Illumination* (York Beach, ME: Weiser, 1989), 205–32.

7. Margaliot, *Sefer ha-Bahir*, 33; Kaplan, *The Bahir*, §§51, 52–53. See also Gershom Scholem, *Origins of the Kabbalah* (Philadelphia: Jewish Publication Society, 1987).

The tenth Sefirah [attribute/emanation] called *Shekhinah*, is the crown....
And it is [i.e., symbolized by] this world, for the guidance of this world
is affected by [the pleroma] that comes to it from the... seven upper
Sefiroth.... And it is called "angel" and "the angel of God" ... and it is the
bride of the Song of Songs who is called "daughter" and "sister"; and it is
Kenesseth Yisra'el [literally, "Gathering of Israel"], in which everything is
ingathered. It is the supernal Jerusalem and in prayers it is known as Zion.[8]

In the second millennium, kabbalah transformed the Godhead and propounded a dynamic conception of the divinity as a unity of contrasts. Poured into the being of God was human bisexuality and the transformations contained within it that are connected with unity, conception, pregnancy, birth, and fertility. The kabbalists dared to do this against the conventions of the monotheistic tradition, which separates the divine from the human and the abstract from the material. They took this path because of the terrible physical annihilation of the Jewish congregations along the Rhine by the Crusaders and the dismaying breakdown of the continuity of life. The news that Jews were murdered for no reason created in the kabbalists a deep need for protest against the arbitrariness of history and the destruction of Jewish life in Ashkenaz (Germany) among the Jewish thinkers in southern France and northern Spain.[9] They articulated this protest by creating a new language based upon an imaginary heavenly world with a masculine divine figure and a feminine divine figure. The masculine divine figure, the "Holy One, Blessed be He," who gave the Torah, is described with the terms husband, king, bridegroom, and light or source. The feminine divine figure, the Shekhinah, the Oral Torah, is portrayed as a bride, daughter of the king, daughter of light, the number thirty-two or heart (in gematria the heart, לב, is equal to thirty-two), garden, and tree. Between the two a relationship of union, mating, unification, fertility, birth, and continuity is played out. As a consequence of this relationship, new souls among the children of Israel are born who wait in the treasury of souls in the garden of Eden until the moment arrives in which they come into the world.[10]

---

8. Scholem, *On the Mystical Shape of the Godhead*, 172.

9. See Robert Chazan, *European Jewry and the First Crusade* (Berkeley: University: University of California Press, 1987).

10. See Isaiah Tishby and Fischel Lachower, eds., *The Wisdom of the Zohar: An Anthology of Texts*, trans. David Goldstein, 3 vols. (Oxford: Oxford University Press, 1989), 2:677–83.

The Zohar, which is attributed by tradition to the Tanna Rabbi Shim'on bar Yochai from the circle of sages of the Oral Torah, was composed toward the end of the thirteenth century in Spain by Rabbi Moses de Leon. He wanted to break apart the boundaries between the written past and the present revealed in the dream, between the hidden and the revealed. This breach would be achieved through the mysteries of the Holy Language, which reveals the path of the transition from exile to redemption, the path of the mystical union of Written and Oral Torah as bridegroom and bride. In his book written in Hebrew and Aramaic, he treats the Shekhinah as a feminine dimension of the divinity in more detail than any other author before him when he describes the wedding night that is consummated on Shavuot, the feast of remembrance of the eternal covenant of Sinai and the annually renewed gift of the Torah. In the first part, it says:

> R. Shim'on sat there and concerned himself with the Torah in the night, in which the bride unites with her spouse, as we have learned it: All the companions of the sons of the temple of the bride must, in that night in which the bride makes herself ready to stand on the following day with her spouse under the *Chuppa* (bridal canopy), be with her the whole night long and rejoice with her in all the things that she has experienced that have led to her perfection [*tiqqunim*]: to concern herself with the Torah—from the Torah to the Prophets, from the Prophets to the Writings—with the *aggadic* exegesis of verses, and with the secrets of Wisdom, for these are the things that lead to her perfection and are her ornaments. She enters with her maidens, stands at the head of them, and is made perfect through them the whole night long and delights in them. And when she takes her place under the *Chuppa*, then does the Holy One, blessed be He, inquire about them, blesses her, and crowns her with the diadems of the bride. Happy is their lot! (Zohar 1:8a)[11]

In another version of the *tiqqun* for the night of the feast of Shavuot, the unification of the bridegroom, who gives the written Torah in the language of revelation, the bride, who is the Shekhinah, the "Assembly of Israel," which creates the Oral Torah in every generation, is described as such:

> The secret of the feast of Shavuot.... The old ones of blessed memory, the pillars of the world, those who knew how to draw wisdom from the heights, were in the habit of not sleeping in these two nights of Shavuot.

---

11. English translation by Tishby and Lachower, *Zohar*, 3:1318.

The whole night they read in the Torah, the Prophets, and the Writings; from there, they go over to the Talmud and to the *Aggadot* and read until dawn in the Wisdom literature in the secrets of the Torah, and this was passed down by their fathers.... And on them [the days of the *Omer* reckoning] the Bride adorns herself and enters into the presence of the Highness, and that fiftieth night, this is the night for the Lord for uniting the written Torah with the Oral Torah. Her only sons on earth lead her under the *Chuppa*, and they are recorded and inscribed in the Book of Memories, for they strike up songs of joy and jubilation over the Torah in the night of the Bride's joy.... For this reason, they, for jubilation over the Torah, need not pay any ransom for their souls, for they are inscribed before the Lord.... Then the Lord will listen; He will hear and will inscribe the memory of it before Himself with jubilation. (Schocken MS 14, folio 87.1–2)[12]

The innovation that kabbalah brought lay in the fact that it presented a completely new understanding of traditional religious conduct. It did so by identifying the Shekhinah with the commandments and the halakot; it claimed that every action that the human being carries out in thought, speech, and conduct and that has to do with the Torah and the commandments, the halakah and prayer, the duties and prohibitions, as well as with the ethics of justice and injustice exercises a decisive influence upon the cosmic struggle between the powers of exile and redemption, between the Shekhinah and the "shell" (*qelippa*). Every action in the language of kabbalah is termed intention (*kavanah*), unification (*yikhud*), contemplation (*hitbonenut*), ecstasy (*hitpa'alut*), or devotion (*devequt*). Such action influences the perpetual, cosmic struggle carried out in heaven and on earth between the "holy side" (*sitra' qedusha*) and the "other side" (*sitra' 'akhra*), between the messiah and Samael, or between the powers of good and evil. Every such religious action in every dimension that is accompanied by the intention of unification and devotion contributes directly to the redemption of the Shekhinah out of the pit of imprisonment, to the liberation of the messiah from his fetters, to the acceleration of the end, and to the coming of redemption.

---

12. Cited in Jakob David Wilhelm, "Sidre Tiqqunim" [Hebrew], in *Alei Ayin: The Salman Schocken Jubilee Volume; Contributions on Biblical and Post-biblical Hebrew Literature, Poetry and Belles-lettres; Issued on the Occasion of His Seventieth Birthday by a Circle of His Friends* (Jerusalem: Schocken, 1952), 126. Cf. Tishby and Lachower, *Zohar*, 3:1258.

The kabbalists began to transform the historic exile of the people of Israel in evident reality into the exile of the Shekhinah in hidden reality. They did so by identifying the Shekhinah with the emanated level of the divinity and by ascribing a feminine character to this emanated divinity. They further identified the emanated divinity with the exiled "assembly of Israel," with the Oral Torah and with the entirety of halakic conduct. The Shekhinah was the conduit through which the divine plenitude or the life force flows from the divine world into the lower worlds. The Shekhinah was also associated with the daily conduct of the world through divine providence. They converted the deep yearning for the redemption of the exiles in historical reality into the redemption of the Shekhinah in heavenly reality. They thus shifted the historical event in past, present, and future to the hidden cosmic sphere. This sphere is created by the power of imagination of those who learn by means of their study, exegesis, and faith. Since the days of the Sefer Habahir, in conjunction with the intentional performance of the commandments and the halakot through the earthly "Assembly of Israel," this cosmic sphere exerts influence on the "Shekhinah-bride-heavenly assembly of Israel" and its unification with the "Holy one, Blessed be He."

As the suffering of exiles during the Crusades in Europe grew following Israel's conquest by the Crusaders (1099–1291), the more the ability of the exiles to act in the historical sphere diminished. As a consequence, the activity of those who expected redemption in the cosmic sphere increased. To this purpose, they conferred a divine character on the human being and a human character on God. On the human being, they conferred a divine soul, bound bodily parts together with the Shekhinah and with the hidden world of the *sefirot*. They promised the human being a life that breaks out of the constraints of this world through his strong influence upon the Shekhinah and the heavenly "world of the *sefirot*" that was called the "primordial human being" (*'adam qadmon*). They depicted God anew as source of emanation and of the emanated sphere, or of the masculine and the feminine, who are bound together with the "world of the *sefirot*" in a relationship of unification and separation. Their repair, "restitution of the harmony of the world" (*tiqqun*), is conferred upon the human being in the performance of the commandments, the observance of halakah, and the orientation of intentions in the preservation and observance of them.

The Shekhinah distinguishes herself in the Zohar through a decidedly changeable character. There she is queen, diadem, matron, the redemptive angel; she has changed from a masculine to a feminine figure, the

Mishnah, the "Lily Assembly of Israel." She is also the exiled Shekhinah, the "Assembly of Israel that lays down in exile or in the dust." She changes, as her many names testify, in different contexts, since she expresses, in the consciousness of the authors who preserve the Written Torah and create the Oral Torah, the hope in the transition from the suffering of exile to the longed-for reality of redemption.[13]

The kabbalists created a new shape for the deity with a masculine and a feminine dimension. The masculine dimension is termed as "the Holy One, Blessed be He," beloved, bridegroom, or husband; it is connected with the *sefirot* "crown" (*Keter*), "wisdom" (*Hokmah*), "splendor" (*Tif'eret*), "eternity" (*Netzakh*), and "foundation" (*Yesod*), and with the Written Torah coming from an eternal, divine source. The feminine dimension is designated as the Shekhinah, bride, "Assembly of Israel," diadem; this dimension is connected with the Oral Torah and the world of speech, the *sefirot* "intelligence" (*Binah*), "knowledge" (*Da'at*), "majesty" (*Hod*), and "kingdom" (*Malkut*) and the collective halakic and haggadic creation of Israel, which goes on continually. In kabbalistic literature, the description of these two sides, which was mentioned in part in the above discussion, was deepened. For this reason, the Zohar creates the title "new-old things" for its new creation.

The kabbalists, in their consciousness, opened a new vertical channel between earth and heaven bound together with the influence of the lower human world upon the upper divine world; they called this vertical channel the "impulse from below to above" (*'it'aruta' diletata*). Likewise, they opened a new vertical channel between heaven and earth that they called the "impulse from above to below" (*'it'aruta' dile'ela*) that is bound together with the world of the *sefirot*, which are found between the two channels. The Shekhinah is the lowest *sefira* in the world of the *sefirot*. When she is awakened and strengthened by the powers that awaken from the bottom to the top, she unites with the "grandeur" of the *sefira* which carries the name of the "Holy One, Blessed be He," and is filled with a new abundance, which she pours out from above to below or from the upper into the lower world. The world of the *sefirot*, which is an image for the ten levels in the hidden world, is taken from the Sefer Yetzirah that tells its readers that the world was created "through thirty-two wonderful paths of wisdom" that

---

13. See Scholem, *On the Mystical Shape of the Godhead*, 140–96; Tishby and Lachower, "Shekhinah," in *Zohar*, 1:371–422.

are made up of "twenty-two basic letters and ten infinite *sefirot*." The *sefirot* are divided into ten parts that are connected with the body of the human being as well as a masculine and a feminine dimension. In the words of the Zohar: "The secret of the matter is: The blessings are found only where the masculine and the feminine are found" (Zohar 1:182a). The author of the Sefer Habahir explains that the Shekhinah stores within herself the thirty-two wonderful paths of wisdom, through which the "Holy One, Blessed be He," according to the words of the Sefer Yetzirah, created the world, and he further explains that the "Holy One, Blessed be He" has hidden all the commandments in the body of the Shekhinah, called "the Eternally Living One." The mystical location of all the commandments, thus, is "the Eternally Living One," that is, the Shekhinah, who is mentioned in the prayer. When human beings on earth concern themselves with the study of the Torah, prayer, the benedictions, and the commandments, and when they create the Oral Torah, then they awaken the Shekhinah from below to the top, so that she may shower them with plenitude from the top to the bottom, from the origin of the Written Torah.

In the difficult days of exile in the first centuries of the second millennium, the Shekhinah was imagined, on the one hand, as sitting in the lap of God, but she was also described repeatedly as in a prison pit found under the domination of the "other side." The author of the Zohar wrote:

> When the Temple was destroyed and the sins led to the fact that Israel was banished from the land, the 'Holy One, blessed be He' disappeared far above and did not look upon the destruction of the Temple and His exiled people, and there went the Shekhinah with them into exile.... And all those above and those below wept for them and grieved. What does this mean? That the 'other side', which ruled over the holy land, also ruled over them. (Zohar 1:210a–b)

The divine Shekhinah was described as being in "upheaval," a word that Genesis applies to the destruction of Sodom, creating a tragic comparison between the Jewish congregation that was persecuted in the Christian world by the Crusaders and the Church and persecution in the Muslim world by the Almoravids and Almohads. The author of the Zohar frequently resorts to the foundation of memory among the exiles: "When the Temple was destroyed ... the sanctuary was burned down, the people were exiled, the matronita [= Shekhinah] was expelled, and the house destroyed" (Zohar 1:75a). On the basis of this perception, marked by despair, of the happenings in the cosmic and earthly reality, the redemption of the Shekhinah, the matron, from her imprisonment and her liberation from the fetters in the sphere of the "other side" equated the Shekhinah with the study of the Torah and the halakah and the observance of the commandments with the release of the Shekhinah from her prison.

The kabbalists, who worked in the depths of exile and in the depths of despair, protested against this harsh reality by dividing the whole world, both heaven and earth, into two opposing sides: the "holy side" and the "other side," which was the side of impurity. They connected the first side, the "holy side," which represented their hopes, with the emanating and emanated powers of the good in heaven, which they called the "Holy One, Blessed be He," "Shekhinah," "messiah," and the "ten *sefirot* of holiness, unification, and redemption." They connected the second side, which represented their hard trials in historical reality, the "other side," "*sitra' 'akhra*," with the powers of evil, which they called "Satan," "Samael" (*sitra' mesa'abuta'* = side of impurity), "Lilith," "world of the shell" (*Qelippa*), and the "ten *sefirot* of impurity, separation, and exile." In their earthly reality and in their spiritual reality, of which their creative consciousness bears witness, as seen in Pesiqta Rabbati, Sefer Zerubbabel, and the Zohar, the messiah whose redemption they expected was locked up in prison:

> "One humbled and riding on a donkey" (Zech 9:9). That is the Messiah. And why is he called by the name "one humbled"? Because he bent down (humbly) all those years in prison. (Pesiq. Rab. 34.8)[14]

> Because he was bound in prison. For in those days the peoples of the world gnashed their teeth ... as it is said (Ps 22:7): "All who see me sneer at me." (Pesiq. Rab. 37.3)[15]

The Shekhinah, for whose comfort they yearned, was imprisoned, since the "other side" that ruled over the holy land also ruled over them.

According to the words of the kabbalists, after the destruction of the second temple these dimensions of divinity—the masculine and the feminine—were not in their proper place in a condition of union and in

---

14. Translation by Denis Slabaugh based on Arnold Maria Goldberg, *Erlösung durch Leiden: Drei rabbinische Homilien über die Trauernden Zions und den leidenden Messias Efraim (PesR 34.36.37)* (Frankfurt am Main: Gesellschaft zur Förderung Judaistischer Studien, 1978), 75.

15. Translation by Denis Slabaugh based on Goldberg, *Erlösung durch Leiden*, 269–70.

combination in cosmic space, but rather were in a condition of separation and disintegration, in exile, in a broken and shattered world. In the eternal cosmic struggle between the powers of impurity and the powers of holiness, the great struggle between the powers of exile and the powers of redemption, the powers of destruction, breaking, and devastation gained the upper hand. The Shekhinah, the "Assembly of Israel," was described as a prisoner in custody, or as a wife who was torn away from her husband and who fell into the hands of the "other side" and was raped by it. Many placed this traumatic condition in relationship with the collapse of the worlds and the "shattering of the vessels," which were bound together with the destruction of the temple and the exile of the Shekhinah; others characterized this traumatic condition as the struggle of the "other side" against the "holy side," the struggle of the "shell" against the Shekhinah, or Samael's struggle against the messiah. All, however, were agreed on the fact that the earthly "Assembly of Israel," in the historical reality, which had been banished, forcibly converted and persecuted and subject to injustice,[16] is found in a bitter exile and watches for the longed-for redemption—on the basis of the crisis in the cosmic reality. In this reality, in which the powers of destruction, injustice, evil, and impurity have gained the upper hand over the powers of building up, justice, the good, and holiness, and the Shekhinah, the "Assembly of Israel" in heaven and on earth has fallen into the hands of the "shell." This was a moment of cosmic rupture, called the "shattering of the vessels" (*shevirat hakelim*) and "collapse of the worlds," from which point on nothing is any longer found in its place and the entire existence is in exile.[17] This moment was connected with the destruction of the temple, the disappearance of the Shekhinah, and the victory of the powers of the "shell" and the "other side." The long historical suffering brought by exile became part of a cosmic event in the struggle of evil against the good or in the struggle of the powers of breakage and destruction against the powers of building up and restoration. Kabbalah declared that the human being is obligated to help the Shekhinah.

The exile of the Shekhinah was combined with the exile of Israel, and the redemption of the Shekhinah was placed in relationship with the

---

16. For a concise presentation of the facts connected with the physical suffering, see Rachel Elior, *Israel Ba'al Shem Tov and His Contemporaries: Kabbalists, Sabbatians, Hasidim and Mitnaggedim* [Hebrew], vol.1 (Jerusalem: Carmel, 2014), 36–39.

17. See Isaiah Tishby, *The Doctrine of Evil and the Kelippah in Lurianic Kabbalism* [Hebrew] (Jerusalem: Magnes, 1984).

redemption of Israel. Both were placed in correlation with the decisive human influence upon the divine world and the interdependence between both. In order to lead broken reality back to harmony, the kabbalists said that the Shekhinah, that is, the Mishnah and the halakah, is created through those who study it and is connected intrinsically with the 613 commandments and the regulations of the halakah. It is for this reason that every commandment that the human being fulfills in this world with his 613 members and every halakah that he observes strictly leads to a change in the power relationships between good and evil and contributes toward the process of leading the Shekhinah out of her prison pit from the hands of the "other side" and toward her salvation.

The reunification of the "Holy One, Blessed be He" and the Shekhinah, who were together described as divorced and divorcée, but also as bridegroom and bride, king and daughter of the king, God and widow, find themselves in the world of exile, of separation, of the "shell," of impurity and of breakage. This reunification was imposed in the kabbalist tradition upon every Jewish human being who, in accordance with this tradition, was obligated not only to strict observance of the commandments and to precise fulfillment of the halakhah, but also to "restitution of the harmony of the world" (*tiqqun 'olam*), to "bringing up of the sparks" (*ntizotzot*), and to leading the Shekhinah up from out of her imprisonment in the "world of the shell." Every Jew was obligated to say before every commandment that he fulfills in the course of the day that he has the intention to do this only "for the sake of the unification of the 'Holy One, Blessed be He,' with his Shekhinah." The Jew was required to say this formula, whose content, as we have seen, is the unification of the masculine side of the divinity, of the "Holy One, Blessed be He," with its feminine side, the Shekhinah, or the unification of the "grandeur" of the *sefirot* and "kingdom," every time before he prays the Shemoneh 'Esreh; he speaks it every day in the condition of sanctity, or every time when he concerns himself with the study of the Torah, which he fulfills in the condition of sanctity. Thereby, he had to orient his entire practical religious activity toward this goal of the redemption of the Shekhinah and of her restitution to her partner. In the Zohar, in the *'Idra' Zuta'* (Little Assembly), Zion is the womb of the Shekhinah, in which the "Holy One, Blessed be He" begets blessing and fullness for the world (Zohar 3:296a–b).

Kabbalah opened a vertical channel between the earthly and the heavenly, the revealed and the hidden, the historical and what was above history, and the kabbalists and the "Assembly of Israel" designated as

Shekhinah; this is documented on thousands of pages in the kabbalistic library. Kabbalah taught its readers that the redemption of the Shekhinah, which precedes the redemption of Israel and is a condition for it, is imposed upon them and only them in the world of thought and in the world of deeds. They must concern themselves with the "restoration of the harmony of the world, the "unification of the 'Holy One, Blessed be He,' with his Shekhinah," and with the "bringing up of the sparks." However, the coming of the messiah was left to God only and was combined with the bitter fate of the martyrs. As the number of the innocents killed and murdered by their persecutors grows, the more, according to the mystic messianic tradition, the coming of the messiah is accelerated; this is the avenging messiah clothed in a purple robe (the *Porfira*) upon which the names of all the innocently murdered martyrs are embroidered to their eternal memory. According to the words of the Zohar, the weeping messiah sits and waits in the "Temple of the Bird's Nest" in the garden of Eden, in which the names of all the annihilators and destroyers, persecutors and murderers are registered until the measure of suffering will become full and he will set forth to take revenge upon the murderers and to redeem the remnant left after the murdering is over.

3. Joseph Karo's Apparition of the Shekhinah

After the forced mass conversions in Spain in 1391, the expulsion of the Jews from Spain in 1492 in which a third of the people of Israel was lost, the forced mass conversions of tens of thousands in Portugal in 1497, and the mass murder of thousands of Jews in Lisbon in 1507, the feeling of suffering in exile and the depth of the expectation of redemption led to the opening of new horizons in mystical literature. The Shekhinah no longer remained a merely literary-mystical-halakic figure in the mystic-kabbalist imagination that was bound together with a ritual cycle and was said anew every time before prayer and study. Rather, the Shekhinah was a voice that was written down in the literature of the midrash. Kabbalah became, surprisingly, in the circles of the kabbalists, a speaking voice that was testified to in the autobiographical mystical literature written by them. Kabbalah exerted influence upon the renewal of prophecy and acknowledged the presence of speaking divine voices in the human reality of the present. In the world of one of the greatest rabbinic-halakhic authorities of the sixteenth century, Rabbi Joseph Karo (1488–1575), the Shekhinah was changed from a written presence into a living and speaking feminine divine presence.

Rabbi Joseph Karo was born in Spain, fled to Portugal, and, from there while still a child went with his family to the Ottoman Empire. He was granted an audition of the Shekhinah, or the hearing of the voice of the Shekhinah, which spoke in feminine form through his mouth. This occurred at the feast of Shavuot, the feast of the renewal of the covenant, in the year 1533, on the exact day when the bitter news of the terrible death of his friend, the kabbalist Schlomo Molcho (1500–1532), reached him. Molcho was a Portuguese Marrano (forced convert) who, at the age of twenty-three after he had occupied a high office at the court of the Portuguese king, returned to Judaism. He then left Portugal, was apprehended by the Catholic Inquisition, and was burnt alive at the stake in November 1532 in the Italian city of Mantua.[18]

The bitter news of the death of his kabbalist friend reached Karo on the eve of the Shavuot feast, a day full of joy and on which, according to Jewish tradition, it is forbidden to grieve, since the day is considered in the tradition of the Zohar to be the eve of the wedding feast of the Shekhinah and the "Holy One, Blessed be He." It is the day that lets the revelation on Sinai and the covenant that was concluded between the "Holy One, Blessed be He," and the "Assembly of Israel" occur anew in an updated form in accordance with the tradition of midrash and Kabbalah that connects the making of the covenant on Sinai with the Song of Songs.[19] This created a cognitive dissonance between the deep grief over his martyred friend and the joy of the Shavuot feast, on which the bride, the Shekhinah, is adorned for her wedding. This dissonance awakened in Karo's mind the "apparition of the Shekhinah," or the renewal of the divine speech on the night of Shavuot, a night when, according to kabbalistic tradition, the eternal covenant is concluded anew between the Written Torah and the Oral Torah, and which, in the hands of the "Assembly of Israel-Shekhinah" is renewed, handed down, and created as "new-old."

---

18. See Rachel Elior, "Joseph Karo and Israel Baal Shem Tov: Mystical Metamorphosis, Kabbalistic Inspiration, Spiritual Internalization," *Studies in Spirituality* 17 (2007): 267–319; R. J. Zwi Werblowsky, *Joseph Karo, Lawyer and Mystic* (Philadelphia: Jewish Publication Society, 1977).

19. Rachel Elior, "The Unknown Mystical History of the Festival of *Shavu'ot*," *Studies in Spirituality* 26 (2016): 157–96.

The voice of the Shekhinah, the bride, the diadem, which sounded in the city of Nikopol in the Ottoman Empire in the night of Shavuot as a prophetic moment of living divine speech came from the throat of Rabbi Joseph Karo as witnessed by his companions who studied with him in his house, in accordance with the tradition of the Zohar. Rabbi Karo spoke Hebrew in the feminine form in the voice of the grieving daughter of Zion from Lamentations who describes herself as the figure of a bride whose diadem was thrown away. This is attested by Karo's kabbalist friend Schlomo Alqabez, the author of the well-known *piyyut* "Go, my Friend, to Meet the Bride" (*Lekha dodi liqrat kala*), which is concerned with leading the Shekhinah at the beginning of the Sabbath up from out of the catastrophe or the pit in which she is held captive on the other six days of the week. Rabbi Schlomo Alqabez described the occurrence of the revelation of the Shekhinah that he experienced together with Rabbi Joseph Karo on the night of Shavuot of the year 1533 in a letter that he sent to his kabbalist friends in various Jewish congregations in the Ottoman Empire. Rabbi Jesaja Halevi Horovitz cites the letter in his 1649 work "The Two Tablets of the Covenant" (*Schene luchot habrit*). The voice of the Shekhinah that Alqabez describes introduced herself at the start of her revelation in Karo's mouth in the feminine form as the exiled daughter of Zion from Lamentations who had been thrown into the dust, wallows in rubbish, experiences immeasurable agonies, and embodies the suffering of exile and destruction as it is described in Lamentations. She is the voice that Moses hears on the day of the dedication of the altar in the tent of the covenant above the *kaporet* (covering plate of the Ark of the Covenant) between the two cherubim (Num 7:89). She is the voice of the Oral Torah, the Mishnah, which, as described above, is created in the house of learning "everywhere where three study the Torah, there is the Shekhinah found among them." The voice mentioned further the revelation on Sinai that occurred at the feast of Shavuot, and concluded with the commitment to immigrate into the land of Israel for the sake of the redemption of the Shekhinah:

> Know that we, the pious one—may the merciful one preserve him and redeem him [Rabbi Jospeh Karo]—and I, his servant and your servant from the companions, agreed on devoting our souls in the Shavuot night and on not letting our eyes find any sleep.... When we began to study Mishnah and had already studied two tractates, it was granted to us by our Creator to hear the voice speaking to itself [*haqol middabber* (Num 7:89)] from out of the mouth of the pious one—may the merciful one preserve him and redeem him—a powerful voice with a distinct utterance,

and all the neighbors heard, but understood nothing. The pleasantness was great, and the voice intensified more and more. We fell upon our face and in no one was there enough spirit to lift his eyes and his face and to look, out of pure dread and fear. And this speech spoke with us. She began and said: "Hear, my friends, the strictest among the strict, my friends, my beloved, peace be with you. Fortunate are you and fortunate the women who bore you, fortunate are you in this world, and fortunate are you in the future world, since you have chosen to adorn me in this night after, already several years ago, the diadem fell from my head and I have no comforter,[20] I have been thrown into the dust and I wallow in rubbish.[21] Now you have given the old radiance back to me. Strengthen yourselves, my friends, strive, my friends, rejoice and be happy, and know that you belong to the chosen. It has been granted to you to belong to the sons of the royal Temple, and the voice of your teaching and the breath of your mouth have ascended to the presence of the 'Holy One, blessed be He,' and, before they ascended, they have broken through several firmaments and several atmospheres. The angels kept silence, the seraphim fell silent, the living beings stood still,[22] and the whole heavenly host and the 'Holy One, blessed be He,' hear your voice. And behold, I, the Mishnah, the mother who chastises the human being, have come to speak to you. And if you would have been ten, you would have exalted yourselves further and further. But, in spite of everything, you have exalted yourselves; fortunate you are and fortunate are the women who bore you, my friends, who have let your eyes find no sleep. Through you I have raised myself in this night, through the companions in the great city, a city and mother in Israel. You are not like those who lay themselves down on ivory beds for sleep that is one sixtieth of death, and sin in their cradle. You are devoted to Y-H-W-H and He rejoices over you. For this reason, my sons, strengthen yourselves, be courageous, and rejoice in my love, in my Torah, in the fear of me. If you could imagine only a thousandth of the ten thousand and thousands upon thousands of the sufferings, in which I find myself, then no joy would appear in your heart and no smile

---

20. Cf. Lam 5:16: "The diadem fell from our head"; note also 1:16: "Far from me is every comforter"; 1:2: "I have no comforter."

21. Cf. Lam 4:5. The word for "rubbish" (*'ashpatot*) is a *hapax legomenon* that appears only in Lamentations.

22. The formulation refers to the revelation on Sinai. Cf. Exod. Rab. 29:9: "When namely God gave the law, said R. Abahu in the name of R. Johanan, the bird did not chirp, the birds did not fly, the ox did not bellow, the Ophanim did not fly, and the seraphim did not cry: Oh, Holy One! The sea did not billow, the human beings did not speak, but rather a general silence prevailed. Only the divine voice let the words be heard: 'I am the Eternal, your God.'"

on your mouth while you recall that I was cast into the dust for your sake. Thus, be strong, be courageous, rejoice, my sons, my stern friends, and do not interrupt your study. For comeliness has come upon you and your study is pleasing before the 'Holy One, blessed be He.' Therefore, rise to your feet, my sons, my friends, and lead me up, and speak with a loud voice as on the Day of Atonement: Blessed be the name of His honored kingdom for ever and ever."

We rose to our feet, our loins became weak, and we said with a loud voice: Blessed be the name of the splendor of His kingdom forever and ever. She began again and said:

"Fortunate are you, my sons; return to your study and don't interrupt it for even a moment, and go up to the land of Israel. For, not all times are alike, and salvation is not hindered by many or few. Do not feel sorry about your property, for you will eat from the good of the highest land. If you desire and listen to me, then you will eat from the good of the land. So hurry and go up. For, I am the provider of your nourishment and will feed you. Peace will be on you, your houses, and everything that belongs to you. The Lord will give His people strength; the Lord will bless His people with peace…. Know that you belong to the chosen…. You are devoted to me, and comeliness has come over you. And if it would be permitted to the eye, then you would see the fire that surrounds this house."

All of this she spoke to us and our ears heard it…. We all broke out in tears of joy and also because we perceived the distress of the Shekhinah for our sakes and heard her voice like that of a sick person who beseeches us.[23]

Alqabez continues and describes the revelation of the Shekhinah in the mouth of Rabbi Joseph Karo that took place again in the second night of the feast of Shavuot, which is represented as a renewal of the revelation on Sinai when the mountain stood in flames. He quotes the words of the Shekhinah that confirm once again the task of the kabbalists in the redemption of the Shekhinah:

> Fortunate you are, friends, fortunate those who lead me up…. Do not fear ignominy caused by human beings, and have no fear of revilement, for you are the ones who lead up the "Assembly of Israel." Know that you belong to the chosen…. You are devoted to me, and splendor covers your heads; comeliness has come over you. And if it would be permitted to the eye [to see], then you would see the fire that surrounds this house. So, be

---

23. Joseph Karo, *Maggid Mesharim* [Hebrew] (Jerusalem: Orah, 1960), 18–19.

strong and courageous; do not interrupt the connection to bringing me up, and speak with a loud voice: "Hear, Israel" and "blessed be the name of His honored kingdom for ever and ever" as on the Day of Atonement.[24]

Rabbi Joseph Karo, Shlomo Alqabez, and the other kabbalists who lived in exile in the Ottoman Empire after their expulsion from Spain heard these forceful words from the mouth of the Mishnah-Shekhinah that came from Karo's throat. They then set off and immigrated in 1535 to the land of Israel (a land that, since 1517, had been a part of the Ottoman Empire). These kabbalists founded the city of Tzfat (Safed) in order to lift up the Shekhinah, who in her own words had connected her own rise from the rubbish with the kabbalists' move to the Holy Land. The Shekhinah came to the end of her dramatic words and spoke the key sentence in which the exiles expecting redemption became the redeemers, while the one on whom the hope for redemption rested became herself, through the exiles, the redeemed one:

> You all rise up before the Lord, and He sanctifies Himself in you, and *through you the "Assembly of Israel" will rise and soar up*. And the fact is that what is said: "She has fallen and will not rise again" means that *she will not rise again by herself, but rather through those who bring her up and unite her with her beloved*.[25]

The new emphasis upon the central significance of human action as uttered by the mouth of the Shekhinah-Mishnah was a strong factor in the integration of the contemplative ideal (consideration, devotion) into the activist ideal (unification, the bringing up of the Shekhinah, the bringing up of the sparks) in the framework of the effort to induce a change in heaven and on earth. This was a result of the change in definition of the human ideal and in the determination of the human being from redeemed to redeemer. The "sons of the royal Temple," to whom the Shekhinah turns are the group of those studying the Torah, the elite, those who "build up" this world through their devotion to the upper world and through their commitment to the redemption of the Shekhinah, like the group gathered around Rabbi Shimʻon bar Yohai in the Zohar. Subsequently, the speaking voice, which had found this mystical

---

24. Karo, *Maggid Mesharim*, 19.
25. Karo, *Maggid Mesharim*, 157–58.

group on the night of the feast of Shavuot, introduced herself to Rabbi Joseph Karo, the leader of the group. For the rest of his life, he continued to hear her and write down her words, under an abundance of names, among them: "the Mishnah" ("I am the Mishnah that speaks from your mouth"); "soul" ("I am the Mishnah that speaks from your mouth; I am the soul of the Mishnah, and I, the Mishnah, and you unite to become one"); the redeeming angel; "the voice of my friends"; "the mother who chastises the human being"; the Torah; the exiled "Assembly of Israel," and "the Shekhinah." The voice repeated her demand for absolute devotion: "Wherever you are, do not separate your thoughts from me ... for you will be the repository of the Shekhinah, and the Shekhinah will speak through your mouth."

4. The Shekhinah in Hasidism

The demand from the Shekhinah for absolute devotion of her chosen mouthpiece, as attested dozens of times in the mystical diary *Maggid Mesharim* was addressed solely to Rabbi Joseph Karo, but it was then taken over by the founder of Hasidism, Rabbi Israel Baal Shem Tov (the "Besht," 1698–1760) as a collective instruction for all his Hasidim. He integrated it into his consciousness as though the Shekhinah had spoken to him and as though her words had been spoken through him. He did this after he had read the printed edition of the diary that was published for the first time in 1646 in Lublin and afterward in many editions, although the author, who died in 1575, never had the intention of presenting his mystic experiences to the public.[26]

Rabbi Israel Baal Shem Tov declared in his "Holy Letter" (*'Igeret Haqodesh*) that he had learned from the mouth of the messiah, with whom he had spoken in 1746 on Rosh Hashanah (Jewish New Year) during an "ascent of the souls," "that worlds, souls, and the deity are found in every letter."[27] He added that the Shekhinah, "the world of speech," is found in every letter of speech in the Holy Language, which is spoken by every Jew. He added further, referring to the kabbalistic concept "the limbs of the Shekhinah are Israel," that "every individual from Israel is a member of the limbs of the Shekhinah." The mystical world of perception in regard

---

26. See Elior, "Joseph Karo and Israel Baal Shem Tov."
27. See Elior, *Israel Ba'al Shem Tov*, 2:79–126.

The Feminine Dimension of God in the Mystic Tradition

to the messiah and the Shekhinah, who are found in heaven, was revitalized in the consciousness of Rabbi Israel Baal Shem Tov and Rabbi Joseph Karo in the sense that they related it to human beings and to the mystical linguistic teaching that the creative power of God finds in its expression in His word—"By the word of the Lord the heavens were made, and by the breath of His mouth all their host" (Ps 33:6). The combination of the creative power of the human being speaking in the Holy Language revives the Shekhinah: They heard how the messiah and the Shekhinah in heaven and on earth spoke with them directly. The disciples of the Besht and their disciples wrote down his words in dozens of books and quoted his words about the Shekhinah in hundreds of quotations. Thus, for example, it is said in his name:

> For she is not in Heaven, the Shekhinah of His power, for the 'Holy One, blessed be His name,' let His Shekhinah dwell among us, in the mouths of His people the Children of Israel, as the holy Zohar says: "The kingdom [*Malkhut*] is mouth, for the Shekhinah is found in the mouth of the human being."[28]
>
> And he should remember that the world of speech speaks to him, such a great world through which all worlds are created.... And through this he may remember His—blessed be He—splendor. All the life force of the worlds comes from speech, and speech is the world of reverence. The Shekhinah constrains herself, so to say, and dwells during his act of speaking in his mouth, as it stands written in the Sefer Yetzirah: 'He has put it in the mouth'. And if speech is so, what is the world of thought.... He may remember, that the world of speech speaks to him, and outside of him she cannot speak.[29]
>
> When the human being begins to pray, immediately when he says 'Lord, open my lips', the Shekhinah takes possession of him and speaks the words in him.[30]
>
> The main thing, however, is: When a human being thinks that the speech does not speak at all, but the Shekhinah speaks from his throat, which is called world of speech, then that is well known ... about the exile of the Shekhinah, therewith is meant that speech is in exile.[31]

---

28. Avraham ben Dov Baer von Mezhirech, *Chesed le-Avraham* (Jerusalem, Lewin-Epstein, 1973), folio 52, 2.

29. Dov Baer von Mezhirech, *Maggid devarav le-Ya'akov*, ed. Rivka Schatz-Uffenheimer (Jerusalem: Magnes, 1976), 183–84.

30. Dov Baer von Mezhirech, *Maggid devarav le-Ya'akov*, 13.

31. Dov Baer von Mezhirech, *Maggid devarav le-Ya'akov*, 271.

With the help of the kabbalistic world of conception, which was renewed in the spirit of the founder of Hasidism, the Besht liberated his hearers from the fetters of the material world and opened new horizons for them. He deciphered the depth of the expressions, in all the richness of their meanings, in the text that forms the foundation of the kabbalistic creation, and learned from it explicitly and in allusions about the existence of many worlds hidden from the eye, which reveal themselves to the student who searches for the spiritual nature of being and its eternal foundations that are bound together with divine speech and the letters of the Holy Language. The hearers and readers of the Besht conceded a central place to the "contemplation" of the "Shekhinah-the world of speech," the "devotion to the Shekhinah," the "unification of the Shekhinah," the leading upwards of the Shekhinah, "the leading upwards of the sparks" and the "contemplation" of the Holy Language and the letters of the world of speech, in all of which, as has been said, "worlds, souls, and the deity" are found. The distressed, helpless exiles thus became the redeemers of the Shekhinah, or "sons of the upper world," those in whose eyes this world, when it is uncoupled from its divine origin, is nothing but an insignificant "mustard seed." From that moment on in which the deeds and thoughts of the human being, in the teaching of the Besht, became detached from the limitations of this world and became a part of the fabric of the hidden worlds—the "Shekhinah-the world of speech," the "worlds, souls, deity," the sparks, the *sefirot*, the spiritual letters, the "world of speech," the "thirty-two wonderful paths of wisdom"—his students obligated themselves behind their material guises to consider the truth of the divine reality and to conduct a creative dialogue with the infinite possibilities that are hidden in the holy text and which, in the kabbalistic reading, is interpreted anew beyond the clarity of the literal sense. In the teaching of the Besht, the human being is the one who redeems the Shekhinah when he adheres to her as world of speech. He is called to concentrate all his aspiration upon the world hidden from the eye, which is well known in mystical language, is bound together with the divine presence in a mode of being, which is called the Shekhinah, diadem, assembly of Israel, world of speech, and Oral Torah, and is also bound together with the world of the *sefirot* and the "Holy One, Blessed be He" and with the tree of the souls in the garden of Eden, with the sparks and the upper sanctuaries, with the messiah and the letters of the Holy Language. The human being is to take a position of complete indifference in regard to material existence in exile, which is connected with "Samael, the villain, the prince of Rome," with Lilith, with *nuqba detehom raba* (the mythical feminine dimension of the great abyss), with the "shells," with Satan, with Hell, with the dark land, with "criminal Rome," with Amalek, and with Edom. This starting position finds expression in the constant pursuit of devotion to the Shekhinah, which demands "equanimity" (*hishtavut*), "negation of the existent," and "divestiture of the material," for, as it is said, "in accord with the thoughts of human beings, there are worlds above him."

The teachers of Hasidism took the hidden divine world, which was divided in the books of the kabbalists into the "Holy One, Blessed be He," and the Shekhinah, and made it present in the mouth, in thought, in remembrance, and in the speech of every human being. The Shekhinah, the "world of speech," was seen as an expression of the divine presence and as a unifying factor among all the congregations of Israel who learn, speak benedictions, pray, and read and write in the Holy Language. The Shekhinah was connected with the world of divine speech that speaks in the mouth of the human being and that makes speech an area of freedom and infinite creation. She was connected with the Oral Torah, which revives the Written Torah in a learning process and recreates it and makes it present every day in the community of learners. She had a double foundation: the Written Torah which preserves the Holy Language and the Oral Torah which is created anew in the Holy Language during the study of the written Torah. This fact was of great importance in the exilic congregation, to whom freedom had remained in no other dimension of their life except in the freedom of learning and creation. This personal freedom was identified with the Shekhinah, because the letters of the Holy Language were given over in the same way to every person who reads and speaks Hebrew, who reads the Written Torah and from it continues to create the Oral Torah, while he revives its origin and its renewal in his study and in his practice of the commandments.

Before the twentieth century, Jewish woman could not participate in any study circles of holy texts in the Holy Language of the Bible and the Mishnah or in the Aramaic of the Talmud. The study language was the sole domain of men, who were obliged to study the "language of the fathers," Hebrew and its sister language Aramaic. Nor could women participate in the liturgical and mystical circles in the synagogue, in Hebrew or Aramaic, which were totally monopolized by men for thousands of years. This religious-intellectual reality of the past begs the question of the relation and relevance of the Shekhinah to the lives of actual Jewish women who could not speak Hebrew, read the Holy Language, or study Torah.

The Shekhinah was created by postexilic Hebrew readers and writers and by Hebrew speakers, thus limited to the male members of the Jewish community for numerous generations. Women were not affected by the new religious concept that pertained to a female dimension in the Godhead, nor did they contribute to its multifaceted development. However, in the twentieth century, when Jewish women started to study Hebrew as equal members of the community and started to attend schools, secondary schools, colleges and universities, and rabbinical academic institutions, the patriarchal block that excluded them from any study related to holy texts changed profoundly. Human rights, feminism and new ideas about freedom and equality as foundations of human dignity affected the Jewish community in many ways in the decades that followed World War II.

Modern Jewish women influenced by feminist ideas, human rights, and intellectual curiosity started to study Hebrew and Aramaic as part of their communal heritage. They started to explore the vast ancient rabbinic tradition as well as the rich Jewish mystical heritage, and they started gradually to incorporate the figure of the Shekhinah in their intellectual, spiritual, personal, and emotional search, as well as in their historical and philological interests, or in their internal religious life. Female scholars of three generations, who study philosophy or Jewish thought, such as Tamar Ross, Susannah Heschel, Haviva Pedaya, Dalia Marx, Beracha Zak, Shifra Assulin, Tsippi Kauffman, Bitty Roi, Ruth Kara Ivanov-Kaniel, Iris Felix, Lea Morris, Lior Saks Shmueli, Diana Lobel, and many others, contributed to the intellectual and religious-spiritual renewed interest in the feminine aspect of the divine.

It is too early to assess the significance of the new phenomena that commenced in feminist religious circles about two decades ago, but today study circles of women are engaged in conversations about the Shekhinah, in studying relevant sacred traditions about it, and in reevaluating the role of the traditional patriarchal order from current feminist perspectives.

The Biblical Woman Who Is Not Mentioned in the Bible: Feminine Imagery in Kabbalah

Felicia Waldman

1. Introduction

One of the most significant moments in the one thousand years of medieval Judaism, a period characterized by the geographic dispersion of the Jews living "under Crescent and Cross,"[1] was the emergence toward the end of the twelfth century of kabbalah. Kabbalistic thought revolutionized the Jewish world and its outlook on everything, from daily life to social interaction and even international relations. It presented ideas that challenged the establishment, sometimes even verging on heresy, but which were always daring and eventually managed to win the support of a vast number of the members of the Jewish elite class.

Kabbalah was in fact a sort of renaissance *avant la lettre*, a return to ancient wisdom in all its aspects, not just religious but also mythic, legendary, folkloric, and, above all, mystic, or, as Elliot Wolfson more appropriately calls it, "esoteric."[2] After undergoing a process of "arcanization," to use Moshe Idel's term,[3] Jewish mystical thought bloomed, or rather boomed, quite suddenly with a number of writings that seem to have sprung out of nowhere. These writings refer to notions and terms not found in the previous literature that had survived. This was the case,

---

1. As Mark Cohen, *Under Crescent and Cross* (Princeton: Princeton University Press, 2008), so elegantly puts in the title of his book dedicated to this topic.
2. Elliot Wolfson, "The Mystical Significance of Torah Study in German Pietism," *JQR* 84.4 (1993): 43.
3. Moshe Idel, "Magical and Magical-Mystical Arcanizations of Canonical Books," in *Absorbing Perfections: Kabbalah and Interpretation* (New Haven: Yale University Press, 2002), 137–63.

for instance, with the Sefer Habahir (the Book of Brilliance), a short and enigmatic anonymous work that appeared circa 1180 in Provence.[4] The Sefer Habahir deals with the esoteric meaning of certain biblical verses, the Hebrew letters, and the ten *ma'amarot* (commandments) through which the hidden God reveals his divine being. This collection of theosophical explanations, quoting talmudic rabbis as sources, some real but most imaginary, was seen by Gershom Scholem as a type of exegesis whose unexplained notions, instead of deciphering the sacred text, further and more deeply codified it.[5] The growth and spread of the kabbalistic movement also infused new life into the older (ca. second century CE) but equally enigmatic Sefer Yetzirah (the Book of Formation). This short but seminal book, also anonymous, speaks about the creative and implicitly destructive power of letters and numbers as instruments of the divine creation. Then came the Sefer Hazohar (the Book of Splendor), commonly referred to as the Zohar, a mystical journey through the Torah, Jewish law, and lore compiled by Moses de Leon and others in the thirteenth century from various earlier sources, some real and some imaginary; it is considered today the foundational work of kabbalah. The Zohar has been defined by Gershom Scholem as the embodiment of Judaic theosophy, the mystical doctrine whose main aim is the knowledge and description of God's mysterious work. The Zohar grew over time into a corpus of books that includes commentaries on the mystical aspects of the Torah, scriptural interpretations, as well as works on mysticism, mythical cosmogony, and mystical psychology. It contains discussions of the nature of God, the origin and structure of the universe, the nature of souls, redemption, the relationship of the Ego to Darkness and the "true self" to "The Light of God," and the relationship between the cosmos and humanity, as well as the origin and nature of evil and how to combat it. During the next four centuries, kabbalah developed exponentially in Europe and in the Holy Land.

It can thus be said that kabbalah managed to recover diverse, dispersed, and even forgotten elements of earlier Judaism and put them together in a coherent system, giving them new value and significance.

---

4. See the essay by Rachel Elior in this volume for a discussion of excerpts of the Sefer Habahir.

5. Gershom Scholem, *On the Kabbalah and Its Symbolism* (New York: Schocken, 1965), 90.

2. The Feminine Aspect of God

In discussing the nature of God starting with the sacred text of the Torah, kabbalists gave particular attention to the verses in Gen 1 and 2, which deal with the creation of humankind. Giving a mystical twist to an older practice,[6] they interpreted Gen 1:27—"God created man in his own image, in the image of God created he him; male and female created he them"—as implying that the One God has a masculine part and a feminine part. Thus in the face of a tradition impregnated by the masculine God of the Bible, the kabbalists actually develop an outlook that sees key feminine elements within the Godhead.[7] In the kabbalistic view the divine is *Ein Sof*, the Infinite, of which humanity can only perceive ten manifestations, or aspects (*sefirot*), that function like a system. The feminine part of God is embodied in two of these aspects: the second, *Binah*, and the tenth and last, *Malkut*. *Binah* (understanding or emotion), coming after *Keter* (crown) and *Hokmah* (wisdom or cognition), is the stage at which the divine creative impulse starts acquiring a distinct shape.[8] If *Hokmah* is the "sperm" that contains the "genetic code," *Binah* is the "egg" or the "womb," in the absence of which the potential cannot become viable. It is also called the "superior mother," by contrast with *Malkut*, the "inferior mother." Coming after *Hesed* (lovingkindness or mercy), *Gevurah* (rigor or judgment), *Tif'eret* (beauty or harmony but also compassion), *Netzakh* (victory or endurance), *Hod* (splendor or glory), and *Yesod* (foundation), *Malkut* (kingdom) synthesizes all the preceding *sefirot* and serves as a link between them and the rest of reality (i.e., the physical world). As the last stage of reception, *Malkut* gathers all that comes from the upper levels. It is also called Shekhinah and is associated with God's presence in the world. The kabbalists believed that the ideal situation for both the divine world and the rest of creation would be when *Yesod* and *Malkut*, seen in a

---

6. There is evidence that early Canaanite Judaism identified Yahweh with El and saw him as reigning over an assembly or council of gods together with the former Canaanite goddess Asherah. See Rosemary Radford Ruether, *Goddesses and the Divine Feminine: A Western Religious History* (Berkeley: University of California Press, 2005), 74.

7. Biti Roi, "Divine Qualities and Real Women: The Feminine Image in Kabbalah," *Havruta* 5 (2010): 63.

8. It is interesting to note that, while *Hokmah*'s biblical personification is feminine, in kabbalah it is masculine and even called the Superior Father.

simplified vision as the masculine and feminine aspects of the divine, the transcendent and the immanent, become integrated through the righteous action and meditation of the mystic. According to the Zohar, in the beginning the union was permanent. It was the Adamic sin that determined the "exile of the Shekhinah" and it is therefore humanity's duty to reinstate the (broken) original harmony. Tiqqunei Zohar (21:52b), goes even further and establishes an equality between the Torah and Israel, viewed in its turn as a mystical body. But the mystical body of the community of Israel does not refer to the Jewish people only; it also represents an esoteric symbol of God's presence, the Shekhinah. The exile of the Jewish people is seen as the physical embodiment of the exile of the Shekhinah after the sin of Adam, which explains the constant interconnection of the two motifs.

In the kabbalistic evolution of the notion of Shekhinah, one can perhaps find the most interesting examples of how mysticism combined theology with mythology. In talmudic literature and rabbinic Judaism, Shekhinah simply referred to God's presence in the world. It was the kabbalists who transformed it into a queenly personification of the Godhead. Thus, in kabbalah this notion renders an aspect of the Divine from two different but complementary perspectives. On the one hand, *Binah*, as superior mother, represents the feminine aspect of the demiurgic potency. On the other hand, *Malkut*/Shekhinah, the seventh and last *sefira* (manifestation of the Divine Being) that emanated from *Binah*, represents the feminine in general, seen as mother, wife, daughter.[9] Because the six *sefirot* above it are seen as the male foundation, this explains why *Yesod* is sometimes identified with the *tzaddiq* (the wise man). *Malkut*/Shekhinah appears as a completion of the virile manhood and as a providential channeling of creation. Moreover, in Kabbalah, Shekhinah is identified with the mystical community of Israel, on the one hand, and with the *Neshamah* (soul), on the other hand. Starting from the talmudic interpretation of the Song of Songs, according to which the mother and daughter are symbols of the Community of Israel, kabbalists transferred this vision upon the Shekhinah, proposing a previously nonexistent identity. Thus, kabbalists such as Ezra of Gerona interpret the description in the Song of Songs as

---

9. It is not by chance that in his mystical work Sha'arey Orah (Gates of Light), composed at about the same time as the Zohar, Rabbi Joseph Gikatilla says: "The *Shekhinah*, in the time of Abraham our forefather, is called Sarah, and in the time of Yitzhak our forefather is called Rivkah, and in the time of Ya'akov our forefather is called Rachel" (quoted in Roi, "Divine Qualities and Real Women," 64).

symbols of the theosophical processes taking place between the two lower *sefirot*, that is, *Yesod*, seen as husband, and *Malkut*, seen as wife, which in turn reflect events in the intradivine structure. To this we may add the symbolism of the Shekhinah seen as one of the five levels of the soul and even as a dwelling place of the psyche. Paradoxically, this symbolism is double. On the one hand the male aspect is represented by the *Tzaddiq*, the wise man, and the female aspect is represented by God's presence in the world, or the lower divine potency, Shekhinah. On the other hand, the male aspect is associated with the divine and the female aspect with the human soul. The origin of the soul in the feminine sphere of the divine has a huge significance in kabbalistic psychology.

Since it contains components of all the previous *sefirot*, the purely receptive Shekhinah is the manifestation place of both the forces of mercy and the forces of judgment.[10] In Scholem's interpretation, some of the early kabbalists saw as the source of evil the superabundant growth of God's power of judgment, which was made possible by the substantification and separation of the quality of judgment from its customary union with the quality of lovingkindness.[11] There is a state of the world in which the Shekhinah is the target of a certain violence partially originating in *Gevurah*, the *sefira* of Judgment, which penetrates the Shekhinah by force. The Zohar says that "at times the Shekhinah tastes the other, bitter side, and then her face is dark."[12] This is how the symbolism of the "tree of death" is born, by a demonical separation from the "tree of life." If the Shekhinah is Israel's merciful mother, it can also be, at the very same time, the tool of God's judgment and punishment. The two aspects are nevertheless separated: the third *sefira* is exclusively demiurgic, in a full and positive sense, and the tenth has quasi-demonic traits as well. This ambivalence of the Shekhinah, which evolves in alternative phases, is tightly connected to its exile.

The representation of an exile of the Shekhinah is also taken by the kabbalists from the Talmud (b. Meg. 29a), but in their theosophy this concept

---

10. In Moshe Cordovero's view, for instance, "Shekhinah has no light of her own: she is like the moon that only reflects the brightness of the sun; she receives from the upper Sefirot in a posture of openness and submissiveness; she awaits the overflow of divine blessing into her as the sea receives the intersecting currents of river water." Quoted from Eitan P. Fishbane, "A Chariot for the Shekhina: Identity and the Ideal Life in Sixteenth Century Kabbalah," *Journal of Religious Ethics* 37 (2009): 402.

11. Gershom Scholem, *Kabbalah* (New York: New American Library, 1974), 123.

12. Scholem, *On the Kabbalah*, 107.

acquires a new meaning: it is translated as an exile of God within himself. In kabbalah, the exile of the Shekhinah becomes a representation of both the exile of Israel's community and the exile of the soul from its origin. The idea that this double exile dates back to the beginning of creation only appears in Lurianic kabbalah. In the first kabbalistic writings, the separation of the male and female sides of God is seen as a result of the original sin. It was because Adam was not able to participate in the achievement of the divine union; instead of unifying all the *sefirot* through his contemplation he actually separated them. What was up was separated from what was down and the male side of God was separated from the female side. This separation was rendered through many symbols: for example, the separation of the tree of life from the tree of knowledge, and the seperation of life from death. God's reunion with his Shekhinah thus became the very aim of redemption. The uninterrupted union of the male and female parts of the divine will make possible, once again, the outflow of the generative forces through all the worlds. From here to seeing this union as a marriage took only one step; that step was taken by the author(s) of the Zohar, although the ritual itself was actually older. Thus, starting from the process taking place inside God between the two *sefirot*, *Yesod* and *Malkut*, in their capacity as aspects of the divine, by enriching the symbolism of the Shekhinah, kabbalists came up with the idea of a wedding between God as the groom and the Community of Israel as the bride. From this perspective the quasi-demonic traits of the Shekhinah, in its capacity as the origin of the soul, are even the more interesting.

The Zohar speaks of a dynamic relationship between the Godhead and the Shekhinah, seen as his queen (*matronit*) and lover. But we should not forget that in the Zoharic tradition she is also the connecting point between the heavenly realm and the physical world. As such, God's self-consciousness in the Shekhinah is radically vulnerable to the responses, actions, and even thoughts of the human partners.[13] Therefore kabbalists went even further and tried to find ways to bring the Shekhinah close, not virtually, but quite literally. For instance, the idea that Torah study provides the occasion for the visible manifestation of the divine glory or Presence was a point made as early as the late twelfth to early thirteenth century in several passages of the pietistic writings.[14] It is not by

---

13. Michael E. Lodahl, *Shekhinah/Spirit, Divine Presence in Jewish and Christian Religion* (New York: Paulist, 1992), 89.

14. Wolfson, "Mystical Significance," 61.

chance either that a kabbalist like Eliyahu de Vidas says "the *Shekhinah* only dwells [on the person] as a result of *simhah*," referring to the fact that God's presence can only be felt by those who fulfill God's commandments with joy.[15] Furthermore, in halakic midrashim the term Shekhinah refers to God's manifestations, descents and goings forth in Israel's midst, suggesting not just divine presence, but also divine nearness and even intimacy.[16] Kabbalists regarded this Presence as a very visible and palpable thing, sometimes in the form of consuming fire, other times in the form of light, and therefore they expected to literally see it, especially when they studied together. They tried to develop special techniques designed to help them reach the pre-fall state of the Primordial Man to enable them to enter again the radiance of the Shekhinah and even a certain erotic relationship with the Divine Presence.[17] By letter combinations, as well as unifications and reversals of letters, they invoked the tree of knowledge of good and evil and the ten *sefirot*; they meditated together so that they could watch each other and see to what extent the encounter with the divine radiance made them, in their turn, radiate the light.[18]

3. The Biblical Woman Who Is Not Mentioned in the Bible

Strangely (or perhaps not), despite all this overwhelming attention paid to the feminine side of God, kabbalists did not dwell too much on any of the women mentioned in the Torah. Notwithstanding brief references to certain characters, such as Delilah (whose adventure with Samson in a vineyard is interpreted in view of the talmudic story of the four sages who entered the Pardes), Deborah (after whose palm tree Moshe Cordovero named one of his seminal books), or the matriarchs Sarah, Rivka, and Rachel (who are mentioned, for instance, in Joseph Gikatilla's book Sha'arey Orah), for many of the kabbalists the most important biblical

---

15. Quoted by Fishbane in "A Chariot for the Shekhina," 409.

16. Ephraim Urbach, *The Sages: Their Concepts and Beliefs* (Jerusalem: Magnes, 1979), 43.

17. For a comprehensive view on this, see Moshe Idel, *Kabbalah and Eros* (New Haven: Yale University Press, 2005).

18. For more on this, see Felicia Waldman, "Edenic Paradise and Paradisal Eden: Moshe Idel's 'Reading of the Talmudic Legend of the Four Sages Who Entered the Pardes,'" *Journal for the Study of Religion and Ideology* 6.18 (2007): 79–87.

woman was one who was actually not mentioned in the Bible, but was only alluded to, in an attempt, they believed, to hide her existence: Lilith.

It all began with Gen 1:27 where it is written that "God created man in his own image, in the image of God created he him; male and female created he them," and Gen 2:18 and 22 which state: "And the Lord God said: it is not good that the man should be alone; I will make a help mate for him.... And the rib, which the Lord God had taken from man, made he a woman, and brought her unto the man." The kabbalists were dissatisfied with the rabbinic explanation of this apparent contradiction, which held that, as human archetype, 'adam qadmon (the Primordial Man) must have had both features, and just as the divine unity was divided in two (the separation of the waters by the firmament) to create the universe, so too was humankind created by the separation of the Primordial Man into its two halves, male and female. Instead, kabbalists came up with a more attractive explanation in which religion met mysticism and mythology. This was a story at which Genesis vaguely hinted: the story of Adam's first wife, Lilith.

In fact, the idea was not new. As with many other subjects, the kabbalists actually (and naturally) built upon older traditions, which they skillfully interwove. Apparently the first text which clearly stated that Lilith was Adam's first wife was The Alphabet of Ben Sira, a book whose appearance scholars place sometime between the eighth and tenth centuries CE, long before kabbalah emerged. The anonymous author of this work in his turn combined two different older motifs into a new one: a folktale (complemented by superstition and magical practice) about a demon with a talmudic interpretation of Adam's sins.

In the Bible, the word "Lilith" appears only once, in Isa 34:14, which says, "the wild beasts of the desert shall also meet with the wild beasts of the island, and the satyr shall cry to his fellow; Lilith shall also rest there and find for herself a place of rest." The lack of any other references to it in the sacred text (or elsewhere for that matter) makes it very unclear whether at the time it was meant as a proper name or as a common noun meaning "creature of the night," as it was sometimes translated. This translation was based on the similarity with the Hebrew word for night (*layla*) as well as on the existence in Hebrew of the word *lilin*, which may be generically translated as demons.[19]

---

19. Etymologists have found a possible source in the Assyrian-Babylonian word *lilitu* (female demon or wind spirit), part of a triad used in magic invocations. Taking this view, it probably entered the Hebrew language because of its similarity with the

Later, however, the name was clearly used to denominate a specific demon that endangered the lives of newborn babies, mothers in child labor, and men who slept alone. In this way, Lilith was in fact quite similar to the Greek Lamia or to the Arab Qarina.[20] The demon could be warded off by amulets bearing the names of three angels assigned to keep her away, the very un-Hebrew sounding Senoy, Sansenoy and Semangeloph. According to Rafael Patai, such amulets seem to have been in use in the Jewish world even before the Talmudic period.[21]

Not surprisingly, the Babylonian Talmud includes several direct references to Lilith:

> Rabbi Hanina said: one may not sleep alone in a house, for Lilith takes hold of whoever sleeps alone in a house. (b. Sabb. 151b)

> Rabbi Jeremiah ben Eleazar said: during those years (after their expulsion from the Garden), in which Adam, the first man, was separated from Eve, he became the father of ghouls and demons and *lilin*. Rabbi Meir said: Adam, the first man, being very pious and finding that he had caused death to come into the world, sat fasting for 130 years, and separated himself from his wife for 130 years, and wore fig vines for 130 years. His fathering of evil spirits, referred to here, came as a result of wet dreams. (b. ʿEruv. 18b)

> Lilith is a demoness with a human appearance except that she has wings. (b. Nid. 24b)

Incidentally, a close look at these descriptions will reveal that Lilith looked in fact very much like the cherubim, a detail that became very significant in later kabbalistic literature, especially since the Shekhinah was

---

Hebrew word *layla* (night). In their book *Hebrew Myths, The Book of Genesis* (New York: Greenwich House, 1983), Robert Graves and Raphael Patai find the source of the Lilith story in a "careless weaving together of an early Judean and a late priestly tradition" (p. 7). In their view, Lilith typifies the Anath-worshiping Canaanite women, who were allowed prenuptial promiscuity, and whose example the Israelite women followed, to the despair of prophets who kept denouncing these practices, alas to no visible avail.

20. See Raphael Patai, *The Seed of Abraham* (New York: Scribner's Sons, 1986), 227 and Scholem, *Kabbalah*, 357.

21. For more on this topic, see Graves and Patai, *Hebrew Myths*.

thought to dwell in the ark.[22] These talmudic passages warned men that they should not sleep alone because this makes them prone to having wet dreams, allowing Lilith to steal their seed and bear demons. The passages are a direct invitation to fulfill the first commandment of the Torah: grow and be fruitful (i.e., set up a family and have children), otherwise you are easy prey for demons. Not surprisingly, by the end of the talmudic period, the Lilith legend as a succubus was already extensively developed.

It was, however, the author of the Alphabet of Ben Sira[23] who came up with a comprehensive view bringing the two traditions together in a story that started making sense. According to him, the problem with the primordial marriage was the interpretation of the position of the two partners in relation to each other, from all points of view (including sexually). This had to do primarily with the fact that Adam apparently thought only he was created in God's image and was therefore superior to Lilith. Consequently, he tried to dominate her. Lilith went straight to God and lulled him into revealing his Ineffable Name to her. Uttering it, she was freed and fled the garden of Eden, finding her refuge in a cavern by the Red Sea, where she gave birth to legions of demons. Meanwhile, Adam started to regret his loneliness. Upon his request, God sent three angels to Lilith persuade her to return. These angels, Senoy, Sansenoy, and Semangeloph, told her that if she refused to return, her children would be killed at a rate of one hundred a day. Even this fate was preferable to Lilith who, in turn, promised to kill Adam's children: the girls in the first twenty days of their life and the boys in the first eight days, mothers in labor and men in their sleep when she could steal their seed to bear new demons. Nevertheless, Lilith agreed to spare those protected by amulets bearing the names of the three angels.

But Adam had problems with Eve, too. If Lilith was (and remained in mythology) a seductress, Eve remained legendary for being much too easy to seduce. Lilith, representing the will, could not be maneuvered, while Eve, representing the lack of will and submission, was easy to maneuver. To explain the ease with which Eve gave in, one interpretation proposed that Lilith returned to take her revenge in the form of the snake. Thus, under the name of Lilith the Elder or the Northern, she was seen as the wife of Samael, the fallen angel, together with whom she plotted to punish

---

22. For more on this, see Wolfson, "Mystical Significance," 72.

23. Norman Broznick, trans., "Alphabet of Ben Sira," in *Rabbinic Fantasies: Imaginative Narratives from Classical Hebrew Literature*, ed. David Stern and Mark Jay Mirsky (Philadelphia: Jewish Publication Society, 1990), 167–202.

Adam. In this version Lilith was the snake's body and Samael his voice. The result of this joint venture was, as we all know, the expulsion of Adam and Eve from Heaven. Adam blamed Eve and left her for a while in order to repent. But, as he could not stay alone, during the temporary separation he lived again with Lilith, who bore new monsters. This might be the source of the rabbinic interpretation in which Lilith represented all that distracted man from the true path of God, making him repeat the Adamic sin over and over again. Israel Gutwirth, for instance, describes a work called Kav ha-Yashar, which contains several stories about Lilith who was said to appear in the guise of a beautiful woman to attract men and turn their heads.[24] Regarded from this perspective, Lilith was sometimes imagined as a beauty from the waist up and as a monster, ugly and hairy, from the waist down, or even as half-woman and half-man. In this version she was also identified by the biblical exegesis in the image of the Queen of Sheba, who tried to seduce King Solomon. But Solomon, suspecting with whom he was dealing, had her believe the floor was covered in water and made her raise her skirts, thus revealing her hairy legs. Of course, this was ultimately a metaphor. Lilith represented that which appeared beautiful on the outside but actually was sex, indulgence, and everything that one desired to do that broke the laws of God. She stood for all the things in life that distracted men from the true path, showing her real face only after having seduced them.

Kabbalah took over the symbolism related to Lilith and enriched it with new significance. The first kabbalist who took a particular interest in her was Rabbi Isaac Cohen, who wrote, in the thirteenth century, the famous *Treatise on the Left Emanation*,[25] in which he exploited and explained a vast symbolism related to her. Although the *Treatise* does not seem to have been directly influenced by the Alphabet of Ben Sira, it is highly probable that Rabbi Cohen knew the book.

Cohen was the first Jewish mystic in the Middle Ages to present a mystical mythology in the form of an eschatology. Moreover, as the title shows, he was the one who connected the older demonology[26] with the

---

24. Israel Gutwirth, *The Kabbalah and Jewish Mysticism* (New York: Philosophical Library, 1987), 111–12.

25. Isaac b. Jacob ha-Kohen, "Treatise on the Left Emanation," in *The Early Kabbalah*, ed. Joseph Dan (New York, Paulist, 1986).

26. About which Harold Bloom says that "God, after the Babylonian exile, reigns over a cosmos of angelic orders, and is no longer the solitary warrior-god, Yahweh,

emanation theories of kabbalah. In fact, the *Treatise* was one of the most important books in the evolution of kabbalah; it introduced what some scholars, including Gershom Scholem, call a "Gnostic dualism" into kabbalistic symbolism. As Joseph Dan puts it:

> While earlier Kabbalists regarded the problem of evil in a manner very similar to that of the philosophers, Rabbi Isaac created a demonological parallel structure of evil emanatory powers ruled by Asmodeus, Satan, Lilith, and their hosts, deriving from the left side of the *Sefirotic* tree. And in fine mythic form, these various demons are seething with lusts and desires, jealousies and hatreds, flailing about madly in their demon world, waiting to pounce on the hapless humans below.[27]

It was the *Treatise* that brought in the new vision which saw Lilith as the partner of Samael, and therefore the queen of the *sitra' 'akhra* (the realm of evil). She fulfilled a function parallel to that of the Shekhinah (as divine presence): just as the Shekhinah was the mother of the House of Israel, so Lilith was the mother of the unholy folk and ruled over all that which was impure.[28] At the same time, the symbolism in the *Treatise* related to Lilith appears for the first time in combination with the symbolism of *merkabah* mysticism (the ecstatic ascension to the Divine Chariot and the Throne of Glory). Thus Lilith together with Samael, seen in perfect parallelism with Adam and Eve, lived in the Inferior Palaces crossed by the mystic on his way to the Throne of Glory. Moreover, the *Treatise* differentiated between Lilith the Older or Northern and Lilith the Younger. It mentions that Samael and Lilith the Northern were emanations from under the Throne of Glory. The image of the creature with the upper half female and the lower half male, however, was not seen as a monster but rather as "burning fire." It was identified by Rabbi Cohen with Lilith the Younger, the wife of Asmodeus the King of the Demons, reigning over the lower realms. Lilith the Elder would share the fate of her partner, Samael, when in the final battle between good and evil they will be defeated by

---

who employed a handful of Elohim as his messengers and agents. Out of Babylon came not only angelic names but angel-bureaucrats, princes and functionaries" in *Omens of Millennium: The Gnosis of Angels, Dreams, and Resurrection* (New York: Riverhead, 1996), 45.

27. Dan's description is very much, in fact, like the gods of Greek mythology. See the introduction in *Early Kabbalah*, 37.

28. Scholem, *Kabbalah*, 358.

Gabriel, prince of might (*sefira Gevurah*) and Michael, prince of kindness (*sefira Hesed*).

The Zohar continued this tradition, taking over most of its motifs and symbols but also adding new dimensions. Thus, following talmudic legends, the Zohar stresses the origin of certain classes of demons born from sexual intercourse between humans and demons.[29] On the other hand, harking back to earlier times, the evil spirits could be driven away not only with the names of the three angels but also with the divine name *Shaddai* crowned with the Supreme Crown.[30] The seduction of Eve by the Snake (as represented by Samael) was seen not only as a verbal manifestation but as a physical one as well, leading to the birth of Cain in his capacity as an assassin. A reverse model appears in Sitrei Torah (1:147b–148a) in the chapter entitled Jacob's Journey, where Adam is seduced by the Snake (as represented by Lilith). Further on, however, the seeming contradiction is solved by the explanation that the Snake represents the demonic and had in his turn an implicit double aspect: female and male at the same time. Developing this motif, Moses Cordovero showed in *Pardes Rimmonim* (Pomegranate Orchard; see 186d) that Samael and Lilith could only exist through the emanation of evil from one another.[31]

But kabbalah did more than simply comment on the symbols related to Lilith that it had taken over from the previous tradition and mythology. In the kabbalist's overall view on the world, Lilith came to represent all those things that God frowned upon, not only in regard to the Israelites but also as to the entire world. By extension, Lilith symbolized the ways of the pagans living around the Jews. She also symbolized all those who would break the Torah and anyone who would attack the Israelites. From this perspective, Lilith was identified in apotheosis with Babylon itself. It is highly probable that this equivalence was also based on the legend of the Tower of Babel, seen as a failed project of mass ascension towards unification with the divine (physical and/or spiritual). It is not by chance that the Zohar links the end of Lilith to the fall of Rome: "When the Holy One, blessed be He, will bring about the destruction of the wicked Rome, and turn it into a ruin for all eternity, He will send Lilith there, and let her dwell in that ruin, for she is the ruination of the world. And to this refers

---

29. Scholem, *Kabbalah*, 321.

30. Raphael Patai, *The Hebrew Goddess* (Detroit: Wayne State University Press, 1990), 227.

31. Quoted by Patai, *Hebrew Goddess*, 246.

the verse, 'And there shall repose Lilith and find her a place of rest' (Isa 34:14)" (Zohar 3:19a).[32]

The most shocking outlook proposed by kabbalah in connection with Lilith was probably that which saw her as God's partner. Thus, in her capacity as both God's presence in the world and Israel's mystical community, the Shekhinah was regarded as the wife of the wise man (*tzaddiq*) and, by extrapolation of God himself, seen in one of his aspects. In this circumstance, it is obvious that there was one single place where such divine union could be consummated: the temple of Solomon. Once the temple was destroyed (70 CE), Shekhinah (i.e., the Israelite people) was "taken captive" by the pagans and "raped" continuously. God refused to meet her in impurity. On the other hand, however, a God without a female aspect was an incomplete divinity, which was impossible. This was again reminiscent of the Canaanite mythology with its deities, the male El and female Asherah, and the male Baal and female Anath.[33] That was why, in order to maintain the balance, Adonay took Lilith (i.e., the peoples who kept the Shekhinah captive) as his partner (Zohar 3:69a).[34] Given her impurity, God would have had no reason to regret his union with Lilith who was thus not his wife but only his harlot. Lilith thus became the Dark Shekhinah, the polar opposite of God's demiurgic female aspect, preserving however, at the same time, her quality of image (presence) that humankind reserved to God. Here once again the kabbalist's task was to participate in what sixteenth-century kabbalist Isaac Luria called *Tiqqun 'Olam* (the repair of the world). Through his actions—meditation, contemplation, fast, prayer, charity, et cetera—the mystic helps reunite God with his Shekhinah in the days of Shabbat, holy days in which Lilith could not remain near the divinity. Moreover, we should also recall at this point that in kabbalistic thinking there was a close connection between the divine reunion of God and the Shekhinah on the one hand and the relation between man and his wife on the other hand. Just as God was complete only when both his male and female aspects were together, so a human being was complete only when man and woman were together. Furthermore, the very coupling of man and wife—if done properly, of course, according to the Torah prescriptions, but also with joy—was

---

32. Quoted by Patai, *Hebrew Goddess*, 237.

33. In some sources Anath is Baal's sister and consort, which was not unusual in the ancient world.

34. Quoted by Patai, *Hebrew Goddess*, 249.

believed to exert a mystical influence on the divine realm by bringing together the male and female aspects of the divine, thus inducing balance among the *sefirot* and regaining the original harmony broken by Adam and Eve. This explains why for the kabbalists sex had cosmic effects, not just in theory but also in practice, as a way to drive Lilith away from both man and God.

4. Conclusion: Lilith's Relevance Today

One must admit that for a character who is not even mentioned in the Genesis story, Lilith's evolution is impressive. Under the circumstances it is no wonder that she has been adopted as the symbol of the feminist movement. Clearly, the first Eve version of the biblical account gives women a role to identify with not only in Judaism but also in other religious traditions. Lilith can be regarded as the model of an independent woman who challenges the system in which she is placed. Killing children may be interpreted as the expected amount of madness that results from solitude and exclusion or simply as a rejection of the child-rearing role expected of women in the patriarchy. Moreover, her career would make any woman envious; as Raphael Patai puts it, she "started out from the lowliest of origins, was a failure as Adam's intended wife, became the paramour of lascivious spirits, rose to be the bride of Samael the Demon King, ruled as Queen of Zemargad and Sheba, and ended up as the consort of God Himself."[35] On the other hand, the fact that her advancement was based on her seductive power is not a characteristic that feminists are likely to admire.

The open-ended nature of Lilith's symbolism has allowed her use in the most diverse and even contradictory ways, from being a symbol of feminine power to a symbol of a destructive female. Feminists see Lilith as the first independent woman—and there is a well-known Jewish feminist magazine called *Lilith*, which labels itself as an "Independent Jewish Woman's Magazine." There are people, however, who still see her as a demoness, wicked and dangerous for men; thus they think of feminists as men-haters.

These multiple aspects of Lilith explain why she has been made the object of both medieval and modern art. She can be seen in Filippino Lippi's vault fresco of Adam in Filippo Strozzi's burial chapel in the Santa

---

35. Patai, *Hebrew Goddess*, 221.

Maria Novella Dominican Church of Florence.[36] We can find her, too, in Hieronymus Bosch's triptych "The Garden of Earthly Delights," although most art critics have missed it,[37] or later on in Dante Gabriel Rossetti's 1868 painting "Lady Lilith" and John Collier's 1887 painting "Lilith." She is also present in fantasy novels such as George MacDonald's 1895 work *Lilith*.

Today Lilith remains a symbol of power simply by virtue of her survival. As Patai puts it, "a citizen of Sumer ca. 2500 BCE and an East European Hassidic Jew in 1880 CE had very little in common as far as the higher levels of religion were concerned. But they would have readily recognized each other's beliefs about the pernicious machinations of Lilith, and each other's apotropaic measures for driving her away or escaping her enticements."[38] There are only a handful of other mythological characters who can easily claim such universal fame and overarching longevity.

---

36. Robin O'Bryan, "Carnal Desire and Conflicted Sexual Identity in a 'Dominican' Chapel," in *Images of Sex and Desire in Renaissance Art and Modern Historiography*, ed. Angeliki Pollali and Berthold Hub (New York: Routledge, 2018), 44.

37. See Virginia Tuttle, "Lilith in Bosch's 'Garden of Earthly Delights,'" in *Simiolus: Netherlands Quarterly for the History of Art* 15.2 (1985): 119–30.

38. Patai, *Hebrew Goddess*, 251.

The Figure of Ruth as a Convert in the Zohar

Yuval Katz-Wilfing

1. Introduction

The biblical figure of Ruth is the protagonist of the book of Ruth or the scroll of Ruth (*Megillat Ruth*), a rather small book of only four chapters in the Hebrew Bible. According to the story, Ruth is the Moabite wife of an Israelite living in the land of Moab. She is married to a son of Elimelech and his wife Naomi who come to Moab to escape a famine. After Elimelech and his two sons die, Naomi decides to return to the land of Israel. Despite Naomi urging her to stay in Moab, Ruth insists on accompanying Naomi to Israel. There, through her gleaning in his field, Ruth meets one of Naomi's kinsmen, a man called Boaz. With Naomi's encouragement, Ruth marries Boaz and gives him children, whose descendants are the Davidic kings of Judah. Her firstborn son is given to Naomi to raise as the titular successor to the line of Naomi's husband, Elimelech.

This essay will examine Ruth's many roles as she emerges from the pages of kabbalistic literature through the books of the Zohar. The Zohar texts can be seen as a late piece in the chain of midrashic texts; they reflect the former traditions as laid out in different midrashim and build another layer of exegesis, a layer rich in reference to the unseen esoteric side of the Jewish tradition. Ruth the outsider becomes not only an integral part of the nation but its center, the aristocratic matriarch in political terms and the messianic matriarch in theological thought.

Moreover, Ruth is likened to the *sefira* of *malkut*, which is the lowest *sefira*.[1] She is thus linked to the divine and is also closest to the people of

---

1. There are ten *sefirot* in the kabbalistic model of the unfolding of reality from the divine realms to our human reality. The lowest one and the closest one to our real-

Israel. In this way, Ruth becomes both Israel's spirit representative towards the divine and the divine's emissary to the earthly people of Israel:

> Ruth in the image of the lower world, saturating the blessed Holy one with songs and praises perpetually. Ruth, like the name *tor*, turtledove. As the turtledove has a unique song among all others, so the assembly of Israel has a song of praise unique among all other calls—praise of *thor*, awakening. The turtledove emits two calls as one: one high and one low—all as one. The Assembly of Israel, too, arouses above and arouses below—all at once and with a single voice.[2]

Ruth is a prominent yet surprising figure in Jewish literature. She is not initially part of the people of Israel, yet she makes her way to the center of how Jews define themselves. Ruth is a somewhat passive figure in the biblical story while her mother-in-law Naomi not only returns to the land of Israel but also regains her status as a matriarch. Ruth is the Esther to Naomi's Mordechai. Naomi uses Ruth as an obedient pawn in her struggle to regain her deceased family's status through Ruth's marriage to Boaz, as Mordecai used Esther to save the Jews in Achashverosh's Persian court from extermination. Ruth's most independent moment is when she insists on following Naomi to Israel, thus forsaking her own homeland of Moab. With that moment of devotion she becomes the ultimate manifestation of a convert's subservience to God even though, for reasons of gender, she may not have been the perfect candidate. Ruth's problematic attributes as a *giyoret* (a woman convert to Judaism) and how the Zohar deals with them is the focus of this article.

2. Kabbalah and the Zohar

Kabbalah can be defined as a worldview that encompasses all fields of life and existence and seeks solutions for the world's mysteries and life's upheavals from a religious, mystical approach. At its heart lies the secret of knowing the divine. Kabbalah deals with the hidden areas of the divine life and the human as an individual, as well as the relationship between them.[3]

---

ity is *malkut*. For further details, see Moshe Hallamish, *Introduction to the Kabbalah* (Albany: State University of New York Press, 1992).

2. Joel Hecker, *The Zohar: Pritzker Edition, with Translation and Commentary*, vol. 11 (Stanford, CA: Stanford University Press, 2016), 196.

3. Hallamish, *Introduction to the Kabbalah*, 13.

The tradition of kabbalah can be seen as an answer to the philosophical quandaries which occupied Jewish thought at the end of the first millennium and the beginning of the second.[4] During this period, kabbalah emerged as a new genre of rabbinic literature. This is the fourth form of the four-tiered reading scheme known as *PaRDeS*, which is an acronym for *peshat, remez, drash,* and *sod*.[5] The last of these, *sod*, is the esoteric understanding of the biblical texts as transmitted through *kabbalah*, which is translated as "reception." The kabbalah tradition was very influential, and some of the most prominent figures in Jewish thought and law are kabbalists or at least well versed if not immersed in kabbalah thought and practice.[6]

The Zohar is a collection of writings and texts that is traditionally attributed to Rabbi Shimon bar Yochai, who lived in the second century CE. However, the scholarly consensus is that this work came out of medieval Europe. The content of the Zohar's first three books follows the order of the weekly reading portion of the Pentateuch. The first two books are dedicated to Genesis and Exodus, and the third one deals with Leviticus, Numbers, and Deuteronomy. The Zohar also contains the new Zohar, known as Zohar Hadash (abbreviated ZH), which may, however, include some of the earliest Zoharic material.[7] This part includes more texts on the Pentateuch as well as on Ruth, Lamentations, and the Song of Songs.[8]

The Zohar first appears at the end of the thirteenth century in Castile.[9] Major researchers, such as Heinrich Graetz and Gershom Scholem, have reasoned that Rabbi Moses de Leon in Spain was its sole creator.[10] Later scholars have argued that the Zohar is a collaborative work and may reflect a much bigger circle than merely one person. For the purpose of this work, the Zohar can be said to represent wider circles in regard to its view of female figures in general and Ruth specifically.

---

4. Hallamish, *Introduction to the Kabbalah*, 11.

5. *Peshat* is the literal, accepted reading; *remez* is allegorical; *drash* is the midrashic reading; and *sod* is the mystic reading. See also Gerhard Langer, *Midrasch* (Tübingen: Mohr Siebeck, 2016), 260–66.

6. Hallamish, *Introduction to the Kabbalah*, 13.

7. See volumes 9 and 11 of *Zohar: Pritzker Edition*.

8. For more information, see the preface to volume 11 of Hecker, *Zohar: Pritzker Edition*; Arthur Green, *A Guide to the Zohar* (Stanford, CA: Stanford University Press, 2004), 63.

9. Green, *Guide to the Zohar*, 162.

10. Green, *Guide to the Zohar*, 64–65.

Even though the book emerged at a specific time in the Middle Ages, it is possible that it is only a compilation of older traditions that have not reached us directly. This may be both because of their esoteric nature and because of the oral tradition in which they were preserved. As Herbert Basser has said: "It may be that the Zohar is not woven from fragments found here and there but that it preserves the ancient warp and woof of a tradition more antique than Sifre and Midrash Tannaim."[11]

3. Conversion in Kabbalah

The Zoharic kabbalists use Ruth's story as a vehicle to discuss converts and gentiles.[12] The kabbalistic view, which is clear already in the thirteenth century, differentiates sharply between the soul of a Jew and that of a gentile.[13] This view draws from the general distinction between the forces of holiness (*qedusha*) and defilement (*tuma'a*). These forces are represented in reality by Israel and the gentiles. This is sometimes manifested by a radical resistance to mixed marriage and an aversion to *giur* (conversion), as can be seen in the writings by Isaac Luria (as known as the ARI, 1534–1572).[14] These attitudes would make it difficult to have a positive view of Ruth's story, as she is an example of a mixed marriage. Indeed, both her marriages—the first to Elimelech's son Mahlon and the second to Boaz—could be considered mixed marriages. But even the preferred reading of Ruth as a convert may be viewed negatively because of the deep seated resistance to conversion.

A uniquely positive view about conversion can be seen in the writings of Rabbi Isaac ben Samuel of Acre during the thirteenth and fourteenth centuries CE: "All those people from the nations of the worlds which undergo *giur* (conversion), their soul was from the souls of the sons of Israel, and that is why the Lord has brought them under his wings so no one is lost to Him."[15] This may mean that converts to Judaism are actually

---

11. Herbert Basser, "Midrash Tannaim," in *Encyclopedia of Midrash: Biblical Interpretation in Formative Judaism*, ed. Jacob Neusner and Alan Avery-Peck, 2 vols. (Leiden: Brill, 2005), 1:516.
12. Volumes 11 and 12 of Hecker, *Zohar: Pritzker Edition*.
13. Hallamish, *Introduction to the Kabbalah*, 213.
14. Hallamish, *Introduction to the Kabbalah*, 214.
15. Translation based on Menachem Recanati, *Perush 'al ha-Torah* (Lemberg, 1880), 35b.

descendants of Jews who had left Judaism. However, there was another view that saw the bond with God as dependent on the fulfillment of God's laws, so that any person obeying the laws would be considered as a full member of the Jewish people.[16]

In the case of Ruth, there is no doubt that she is viewed positively. Kabbalistic texts, among them the Zohar, explain Ruth's special status in the legacy of the Jewish people despite her possibly dubious gentile background. Ruth is transformed from a literary figure in a particular narrative and background to a universal figure signifying much more than her role in the original narrative. Ruth gains a place in the Zoharic view of the world by being linked to a certain *sefira* and thus incorporated into the relationship of the divine and this world. Her role is still seen as feminine, and just like the Torah she is given feminine attributes. Ruth becomes a symbol for the people of Israel, and thus grants her feminine attributes to the people of Israel.

4. The Importance of the Convert and the Feminine in the Zohar

In the Zohar, Ruth the convert is used metaphorically to reimagine the structure of the relationship between God, his Torah, and his people. Intertwined with Ruth's role as a convert, someone who was not part of the people of Israel but becomes central to them, is the important role that the feminine played in kabbalah. An example of the importance of the theology of the *ger* (alien or foreigner) is shown in the famous parable of the maiden in the part of the Zohar linked to the weekly reading portion of Mishpatim, called Saba de-Mishpatim.

In this text the Torah and her secrets are likened to a fair maiden. The parable uses the same language that is later used to describe the secret layer of the Torah. In the narrative of the parable of the maiden, the old man (*saba'*) telling the story describes a maiden in a palace who briefly opens her window to her lover below, but only to close it again to conceal herself. It can be understood that this parable develops the example of the way in which the hidden secret is revealed to the converts' souls and then hidden again from them. This could be as a result of the contemporary uselessness of the *ger* concept to medieval kabbalists; perhaps there were not many converts in those days and the original concept of *ger*, as a resident alien,

---

16. Hallamish, *Introduction to the Kabbalah*, 215.

was thus no longer relevant. This lack of relevance in the contemporary world of the writer may have driven him to seek for a deeper meaning. Here the *ger* is a metaphor for the strange soul in our (lowly) world. This approach maintains the original meaning of *ger* as an alien rather than a convert, as it is usually seen.

Let us look at the relevant verses: "In numerous places the blessed Holy One has cautioned us concerning the stranger (*ger* could also be a convert), so that the holy seed should be mindful of him. Afterward the concealed matter emerges from its sheath, and as soon as being revealed it returns to its sheath, clothing itself there."[17] The secret explained regarding the souls of *gerim* is here linked to the scriptural text, the recurring theme of protecting the *ger* and to their importance in the behavior of the higher souls. The following verses continue the explanation:

> Once he had cautioned concerning the stranger, in all these places, the matter emerged from its sheath, declaring *you know the stranger's soul* (Exod 23:9). Immediately it enters its sheath, returning to its garment, hiding away, as it is written: *for you were strangers* [*gerim*, possibly also converts] *in the land of Egypt* (ibid.)—for scripture supposes it clothed itself immediately, no one noticed it. Through this stranger's soul, the holy soul perceives things of this world, enjoying them.[18]

Here we see the idea that the holy *neshamah* (a part of the soul) of a Jew cleaves to the *nefesh* (another part of the soul) of the *ger*.[19] The role of the *nefesh* of the *ger* seems crucial to the ability of the *neshamah* to encounter the world. Without it the *neshamah* could not take part in the world. Later, the old man explains how the soul of a convert is dealt with in regard to his body and the raising of the dead in the world to come (Saba de-Mishpatim 100a). The verses cited here show the importance and centrality of the *ger* when illustrating the concepts of the souls, their origin, and dynamics. The verses also demonstrate the unique application of traits thought of as feminine, such as the revealing and concealing aspects of the various parts of the soul and especially the souls of converts, to explain how the Torah

---

17. Daniel C. Matt, *The Zohar: Pritzker Edition, with Translation and Commentary*, vol. 5 (Stanford, CA: Stanford University Press), 31. See Saba de-Mishpatim 98b.

18. Matt, *Zohar: Pritzker Edition*, 5:31–32.

19. According to this worldview the soul has several parts, which cleave to each other to make an entire soul. These parts can come from different sources. For more details see Hallamish, *Introduction to the Kabbalah*.

and the Jewish people relate. The figure of Ruth as a female convert allows for the elements shown above in the parable of the maiden to emerge with full force in the Zohar.

Alongside the positive relationship of Torah to a feminine figure, we also find a very negative attitude toward women in the Zohar. Women are seen, probably because of their sexuality and the sexual emotions they evoke in men, as the source of all evil: "From females come all forms of magic and witchcraft, and all evil thoughts. If not for 'her hands are fettered' (Eccl 7:26) and her being restricted, woman would murder and bring death to the entire world—always, everywhere" (Midrash Ha-Nelam Ruth, ZH 81c).[20] Similarly, we see a suspicious and antagonistic attitude toward the convert:

> Come and see: slime of a Gentile.[21] Even if he converted, it is hard to slough. Such slime lasts for three generations—all the more so for one who has remained a Gentile. The best among them: Ruth—and no blemish was found in her at all. This is an intellectual soul. Orpah, bestial soul, returned at once to her stench and degradation. (Midrash Ha-Nelam Ruth, ZH 82b)[22]

There is a great tension between the centrality of the feminine figure versus the potential danger coming from her. There is also an unbearable tension between the centrality of the convert figure versus the possible unholiness or filth she carries. Both tensions are expressed in the figure of Ruth, making her a uniquely important and dramatic figure. Those who walk near the edge of a cliff risk being delegitimized if they cross over the edge. The text of the Zohar creates the security rails, making sure that Ruth does not fall into disrepute.

5. Ruth as the Exemplary Convert

Ruth is made into a model woman convert (*gioret*) by the midrashic literature of the Middle Ages.[23] She is the ultimate outsider who gained a

---

20. Cited by Hecker, *Zohar: Pritzker Edition*, 11:136.

21. The idea of human filth that can be washed off can be seen in b. Shabb. 145b–146a. There we can see that the filth was removed from the Israelites at Sinai but it remained on gentiles and it stays with converts for three generations. The filth here is internalized and made into spiritual filth in the soul.

22. Cited by Hecker, *Zohar: Pritzker Edition*, 11:150.

23. Paulina Bebe, *Isha, Frau und Judentum, Enzyklopädia* (Egling an der Paar: Verlag Roman Kovar, 2004), 292.

place in the heart of the Israelite nation as a foremother of the eternal house of David, of the kings of the mythic golden age of Judea, and of the future messiah and redeemer of the Jews. Even though the book in which she is the titular protagonist does not explicitly talk of her conversion to Judaism—the word *giur* is not used in any form there—the story is nevertheless one of her integration into the Judean society and family structure. A story of affiliation is carried out because of the affection Ruth has for Naomi, the mother of Ruth's late husband.

Reading Ruth's biblical narrative, it does not seem obvious that she would be a model *gioret*. First, there is no real mentioning of a *giur* process. Even more than that, Ruth seems like a very inappropriate candidate for conversion to Judaism. Her past as the Moabite widow of a Judean man places her not only as someone whom the Torah explicitly forbids to integrate into Judean society but also as a model of the foreign temptress who leads Judean men away from their own tradition. In the time of her marriage to Boaz, she is a helpless refugee in Judea, someone who has completely surrendered herself to the wishes of her mother-in-law. After the marriage she is reduced to a biological vehicle, a mother to children who are considered more Boaz's and Naomi's than her own. Ruth seems to have three strikes against her: her past as a daughter of an unwanted nation, her present as an unlikely wife to Boaz dominated by the older family connection via her mother-in-law, and the future of her bloodline as her motherhood is confiscated by her dead husband's family and her son is given to Naomi to nurture and raise.

In the Zohar we find two ideas about the main point of the story of Ruth. One is to present us with a model convert rather than to legitimize the Davidic line:

> Rabbi Yose son of Qisma: "I would be astonished if this scroll came only to trace the lineage of David back to Ruth the Moabite and nothing more!... But actually, all of this is necessary because the righteous woman came to convert and to be enveloped by beneath the wings of Shekhinah—teaching about her humility and modesty." (Midrash Ha-Nelam Ruth, ZH 78b)[24]

The second idea found in the Zohar is to hold Ruth as the appropriate mother of David's line and thus to legitimize the Davidic lineage:

---

24. Cited by Hecker, *Zohar: Pritzker Edition*, 11:92.

Rabbi El'azar son of Rabbi Yose said: "It comes to teach us that the lineage of David is like silver smelted in an earth crucible (Ps 12:7) for the silver of Obed is clarified silver, smelted again and again. If you say, 'If so, why did they come from such mothers, with this kind of background?' This is as is written: You shall love the lord your God with all your heart (Deut 6:5), with both your impulses with the good impulse and with the evil impulse—everything as one, as necessary—and the lineage of David, necessarily so." (Midrash Ha-Nelam Ruth, ZH 78b–c)[25]

As seen in these two passages, the Zohar addresses both aspects of Ruth's story, and one could say that it must address both. The two ideas are dependent on each other: Ruth as a model convert legitimizes the Davidic line, and the legitimization of the Davidic line stresses how perfect was Ruth as a convert.

As I outline in the following sections, the Zohar deals with all three aspects of Ruth: her past as a daughter of a king is legitimized; her present as a wife is elevated so that she becomes a great woman with extraordinary traits of her own; and her future as a mother of the greatest Judean dynasty is glorified. Let us now turn to the Zohar texts themselves to explore how these three dimensions are handled in detail.

6. Ruth's Past as a Daughter

In Deut 23:4 we read: "And an Ammonite and a Moabite will not come in the midst of the congregation of the Lord, also the tenth generation will not join in the Lord's congregation forever." This explicit law would seem to make any marriage or even conversion (*giur*) of Ruth impossible. As a Moabite woman she cannot join the Israelites no matter what she does. However, the Zohar makes her an appropriate candidate for joining the people of God by describing her in this way: "So was Ruth fit to join the congregation. For the law had already been established: 'an Ammonite but not an Ammonitess; a Moabite but not a Moabitess.'"[26] The Zohar includes a quote from Ruth Rab. 4 and thus uses Ruth's gender to legitimize her despite her birth in the country of Moab. The text claims that since Ruth is not a Moabite but a Moabitess, she can actually join the Lord's people.

---

25. Cited by Hecker, *Zohar: Pritzker Edition*, 11:92.
26. Hecker, *Zohar: Pritzker Edition*, 11:88.

The prohibition in Deut 23:4, according to the Zohar's explanation, applies only to men.

Ruth's past is not only legitimized in the Zohar but also glorified. Ruth's lineage is given a royal ancestry in the following passage:

> In the days of the judges, Ruth issued, and she was the daughter of Eglon, king of Moab. Eglon died, killed by Ehud, and another king was appointed; and this daughter of his was orphaned, and she was placed in the home of a guardian, in the fields of Moab. When Elimelech went there, he married her to his son.[27]

In Judg 3, we are told about a Moabite king by the name of Eglon who occupied territories east and west of the Jordan River and also parts of the land of the tribe of Benjamin for eighteen years. According to the biblical narrative, this king is killed by an Israelite by the name of Ehud ben Gera (see Judg 3:15–30).

Based on this narrative, the Zohar associates Eglon with another important Moabite, Ruth, a connection that is already made in the Talmud: "Rabbi Yosei, son of Rabbi Ḥanina, says: Ruth was the daughter of the son of Eglon, the son of the son of Balak, king of Moab" (b. Hor. 10b).[28] Although Eglon was a king, he is not described as a righteous man whom God should reward. The narrative of Judges 3 describes how Ehud went with a hidden knife to see the king, telling him that he had a message for him alone, thus ensuring that Eglon's guards would leave. Once they left, Ehud told Eglon that he had a word from God, and when Eglon rose from his throne, Ehud stabbed him in the belly. Building on this narrative, the following passage from the Zohar explains why Eglon is worthy to be the forefather of the Davidic dynasty:

> They [Ruth and Orpah] were the daughters of Eglon the king of Moab. And what was the reason for Eglon's merit? Rabbi Rechumai explained, "When Ehud came and said to him, 'I have a message from Elohim for you,' immediately he arose from his seat (Judg 3:20). The blessed Holy One said to him, "You rose from your seat for My honor; by your life,

---

27. Hecker, *Zohar: Pritzker Edition*, 11:89.

28. The royal genealogy of Ruth can also be seen in a few more places in talmudic literature: b. Sotah 47a; b. Sanh. 105b; b. Naz. 23b; and Ruth Rab. 2:9. See Hecker, *Zohar: Pritzker Edition*, 11:282 n. 102.

from you will be the forebear of one who will sit upon my throne!" This is said, "Solomon sat upon the throne of the Lord" (1 Chr 29:23).[29]

The fact that Eglon rose from his throne for the word of God is the justification used by the Zohar to paint Eglon as a righteous man worthy of begetting King Solomon. Through Eglon and his story, the text proves that Ruth's ancestry is not a liability but an advantage to her legitimization as a convert.

As a part of Ruth's legitimization, the Zohar further demonstrates her past as a part of her qualifications to be a proper convert. We find this quote:

> If you say that Elimelech converted her [Ruth] there,—no! Rather, she learned all the household customs, and the food and the drink, before she was converted. Only afterwards, when she went with Naomi, did Ruth say "Your people are my people, and your God is my God" (Ruth 1:16).[30]

Here we see that Ruth had not converted in order to marry Elimelech's son Mahlon; however, she learned some customs from sharing their household. This text demonstrates that knowing Jewish customs and practice does not constitute a convert (*giur*). That would only happen with the commitment to the Israelite people and their God. However, Ruth's time with her husband's family was not in vain. It was a part of the process where she gained her practical knowledge about Judean practices and beliefs and perhaps her devotion to her mother-in-law, her people, and her God. Thus Ruth's past as a potential Moabite danger to the household's practice of Judean law and worship of God is negated by her acceptance of the customs and practices of the household.

7. Ruth's Present as a Wife

The legitimacy of Ruth's conversion was not only achieved by the rehabilitation of her past but also by illustrating how, at the time of her marriage to Boaz, she seemed to possess some special traits that made her a model convert. Her actions seem to originate in a noble cause: an act of kindness toward her dead husband. The Zohar explains:

---

29. Hecker, *Zohar: Pritzker Edition*, 11:89.
30. Matt, *Zohar: Pritzker Edition*, 9:282.

> Further, on her rising, as is written she rose before one person could recognize another (Ruth 3:14). That day, she really rose—for Boaz united with her to raise in the name of the dead upon his inheritance (Ruth 4:10) so from her were raised all those kings and the eminence of Israel. (Vayera, Zohar 1:111a)[31]

Ruth's efforts in approaching Boaz and Boaz's consent were to honor the dead, and they were rewarded with being the ancestors of all the exalted men in Israel. Her physical rising (קימה) and her rising in status after her relationship with Boaz for the sake of the dead were rewarded with the rising (הוקם), that is, begetting the great men of Israel. In this light, the Zohar explains the great kindness she was doing:

> This corresponds to what is said: I praise the dead, who have already died (Eccl 4:2), because when they were first alive, they were not praiseworthy, but later they were. Both of them exerted themselves to act kindly and faithfully towards the dead, and the blessed Holy One assisted in that act. All was fitting! "Happy is one who engages in Torah day and night, as it is written meditate on it day and night" (Josh 1:8).[32]

Here we see that the Zohar sees a need to excuse the deeds of Ruth and Tamar, both of whom were foreigners who birthed sons to continue the lines of their deceased Judean husbands. In this manner, the text gives Ruth's actions legitimacy. The text takes the descendants of these women and their biological fathers and gives the credit for those descendants to the women's already dead husbands, thus turning an act of intercourse with one man into the culmination of loyalty and kindness to another (their deceased husbands). The efforts of Tamar and Ruth are likened to Torah study, which should also be done in the night and not only in the day.

Furthermore, Ruth's loyalty to her husband is so great that even though he was already dead and she no longer feared him, she still kept to his family's law:

> "And Ruth clung to her" (Ruth 1:14)—Just as she had accepted [its yoke] during her husband's lifetime, so did she cling to her faith afterwards.

---

31. See Matt, *Zohar: Pritzker Edition*, 2:161.
32. Matt, *Zohar: Pritzker Edition*, 3:149–50.

> Come and see: How exemplary is Ruth! Even without fear of her husband, she clung to her faith. (Midrash Ha-Nelam, ZH 82a)[33]

The text assumes that Ruth was converted to some extent when she married Naomi's son and that she stuck to the faith. Moreover, Ruth has other important traits besides her unending loyalty to her husband, his family, and their law which make her a potential convert. She is viewed in the Zohar as having special, almost divine qualities:

> It is written: listen my daughter, do not go to glean in another field. What was written previously? Ruth said: "I shall go to the field and glean among the ears of grain." This teaches that the holy spirit sparkled within her. Ruth said: "Let me go in the field." Which field did she scrutinize with great faith? Which field was it? The field blessed by the Lord, and that is the Field of Apples. (Midrash Ha-Nelam, ZH 85c)[34]

From this text, we see that Ruth has divine sparks that make her a perfect match for conversion and for being a part in the divine plan. With her divine spark, Ruth seems to access the field of great faith. In this field there is special fruit, literally apples in modern Hebrew, although usually in kabbalah the word refers to citron. These fruits can stand for the divine presence (Shekhinah) or for the people of Israel. In this case, the word could be read as referring to the people of Israel. Thus, the picture painted is one in which Ruth can join the people of Israel as a convert and can enter the dwelling place of the divine presence and faith. Ruth's image seems to be elevated to one of a great devotional mystic. Through her devotion and her special divine spark, she seems to be able to reach the highest spiritual realities where she can join the divine presence and the people of Israel.

Ruth's story also demonstrates to the rabbis of the Zohar what they should have in mind when assessing candidates for conversion, such as how they should treat them and what traits they should find in them:

> Naomi said to her daughters-in-law: "Turn back my daughters." But Ruth replied: "Do not urge me to leave you." Orpah had returned to her people and her gods. This is when one examines a convert to ensure that

---

33. Cited by Matt, *Zohar: Pritzker Edition*, 3:144.
34. As cited by Hecker, *Zohar: Pritzker Edition*, 11:203.

they will endure under the wings of the Shekhinah (divine presence) like Ruth, with a perfect heart. (Midrash Ha-Nelam, ZH 82c)[35]

The rabbis should do as Naomi did; they should send away any potential converts to test their faith and loyalty to God and his people. In Naomi's case, not once but three times did she send Ruth and her other daughter-in-law Orpah away. If they react like Orpah, who stayed in Moab, they are not worthy of *giur*; only if they persist like Ruth do they show a genuine and deep intention to convert and can thus be allowed into the people.

The Zohar also holds up Boaz as a model of perception in identifying necessary traits in a potential convert and states: "Even though she was fit, her suitability was not apparent until she was clung to that righteous one (Boaz). Come and see, Ruth was most fit among the nations" (Midrash Ha-Nelam, ZH 85c).[36]

Elsewhere the Zohar states regarding the matter:

> In fact, there is a mystery here, and it was uttered in the Holy Spirit. For Boaz, the judge of Israel, saw the humility of that righteous woman—who did not move her eyes to look anywhere but in front of her, and saw whatever that saw with a benevolent eye, and had no impudence in her. So he praised her eyes. (Va-Yaqhel, Zohar 2:217b)[37]

The text illustrates that Boaz had a special gift, using the Holy Spirit to see things in Ruth. The Zohar states further:

> But in her he saw (Boaz) a benevolent eye, for she gazed upon everything benevolently. Furthermore, he saw that everything prospered in her hands: the more she gleaned, the more was added in the field; and Boaz perceived that the holy spirit settled upon her.... rather, he was referring to her eyes, which stimulated blessing and many gleanings. Thus, and follow after them—after *your eyes*. (Va-Yaqhel, Zohar 2:218a)[38]

The passage describes Ruth as having special eyes, perhaps a sort of magical ability, a kind of the opposite of evil eye. Ruth's "benevolent eye" is her

---

35. As cited in Hecker, *Zohar: Pritzker Edition*, 11:151.
36. As cited in Hecker, *Zohar: Pritzker Edition*, 11:202.
37. As cited in Matt, *Zohar: Pritzker Edition*, 6:241.
38. As cited in Matt, *Zohar: Pritzker Edition*, 6:242.

fruitfulness, her ability to raise crops and children. Ruth is the one raising the house of David in the field of Judah.

Boaz plays a major role in "discovering" Ruth and in bringing out her potential as an appropriate convert. She may be appropriate, but the "seal of approval" was given by Boaz, as he had previously approved her advances to him. Even though in the biblical narrative Boaz has a more passive role at the start of the relationship, a relationship instigated by Naomi, Boaz's role becomes an active and crucial one as he makes her appropriateness as a convert apparent:

> Parcel of land (Gen 33:19)—a parcel of land of the righteous. She [Ruth] had gone there, entering into a particular section, learning its way, becoming expert in it from these reapers. Who are they? Scholars, called "reapers of the field." Meanwhile, presently, Boaz arrived (Ruth 2:4). Look, righteous one arrived, laden with blessing and bountiful sanctifications. And he created the reapers—who were the reapers? Heavenly court, great Sanhedrin above. The Lord be with you! Now he bestows blessings from holy ones. and they responded, the Lord blesses you, granting him power to draw from source of life, from the midst of the world that is coming. (Midrash Ha-Nelam, ZH 85c)[39]

The text above describes the conversion process with its earthly and otherworldly parts; a convert should come to the sages and learn from them. Then the righteous person, probably a great rabbinical figure, can come in front of the court and ask for the conversion to be fulfilled. The conversion is fulfilled with the drawing of life force, maybe a new soul from the otherworldly dimension. What this process may entail we learn from a different text in the Zohar:

> When a proselyte converts, a soul flies from that palace and enters beneath the wings of the Shekhinah. She kisses her, since she is the fruit of the righteous; and she sends her into that convert, within whom she dwells. From that time on, he is called *ger tsedeq*, convert of rightness.[40] This accords with the mystery that is written: the fruit of the righteous

---

39. As cited in Hecker, *Zohar: Pritzker Edition*, 11:204.
40. The rabbinic tradition differentiates between a *ger tzedeq*, a righteous convert who accepts all of the Jewish law and joins fully the Jewish people, and a *ger toshav*, a resident convert who accepts a small part of the Jewish law and only lives among Jews in the land of Israel without becoming a full member of the Jewish people.

is a tree of life (Prov 11:30) just as the tree of life yields souls, so, too, the fruit of the righteous person yields souls. (Rav Metivta, Zohar 3:168a)[41]

From this passage we understand that the righteous actually create souls for converts in heaven, souls that the converts need access to in order to complete the conversion process and become fully Jewish. The text about Ruth and Boaz may demonstrate how these souls, these divine life forces, are accessed via the power of the *tzaddiq*, the great righteous man. This process places all the authority in the conversion process into the hands of the Torah-studying, masculine elite and the rabbis, in contrast to the book of Ruth, which gives a major role to Naomi and Ruth herself. Boaz the righteous may be likened to the Rabbis who should only passively accept converts and not actively pursue them. It is their duty to examine the candidates and to accept the worthy.

The Zohar analyzes Ruth's conversation with Boaz, reading into it her utmost dedication to the Lord. It finds in Ruth bits of the divine spark, hinting at her possible "Jewish" soul or her special relationship with the divine. Boaz's importance is stressed again and again, as a judge, a teacher, and a righteous person. The Zohar diminishes the active importance of both Ruth and Naomi but makes sure that Ruth really possesses all the qualities needed to join the people of God and to beget their royal dynasty.

8. Ruth's Future as a Mother

Ruth's children are actually seen as Naomi's, her mother-in-law's, children. In this sense, the Davidic line can be said to stem from Naomi more than Ruth. Indeed, Ruth is given only the role of a biological mother, while the spiritual motherhood is given to Naomi. In the biblical tale, Ruth's role is reduced to a passive part of the story. Her only real decision is to join Naomi. Subsequently, she turns into a tool of Naomi's and is a puppet in both her hands and later in the hands of Boaz. The only meaningful independent act she makes is her resistance to her mother-in-law's plea to return to Moab; in that act, she is almost reminiscent of a slave who is unwilling to go free.[42] But as such a slave is treated with contempt in the

---

41. As cited in Matt, *Zohar: Pritzker Edition*, 9:105.

42. The rabbinical term would be *eved nirzaa* after the law prescribing the ceremonial mutilation of a slave's ear who does not want to regain his freedom for love of his master, as described in Exod 21:6.

rabbinical texts, Ruth, who ends up serving God as her master, is very much appreciated. Ruth's quality is based on her devotion and unending loyalty. With those attributes of subservience, she wins her place in Jewish history. Ruth's devotion has made her a part in God's future for Judea and the people of Israel.

Another passage of the Zohar states: "The blessed Holy One draws Ruth after Him, extracting her from among the nations, drawing her towards Him, causing troops and holy camps to issue forth from Her" (Midrash Ha-Nelam, ZH 85c).[43] Here we see that Ruth must be a legitimate convert since God himself picked her out from among the nations and selected her for a higher purpose: to beget his future servants. We see that she is picked by God to be a mother. Her biological function as a woman is her purpose in this text's view. Her behavior as a temptress, which is alluded to in the biblical tale, is looked upon in the Zohar in the context of the future of Judea, in which her special role in Jewish history is stressed:

> As for Ruth, her husband died and then she engaged in this act with Boaz, as it is written: "She uncovered his feet and lay down" (Ruth 3:7). Engaging with him, she later gave birth to Obed. Now, you might ask "why didn't Obed issue from another woman?" but precisely she was needed, no one else. "From those two," the seed of Judah was established and consummated. Both of them acted properly, acting kindly towards the dead so that the word would later be enhanced. (Va-Yeshev, Zohar 1:188b)[44]

Her actions are seen as a part of a divine plan; only she could carry the seed of Judah forward. Boaz seems to see that with his divine powers and thus approve of her conversion: "Through the holy spirit, Boaz saw that the superior holy eyes (i.e. kings) were destined to issue from her" (Va-Yaqhel, Zohar 2:218a).[45] Ruth's future legacy as a mother required legitimizing her conversion. Her devotion as a wife further legitimized her as the person from whom future kings were descended. God has a plan in which Ruth's past, present, and future take part in the story of the Jewish people.

---

43. As cited in Hecker, *Zohar: Pritzker Edition*, 11:199.
44. As cited by Matt, *Zohar: Pritzker Edition*, 3:149.
45. As cited by Matt, *Zohar: Pritzker Edition*, 3:242.

9. Conclusion

We have seen that the Zohar has a unique esoteric approach to conversion. The conversion process does not happen exclusively in the material or social world. It also has hidden, otherworldly elements. The candidate for conversion may have special attributes, abilities, "magical" eyes or divine sparks, possibly hinting at the candidate's divine connection or at least a special connection with God and his people. The one performing the conversion process must also have special abilities, help from the Holy Spirit, and an access to hidden and elevated dimensions of reality.

The three aspects of Ruth which have been discussed above—past-present-future and daughter-wife-mother—are combined in the following passage from the Zohar:

> Ruth, on account of the name, turtledove [*tor*]. Just as the latter is fit for the altar, so was Ruth fit to join the congregation. For the law has already been established: "An Ammonite (Deut 23:4), but not an Ammonitess; a Moabite, but not a Moabitess." "Ruth, forebear of a son who, satiated the blessed Holy One with songs of praises. Ruth, wife of Mahlon, came into the congregation." (Midrash Ha-Nelam, ZH 78b)[46]

At the heart of this passage is a quote from Ruth Rab. 4, which uses Ruth's gender to legitimize her despite her past; the text claims that since Ruth is not a Moabite but a Moabitess, she can join the people of the Lord. This passage opens and closes with the present. It uses her name Ruth and the letters spelling it to treat her like a dove, which is an appropriate sacrifice, hinting at her special attributes. The text calls her the wife of Machalon (son of Naomi), reminding us of the kindness she has shown him. Her legitimacy as a convert and a member of the people is also won by her motherhood. Her descendants' extra services to God in song and praise show her central place among the people of the Lord. These three roles are summarized succinctly by Elliot Wolfson:

> There are several distinct feminine images of the Torah in the body of classical rabbinic literature. I would like to mention here three of the more salient images: daughter of God, or sometimes expressed as the daughter of the king, the bride, and the mother.[47]

---

46. As cited in Hecker, *Zohar: Pritzker Edition*, 11:88–89.

47. Elliot R. Wolfson, *Circle in the Square: Studies in the Use of Gender in Kabbalistic Symbolism* (Albany: State University of New York Press, 1995), 3.

Thus the three dimensions of Ruth's legitimization as a convert are the three ways women can be seen in relation to men: daughter, wife, mother. It is no coincidence that in kabbalah the Torah itself, when likened to a woman, also has these three dimensions: daughter of a king, who is God; wife from whom learned men derive pleasure and to whom they need to be loyal; and mother who both protects the people of Israel and requires obedience.

Art

Female Protagonists in Medieval Jewish Book Art

Katrin Kogman-Appel

From the time that Jewish culture embraced the visual arts, various forms of cyclic or programmatic visualization of biblical history came into being. Embedded within a narrative framework, cyclic treatments of biblical events allow us to investigate the way in which medieval Jewish visual language approached any particular group of protagonists. Image cycles reflect selections made by either the team who produced them, the manuscript's patron, or both. The selection of specific themes underscored the specific interests of the patronage. The themes chosen conveyed these agendas and are indicative of the reception of the contents on the part of those who designed and commissioned the cycles. Selection means emphasis, and it guides the reader through the viewing of the cycle. The pictorial narratives in medieval Hebrew books were no exception.

The following discussion focuses on two women, Rebekah and Zipporah, neither of whom stands out in any way in the biblical narrative. They married their husbands, mothered their children, and assumed various roles in the story as biblical history unfolded. Both also interacted with God. Although the Bible tells their stories, rabbinic exegesis has its own take on them and for the most part downplays their input and status. For example, whereas the Bible has Rebekah consulting God about her pregnancy, the rabbinic tradition emphasizes that she needed a human mediator for the interaction. Likewise, whereas the Bible has Zipporah circumcising her son with her own hands, some rabbinic traditions insist that she sought a male protagonist to perform the ritual. The observations presented here demonstrate that medieval visual renderings of Rebekah and Zipporah occasionally altered the rabbinic image of these women and created alternative narratives indicative of a different path of reception of the biblical content.[1] These images do so in two different ways: they assign both women central roles in salvation history and they also present them as gender-relevant role models for certain religious values as these values changed over time and in varying social circumstances.

1. Cyclic Imagery in Medieval Jewish Book Art

The following section briefly surveys the principal stages in the development of pictorial cycles in Jewish contexts and then offers a short discussion regarding the relevant scholarship. The earliest extant visual treatment of the biblical narrative goes back to third-century Syria. The spectacular discovery of the synagogue of Dura Europos in 1932 revealed a rich set of narrative murals arranged not in chronological sequence but rather in a programmatic approach.[2]

The fourth to the sixth centuries saw some biblical themes represented on mosaic pavements, but Jewish narrative art stopped developing at some point toward the end of the late antique period, only to reappear around the 1230s. Many scholars have suggested that the reason for this hiatus lies in the fact that most Jews were then living within an Islamic cultural environment and thus adopted a stringent approach to the prohibition to create and use images.[3] As I have shown elsewhere, however, it is likely that the preference for figural or abstract art had to do with Jewish cultures

---

1. In a recent paper on biblical models and Jewish daily life, Elisheva Baumgarten points to the centrality of biblical teachings among medieval non-scholarly groups and suggests that understanding the reception of the Bible and its interpretation can reveal much about the role of biblical models in the life of medieval Jews. See "'Like Adam and Eve': Biblical Models and Jewish Daily Life in Medieval Christian Europe," *ITQ* 83.1 (2018): 44–61.

2. For the archaeological report, see Carl Kraeling, *The Synagogue: The Excavations at Dura Europos: Final Report VIII, Part 1* (New Haven: Yale University Press, 1956). Among the most important efforts to contextualize the imagery, see Annabel J. Wharton, "Good and Bad Images from the Synagogue of Dura Europos: Contexts, Subtexts, Intertexts," *Art History* 17.1 (1994): 1–25; Jas Elsner, "Cultural Resistance and the Visual Image: The Case of Dura Europos," *Classical Philology* 96 (2001): 269–304; Steven Fine, "Jewish Identity at the *Limus*—The Earliest Reception of the Dura Europos Synagogue Paintings," in *Cultural Identity in the Ancient Mediterranean*, ed. Erich S. Gruen (Los Angeles: Getty Publications, 2011), 289–306.

3. Among the more recent scholars to suggest so is Shalom Sabar, "'The Right Path for an Artist': The Approach of Leone da Modena to Visual Art," *Hebraica hereditas* (2005): 255–56.

adopting and adapting to the tastes and fashions of their environments. It is thus also reasonable to interpret the revival of figural art as a reaction to changing Jewish perceptions of Christianity.[4] From the thirteenth century on, Jewish manuscript painting became increasingly popular all over Europe, developing simultaneously in the cultural centers of Iberia, France, the Roman Empire, and Italy. Bibles and Passover haggadot as well as other prayer books were being decorated with rich and versatile iconographic programs. Some of these now extant books include lengthy pictorial cycles that retell the biblical narrative of Israelite history, and it is to these that I turn my attention in the present essay.

Particularly outstanding are ten manuscripts of the Passover haggadah from Iberia, mostly Catalonia; among them is the Sarajevo Haggadah (Aragon, ca. 1330s), which was the first Jewish work of art to attract scholarly attention at the end of the nineteenth century.[5] The haggadah, normally a small book, includes the text to be read at the ceremonial meal on the eve of the Passover holiday. While for centuries it was attached to the general prayer book, the haggadah eventually turned into an independent, small-sized volume at an unknown date during the thirteenth century. This format left plenty of space for artistic treatment and a pictorial cycle was one of the ways of enriching the Passover ritual for a range of different audiences, scholarly and unscholarly alike. One specific example discussed here is the Golden Haggadah in London (ca. 1320).[6] A manuscript that is closely related to it is also in the British Library (BL Or. 2884, ca. 1325).[7] The Rylands Haggadah is in Manchester

---

4. Katrin Kogman-Appel, "Christianity, Idolatry, and the Question of Jewish Figural Painting in the Middle Ages," *Speculum* 84 (2009): 73–107.

5. Julius von Schlosser and David Heinrich Müller, *Die Haggadah von Sarajevo: Eine spanisch-jüdische Bilderhandschrift des Mittelalters* (Vienna: Hölder, 1898); Mirsad Sijarić, ed., *The Sarajevo Haggadah: History and Art*, with a commentary volume by Shalom Sabar (Sarajevo: The National Museum of Bosnia and Herzegovina, 2018).

6. British Library, Add. MS 27210, http://www.bl.uk/manuscripts/Viewer.aspx?ref=add_ms_27210_f001r. For a facsimile edition, see Bezalel Narkiss, *The Golden Haggadah: A Fourteenth-Century Illuminated Hebrew Manuscript in the British Museum* (London: Eugrammia, 1970); Bezalel Narkiss, Aliza Cohen-Mushlin, and Anat Tcherikover, *Spanish and Portuguese Manuscripts*, vol. 1 of *Hebrew Illuminated Manuscripts in the British Isles* (Jerusalem: Israeli Academy of Sciences; Oxford: Oxford University Press, 1982), 58–67.

7. MS Oriental 2884, http://www.bl.uk/manuscripts/Viewer.aspx?ref=or_2884_fs001r; Narkiss et al., *Spanish and Portuguese Manuscripts*, 67–78.

(ca. 1330–1340).[8] A very similar book is also in London (BL Or. 1404, ca. 1330–40).[9] All of these manuscripts originated in Catalonia.

Medieval Ashkenaz also developed a rich visual language, even though cyclic treatments of biblical history were less common. The Schocken Bible (ca. 1300) from the Upper Rhine region has a single, large initial panel decorating the word *bereshit*, "in the beginning." The initial is surrounded by forty-six grisaille medallions that offer a rich narrative sequence that runs from the temptation of Adam and Eve to the story of Balaam.[10] Finally, there is an outstanding pair of richly illustrated Ashkenazic Passover haggadot. The first, commonly known as the Second Nuremberg Haggadah, is in a private collection in London; the second, known as the Yahuda Haggadah, is in the Israel Museum. Judging from their style and technique they were perhaps produced in Franconia during the 1460s.[11] Both visualize the stories of Genesis and Exodus together with a few events from other biblical books.

Comparative iconography easily reveals that Jewish figurative art evidences various relationships to Christian art. Studies on the impact of late antique rabbinic exegesis on the imagery have shown that the interpolation of extrabiblical narrative elements from commentary literature helped Jewish patrons and artists transform Christian motifs into imageries that projected specific Jewish visual idioms.[12] However, any narrative image

---

8. Manchester, John Rylands University Library, MS Heb. 6. For a facsimile edition, see Raphael Loewe, ed., *The Rylands Haggadah* (London: Thames & Hudson, 1988); Narkiss et al., *Spanish and Portuguese Manuscripts*, 86–93.

9. MS Oriental 1404, http://www.bl.uk/manuscripts/Viewer.aspx?ref=or_1404_fs001r (15.8.2017); Marc M. Epstein, ed., *The Brother Haggadah: A Medieval Sephardi Masterpiece in Facsimile* (London: Thames & Hudson, 2016); Narkiss et al., *Spanish and Portuguese Manuscripts*, 93–101.

10. Private collection; formerly Jerusalem, Schocken Institute for Jewish Research, MS 14840. For a good publication of the image, see Bezalel Narkiss, *Hebrew Illuminated Manuscripts* (Jerusalem: Keter, 1969), pl. 31.

11. London, private collection of David Sofer. For a description and scans of earlier photographs, see http://cja.huji.ac.il/browser.php?mode=set&id=30. Jerusalem, Israel Museum, MS 180/50. For a description and scans of earlier photographs, see http://cja.huji.ac.il/browser.php?mode=set&id=11; Katrin Kogman-Appel, *Die Zweite Nürnberger und die Jehuda Haggada: Jüdische Künstler zwischen Tradition und Fortschritt* (Frankfurt am Main: Lang, 1999).

12. This has been demonstrated for the Dura murals, e.g., by Eliezer L. Sukenik, *The Synagogue of Dura Europos and Its Wall Paintings* [Hebrew] (Jerusalem: Bialik Institute, 1947). For the Sephardic Golden Haggadah, see Narkiss, *Golden Haggadah*.

cycle produced in the thirteenth to the fifteenth centuries, whether composed by Christians or by Jews and whether newly designed or based on earlier sources, was the result of an individual process of the visualization of Scripture, performed under various circumstances, serving different purposes, and aimed at diverse audiences. Art historical research in recent decades has approached these cycles with the goal of contextualizing them within broader frameworks of cultural history. Often relying on theories developed outside the field of art history, such as narratology, reception theory, and *Annales*-style studies of *mentalités*,[13] these efforts have significantly changed our understanding of how the visual language functioned in Jewish cultures. Other contextualizing approaches have resulted in attempts to solve questions of text-image relationships, patronage, and functionality.[14] The question of the relationship between Jewish and Christian cycles, which was the focus of early research on issues of iconographic prototypes and model-copy connections, gave way to a discourse on cultural interaction and exchange, cultural resistance, and polemical imagery.[15] Gender theoretical approaches were employed in any number of projects concerned with medieval Christian art, but less so in the context of Jewish works.[16]

2. Female Protagonists Visualized: Two Case Studies

In seeking prominent female protagonists in pictorial cycles in Hebrew manuscripts, one soon observes that two figures stand out: Rebekah and Zipporah. I first present the visual renderings in their relation to the relevant biblical narratives and midrashic elaborations and submit that they suggest a parallel story line meant as some sort of alternative narrative.

For the Second Nuremberg and the Yahuda Haggadah, see Kogman-Appel, *Zweite Nürnberger*, 33–90.

13. One example is Marc M. Epstein, *The Medieval Haggadah: Art, Narrative, and Religious Imagination* (New Haven: Yale University Press, 2010).

14. Wharton, "Good and Bad Images"; Katrin Kogman-Appel, *Illuminated Haggadot from Medieval Spain: Biblical Imagery and the Passover Holiday* (University Park: Pennsylvania State University Press, 2006).

15. Kogman-Appel, *Illuminated Haggadot*, 47–110, 135–86; Elsner, "Cultural Resistance"; Julie A. Harris, "Polemical Images in the Golden Haggadah, BL, Add. MS 27210," *Medieval Encounters* 8 (2002): 105–22.

16. For an example, see Julie A. Harris, "Love in the Land of Goshen: Haggadah, History, and the Making of British Library, MS Oriental 2737," *Gesta* 52.2 (2013): 161–80.

The images were produced under different historical situations in different Jewish societies with different halakhic agendas. Hence the observations regarding the visual language employed are discussed against the background of these varying circumstances and thus contextualize the images within the framework of the societies that produced and used them.

Rebekah appears in the haggadah cycles as the driving force behind the actions taken to ensure that Jacob will become the heir of Israel instead of the firstborn Esau. In some cycles Rebekah's role is visualized from the moment she arrives at Isaac's tent. The Sarajevo Haggadah includes this scene in the earliest cycle (fig. 1). Isaac is shown as a young man to the left "wandering about the field," as a nearby caption explains, quoting the book of Genesis. Eliezer, Abraham's servant who had been sent out to seek a wife for Isaac, and Rebekah, whom he had brought from Aram Naharaim, are approaching on donkeys (Gen 24:63).[17] What has been translated in the English version of the Bible as "wandering" appears in the Hebrew text as לשוח. The midrash Genesis Rabbah references one of Rabbi Eliezer's hermeneutical rules (paronomasia) based on the similar grammatical roots of words: "Towards evening Isaac went out to wander [לשוח] in the fields: there is no wandering [שיחה] other than prayer," interpreting the word לשוח as a relative of the word שיחה (conversation). Thus, the biblical verse is understood as "toward evening Isaac went out to pray" (Gen. Rab. 60:16 on Gen 24:61–63).[18] This understanding alters the meaning of the couple's first encounter: Isaac is not just walking about in the fields; instead, Rebekah sees him as a pious man in the midst of prayer. This highlights the aspect of the story showing that she had been found to be a worthy bride for this outstandingly devout man.

The Second Nuremberg and the Yahuda Haggadot also emphasize this aspect of the story. Common in both these manuscripts, we find an unframed marginal narrative covering both the lower and the outer margins (fig. 2). Rebekah and Eliezer approach at the bottom of the page, but Isaac also appears in the upper right-hand corner head down as if he were

---

17. For the English text of the Bible, occasionally adapted here for accuracy and clarity, see *The Jewish Bible: Tanakh—The Holy Scriptures: The New JPS Translation According to the Traditional Hebrew Text* (Philadelphia: Jewish Publication Society, 1985).

18. Text from Yehuda Theodor and Hanoch Albeck, eds., *Genesis Rabbah* [Hebrew] (Jerusalem: Wahrmann, 1965); for an English version, see *Genesis Rabbah: The Judaic Commentary of the Book of Genesis: A New American Translation*, trans. Jacob Neusner (Atlanta: Scholars, 1985).

Fig. 1. Sarajevo, National Museum of Bosnia and Herzegovina, Aragon, ca. 1330 ("Sarajevo Haggadah"), fol. 8r, Isaac and Rebekah meet

falling from heaven. An accompanying rhymed caption in the Yahuda Haggadah explains: "Isaac returned glorified, because he arrived from the upper realms." The parallel in the Second Nuremberg Haggadah reads: "Isaac returned from the garden that God had planted for our protection."[19]

Rebekah thus encounters not just any pious man but one who, at the very moment of their first meeting, returns from paradise. Midrashic elaborations of the biblical story about the binding of Isaac in Gen 22 added a significant motif in which Abraham had harmed Isaac, who died and visited paradise to be resurrected and to return only when Rebekah arrived with Eliezer. The idea that Abraham touched Isaac's throat and that the latter's soul disappeared for a time appears in late antique and early medieval midrashim as an explanation of the fact that Isaac is not mentioned in Genesis between the binding scene on Mount Moriah and the arrival of Rebekah (see, e.g., Pirqe R. El. 31).[20] Later midrashim declare more explicitly that Isaac was hurt.[21] The late medieval readers of the Yahuda Haggadah viewed the tale not solely from the point of view of Isaac's righteousness, but also saw it from the perspective of Rebekah's place as a witness to his return, thus presenting her as a worthy bride for a man who was willing to sacrifice his life for the love of God, a martyr.

Whereas the cycles in Iberian haggadot do not relate to the biblical narrative until the birth of the twin brothers, Jacob and Esau, in the Franconian haggadot Rebekah's first encounter with her future husband is immediately followed by a depiction that highlights her role in fulfilling her domestic duties. After their first meeting, the couple is officially introduced by Eliezer and married by Abraham (Gen 25:21).[22] The scene is set in front

---

19. For a publication and translation of the captions, see *Index of Jewish Art*, https://tinyurl.com/SBLPress6014b.

20. For an English translation, see Gerald Friedlander, ed. and trans., *Pirkê de Rabbi Eliezer* (London: Kegan Paul, 1916).

21. See, e.g., Dov Heiman et al., eds., *Yalqut Shim'oni* (Jerusalem: Kook Institute, 1973), 1:101. On the midrashic tradition, see Shalom Spiegel, "*Aggadot* on the Binding of Isaac: A *Piyyut* about the Slaughter of Isaac and His Resurrection by R. Ephraim of Bonn" [Hebrew], in *Alexander Marx Jubilee Volume on the Occasion of His Seventieth Birthday* (New York: Jewish Theological Seminary of America, 1950), 484–91. On visualizations of the binding of Isaac in medieval Ashkenaz contextualized within their cultural and religious settings, especially martyrdom, see Shalom Sabar, "'The Fathers Slaughter Their Sons': Depictions of the Binding of Isaac in the Art of Medieval Ashkenaz," *Images* 3 (2009): 9–28.

22. Second Nuremberg Haggadah, fol. 32r; Yahuda Haggadah, fol. 31r.

Fig. 2. Jerusalem, Israel Museum, MS 180/50, Franconia, ca. 1465 ("Yahuda Haggadah"), fol. 30v: Rebekah arrives

of a large tent that covers most of the outer margins of the page. Below and above the tent, two captions characterize Rebekah in some detail:

> Eliezer brought Rebekah to the tent, and Isaac was consoled by her of his mother['s death]. When Sarah died, three things ceased [to exist], and when Rebekah arrived, they reappeared; a cloud spread above the tent and there is a blessing on the dough, and the candle burns from Sabbath eve to Sabbath eve.

The motif that Isaac was consoled for the death of his mother by the piety of his wife is based on Genesis Rabbah (60:16).[23]

As the union remains childless for some time, Isaac prays to God "in the presence of his wife, because she was barren" (Gen 25:21). It is not quite clear how "in the presence of his wife" should be understood: Did Isaac pray together with his wife? on behalf of his wife? for his wife? The image shows both Isaac and Rebekah in prayer, while the caption notes that God heard his prayer and not hers (fig. 3). The rabbinic tradition implies that it is not clear who was barren, but insists in any case that it was Isaac's prayer and not Rebekah's that was heard by God (*Midrash Aggadah* on Gen 25:21).[24]

Once pregnant and with the two boys struggling in her womb, Rebekah confers with the Lord about her pain (Gen 25:22). Images in the Second Nuremberg and the Yahuda Haggadot again follow the midrash and have her consult the rabbinic school of Shem, as God never converses directly with a woman. There she learns about the two nations struggling in her womb (fig. 3) (Gen. Rab. 63:6). The twins' birth is shown in both the Sarajevo Haggadah and the two Ashkenazic cycles, but it is only in the latter that Rebekah undertakes the education of her sons, another midrashic motif (fig. 4). The tale about the twins being educated is an important part of the rabbinic plot, as it is at that point that their differences in character are highlighted by contrasting Jacob's scholarliness with Esau's roughness. In the Bible we read: "When the boys grew up, Esau became a skillful hunter, a man of the outdoors; but Jacob was a mild man who stayed in camp" (Gen 25:27). Numerous midrashim comment on the verse and explain

---

23. The allusion to the dough and the Sabbath candles relies on a common motif, the commandments of dough, ritual cleaning, and candle lighting on the Sabbath eve (מצות חנ"ה), the three main responsibilities of women; for more see below. The depicted miracles, thus, highlight Rebekah's role as the pious wife of a martyr.

24. *Midrash Aggadah*, ed. Solomon Buber (Vienna: n.p., 1884).

Fig. 3. Jerusalem, Israel Museum, MS 180/50, Franconia, ca. 1465 ("Yahuda Haggadah"), fol. 31v: Isaac and Rebekah pray for offspring; Rebekah consults Shem

that Jacob's mildness has to do with his eagerness to study. The rabbinic tradition explains that when still in their mother's womb, Jacob tended toward the study houses and Esau toward the sites of idolatry (b. Meg. 17a).[25] Later both boys were educated, but after thirteen years of study it is only Jacob who remained in the houses of study, whereas Esau became an idolater (Gen. Rab, 63:10). Rebekah is mentioned in these midrashic tales. However, in the Ashkenazic haggadah cycles, it is she who takes the boys to school. Thus, the imagery not only elaborates on the biblical narrative by means of the midrash, but goes beyond the rabbinic image of Rebekah and turns her into the major agent of the story.

The highlight of this entire series is the image of Isaac blessing Jacob as the firstborn, which is included not only in the most extensive cycles, but also in the Golden Haggadah (fig. 5) and BL Or. 2884 (fol. 4v). The biblical narrative has Isaac, having grown old and blind, converse with Esau, the firstborn. He sends him out to hunt for venison, to bring it home, have a meal prepared, and receive his father's blessing. Rebekah, having overheard the conversation, advises Jacob to slaughter an animal from the flock, to prepare a meal, and to go to his father disguised as Esau so that he will receive the blessing instead. Rebekah is also the one who prepares a kid's skin to be put on Jacob's arm to have him appear as hairy as his brother. However, there is no mention of Rebekah when Jacob goes to his father (Gen. 27:1–29).

Even though she is not mentioned in this scene in the biblical text, Rebekah appears in all the visualizations of the actual blessing, as if to underscore that she was the driving force behind Jacob's actions. The depiction in the Sarajevo Haggadah adds a significant detail to the imagery (fig. 6). Whereas the Golden Haggadah shows Rebekah inside the room where the blessing takes place, the Sarajevo Haggadah has her at some distance within a separate architectural unit holding Esau's garment for Jacob to wear, a detail not found in any of the other renderings. The images add her figure to the scene and underscore her role in the narrative, thus acknowledging that it was her actions that made it possible for Jacob to become the father of the nation.

This last point is particularly stressed in the Sarajevo Haggadah. The garment Rebekah is holding in her hands is mentioned in the bibli-

---

25. For an English version, see Isidore Epstein, ed., *Hebrew-English Edition of the Babylonian Talmud* (London: Soncino, 1984).

Female Protagonists in Medieval Jewish Book Art

Fig. 4. London, Collection David Sofer, Franconia, c. 1465 ("Second Nuremberg Haggadah"), fol. 33r: Birth of Jacob and Esau; Jacob and Esau on the way to school

Fig. 5. London, British Library, Add. MS 27210, Catalonia, c. 1320 ("Golden Haggadah"), fol. 4v: Isaac blesses Jacob

Fig. 6. Sarajevo, National Museum of Bosnia and Herzegovina, Aragon, ca. 1330 ("Sarajevo Haggadah"), fol. 9v: Isaac blessing Jacob

cal text (Gen 15): "Rebekah then took the best clothes of her elder son, Esau, which were there in the house, and had her younger son Jacob put them on." This, however, does not account for the prominent position of the garment occupying the left side of the panel. A midrash elaborates on the garment, noting that it was originally in Nimrod's possession, but was acquired by Esau. The midrash also attempts to explain why it was kept in Rebekah's dwelling, indicated by the architectural structure behind her. This commentary is included in late antique sources and is quoted in the medieval anthology Yalqut Shimoni (115).[26]

The visual narratives not only differ slightly from the textual ones, but also focus specifically on certain aspects. The Bible underscores the family connections between Abraham and Laban and the efforts to find a non-Canaanite wife. Once pregnant, Rebekah becomes a major protagonist learning about the two nations in her womb and that "the older shall serve the younger" (Gen 25:23). When she overhears the conversation between

---

26. Kogman-Appel, *Illuminated Haggadot*, 162.

Isaac and Esau in preparation of the firstborn's blessing, remembering what God told her, she intervenes and makes sure that the younger son receives the blessing. Isaac's performance of the blessing is the most crucial moment of the narrative.

Whereas Rebekah appears in the biblical story along with the male protagonists who account for the main aspects of the plot, the visual representations define her role with greater precision. Above all, her worthiness is underscored in all the cycles. In later Ashkenazic renderings, she even becomes a witness to Isaac's miraculous resurrection. She is pious like her mother-in-law, and she is the one who notices the boys' different characters.

In the rabbinic tradition Jacob and Esau became key figures in the discourse about the Jewish-Christian divide. Jacob is associated with Israel and Esau first with Rome and eventually with Christianity;[27] the differences in their characters underscore their identities even while they are still in their mother's womb. Mildness and roughness are explained in terms of differentiating between Jews and gentiles. Dedicating an entire illustration to Rebekah's understanding of the diverging nature of her sons' characters highlights her role. Not only are the boys shown doing different things (for instance, as in the Sarajevo Haggadah), but Rebekah is portrayed as coming to terms with it. The image of the boys on the way to school clearly underscores this message: Rebekah had taken care of the boys' education and thus was able to see which of the two was worthy to be chosen by God. The midrash emphasizes that despite a proper Jewish education, Esau chose the houses of idolatry. Although it is not clear among those who composed the midrashim who were envisioned as idolaters, there can be no doubt that for the viewers of the medieval Ashkenazic haggadot, these were Christians. Rebekah is portrayed as the principal agent ensuring that God's promise will be fulfilled.

Christian exegesis appropriated the role of Jacob, the real Israel, and at the same time assigned the part of Esau to the Jews. Rebekah's actions in a Jewish image cycle thus represented a proper answer to Christian claims of *verus Israel*. She became a visual vehicle of Jewish challenges to the Christian contention. This is true of both the Iberian and the Ashkenazic

---

27. y. Taʿan. 4:8, 68d. For an English version of the Jerusalem Talmud, see Jacob Neusner, ed., *The Talmud of the Land of Israel* (Chicago: University of Chicago Press, 1987). On Esau see also the discussion by Israel J. Yuval, *Two Nations in Your Womb: Perceptions of Jews and Christians in Late Antiquity and the Middle Ages* (Berkeley: University of California Press, 2006), 1–30.

visualizations of the story. They differ, but they both highlight Rebekah and show her repeatedly in scenes where she is not mentioned in the Bible. In both the Sarajevo Haggadah and the Ashkenazic cycles her role is further highlighted by adjacent depictions of Esau at the hunt, as his identity as a hunter emphasizes his association with Christianity. Depictions of a hunt in Hebrew manuscripts have often been interpreted as allegories of Jewish persecution by Christian authorities.[28] Esau's portrayal was not merely an illustration of "Esau became a skillful hunter," but was stylized into a prototype of Christian hostility against Israel and as representative of Jewish persecution.

Another woman who takes Israel's history into her own hands is Moses's wife Zipporah. The most detailed cyclic treatment is, again, found in the two Ashkenazic manuscripts, the Second Nuremberg and the Yahuda Haggadot. Moses, having escaped prosecution in Egypt for killing an Egyptian overseer, travels to Midian. At a well in the desert he encounters the seven daughters of the Midianite priest Re'uel (Jethro) who were being bothered by aggressive shepherds. Moses stands up against the shepherds, drives them away, and helps the young women draw water. When the daughters return to their father to report what has happened, he sends them out again to invite Moses to his camp (Exod 2:15–20). The images show Moses as a traveler on the way, the encounter at the well, and Jethro listening to the story.[29] The pictorial rendering of this last act in the upper left-hand corner of the page diverges from the biblical text and instead of showing all the daughters, it singles out one, apparently Zipporah, Moses's future bride. The caption explains that she described him as a "hero, brave, beautiful and pleasant."

Jethro gives Zipporah to Moses in marriage (Exod 2:21). In the pictorial, however, things do not go as smoothly as in the biblical text. The first image on the next page shows Moses imprisoned after Jethro, who had earlier functioned as one of Pharaoh's counselors, had recognized him as the Hebrew child about whom the king had been warned. Moses appears in a tower and is expected to starve, but is nourished secretly by the brave

---

28. Marc M. Epstein, *Dreams of Subversion in Medieval Jewish Art and Literature* (University Park: Pennsylvania State University Press, 1997), 16–38; Sara Offenberg, "Expressions of Meeting the Challenges of the Christian Milieu in Medieval Jewish Art and Literature" [Hebrew] (PhD diss., The Ben-Gurion University of the Negev, 2008), 97–143.

29. Second Nuremberg Haggadah, fols. 12r–12v; Yahuda Haggadah, fols. 11r–11v.

maiden. Her father, convinced by Moses's miraculous survival, releases him and arranges for the marriage, which is shown on the bottom of the page. This elaboration is based on a midrashic motif, which was particularly popular in the late medieval genre of biblical story telling (Exod 4:20).[30] The couple gets married and two sons are born.

After God reveals himself to Moses at the burning bush and tells him to go back to Egypt to lead his fellow Israelites out of the bondage, Moses "took his wife and his sons, mounted them on an ass, and went back to the Land of Egypt" (Exod 4:20). A few verses later, however, God sought to kill Moses or his younger son (the text is not clear on this point), while the family lodged at an encampment in the desert. No reason is given. It is Zipporah who realizes that Moses had neglected the divine command to circumcise his son: "Zipporah took a flint and cut off her son's foreskin, and touched his legs with it, saying: You are surely a bridegroom of blood to me" (Exod 4:25). It is not clear whose legs Zipporah touched, nor is it clear whom she is referring to as a "bridegroom of blood."

A late thirteenth-century Castilian haggadah, now in London, has an image of the couple on the way: Zipporah and the boys on the donkey accompanied by Moses walking behind them.[31] In other cycles the two episodes are juxtaposed, as in the Catalan examples Or. 1404 in the British Library (fig. 7) and the Rylands Haggadah in Manchester (fig. 8). In the Second Nuremberg and the Yahuda Haggadot the two events appear on the margins of the page, one above the other. Here Moses is missing from the travel scene; he appears only in the upper right-hand corner being swallowed up by a monster (God's attempt to kill him) and, again, to the left, where he meets Aaron (fig. 9).

In all of these portrayals, but in particular in the ones from Iberia, the imagery of the traveling couple creates an immediate association with Christian representations of the Holy Family's flight to Egypt. This was observed and discussed several years ago by Marc Epstein in connection with a depiction of the couple in the Golden Haggadah. The image, Epstein argues, does not simply copy the Christian model but translates it into a visual polemic that contrasts the old, barren figure of the Christian Joseph with a young image of the Jewish Moses traveling with two children. The

---

30. For details, images, and sources, see Kogman-Appel, *Zweite Nürnberger*, 42–44.

31. London, British Library, MS Or. 2737, fol. 67v, http://www.bl.uk/manuscripts/Viewer.aspx?ref=or_2737_fs001r; see Narkiss et al., *Spanish and Portuguese Manuscripts*, 45–51.

Fig. 7. London, British Library, MS Or. 1404, Catalonia, 1330–40, fol. 2r: Moses and Zipporah on the way to Egypt; Zipporah circumcising Eliezer.

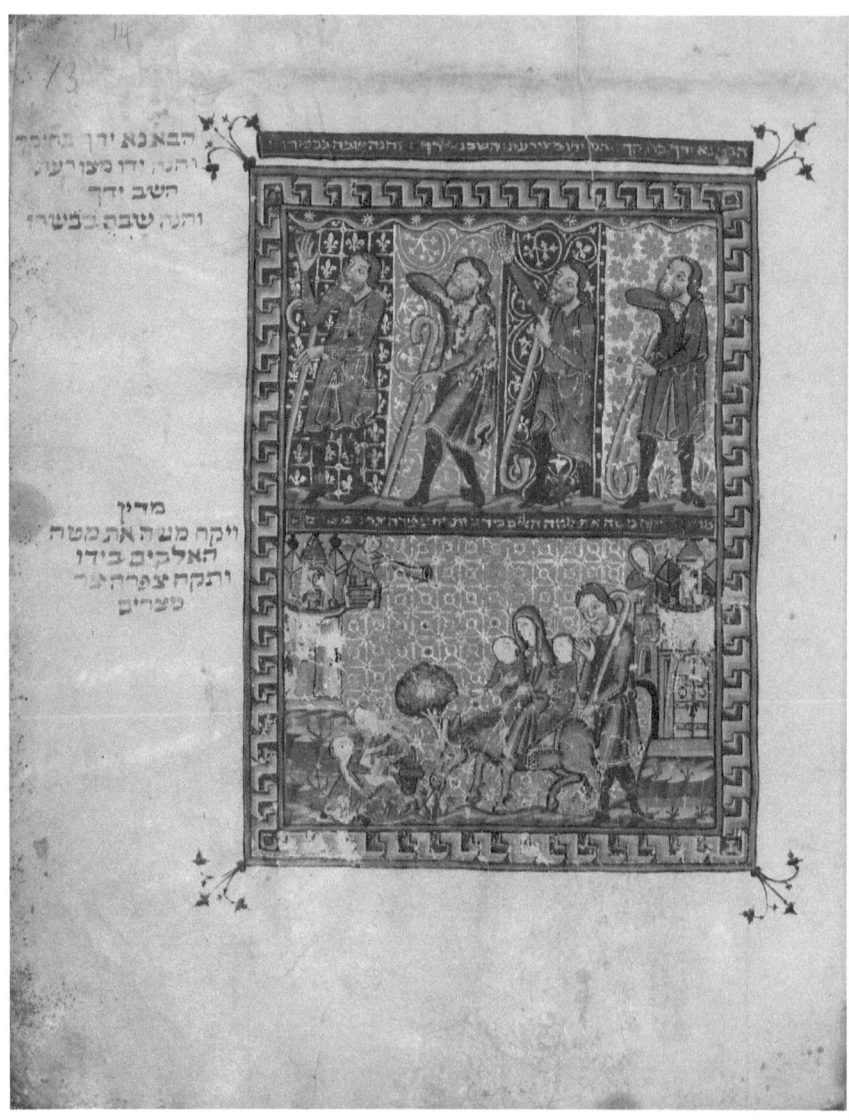

Fig. 8. Manchester, John Rylands University Library, MS Heb. 6 ("Rylands Haggadah"), fol. 14r: Moses and Zipporah on the way to Egypt; Zipporah circumcising Eliezer.

Female Protagonists in Medieval Jewish Book Art

Fig. 9. London, Collection David Sofer, Franconia, ca. 1465 ("Second Nuremberg Haggadah"), fol. 13v: Moses and Zipporah on the way to Egypt; Zipporah circumcising Eliezer.

tree behind Moses should be read as a symbol of Zipporah's fertility, and the donkey should be viewed as a symbol of divine redemption.[32]

The tale of a woman circumcising her son raised halakic questions. Rabbinic views as to whether women may perform circumcisions differed. According to some opinions, they are allowed to perform the ritual, and the story of Zipporah in fact supports that contention. Another opinion prevailing among Iberian Jewish scholars suggests that women can circumcise only if no man is available to fulfill the precept.[33] According to a third view, which became dominant in late medieval Ashkenaz, women are not allowed to circumcise their sons under any circumstances. Those who held this opinion claimed that Zipporah *made* somebody else circumcise her son.[34] This solution appears in versions of Moses in Coucy's *Sefer Mitzvot Gadol* (*Semag*) from thirteenth-century France. However, as Ya'acov Spiegel observes, not all of the manuscripts of the *Semag* have this wording. He lists several that follow the earlier suggestion that Zipporah did perform the circumcision and suggests that later copiers changed the wording, perhaps following glosses they found in their model books.[35] In any event, the view that Zipporah did not perform the circumcision became dominant in the early modern period.[36]

---

32. Marc M. Epstein, "Another Flight into Egypt: Confluence, Coincidence, the Cross-Cultural Dialectics of Messianism and Iconographic Appropriation in Medieval Jewish and Christian Culture," in *Imagining the Self, Imagining the Other: Visual Representation and Jewish-Christian Dynamics in the Middle Ages and Early Modern Period*, ed. Eva Frojmovic (Leiden: Brill, 2002), 33–52.

33. This was discussed in great detail and with abundant sources by Yaakov S. Spiegel, "Woman as Ritual Circumciser: The Halakhah and Its Development," [Hebrew], *Sidra* 5 (1989): 149–57.

34. Moses of Coucy, *Sefer mitsvot gaddol: Positive Precepts* 28, Responsa Project, Bar-Ilan University, Ramat Gan. Eva Frojmovic, "Reframing Gender in Medieval Jewish Images of Circumcision," in *Framing the Family: Narrative and Representation in the Medieval and Early Modern Periods*, ed. Rosalynn Voaden and Diane Wolfthal (Tempe: Arizona Center for Medieval and Renaissance Studies, 2005), 221–43; see 238. Here Frojmovic misinterprets a passage in b. 'Avod. Zar. 27a to the effect that she locates this opinion as early as in the Talmudic period.

35. Spiegel, "Women," 155–57.

36. Avraham Grossman, *Pious and Rebellious: Jewish Women in Medieval Europe* (Waltham, MA: Brandeis University Press, 2004), 190. See also the discussion of Meir ben Barukh of Rothenburg (Maharam, d. 1293), who does not even allow for godmothers, let alone female circumcisers, in Simon ben Tsadoq, *Sefer Ha-Tashbetz* (Warsaw: Levin-Epstein, 1901), no. 397. For a discussion, see Elisheva Baumgarten,

Medieval exegetes of the Bible such as Rashi (d. 1105) or Bahye ben Asher of Saragossa (ca. 1300) described Moses as being either too ill to perform the circumcision or absent from the encampment; hence Zipporah had to fill in, given that the attempt to kill Moses (or Eliezer) represented an emergency.[37] Nahmanides (Moses ben Nahman, Ramban, d. 1270) hardly refers to the episode at all and focuses on Moses.[38]

The visual language of the depictions of Zipporah circumcising her son in Or. 1404 and the Rylands Haggadah, however, seems to address an altogether different issue. They were created in a Sephardic environment, where the rabbis held that in an emergency—as in the case of Eliezer—women are permitted to perform circumcision. Zipporah is shown holding the infant in her lap and, as Eva Frojmovic observes, the portrayal strongly resembles images of the Madonna holding the infant Jesus.[39] Some years ago I suggested that the imagery in Or. 1404 and the Rylands Haggadah is indebted to Italian Christian models. Specific resemblance can be observed in the way Zipporah is shown on the donkey with one child in front of her and the other behind her, with a parallel in an Italian Christian picture Bible from Padua (fig. 10).[40] The point I was making then was to show patterns of cultural interactions between Christian and Jewish workshops and artists, who shared the same visual language. I also showed that Jewish patrons and artists treated their models critically and translated them into a Jewish idiom addressed to a Jewish audience. Interestingly enough, the resemblance between the Christian and the Jewish imagery applies only to the depiction of the traveling family. As far as the circumcision scene is concerned, the Padua Bible shows Zipporah leaning over her son, who is lying on the ground (fig. 10). Thus it appears that the Catalan Jewish artists deliberately altered the composition as if to underscore the parallel with images of the

---

Mothers and Children: Jewish Family Life in Medieval Europe (Princeton: Princeton University Press, 2004), 77–78.

37. Rashi on Exod 4:24; Bahye ben Asher on Exod 4:24 in Haim D. Chavel, ed., *Rabenu Bahye: Bi'ur al hatorah* (Jerusalem: Rav Kook Institute, 1966).

38. Frojmovic, "Reframing," 238–42, based on Haim. D. Chavel, ed., *Perushe hatorah lerabbenu Moshe ben Nahman (Ramban)* (Jerusalem: Rav Kook Institute, 1972); for an English version, see Nachmanides, *Commentary on the Torah*, trans. R. Charles B. Chavel (New York: Shilo, 1971).

39. Frojmovic, "Reframing," 240.

40. Kogman-Appel, *Illuminated Haggadot*, 92–93. The Padua Bible is not as old as the haggadot, so the relationship cannot be a direct one, but should be explained via shared sources.

Fig. 10: London, British Library, MS Add. 15277, northern Italy (Padua?), ca. 1400, fol. 4v: Zipporah circumcising Eliezer.

Madonna, even though it would perhaps make more sense to expect the opposite process: the similarity with the Madonna in the Christian image and the altered version in the Jewish one.

These observations indeed confirm that Zipporah was stylized into a Jewish answer to Mary. Whereas Mary is the mother of the messiah, Zipporah is the wife of the redeemer of Israel. She carries Moses's children on the donkey and in this capacity parallels Mary on the flight to Egypt. She performs the circumcision while holding the infant in her arms as Mary holds Jesus. Realizing that Moses is in danger of being killed as a punishment for having neglected the precept of circumcision and saving him from death makes her an agent in bringing about the liberation of Israel from Egypt. As Frojmovic puts it, the way Zipporah's action is visualized underscores her role as a mediator of salvation in the same way that Mary's parallel role is dominant in Christian culture.[41]

It requires a look at the Ashkenazic parallels to come to grips with a further layer of meaning for this scene. The images of Eliezer's circumcision in the two Ashkenazic haggadot differ from their Catalan counterparts. Unlike the Iberian environment, which suggested that women circumcise in cases of emergency, the culture that brought forth the images in the Second Nuremberg and the Yahuda Haggadot, that is, an Ashkenazic community in the second half of the fifteenth century, in all likelihood no longer allowed for female circumcisers. Furthermore, Zipporah does not echo Mary visually. Rather, she is kneeling on the ground with a huge flint stone in her left hand, with her right hand reaching for the child's penis. Eliezer, naked, is placed on a large cushion in front of his mother (fig. 9).[42] The intimate scene of a mother holding

---

41. Frojmovic, "Reframing," 238–42. Several scholars have observed that rabbinic approaches to women were dynamic; during the late twelfth and the thirteenth century, they were influenced in part by Christian approaches to Mary and the development of the Marian cult during that period, see, e.g., Grossman, *Pious and Rebellious*, 175–77; Peter Schäfer, *Mirror of His Beauty: Feminine Images of God from the Bible to the Early Kabbalah* (Princeton: Princeton University Press, 2002); Arthur Green, "Shekhinah, the Virgin Mary, and the Song of Songs: Reflections on a Kabbalistic Symbol in Its Historical Context," *AJSR* 26.1 (2002): 1–52. The last two publications both analyze the history of the female *shekhinah*; more recently, see Ephraim Shoham-Steiner, "The Virgin Mary, Miriam, and Jewish Reactions to Marian Devotion in the High Middle Ages," *AJSR* 37 (2013): 75–91, who shows that Miriam had been "empowered" in Jewish texts to challenge the Marian cult.

42. Frojmovic, "Reframing," 229, notes in relation to Isaac that the nakedness of

her infant in the Catalan images gave way to a portrayal of Zipporah in a way resembling a priest before an altar slaughtering an animal with a knife. Zipporah thus appears as a visual prototype of the priesthood. Several scholars have dealt with the ritual of circumcision as a type of the sacrificial cult. As Lawrence Hoffman argues, circumcision began to be ritualized when the sacrificial cult ceased after the destruction of the temple. Around the same time, it also became the subject of a liturgy.[43] In the period that followed, but not before the ninth century, according to Shaye Cohen, rabbinic approaches to circumcision began to focus on blood, linking it to sacrificial blood in general and the blood of the Passover lamb in particular, all of which, in Hoffman's words, "are designated as vehicles of salvation."[44] This leads us back to Zipporah, who in the biblical text speaks of a "bridegroom of blood," and it is this verse that is quoted in the captions that accompany the images in both the Second Nuremberg and the Yahuda Haggadot.

One text cited by Hoffman, a section in the early medieval midrashic collection Pirqe Rabbi Eliezer, makes the link between circumcision and sacrifice particularly clear. It speaks of the circumcision of Isaac and explains:

> Rabbi Ishmail said that Abraham shrank from nothing that God commanded him, so when Isaac was only eight days old, he hurried to circumcise him, as it says, "Abraham circumcised Isaac his son when he was eight days old." And he offered him as a sacrifice on the altar. (Pirqe R. El. 29)[45]

How closely circumcision was associated with sacrifice becomes yet more obvious in an earlier image in the Regensburg Pentateuch (ca. 1300; fig. 11). It shows two key scenes from the story of the patriarchs, the circumci-

---

the infant implies willingness to be circumcised; if, indeed the image relates to martyrdom, willingness is certainly a central motif. See, however, the parallel in the Second Nuremberg Haggadah, fol. 13v, where Isaac is shown swaddled.

43. Lawrence Hoffman, *Covenant of Blood: Circumcision and Gender in Rabbinic Judaism* (Chicago: University of Chicago Press, 1996), 102.

44. Hoffman, *Covenant*, 96–110, esp. 102; Shaye J. D. Cohen, "A Brief History of Jewish Circumcision Blood," in *Covenant of Circumcision: New Perspectives on an Ancient Jewish Rite*, ed. Elizabeth Wyner Mark (Lebanon, NH: University Press of New England and Brandeis University Press, 2003), 33–34.

45. On circumcision and sacrifice, see Bona Devorah Haberman, "Foreskin Sacrifice: Zipporah's Ritual and the Bloody Bridegroom," in *Covenant of Circumcision*, 18–29.

Fig. 11. Jerusalem, Israel Museum, MS 180/52, Regensburg, 1300 ("Regensburg Pentateuch"), fol. 18v: Binding of Isaac; Circumcision of Isaac.

sion of Isaac and the binding of Isaac on Mount Moriah. Frojmovic points out that, instead of reading the two scenes simply as a sequence of biblical events, one must realize that their juxtaposition of one above the other has further meaning. The image of the godfather seated on a backless stool holding the infant on his lap shows the child as a sacrificial animal on an altar and thus parallels the circumcision with the binding of Isaac, which reinforces the link between circumcision and sacrifice.[46]

So far our discussion has focused on the images in their relation to the biblical story as well as their midrashic elaborations. In the visual narratives, both Rebekah and Zipporah take on certain roles as types of the biblical notions of chosenness and sacrifice. Whereas Rebekah is shown as the driving force behind Jacob's development into the representative of the Jews as *verus Israel*, the Sephardic Zipporah visually echoes depictions of Mary and assumes the role of a female protagonist in the history of Israel's salvation. The visual equivalence between Zipporah and Mary is not found in the Ashkenazic version, where Zipporah plays a central role in highlighting the links between circumcision and sacrifice.

In these medieval visual narratives Rebekah and Zipporah thus crystallize as biblical protagonists who took Israelite history into their hands. Although the rabbinic reading tends to downplay their roles, the visual renderings, in contrast, highlight them. Whereas the portrayals of Rebekah in the Second Nuremberg and Yahuda Haggadot basically reflect the midrash (figs. 2–4), the fact that the cycle seems to center on her as a protagonist and shows her repeatedly assigns her a role that the rabbis did not necessarily allow for. In the midrash Jacob and Esau are at the focus of the narrative, but the pictorials seem to shine more light on the figure of Rebekah. Singling her out visually while limiting Isaac's paternal role to blessing Jacob underscores her part in making Jacob the ancestor of the Israelite nation. The visual narrative communicates her agency in a particularly strong fashion. The same is true of Zipporah (figs. 7–9). In the fourteenth-century Catalan visual renderings, Zipporah grows into the figure of a Jewish agent of redemption. Her role as a circumciser in times of emergency corresponds with the common Iberian halakic opinion. In the fifteenth-century Ashkenazic images, she performs the ritual as a paradigm of sacrifice. Around that time the view that women could not circumcise and that Zipporah had a man act in her stead would just

---

46. Frojmovic, "Reframing," 229–33.

have begun to dominate. In this context, then, the visual narrative presents a challenging alternative version to the biblical story and the associated rabbinic views. Clearly, the visual language manipulated the rabbinic reception of the biblical stories, but it is by no means apparent that it was actually designed to challenge rabbinic views. In the following I suggest that our visual protagonists, rather, functioned as paradigms to promote values that were fully grounded in the late medieval rabbinic mindset.

3. Paradigms of Rabbinic Values

The potential of medieval biblical imagery to reflect medieval realities is very limited.[47] In particular, depictions of biblical events that convey the realities of Jewish life are very rare, and the images under discussion here have very little to offer as projections of actual practices. One exception is the depiction of Moses's wedding to Zipporah, which, as I have shown elsewhere, faithfully reflects fifteenth-century Jewish realities in Franconia.[48] Likewise, the famous example of the image of Isaac's circumcision in the Regensburg Pentateuch (ca. 1300) mentioned earlier stands out in this regard from other biblical imageries and was indeed interpreted by Elisheva Baumgarten against the background of medieval ritual practice and changing halakic prescriptions. The circumcision takes place in a public space, the synagogue, whereas in the earlier Middle Ages real-life circumcision was commonly performed in the private sphere of the family home, where, since the thirteenth century, women had been consigned to a separate space (fig. 11).[49]

---

47. An attempt to take medieval Jewish art at face value and to reconstruct "Jewish life in the Middle Ages," was made in the 1980s by Mendel and Thérèse Metzger, *Jewish Life in the Middle Ages: Illuminated Hebrew Manuscripts of the Thirteenth to the Sixteenth Century* (New York: Alpine Fine Arts Collection, 1982). This book was criticized by several scholars for its methodology; see Elliott E. Horowitz, "The Way We Were: Jewish Life in the Middle Ages," *Jewish History* 1 (1986): 75–90; Kogman-Appel, *Zweite Nürnberger*, 91–95; Frojmovic, "Reframing," 221.

48. Kogman-Appel, *Zweite Nürnberger*, 91–95.

49. Baumgarten, *Mothers and Children*, 70–76; Frojmovic, "Reframing," 223–38, dealt with the image from a gender perspective focusing on the role of Sarah having been misled by Satan, who had told her that Isaac had actually been killed, as a prototype of the mourning mother. Deborah Elhadad-Aroshas, "Gazing through the Window: Depictions of Women in the *Rothschild Miscellany* manuscript" [Hebrew] (MA thesis, Ben-Gurion University of the Negev, 2014), 38–39, points out that in an

In contrast, the images of Eliezer being circumcised are clearly not in any way instrumental in coming to grips with medieval performances of the ritual. We have seen that the images are not indicative of an actual common practice of women performing circumcision. While Frojmovic suggests that Zipporah's portrayal as circumciser was meant to challenge rabbinic attitudes and reflects practices that transgressed the rabbinic norms,[50] I suggest an alternative reading.

One of the multiple cultural functions of medieval image cycles was also the stylization of biblical figures into paradigms of religious values and models of behavior. From this point of view, the images discussed here address three themes, and the female protagonists assume a determining role in promoting them as central values: Israel as the chosen nation; piety; and martyrdom. I have already discussed Rebekah's and Zipporah's roles in highlighting Israel's chosenness, but I now take a second look at these images to examine how the visual language functions in relation to piety and martyrdom and their status in medieval Jewish societies.

Whereas the Iberian depictions of Rebekah focus only on her role in the story of Israel's chosenness, the Ashkenazic cycles also picture her as a role model of female piety. However, as Avraham Grossman and Baumgarten have shown, there were different approaches to female piety. Rabbinic halakhah does not oblige women to fulfill time-bound positive precepts, but during the high Middle Ages, at a time of general religious revival in Europe, many Jewish women insisted on doing so. Ashkenazi rabbis complied, and women could act as ritual slaughterers and, as we have seen, as circumcisers. However, toward the later Middle Ages, rabbinic criticism over such norms abounded.[51] Thus, the question becomes whether the kind of piety promoted in the Rebekah pictorial implies a role of female pietist activism or, rather, suggests a woman who was entrusted

---

image of a circumcision in the Rothschild Miscellany, produced for an Ashkenazi male patron during the 1470s, women are altogether absent from the composition; this appears in stark contrast to a *Minhagim* book in Yiddish from the sixteenth century, which underscores the role of women before and after the actual ritual act. The *Minhagim* book was intended for a female patronage, on the latter, see Diane Wolfthal, *Picturing Yiddish: Gender, Identity, and Memory in the Illustrated Yiddish Books of Renaissance Italy* (Leiden: Brill, 2004), 72.

50. Frojmovic, "Reframing," 238–42.

51. Grossman, *Pious and Rebellious*, 174–97; Elisheva Baumgarten, *Practicing Piety in Medieval Ashkenaz* (Philadelphia: University of Pennsylvania Press, 2014).

with religious obligations limited to her household.[52] Rebekah, pious enough to be the worthy wife of a martyr, is defined as a woman who takes the place of her mother-in-law, and whose presence in the camp guarantees that "a cloud is spread above the tent, there is a blessing on the dough, and the candle burns from Sabbath eve to Sabbath eve." Two of these phenomena relate to traditional precepts of the female domain, and thus define Rebekah not as a strong woman insisting on fulfilling men's precepts, but one who accepts her limits, as the rabbis of the fifteenth century demanded.[53]

Yet, in two aspects, the portrayals of Rebekah seem to challenge rabbinic positions. As in biblical narration, infertility was a major issue in medieval Jewish societies. Whereas both the rabbinic tradition and the images in the two Ashkenazic haggadot imply that it is not certain that Rebekah was the only one to be blamed for the lack of offspring (fig. 3), in most real-life cases it was only the woman who was examined for abnormal physical conditions that might lead to infertility. Problems with fertility, complications during pregnancy, and difficulty during delivery were associated with laxity in fulfilling the three main precepts imposed on women: setting aside a small amount of dough before baking bread; lighting candles on the eve of the Sabbath; and ritual purity during menstruation.[54] In the Ashkenazic images and their captions, Rebekah is explicitly described as pious to an extent that her piety brought back miracles that had ceased with Sarah's death. The blessing over the dough and the candles that miraculously remained lit from Sabbath to Sabbath are associated with these precepts. The imagery and the caption imply that Rebekah is described as particularly strict in performing them. Yet she did not conceive immediately upon her marriage, and once she did, she experienced excessive pain during her pregnancy. Moreover, although pregnant women were cared for exclusively by midwives and were not expected to leave the house, Rebekah in her pain sought the assistance of sages, implying that she left the house on her own.[55]

---

52. By that I do not question the phenomenon of female pietism; rather I suggest that the images attempt to challenge it.

53. On these precepts, see above.

54. Baumgarten, *Mothers and Children*, 30–32, 41; Baumgarten, "Biblical Models," 51–52.

55. For a discussion of the care for pregnant women, see Baumgarten, *Mothers and Children*, 48–49.

Likewise, even though not implied in either the biblical narrative or its rabbinic readings, the images show Rebekah actively taking care of her sons' education (fig. 4). This, again, contradicts medieval social norms. The roles parents were to assume in their children's education were clearly defined. Women were responsible for the education of their daughters throughout childhood and puberty and for the physical well-being of their sons during early childhood.[56] The latter's schooling, however, was the responsibility of their fathers, and when the time came, the boys were introduced into the male world and brought into the synagogue or their teacher's home by their father.[57]

Finally, martyrdom, as an ultimate expression of piety, is also addressed in the images under discussion here. Martyrdom had become an issue of particular significance in Ashkenazic culture from the time of the Rhineland massacres during the First Crusade (1096).[58] Three Hebrew Chronicles describe in great detail the events that took place in the flourishing communities of Speyer, Worms, and Mainz, as well as elsewhere in the early summer of that year.[59] Active martyrdom appears there as a central motif. Scholars are divided as to what extent these texts should be treated as accurate accounts of historical fact or as literary renderings representing a state of mind from several decades later regarding a phenomenon that undoubtedly evoked a whole range of emotional reactions.[60]

---

56. Elisheva Baumgarten, "Religious Education of Children in Medieval Jewish Society," in *Essays on Medieval Childhood. Responses to Recent Debates*, ed. Joel T. Rosenthal (Donington: Shaun Tyas, 2007), 54–72.

57. In the medieval Rhineland communities an initiation ritual took place for young boys who began schooling during the Feast of Weeks, see Ivan Marcus, *Rituals of Childhood: Jewish Acculturation in Medieval Europe* (New Haven: Yale University Press, 1996).

58. For a detailed discussion of the events and their historical significance, see Robert Chazan, *European Jewry and the First Crusade* (Berkeley: University of California Press, 1987).

59. For a critical edition with a translation into German and discussion, see Eva Haverkamp, ed., *Hebräische Berichte über die Judenverfolgungen während des Ersten Kreuzzugs* (Hannover: Hahnsche Buchhandlung, 2005); for English translations, see Shlomo Eidelberg, *The Jews and the Crusaders: The Hebrew Chronicles of the First and Second Crusades* (Madison: University of Wisconsin Press, 1977); see also, Chazan, *European Jewry*, appendix.

60. Shlomo Eidelberg, "The Solomon bar Simson Chronicle as a Source of the History of the First Crusade," *JQR* 49 (1959): 282–87; Ivan G. Marcus, "From Politics to Martyrdom: Shifting Paradigms in the Hebrew Narratives of the 1096 Crusade

In any event, during the subsequent four hundred years these texts played a crucial role in turning deeds of active martyrdom in the face of forced baptism—both the killing of relatives and suicides—into a religious, ideological, and educational ideal.[61]

Judaism had developed a tradition of martyrdom in late antiquity, but until 1096 the "sanctification of the name of God" (*qiddush hashem*) was normally understood as passive martyrdom expressed in the willingness to be killed for the Jewish faith. Apart from a few exceptional cases, active martyrdom as practiced in the Rhineland communities in 1096 was a new phenomenon. The ideal of active martyrdom was linked to two paradigm motifs from the Bible: the binding of Isaac[62] and the description of the sacrificial cult in the temple. As Ivan Marcus demonstrates, both can be interpreted metaphorically as ritualized acts foreshadowing active mar-

---

Riots," *Prooftexts* 2 (1982): 42–43; Chazan, *European Jewry*, and a critical review by Marcus in *Speculum* 64 (1989): 685–88; Jeremy Cohen, "The Persecutions of 1096 – from Martyrdom to Martyrology: The Sociocultural Context of the Hebrew Crusade Chronicles" [Hebrew], *Zion* 59 (1994): 169–208; Cohen, *Sanctifying the Name of God: Jewish Martyrs and Jewish Memories of the First Crusade* (Philadelphia: University of Pennsylvania Press, 2004); Robert Chazan, *God, Humanity, and History: The Hebrew First Crusade Narratives* (Berkeley: University of California Press, 2000). On the relationship of the texts to one another, see Anna Sapir Abulafia, "The Interrelationship between the Hebrew Chronicles of the First Crusade," *JSS* 27 (1982): 221–39; and the introduction to Eva Haverkamp, *Hebräische Berichte*.

61. Cohen, *Sanctifying*, 55–60; Avraham Grossman, "The Roots of *Qiddush Hashem* in Early Ashkenaz" [Hebrew], in *The Sanctity of Life and Martyrdom: Collection of Studies in the Memory of Amir Yekutiel*, ed. Yeshayahu Gafni and Aviezer Ravitzky (Jerusalem: Zalman Shazar Institute, 1993), 121–27; Simha Goldin, *The Ways of Jewish Martyrdom* (Turnhout: Brepols, 2008).

62. This was discussed first by Spiegel, "Binding of Isaac"; see also Yitzhak Baer, "The 1096 Persecution" [Hebrew], in *Sefer Assaf: Collection of Studies for the Celebration of Prof. Simha Assaf's Sixtieth Birthday*, ed. Umberto Cassuto (Jerusalem: Rav Kook Institute, 1953), 126–40; see also Shalom Spiegel, *The Last Trial: On the Legends and Lore of the Command to Abraham to Offer Isaac as a Sacrifice—The Akedah* (Philadelphia: Jewish Publication Society, 1967); Grossman, "Roots," 115; Elisabeth Hollender and Ulrich Berzbach, "Einige Anmerkungen zu biblischer Sprache und Motiven in Piyyutim aus der Kreuzzugszeit," *Frankfurter Judaistische Beiträge* 25 (1998): 67–68; Lotter, "'Tod oder Taufe,'" 134–43; Goldin, *Martyrdom*, 325–40; Shulamit Elizur, "The Binding of Isaac: In Mourning or in Joy? The Influence of the Crusades on the Biblical Story and Related *Piyyutim*" [Hebrew], *Et Hada'at* 1 (1997): 15–36; more recently also Shepkaru, *Martyrs*, 174–77.

tyrdom.[63] All three of the Hebrew Chronicles describe such acts of active martyrdom by means of "binding"; time and again they use this term in reference to the self-slaughter, comparing it explicitly "to the Binding of Isaac by Abraham" on "Mount Moriah."[64] The notion that Isaac was actually harmed during the binding and that he had temporarily died and come back from paradise was central to the idea that martyrdom brings about redemption, which leads us back to the encounter of Rebekah and Isaac just after the latter's redemption from death. This background to the scene in the Second Nuremberg and the Yahuda Haggadot frames the story within a major discourse that was taking place in Ashkenazic culture. In Iberia, where martyrdom never played the same role as it did in Ashkenaz, Rebekah was found worthy to be the wife of a pious man, whereas in Ashkenaz she was worthy to be the wife of a (redeemed) martyr.

This observation regarding Rebekah calls for a brief sketch concerning the image of women in Ashkenazic and active martyrdom, a subject dealt with by Grossman, Susan Einbinder, and Baumgarten. Women play an outstanding role in the Chronicles that tell of the Crusader attacks, but as for other aspects of these accounts, the historical reliability is uncertain.[65] Women are stylized in these versions as leading exemplars of heroic behavior. In a careful analysis of these narratives and several liturgical poems from the twelfth and thirteenth centuries, Einbinder observes that the image of female martyrs changed over the years. Whereas in mid-twelfth century references, women appear as protagonists active within the public arena, willing to die and willing to kill their own children, in sources from the later twelfth and thirteenth centuries their actions seem to be downplayed and their roles are described as passive rather than active. The deeds of the women in the earlier sources are equated to sacrificial acts, but "the cultic equality of the female martyr has ... disappeared [in the later sources], in favor of attributes portraying passivity and vul-

---

63. Marcus, "Politics," 43 and n. 9, with a reference to Alan Mintz, *Hurban: Responses to Catastrophe in Hebrew Literature* (New York: Columbia University Press, 1984), 96; see also Robert Chazan, "The Early Development of *Hasidut Ashkenaz*," *JQR* 75.3 (1985): 205; Marcus, *Rituals*, 7; Shmuel Shepkaru, *Jewish Martyrs in the Pagan and the Christian Worlds* (New York: Cambridge University Press, 2005), 173–74: Grossman, "Roots," 111, refers to a case of martyrdom in tenth-century Otranto having been compared to the Temple offerings.

64. See the synoptic juxtaposition in *Hebräische Berichte*, 335 and 337.

65. Grossman, *Pious and Rebellious*, 198–211.

nerability to defilement."⁶⁶ Fifteenth-century images presenting Rebekah as a passive observer of Isaac's dramatic return from paradise in a way correspond with Einbinder's conclusions about the changing role of women with regard to martyrdom.

The issue of martyrdom and the role women could play in it also seems to be addressed in the Ashkenazic renderings of Eliezer's circumcision. We have seen that the composition of these images evokes associations with ritual slaughter. Sacrificial service, in turn, was often discussed in medieval texts as yet another paradigm of martyrdom.⁶⁷ Thus, these fifteenth-century images do not necessarily convey a message of female boldness challenging male dominance; instead, they visualize one of the biblical paradigms of (active) martyrdom. Zipporah playing her part in the drama that took place in the desert encampment functions as a metaphor of Jewish women performing martyrdom and sending their children to death for the sanctification of the name of God.

4. Conclusions

The biblical narrative assigns only a minor role to Israelite mothers and wives, and they do not seem to be at all dominant. The narrative voice of Jacob's wives, for example, is strikingly silent. Only rarely does the biblical story break with this attitude. The rabbinic tradition in many ways further weakens the role of women in the biblical tales. Hand in hand with this approach to the biblical narrative, we can also observe that, throughout the Middle Ages, the role of women in the performance of rituals became increasingly limited. The images discussed here comply with these portrayals but also challenge them. They put Rebekah in the spotlight and show Zipporah performing a ritual that is largely associated with men. Image cycles are never literal translations of a text into a visual language. As parallel narratives, they can either represent the rabbinic angle (as they were often shown to do) and tell a story that corresponds with the rabbinic attitude and underscores it; however, at certain points they function as alternative narratives going beyond the biblical plot and diverging from the rabbinic narrative. The

---

66. Susan L. Einbinder, "Jewish Women Martyrs: Changing Models of Representation," *Exemplaria* 12 (2000): 120; but cf. Grossman, *Pious and Rebellious*, 211 critiquing her assumptions as being based on too narrow a range of sources.

67. Goldin, *Martyrdom*, 167–74; Shepkaru, *Martyrs*, 167–68.

examples discussed here highlight certain special roles assumed by female protagonists.

The Ashkenazic and Iberian portrayals of Rebekah and Zipporah differ significantly from one another. In the Sephardic cycles both women actively step in to change the fate of the nation; they take the law into their own hands and they become active agents in salvation history. These portraits of Rebekah and Zipporah do not reflect rabbinic exegesis, nor do they in any way challenge rabbinic stances. They can best be viewed within the context of medieval visual culture and demonstrate how conversant Jewish patrons and artists were with the visual language common in their environment. They were familiar with the image of Mary and her role in Christian life in the thirteenth, fourteenth, and fifteenth centuries, and they offered their own visual challenges to her role in the Christian world. As Mary was visualized as an agent of Christian redemption, Rebekah and Zipporah became mediators in the history of Israel's redemption. This corresponds well with the overall nature of the Sephardic haggadah cycles, which offer visual guidance to the historiosophical approach typical for certain circles in Sepharad. They are part and parcel of these cycles' function in defining the place of history in the Passover ritual.

The Ashkenazic examples take a different approach. They are not as strongly embedded in the surrounding culture as their Iberian counterparts. Nor do they offer much insight into the lives of medieval Jews. Rather, they represent certain values, such as procreation, motherhood, education, piety, and martyrdom, and thus turn Rebekah and Zipporah, the principal female protagonists of these stories, into metaphors of these values and into paradigms of religious conduct. Linking these images, which at first sight appear as naïve pictorials of biblical stories, to abstract notions of religious life seems to be something of a tour de force on the part of the modern observer. However, we have seen that, as in the case of Rebekah's pious conduct, the captions offer information beyond the visual and thus support such a reading. Moreover, piety, martyrdom, persecution, and chosenness while facing the threat of forced baptism were notions that dominated the medieval discourse beyond any "academic" treatments of halakah and ritual. There was oral communication, there were sermons, and there must have been a discourse that addressed these issues besides what we can now read in the sources. The meanings I discussed in this essay would thus have been much more obvious for the contemporaneous viewer. The images metaphorically evoked these notions and they were meant to do so. Moreover, they assuredly teach us a lesson about the Jewish reception of biblical figures in the Middle Ages.

Bibliography

Adler, Elkan Nathan, ed. *Catalogue of Hebrew Manuscripts of the Collection of Elkan Nathan Adler*. Cambridge: Cambridge University Press, 1921.
Agus, Irving. *Urban Civilization in Pre-Crusade Europe*. 2 vols. New York: Yeshiva University Press, 1965.
Alexander, Philip. *The Targum of Canticles. Translated with a Critical Introduction, Apparatus and Notes*. London: Routledge, 2008.
Alfonso, Esperanza. *Islamic Culture through Jewish Eyes: Al Andalus from the Tenth to the Twelfth Century*. London: Routledge, 2008.
Alster, Baruch. "Human Love and Its Relationship to Spiritual Love in Jewish Exegesis on the Song of Songs." PhD diss., Bar Ilan University, 2006.
Ansberry, Christopher B. *Be Wise, My Son, and Make My Heart Glad: An Exploration of the Courtly Nature of the Book of Proverbs*. Berlin: de Gruyter, 2011.
Astell, Ann W. *The Song of Songs in the Middle Ages*. Ithaca, NY: Cornell University Press, 1990.
Atzmon, Arnon. "Mordechai's Dream: From Addition to Derashah" [Hebrew]. *Jewish Studies: An Internet Journal* 6 (2007): 127–40.
———. "Old Wine in New Flasks: The Story of Late Neoclassical Midrash." *European Journal of Jewish Studies* 3 (2009): 183–203.
Baer, Yitzhak. "The 1096 Persecution" [Hebrew]. Pages 126–40 in *Sefer Assaf: Collection of Studies for the Celebration of Prof. Simha Assaf's Sixtieth Birthday*. Edited by Umberto Cassuto. Jerusalem: Rav Kook Institute, 1953.
———. "The Religious and Social Tendency of *Sefer Hasidim*" [Hebrew]. *Zion* 3 (1937–1938): 1–50.
Bakhos, Carol. *The Family of Abraham: Jewish, Christian and Muslim Interpretations*. Cambridge: Harvard University Press, 2014.
Baldwin, John W. "The Image of the Jongleur in Northern France around 1200." *Speculum* 72 (1997): 635–63.

Baskin, Judith R. "Dolce of Worms: The Lives and Deaths of an Exemplary Medieval Jewish Woman and Her Daughters." Pages 429–37 in *Judaism in Practice: From the Middle Ages through the Early Modern Period*. Edited by Lawrence Fine. Princeton: Princeton University Press, 2001.

———. "Female Prophets in the Babylonian Talmud Megillah 14a–15a." Pages 263–80 in *Rabbinic Literature*. Edited by Tal Ilan, Lorena Miralles-Maciá, and Ronit Nikolsky. BW 4.1. Atlanta: SBL Press, 2022.

———. "From Separation to Displacement: The Problem of Women in *Sefer Hasidim*." *AJSR* 19 (1994): 1–18.

———. "Gender and Daily Life in Jewish Communities." Pages 213–28 in *The Oxford Handbook of Women and Gender in Medieval Europe*. Edited by Judith Bennett and Ruth Mazo Karras. Oxford: Oxford University Press, 2013.

———. "Jewish Traditions about Women and Gender Roles: From Rabbinic Teachings to Medieval Practice." Pages 36–51 in *The Oxford Handbook of Women and Gender in Medieval Europe*. Edited by Judith Bennett and Ruth Mazo Karras. Oxford: Oxford University Press, 2013.

———. "'Like Adam and Eve': Biblical Models and Jewish Daily Life in Medieval Christian Europe." *ITQ* 83 (2018): 44–61.

———. "Male Piety, Female Bodies: Men, Women, and Ritual Immersion in Medieval Ashkenaz." *Journal of Jewish Law* 17 (2007): 11–30.

———. *Midrashic Women: Formations of the Feminine in Rabbinic Literature*. Hanover, NH: Brandeis University Press, 2002.

———. "'She Extinguished the Light of the World': Justifications for Women's Disabilities in *Abot de-Rabbi Nathan* B." Pages 277–98 in *Current Trends in the Study of Midrash*. Edited by Carol Bakhos. JSJSup 106. Leiden: Brill, 2006.

———. "Women and Ritual Immersion in Medieval Ashkenaz: The Sexual Politics of Piety." Pages 131–42 in *Judaism in Practice: From the Middle Ages through the Early Modern Period*. Edited by Lawrence Fine. Princeton: Princeton University Press, 2001.

———. "Women and Sexual Ambivalence in *Sefer Hasidim*." *JQR* 96 (2006): 1–8.

———. "Women Saints in Judaism: Dolce of Worms." Pages 39–69 in *Women Saints in World Religions*. Edited by Arvind Sharma. Albany: State University of New York Press, 2000.

Baumgarten, Elisheva. *Biblical Women and Jewish Daily Practice in the Middle Ages*. Philadelphia: University of Pennsylvania Press, 2022.

———. "Charitable like Abigail: The History of an Epitaph." *JQR* 105 (2015): 312–39.

———. *Mothers and Children: Jewish Family Life in Medieval Europe*. Princeton: Princeton University Press, 2004.

———. *Practicing Piety in Medieval Ashkenaz*. Philadelphia: University of Pennsylvania Press, 2014.

———. "Religious Education of Children in Medieval Jewish Society." Pages 54–72 in *Essays on Medieval Childhood: Responses to Recent Debates*. Edited by Joel T. Rosenthal. Donington: Shaun Tyas, 2007.

———. "Who Was a Hasid or Hasidah in Medieval Ashkenaz: Reassessing the Social Implications of a Term." *Jewish History* 34 (2021): 125–54.

Bebe, Paulina. *Isha: Frau und Judentum; Enzyklopädie*. Engling an der Paar: Verlag Roman Kovar, 2004.

Ben Asher, Bahye. *Rabenu Bahye: Bi'ur al hatorah*. Edited by Haim D. Chavel. Jerusalem: Rav Kook Institute, 1966.

Ben Judah of Worms, Eleazar. *Sefer ha-Rokeach ha-Gadol*. Jerusalem, 1968.

Ben Tsadoq, Simon. *Sefer Ha-Tashbetz*. Warsaw: Levin-Epstein, 1901.

Bercher, Léon. *Ibn Hazm al-Andalusi, Le Collier du Pigeon, Texte arabe et Traduction française*. Alger: Carbonel, 1949.

Berliner, Abraham. *Aus dem inneren Leben der deutschen Juden im Mittelalter*. Berlin: Benzian, 1871.

Bernstein, Marc S. *Stories of Joseph: Narrative Migrations between Judaism and Islam*. Detroit: Wayne State University Press, 2006.

Bernstein, Shimon. *Moses Ibn Ezra. Shire ha-Qodesh* [Hebrew]. Tel Aviv: Verlag Massada, 1957.

Biale, David. ed. *Culture of the Jews: A New History*. New York: Schocken, 2002.

———. *Eros and the Jews: From Biblical Israel to Contemporary America*. New York: Basic Books, 1992.

Bickerman, Elias J. *The Jews in the Greek Age*. Cambridge: Harvard University Press, 1988.

Bloom, Harold. *Omens of Millennium: The Gnosis of Angels, Dreams, and Resurrection*. New York: Riverhead Books, 1996.

Bodendorfer, Gerhard. "Die Diaspora, die Juden und die 'Anderen.'" Pages 193–214 in *"Eine Grenze hast Du gesetzt": Edna Brocke zum 60. Geburtstag*. Edited by Ekkehard W. Stegemann and Klaus Wengst. Stuttgart: Kohlhammer, 2003.

Bonnen, Gerald. "Worms: The Jews between the City, the Bishop and the Crown." Pages 449–57 in *The Jews of Europe in the Middle Ages (Tenth* to Fifteenth Centuries): Proceedings of the International Symposium Held at Speyer, 20–25 October 2002. Edited by Christoph Cluse. Turnhout: Brepols, 2004.

Börner-Klein, Dagmar. *Das Alphabet des Ben Sira: Hebraisch-deutsche Textausgabe mit einer Interpretation.* Wiesbaden: Marix, 2007.

———. *Eine babylonische Auslegung der Ester-Geschichte.* Frankfurt am Main: Lang, 1991.

———. *Gefährdete Braut und schöne Witwe: Hebräische Judit-Geschichten.* Wiesbaden: Marixverlag, 2007.

———. *Pirke de-Rabbi Elieser: Nach der Edition Venedig 1544 unter Berücksichtigung der Edition Warschau 1852.* SJ 26. Berlin: de Gruyter, 2004.

Börner-Klein, Dagmar, and Elisabeth Hollender, eds. *Die Midraschim zu Ester.* Leiden: Brill, 2000.

Bossong, Georg. *Das Maurische Spanien, Geschichte und Kultur.* Munich: Beck, 2007.

Boyd-Taylor, Cameron, trans. "Ioudith." Pages 441–55 in *A New English Translation of the Septuagint.* Edited by Albert Pietersma and Benjamin G. Wright. Oxford: Oxford University Press, 2007.

Brann, Ross. *The Compunctious Poet: Cultural Ambiguity and Hebrew Poetry in Muslim Spain.* Baltimore: Johns Hopkins University Press, 1991.

Braude, William G. *Midrash on Psalms.* New Haven: Yale University Press, 1959.

Brin, Gerson. "Problems of Composition and Redaction in the Bible according to R. Abraham Ibn Ezra" [Hebrew]. Pages 121–35 in *Teudah 8: Studies in the Composition of Abraham Ibn Ezra.* Edited by Israel Levin. Tel Aviv: Tel Aviv University, 1992.

Brine, Kevin R., Elena Ciletti, and Henrike Lahnemann, eds. *The Sword of Judith: Judith Studies across the Disciplines.* Cambridge: Open Book, 2010.

Brinner, William, trans. *Prophets and Patriarchs.* Vol. 2 of *The History of al-Tabari.* Albany: State University of New York Press, 1987.

Brody, Hayyim. *Dîwân des Abû-l-Hasân Jehuda ha-Levi* [Hebrew]. 3 vols. Berlin: Schriften des Vereins Mequitze Nirdamim, 1894–1930.

Brody, Hayyim, and Jefim Schirmann, eds. *Solomon ibn Gabirol: Secular Poems* [Hebrew]. Jerusalem: Schocken Institute, 1974.

Buber, Salomon, ed. *Sifre de-Agadta al megillat Ester.* Rome: Vilna, 1886.

Caponigro, Mark. "Judith, Holding the Tale of Herodotus." Pages 47–59 in *"No One Spoke Ill of Her": Essays on Judith.* Edited by James C. VanderKam. EJL 2. Atlanta: Scholars Press, 1992.

Castelli, Elizabeth. "Allegories of Hagar: Reading Galatians 4:21–31 with Postmodern Feminist Eyes." Pages 228–50 in *The New Literary Criticism and the New Testament*. Edited by Elizabeth Struthers Malbon and Edgar McKnight. Sheffield: Sheffield Academic, 1994.

Chavel, Charles B. *RAMBAN: Commentary on the Torah*. New York: Shilo, 1999.

Chavel, Haim D. *Peruse hatorah lerabbenu Moshe ben Nahman (Ramban)*. Jerusalem: Rav Kook Institute, 1972.

Chazan, Robert. "The Early Development of *Hasidut Ashkenaz*." *JQR* 75 (1985): 199–211.

———. *European Jewry and the First Crusade*. Berkeley: University of California Press, 1987.

———. *God, Humanity, and History: The Hebrew First Crusade Narratives*. Berkeley: University of California Press, 2000.

———. *Reassessing Jewish Life in Medieval Europe*. Cambridge: Cambridge University Press, 2010.

Clines, David J. A. *The Scroll of Esther: The Story of the Story*. Sheffield: Sheffield Academic Press, 1984.

Cluse, Christoph, ed. *The Jews of Europe in the Middle Ages (Tenth to Fifteenth Centuries): Proceedings of the International Symposium Held at Speyer, 20–25 October 2002*. Turnhout: Brepols, 2004.

Cohen, Esther, and Elliott Horowitz. "In Search of the Sacred: Jews, Christians and Rituals of Marriage in the Later Middle Ages." *Journal of Medieval and Renaissance Studies* 20 (1990): 225–50.

Cohen, Gerson. "The Song of Songs and the Jewish Religious Mentality." Pages 3–17 in *Studies in the Variety of Rabbinic Cultures*. Edited by Gerson Cohen. Philadelphia: Jewish Publication Society, 1991.

Cohen, Jeremy. "The Persecutions of 1096—From Martyrdom to Martyrology: The Sociocultural Context of the Hebrew Crusade Chronicles" [Hebrew]. *Zion* 59 (1994): 169–208.

———. *Sanctifying the Name of God: Jewish Martyrs and Jewish Memories of the First Crusade*. Philadelphia: University of Pennsylvania Press, 2004.

Cohen, Mark. *Under Crescent and Cross*. Princeton: Princeton University Press, 2008.

Cohen, Menachem. *Mikra'ot Gedolot 'Haketer': A Revised and Augmented Scientific Edition of 'Mikra'ot Gedolot' Based on the Aleppo Codex and Early Medieval Mss; The Five Scrolls* [Hebrew]. Ramat Gan: Bar Ilan University Press, 2012.

Cohen, Naomi. "Bruria in the Bavli and in Rashi Avodah Zarah 18b." *Tradition* 48.2–3 (2015): 29–40.
Cohen, Shaye J. D. "A Brief History of Jewish Circumcision Blood." Pages 30–42 in *Covenant of Circumcision: New Perspectives on an Ancient Jewish Rite*. Edited by Elizabeth Wyner Mark. Lebanon, NH: University Press of New England; Brandeis University Press, 2003.
———. *Why Aren't Jewish Women Circumcised? Gender and Covenant in Judaism*. Berkeley: University of California Press, 2005.
Cole, Peter. *The Dream of the Poem: Hebrew Poetry from Muslim and Christian Spain (950–1492)*. Princeton: Princeton University Press, 2007.
Cordoni, Constanza. "'For They Did Not Change Their Language' (MekhY Pischa 5): On Early Medieval Literary Rehebraicisation of Jewish Culture." *Medieval Worlds* 11 (2020): 165–86.
———. *Seder Eliyahu: A Narratological Reading*. Berlin: de Gruyter, 2018.
Crenshaw, James L. "The Sage in Proverbs." Pages 205–16 in *The Sage in Israel and the Ancient Near East*. Edited by John G. Gammie and Leo G. Perdue. Winona Lake, IN: Eisenbrauns, 1990.
Dahan, Alon. "Ashkenazic Motifs in the Halachah of the 'Bahir.'" [Hebrew]. *Jerusalem Studies in Jewish Thought* 22 (2011): 159–80.
Dahood, Mitchell J. *Psalms I, 1–50*. AB 16. Garden City, NY: Doubleday, 1966.
Dan, Joseph, ed. *The Early Kabbalah*. New York: Paulist Press, 1986.
———, ed. *Early Kabbalistic Circles* [Hebrew]. Vol. 7 of *History of Jewish Mysticism and Esotericism*. Jerusalem: Zalman Shazar, 2012.
———. *Jewish Mysticism and Jewish Ethics*. Seattle: University of Washington Press, 1986.
———. "A Re-Evaluation of the 'Ashkenazi Kabbalah'" [Hebrew]. *Jerusalem Studies in Jewish Thought* 6 (1987): 138–39.
David, Yonah. *The Poems of Rabbi Isaac ibn Ghiyyat* [Hebrew]. Jerusalem: Achshav, 1987.
DeFranza, Megan K. "The Proverbs 31 'Woman of Strength': An Argument for a Primary-Sense Translation." *Priscilla Papers* 25 (2011): 21–25.
Delcor, Mathias. "Le livre de Judith et l'époque grecque." *Klio* 49 (1967): 151–79.
Dell, Katharine J. *The Book of Proverbs in Social and Theological Context*. Cambridge: Cambridge University Press, 2006.
Dobbs-Weinstein, Idit. "Thinking Desire in Gersonides and Spinoza." Pages 51–77 in *Women and Gender in Jewish Philosophy*. Edited by Hava Tirosh-Samuelson. Bloomington: Indiana University Press, 2004.

Dönitz, Saskia. "Historiography among Byzantine Jews: The Case of *Sefer Yosippon*." Pages 951–68 in *Jews in Byzantium: Dialectics of Minority and Majority Cultures*. Edited by Robert Bonfil, Oded Irshai, Guy G. Stroumsa and R. Talgam. Leiden: Brill, 2012.

———. "Sefer Yosippon (Josippon)." Pages 382–89 in *A Companion to Josephus*. Edited by Honora Howell Chapman and Zuleika Rodgers. Malden, MA: Wiley, 2016.

———. *Überlieferung und Rezeption des Sefer Yosippon*. TSMJ 29. Tübingen: Mohr Siebeck, 2013.

Dov Baer of Mesritsch. *Chesed le-Avraham* [Hebrew]. Jerusalem: Lewin-Epstein, 1973.

———. *Maggid devarav le-Ya'akov* [Hebrew]. Edited by Rivka Schatz-Uffenheimer. Jerusalem, Magnes, 1976.

Drory, Rina. *Models and Contacts: Arabic Literature and Its Impact on Medieval Jewish Culture*. Leiden: Brill, 2000.

Dubarle, Marie-André. *Judith: Formes et sens des diverses traditions*. 2 vols. Rome: Institute Biblique Pontifical, 1966.

Dunsky, Samson. *Midrash Rabah Shir Ha-Shirim: Midrash Hazit*. Jerusalem: Devir, 1980.

Eidelberg, Shlomo. *The Jews and the Crusaders: The Hebrew Chronicles of the First and Second Crusaders*. Madison: University of Wisconsin Press, 1977.

———. "The Solomon bar Simson Chronicle as a Source of the History of the First Crusade." *JQR* 49 (1959): 282–87.

Einbinder, Susan L. "Jewish Women Martyrs: Changing Models of Representation." *Exemplaria* 12 (2000): 105–27.

Eisenstein, Jehuda Dov. *Ozar Midrashim: A Library of Two Hundred Minor Midrashim. Edited with Introductions and Notes*. 2 vols. New York: Noble Offset, 1915.

Elhadad-Aroshas, Deborah. "Gazing through the Window: Depictions of Women in the *Rothschild Miscellany* Manuscript" [Hebrew]. MA thesis; Ben-Gurion University of the Negev, 2014.

Elior, Rachel. *Israel Ba'al Shem Tov and His Contemporaries: Kabbalists, Sabbatians, Hasidim and Mitnaggedim* [Hebrew]. 2 vols. Jerusalem: Carmel, 2014.

———. *Jewish Mysticism: The Infinite Expression of Freedom*. Oxford: Littman Library of Jewish Civilization, 2007.

———. "Joseph Karo and Israel Baal Shem Tov: Mystical Metamorphosis, Kabbalistic Inspiration, Spiritual Internalization." *Studies in Spirituality* 17 (2007): 267–319.

———. "The Unknown Mystical History of the Festival of *Shavu'ot*." *Studies in Spirituality* 26 (2016): 157–96.

Elizur, Shulamit. "The Binding of Isaac: In Mourning or in Joy? The Influence of the Crusades on the Biblical Story and Related *Piyyutim*" [Hebrew]. *Et Hada'at* 1 (1997): 15–36.

———. *Qedushta waShir, Qedushta'ot leShabbatoth haNechamah leRabbi El'azar berabbi Kallir*. Jerusalem: self-published, 1988.

———. "The Use of Biblical Verses in Hebrew Liturgical Poetry." Pages 83–100 in *Prayers that Cite Scripture*. Edited by James L. Kugel. Cambridge: Harvard University Press, 2006.

Elsner, Jas. "Cultural Resistance and the Visual Image: The Case of Dura Europos." *Classical Philology* 96 (2001): 269–304.

Elukin, Jonathan. *Living Together, Living Apart: Rethinking Jewish-Christian Relations in the Middle Ages*. Princeton: Princeton University Press, 2007.

Engel, Helmut. "Der HERR ist ein Gott, der Kriege erschlägt: Zur Frage der griechischen Originalsprache und der Struktur des Buches Judith." Pages 155–68 in *Goldene Äpfel in silbernen Schalen*. Edited by Klaus-Dieter Schnuck and Matthias Augustin. Frankfurt am Main: Lang, 1992.

Epstein, Marc M. "Another Flight into Egypt: Confluence, Coincidence, the Cross-Cultural Dialectics of Messianism and Iconographic Appropriation in Medieval Jewish and Christian Culture." Pages 33–52 in *Imagining the Self, Imagining the Other: Visual Representation and Jewish-Christian Dynamics in the Middle Ages and Early Modern Period*. Edited by Eva Frojmovic. Leiden: Brill, 2002.

———. *The Brother Haggadah: A Medieval Sephardi Masterpiece in Facsimile*. London: Thames & Hudson, 2016.

———. *Dreams of Subversion in Medieval Jewish Art and Literature*. University Park: Pennsylvania State University Press, 1997.

———. *The Medieval Haggadah: Art, Narrative, and Religious Imagination*. New Haven: Yale University Press, 2010.

Exum, J. Cheryl. *Fragmented Women: Feminist (Sub)versions of Biblical Narratives*. Valley Forge: Trinity Press International, 1993.

Falk, Zeev W. *Jewish Matrimonial Law in the Middle Ages*. Oxford: Oxford University Press, 1966.

Fine, Steven. "Jewish Identity at the *Limus*—The Earliest Reception of the Dura Europos Synagogue Paintings." Pages 289–306 in *Cultural Identity in the Ancient Mediterranean*. Edited by Erich S. Gruen. Los Angeles: Getty Publications, 2011.

Firth, David G. "The Third Quest for the Historical Mordecai and the Genre of the Book of Esther." *OTE* 16.2 (2003): 233–43.

Fishbane, Eitan P. "A Chariot for the Shekhina, Identity and the Ideal Life in Sixteenth Century Kabbalah." *Journal of Religious Ethics* 37 (2009): 385–418.

Fishbane, Michael. *The JPS Bible Commentary: Song of Songs*. Philadelphia: Jewish Publication Society, 2015.

Fisher, Charles Dennis. *Cornelii Tacii Historiarum libri*. Repr., Oxford: Clarendon, 1990.

Fleischer, Ezra. *Sirat ha-Kodesh ha'ivrit bi-yeme ha-benayim*. 2nd ed. Jerusalem: Magnes, 2007.

Flusser, David, ed. *The Josippon [Josef Gorionides]: Edited with Introduction, Commentary and Notes* [Hebrew]. 2 vols. Jerusalem: Bialik Institute, 1980–1981.

Fonrobert, Charlotte E. *Menstrual Purity: Rabbinic and Christian Reconstruction of Biblical Gender*. Stanford, CA: Stanford University Press, 2000.

Fox, Michael V. *Proverbs 10–31: A New Translation with Introduction and Commentary*. AB 18B. New Haven: Yale University Press, 2009.

Friedlander, Gerald, ed. and trans. *Pirkê de Rabbi Eliezer*. London: Kegan Paul, 1916.

Frisch, Amos. "The Sins of the Patriarchs as Viewed by Traditional Jewish Exegesis." *JSQ* 10.1 (2003): 258–73.

Frojmovic, Eva. "Reframing Gender in Medieval Jewish Images of Circumcision." Pages 221–43 in *Framing the Family: Narrative and Representation in the Medieval and Early Modern Periods*. Edited by Rosalynn Voaden and Diane Wolfthal. Tempe: Arizona Center for Medieval and Renaissance Studies, 2005.

Frymer-Kensky, Tikva. *Reading the Women of the Bible*. New York: Schocken Books, 2002.

Gafni, Isaiah. *Land, Center and Diaspora: Jewish Constructs in Late Antiquity*. Sheffield: Sheffield Academic, 1997.

Gaster, Moses. *The Exempla of the Rabbis, Being a Collection of Exempla, Apologues and Tales*. New York: Ktav, 1924.

Georges, Karl Ernst. *Ausführliches lateinisch-deutsches Handwörterbuch*. 2 vols. Darmstadt: Wissenschaftliche Buchgesellschaft, 1985.

Goitein, Shlomo Dov. *Bible Studies* [Hebrew]. Tel Aviv: Yavneh, 1967.

——. *A Mediterranean Society: The Jewish Communities of the Arab World as Portrayed in the Documents of the Cairo Geniza*. 6 vols. Berkeley: University of California Press, 1967–1993.

Goldberg, Arnold Maria. *Erlosung durch Leiden. Drei rabbinische Homilien uber die Trauernden Zions und den leidenden Messias Efraim (PesR 34.36.37)*. Frankfurt am Main: Gesellschaft zur Förderung Judaistischer Studien, 1978.

Goldin, Simha. *The Ways of Jewish Martyrdom*. Turnhout: Brepols, 2008.

Graves, Robert, and Raphael Patai. *Hebrew Myths, The Book of Genesis*. New York: Greenwich House, 1983.

Gray, Alyssa. "Married Women and 'Tsedaqah' in Medieval Jewish Law: Gender and the Discourse of Legal Obligation." *Jewish Law Association Studies* 17 (2007): 168–212.

Grayzel, Solomon. *The Church and the Jews in the Thirteenth Century*. New York: Hermon, 1966.

Green, Arthur. *A Guide to the Zohar*. Stanford, CA: Stanford University Press, 2004.

——. "Shekhinah, the Virgin Mary, and the Song of Songs: Reflections on a Kabbalistic Symbol in Its Historical Context." *AJSR* 26 (2002): 1–52.

Greenspahn, Frederick E. "A Typology of Biblical Women." *Judaism* 32.1 (1983): 43–50.

Grintz, Jehosua M. *The Book of Judith: A Reconstruction of the Original Hebrew Text with Introduction, Commentary, Appendices and Indices* [Hebrew]. Jerusalem: Mossad Bialik, 1957.

Grossman, Avraham. *The Early Sages of Ashkenaz: Their Lives, Leadership, and Works* [Hebrew]. Jerusalem: Magnes, 2001.

——. *The Early Sages of France: Their Lives, Leadership and Works* [Hebrew]. Jerusalem: Magnes, 1995.

——. "The Origins and Essence of the Custom of 'Stopping the Service'" [Hebrew]. *Mil'et* 1 (1983): 199–221.

——. *Pious and Rebellious: Jewish Women in Medieval Europe*. Translated by J. Jonathan Chipman. Waltham, MA: Brandeis University Press, 2004.

——. "The Roots of *Qiddush Hashem* in Early Ashkenaz" [Hebrew]. Pages 99–130 in *The Sanctity of Life and Martyrdom: Collection of*

Studies in the Memory of Amir Yekutiel. Edited by Isaiah Gafni and Aviezer Ravitzky. Jerusalem: Zalman Shazar Institute, 1993.
Gruber, Mayer I. *Rashi's Commentary on Psalms.* Leiden: Brill, 2004.
Grundmann, Regina. "Judit, Hanna und Chanukka." Pages 471–82 in *Gefährdete Braut und schöne Witwe: Hebräische Judit-Geschichten.* Edited by Dagmar Börner-Klein. Wiesbaden: Marixverlag, 2007.
Gutmann-Grün, Meret. "Schlafend auf den Flügeln des Umherirrens. Exilsmetaphorik bei Jehuda Halevi." *Judaica* 2.3 (2008): 97–117.
———. *Zion als Frau: Das Frauenbild Zions in der Poesie von al-Andalus auf dem Hintergrund des klassischen Piyyuts.* Bern: Lang, 2008.
Gutwirth, Israel. *The Kabbalah and Jewish Mysticism.* New York: Philosophical Library, 1987.
Haberman, Bona Devorah. "Foreskin Sacrifice: Zipporah's Ritual and the Bloody Bridegroom." Pages 18–29 in *Covenant of Circumcision: New Perspectives on an Ancient Jewish Rite.* Edited by Elizabeth Wyner Mark. Lebanon, NH: University Press of New England; Brandeis University Press, 2003.
Hackett, Jo Ann. "Rehabilitating Hagar: Fragments of an Epic Pattern." Pages 12–27 in *Gender and Difference in Ancient Israel.* Edited by Peggy L. Day. Philadelphia: Fortress, 1989.
Haider, Peter W. "Judith—Eine zeitgenössische Antwort auf Kleopatra III als Beschützerin der Juden?" *Grazer Textbeiträge* 22 (1998): 117–28.
Ha-Kohen, Isaac b. Jacob. "Treatise on the Left Emanation." Pages 165–82 in *The Early Kabbalah.* Edited by Joseph Dan. New York: Paulist, 1986.
Halkin, A. S. *Kitāb al-muḥādara wa'l-mudhākara.* Jerusalem: Mequitze Nirdamim, 1975.
Hallamish, Moshe. *Introduction to the Kabbalah.* New York: State University of New York Press, 1999.
Hanhart, Robert. *Text und Textgeschichte des Buches Judit.* Göttingen: Vandenhoeck & Ruprecht, 1979.
Harris, Julie A. "Love in the Land of Goshen: Haggadah, History, and the Making of British Library, MS Oriental 2737." *Gesta* 52.2 (2013): 161–80.
———. "Polemical Images in the Golden Haggadah, BL, Add. MS 27210." *Medieval Encounters* 8 (2002): 105–22.
Harris, Robert A. "Awareness of Biblical Redaction among Rabbinic Exegetes of Northern France" [Hebrew]. *Shnaton* 13 (2000): 289–310.
———. "The Book of Leviticus Interpreted as Jewish Community." *Studies in Christian-Jewish Relations* 6 (2011): 1–15.

———. "From 'Religious Truth-Seeking' to Reading: The Twelfth Century Renaissance and the Emergence of Peshat and Ad Litteram as Methods of Accessing the Bible." Pages 54–89 in *The Oral and the Textual in Jewish Tradition and Jewish Education*. Edited by Jonathan Cohen, Matt Goldish, and Barry Holtz. Jerusalem: Magnes, 2019.

———. "Jewish Biblical Exegesis in the Middle Ages: From Its Beginnings through the Twelfth Century." Pages 596–615 in *The New Cambridge History of the Bible*. Edited by Richard Marsden and Ann Matter. Cambridge: Cambridge University Press, 2012.

———. "The Rashbam Authorship Controversy Redux: On Sara Japhet's *The Commentary of Rabbi Samuel Ben Meir (Rashbam) on the Book of Job*." *JQR* 95:1 (2005): 163–81.

———. "Rashi's Introductions to His Biblical Commentaries." Pages 219–41 in *Shai Le-Sara Japhet: Studies in the Bible, Its Exegesis and Its Language*. Edited by Moshe Bar-Asher, Dalit Rom-Shiloni, Emanuel Tov, and Nili Wayzana. Jerusalem: Bialik Institute, 2007.

———. "What's in a Blessing? Rashi and the Priestly Benediction of Numbers 6:22–27." Pages 231–58 in *Birkat Kohanim: The Priestly Benediction in Jewish Tradition*. Edited by Martin S. Cohen and David Birnbaum. New York: New Paradigm Matrix, 2016.

Harris, Tracy K. *Death of a Language: The History of Judeo-Spanish*. Newark: University of Delaware Press, 1994.

———. "The State of Ladino Today." *European Judaism 11* (2011): 51–61.

Har-Shefi, Bitkha. *Women and Halakha in the Years 1050–1350 CE: Between Custom and Law*. Jerusalem: Hebrew University of Jerusalem, 2002.

Haverkamp, Eva, ed. *Hebräische Berichte über die Judenverfolgungen während des Ersten Kreuzzugs*. Hannover: Hahnsche Buchhandlung, 2005.

Hecker, Joel. *The Zohar Pritzker Edition: Translation and Commentary*. Vol. 11. Stanford, CA: Stanford University Press, 2016.

Heiman, Dov, et. al, eds. *Yalqut Shim'oni*. Jerusalem: Kook Institute, 1973.

Henten, Jan Willem van. "Judith as Alternative Leader: A Rereading of Judith 7–13." Pages 224–52 in *A Feminist Companion to Esther, Judith und Susanna*. Edited by Athalya Brenner. Sheffield: Sheffield Academic, 1995.

———. "Judith as a Female Moses: Judith 7–13 in the Light of Exodus 17, Numbers 20, and Deuteronomy 33:8–11." Pages 33–48 in *Reflections on Theology and Gender.* Edited by Fokkelien van Dijk-Hemmes and Athalya Brenner. Kampen: Kok Paros, 1994.

Hirshman, Marc. *A Rivalry of Genius: Jewish and Christian Biblical Interpretation in Late Antiquity.* Albany: State University of New York Press, 1996.

Hoffman, Lawrence. *Covenant of Blood: Circumcision and Gender in Rabbinic Judaism.* Chicago: University of Chicago Press, 1996.

Hollender, Elisabeth, and Ulrich Berzbach. "Einige Anmerkungen zu biblischer Sprache und Motiven in Piyyutim aus der Kreuzzugszeit." *Frankfurter Judaistische Beiträge* 25 (1998): 67–68.

Horovitz, Haim Shaul, ed. *Mekhilta de Rabbi Yishmael.* Jerusalem: Bamberger & Wahrman, 1960.

Horowitz, Elliott E. "The Way We Were: Jewish Life in the Middle Ages." *Jewish History* 1 (1986): 75–90.

Hossfeld, Frank-Lothar, and Erich Zenger. *Die Psalmen I. Psalm 1–50.* Würzburg: Echter, 1993.

Humphreys, W. Lee. "A Life-Style for Diaspora: A Study of the Tales of Esther and Daniel." *JBL* 92.2 (1973): 211–23.

Hurovits, Avigdor. *Mishle: 'im Mavo U-ferush: Kerech 2, Perakim 10–31.* Tel Aviv: Am Oved, 2012.

Hüsch, Adolf. *Die fünf Megilloth nebst dem syrischen Thargum genannt "Peschito."* Prague: Senders & Brandeis, 1866.

Huss, Matti. "Pshat o Alegoria—Shirat haChesheq shel Shmuel Hanagid." *Mechqare Jerushalayim beSifrut Ivrit* 15 (1995): 34–72.

Iancu-Agou, Daniele. *Provincia Judaica. Dictionnaire des geographie historique des juifs en Provence medievale.* Leuven: Peeters, 2010.

Idel, Moshe. *Kabbalah and Eros.* New Haven: Yale University Press, 2005.

———. *Kabbalah: New Perspectives.* New Haven: Yale University Press, 1988.

———. "Magical and Magical-Mystical Arcanizations of Canonical Books." Pages 137–63 in *Absorbing Perfections: Kabbalah and Interpretation.* New Haven: Yale University Press, 2002.

———. "Panim: Faces and Re-presentations in Jewish Thought." Pages 71–102 in *Representing God.* Edited by Hava Tirosh-Samuelson and Aaron W. Hughes. Leiden: Brill, 2004.

Ilan, Tal. "And Who Knows Whether You Have Not Come to Domination for a Time Like This? (Esther 4:14): Esther, Judith and Susanna as Propaganda for Shelamzion's Queenship." Pages 127–53 in *Integrating*

Women into Second Temple History. Edited by Tal Ilan. Repr., Peabody, MA: Hendrickson, 2002.

———. "Folgenreiche Lektüren: Gender in Raschis Kommentar zum babylonischen Talmud." Pages 21–49 in *Der Differenz auf der Spur: Frauen und Gender in Aschkenas*. Edited by Christiane E. Müller and Andrea Schatz. Berlin: Metropol, 2004.

"Index of Jewish Art." http://web.nli.org.il/sites/NLI/Hebrew/digitallibrary/moreshet_bareshet/nuremberg-hagada/Documents/Second-NurmbergHaggadah.pdf.

Jakobi, Renate. "The Origins of the Qasida Form." Pages 21–31 in *Qasida Poetry in Islamic Asia and Africa*. Edited by Stefan Sperl and Christopher Shackle. Leiden: Brill, 1996.

Japhet, Sara. "The Anonymous Commentary on the Song of Songs in Ms. Prague: A Critical Edition and Introduction" [Hebrew]. Pages 206–47 in *"To Settle the Plain Meaning of the Verse": Studies in Biblical Exegesis*. Edited by Sara Japhet and Eran Viezel. Jerusalem: Bialik Institute, 2011.

———. *Collected Studies in Biblical Exegesis (Dor Dor Ufarshanav: Asufat Mehqarim be-Farshanut Hamiqra)* [Hebrew]. Jerusalem: Bialik Institute, 2008.

———. *The Commentary of Rabbi Samuel Ben Meir (Rashbam) on the Song of Songs* [Hebrew]. Jerusalem: World Union of Jewish Studies, 2008.

———. "Exegesis and Polemic in Rashbam's Commentary on the Song of Songs." Pages 182–95 and 304 in *Jewish Biblical Interpretation and Cultural Exchange: Comparative Exegesis in Context*. Edited by Natalie B. Dohrmann and David Stern. Philadelphia: University of Pennsylvania Press, 2008.

———. "'Lebanon' in the Transition From Derash to Peshat: Sources, Etymology and Meaning (With Special Attention to the Song of Songs)." Pages 707–24 in *Emanuel: Studies in Hebrew Bible, Septuagint and Dead Seas Scrolls in Honor of Emanuel Tov*. Edited by Shalom M. Paul, Robert A. Kraft, Lawrence H. Schiffman, and Weston W. Fields. Leiden: Brill, 2003.

———. "The Lovers' Way: Cultural Symbiosis in a Medieval Commentary on the Song of Songs." Pages 863–80 in *Birkat Shalom: Studies in the Bible, Ancient Near Eastern Literature, and Postbiblical Judaism Presented to Shalom M. Paul on the Occasion of His Seventieth Birthday*. Edited by Avi Hurvitz. Vol. 2. Winona Lake, IN: Eisenbrauns, 2008.

———. "Rashi's Commentary on the Song of Songs: The Revolution of the Peshat and Its Aftermath." Pages 199–219 in *Mein Haus wird ein Bethaus für alle Völker genannt werden (Jes 56,7): Judentum seit der Zeit des Zweiten Tempels in Geschichte, Literatur und Kult. Festschrift für Thomas Willi zum 65. Geburstag.* Edited by Julia Mannchen and Torsten Reiprich. Neukirchen-Vluyn: Neukirchener Verlag, 2007.

———. "Two Introductions By Rabbi Samuel Ben Meir (Rashbam): To the Song of Songs and Lamentations." Pages 205–23 in *Transforming Relations: Essays on Jews and Christians throughout History*. Edited by Franklin T. Harkins. Notre Dame: University of Notre Dame Press, 2010.

Japhet, Sara, and Robert Salters. *The Commentary of R. Samuel Ben Meir (Rashbam) on Qoheleth*. Jerusalem: Magnes; Leiden: Brill, 1985.

Japhet, Sara, and Barry Walfish. *The Way of Lovers: The Oxford Anonymous Commentary on the Song of Songs*. Leiden: Brill, 2017.

Jarden, Dov. *Divan Shemuel Ha-Nagid: Ben Tehillim*. Jerusalem: privately published, 1966.

———. *Shirey haQodesh le-Rabbi Shlomo Ibn Gabirol*. 2 vols. Jerusalem: American Academy of Jewish Research, 1971–1972.

———. *Shirey haQodesh le-Rabbi Yehuda Ha-Levi*. 4 vols. Jerusalem: privately published, 1978–1985.

Jellinek, Adolf. *Bet ha-Midrash: Sammlung kleiner Midraschim und vermischter Abhandlungen aus der älteren jüdische Literatur*. 6 vols. Repr., Jerusalem: Wahrmann, 1967.

Jordan, William C. *Women and Credit in Pre-Industrial and Developing Society*. Philadelphia: University of Pennsylvania Press, 1993.

Kamin, Sarah. "דוגמא in Rashi's Commentary on the Song of Songs." Pages 69–88 in *Jews and Christians Interpret the Bible*. Jerusalem: Magnes, 2008.

———. *Rashi's Exegetical Categorization in Respect to the Distinction between Peshat and Derash* [Hebrew]. Jerusalem: Magnes, 1986.

———. "Rashi's Commentary on the Song of Songs and Jewish-Christian Polemic" [Hebrew]. Pages 22–57 in *Jews and Christians Interpret the Bible*. Jerusalem: Magnes, 2008.

Kamin, Sarah, and Avrom Saltman. *Secundum Salomonem: A Thirteenth Century Latin Commentary on the Song of Songs*. Ramat Gan: Bar Ilan University Press, 1989.

Kanarfogel, Ephraim. "R. Judah he-Hasid and the Rabbinic Scholars of Regensburg: Interactions, Influences and Implications." *JQR* 96 (2006): 17–37.

Kaplan, Aryeh, trans. *The Bahir: Illuminations*. York Beach, ME: Weiser, 1989.

Kaplan, Debra. "'Because Our Wives Trade and Do Business with Our Goods': Gender, Work, and Jewish-Christian Relations." Pages 241–64 in *New Perspectives on Jewish-Christian Relations*. Edited by Elisheva Carlebach and Jacob J. Schachter. Leiden: Brill, 2011.

Karo, Joseph. *Maggid Mescharim* [Hebrew]. Jerusalem: Orah, 1960.

Katz, Jacob. "Marriage and Sexual Life among the Jews at the Close of the Middle Ages" [Hebrew]. *Zion* 10 (1945): 21–54.

———. *The "Shabbes Goy": A Study in Halakhic Flexibility*. Translated by Yoel Lerner. Philadelphia: Jewish Publication Society, 1989.

———. "Yibbum veHalizah ba Tekufah haBetar Talmudit." *Tarbiz* 51 (1981): 59–106.

Keil, Martha. "Public Roles of Jewish Women in Fourteenth and Fifteenth-Century Ashkenaz: Business, Community and Ritual." Pages 317–30 in *The Jews of Europe in the Middle Ages (Tenth to Fifteenth Centuries): Proceedings of the International Symposium Held at Speyer, 20–25 October 2002*. Edited by Christoph Cluse. Turnhout: Brepols, 2004.

Kimmelman, Reuben. "Rabbi Yokhanan and Origen on the Song of Songs: A Third-Century Jewish-Christian Disputation." *HTR* 73 (1980): 567–95.

Kogman-Appel, Katrin. "Christianity, Idolatry, and the Question of Jewish Figural Painting in the Middle Ages." *Speculum* 84 (2009): 73–107.

———. *Die Zweite Nürnberger und die Jehuda Haggada: Jüdische Künstler zwischen Tradition und Fortschritt*. Frankfurt am Main: Lang, 1999.

———. *Illuminated Haggadot from Medieval Spain: Biblical Imagery and the Passover Holiday*. University Park: Pennsylvania State University Press, 2006.

Koller, Aaron. *Esther in Ancient Jewish Thought*. Cambridge: Cambridge University Press, 2014.

Kraeling, Carl. *The Synagogue: The Excavations at Dura Europos. Final Report VIII, Part 1*. New Haven: Yale University Press, 1956.

Krautheimer, Richard. *Mittelalterliche Synagogen*. Berlin: Frankfurter Verlags-Anstalt, 1927.

Krakowski, Eve. *Coming of Age in Medieval Egypt: Female Adolescence, Jewish Law and Ordinary Culture*. Princeton: Princeton University Press, 2019.

LaCocque, André. *The Feminine Unconventional: Four Subversive Figures in Israel's Tradition*. Eugene, OR: Wipf & Stock, 1990.

Langer, Gerhard. "Die Bibel und die Rabbinen. Exegese und Aktualisierung und noch etwas anderes!" Pages 37–51 in *Gottes Name(n): Zum Gedenken an Erich Zenger*. HBS 71. Edited by Ilse Müllner, Ludger Schwienhorst-Schönberger and Ruth Scoralick. Freiburg: Herder, 2012.

———. *Midrasch*. Tübingen: Mohr Siebeck, 2016.

Lassner, Jacob. *Demonizing the Queen of Sheba: Boundaries of Gender and Culture in Postbiblical Judaism and Medieval Islam*. Chicago: Chicago University Press, 1993.

Lerner, Myron Bialik. "The Works of Aggadic Midrash and the Esther Midrashim." Pages 176–229 in *The Literature of the Sages, Second Part: Midrash and Targum, Liturgy, Poetry, Mysticism, Contracts, Inscriptions, Ancient Science, and the Languages of Rabbinic Literature*. Edited by Shmuel Safrai, et al. Assen: Van Gorcum; Minneapolis: Fortress, 2006.

Levenson, Jon D. *Death and Resurrection of the Beloved Son: The Transformation of Child Sacrifice in Judaism and Christianity*. New Haven: Yale University Press, 1993.

Levine Gera, Deborah. "The Jewish Textual Traditions." Pages 23–40 in *The Sword of Judith: Judith Studies across the Disciplines*. Edited by Kevin R. Brine, Elena Ciletti, and Henrike Lähnemann. Cambridge: Open Publishers, 2010.

———. "Shorter Medieval Hebrew Tales of Judith." Pages 81–95 in *The Sword of Judith: Judith Studies across the Disciplines*. Edited by Kevin R. Brine, Elena Ciletti, and Henrike Lähnemann. Cambridge: Open Publishers, 2010.

Lieber, Laura. *Yannai on Genesis: An Invitation to Piyyut*. Cincinnati: Hebrew Union College, 2010.

Lipsius, Richard Adelbert. "Jüdische Quellen zur Judithsage." *Zeitschrift für wissenschaftliche Theologie* 10 (1867): 337–66.

Liss, Hanna. "The Commentary on the Song of Songs Attributed to R. Samuel Ben Meir (Rashbam)." *Medieval Jewish Studies-Online* 1 (2007): 1–27.

Lockshin, Martin. *Rabbi Samuel Ben Meir's Commentary on Genesis: An Annotated Translation*. Lewiston: Mellen, 1989.

——. "Rashbam as a 'Literary' Exegete." Pages 83–91 in *With Reverence for the Word: Medieval Scriptural Exegesis in Judaism, Christianity and Islam*. Edited by Jane Dammen McAuliffe, Barry D. Walfish, and Joseph W. Goering. Oxford: Oxford University Press, 2003.

——. *Rashbam's Commentary on Deuteronomy: An Annotated Translation*. Providence, RI: Brown Judaic Studies, 2004.

——. *Rashbam's Commentary on Exodus: An Annotated Translation*. Atlanta: Scholars Press, 1997.

——. *Rashbam's Commentary on Leviticus and Numbers: An Annotated Translation*. Providence, RI: Brown Judaic Studies, 2001.

Lodahl, Michael E. *Shekhinah/Spirit, Divine Presence in Jewish and Christian Religion*. New York: Paulist, 1992.

Loewe, Raphael, ed. *The Rylands Haggadah: A Medieval Sephardi Masterpiece in Facsimile. An Illuminated Passover Compendium from Mid-14th-Century Catalonia in the Collections of the John Rylands University Library of Manchester with a Commentary and a Cycle of Poems*. London: Thames and Hudson, 1988.

Lotter, Friedrich. "'Tod oder Taufe': Das Problem der Zwangstaufen während der Ersten Kreuzzugs." Pages 107–52 in *Juden und Christen zur Zeit der Kreuzzüge*. Edited by Alfred Haverkamp. Sigmaringen: Thorbecke, 1999.

Lowin, Shari. *Arabic and Hebrew Love Poems in al-Andalus*. New York: Routledge, 2014.

——. *The Making of a Forefather: Abraham in Islamic and Jewish Exegetical Narratives*. Leiden: Brill, 2006.

Luzzato, Shmuel David, ed. *Diwan R. Yehuda Halevi*. Lyck, 1864.

Lyke, Larry. "Where Does the Boy Belong? Compositional Strategy in Genesis 21:14." *CBQ* 56 (1994): 637–48.

Malter, Henry. "Purim." Pages 274–79 in *The Jewish Encyclopedia*. Vol. 10. New York: Ktav, 1965.

Manix, Pam. "Oxford: Mapping the Medieval Jewry." Pages 405–20 in *The Jews of Europe in the Middle Ages (Tenth to Fifteenth Centuries): Proceedings of the International Symposium Held at Speyer, 20–25 October 2002*. Edited by Christoph Cluse. Turnhout: Brepols, 2004.

Marcus, Ivan G. "From Politics to Martyrdom: Shifting Paradigms in the Hebrew Narratives of the 1096 Crusade Riots." *Prooftexts* 2 (1982): 40–52.

———. "A Jewish-Christian Symbiosis: The Culture of Early Ashkenaz." Pages 449–518 in *Culture of the Jews: A New History*. Edited by David Biale. New York: Schocken, 2002.

———. "Mothers, Martyrs, and Moneymakers: Some Jewish Women in Medieval Europe." *Conservative Judaism* 38.3 (1986): 34–45.

———. *Piety and Society: The Jewish Pietists of Medieval Germany*. Leiden: Brill, 1981.

———. "Review of Robert Chazan, *European Jewry and the First Crusade*." *Speculum* 64 (1989): 685–88.

———. *Rituals of Childhood: Jewish Acculturation in Medieval Europe*. New Haven: Yale University Press, 1998.

———. *"Sefer Hasidim" and the Ashkenazic Book in Medieval Europe*. Philadelphia: University of Pennsylvania Press, 2018.

Margaliot, Reuven, ed. *Sefer Ha-Bahir* [Hebrew]. Jerusalem: Kook, 1978.

Mathews, H. J. "Anonymous Commentary on the Song of Songs: Edited From a Unique Manuscript in the Bodleian Library Oxford." Pages 164–85 and 238–40 in *Festschrift Zum Achtzigsten Geburtstage Moritz Steinschneider's*. Leipzig: Harrassowitz, 1896.

Matter, E. Ann. *The Voice of My Beloved: The Song of Songs in Western Medieval Christianity*. Philadelphia: University of Pennsylvania Press, 1990.

Meir, Tamar. "Ruth: Midrash and Aggadah." *Jewish Women's Archive Encyclopedia*. https://tinyurl.com/SBL6014e.

Metzger, Mendel, and Thérèse Metzger. *Jewish Life in the Middle Ages: Illuminated Hebrew Manuscripts of the Thirteenth to the Sixteenth Century*. New York: Alpine Fine Arts Collection, 1982.

Meyers, Carol. "Esther". Pages 324–30 in *The Oxford Bible Commentary*. Edited by John Barton and John Muddimann. Oxford: Oxford University Press, 2001.

Michels, Evi. "Purimspiel." Pages 53–58 in *Enzyklopädie jüdischer Geschichte und Kultur*. Vol. 5. Edited by Dan Diner. Stuttgart: Metzler, 2014.

Mintz, Alan. *Hurban: Responses to Catastrophe in Hebrew Literature*. New York: Columbia University Press, 1984.

Miqra'ot gedoloth. 10 vols. Tanakh with Traditional Commentaries. New York: Pardes, 1959.

Mireaux, Émile. *La reine Bérénice*. Paris: Albin Michel, 1951.

Mirsky, Aron. *Ha-piyyut: Hitpathuto be-Erets Yisra'el uva-golah*. Jerusalem: Magnes, 1990.

Mondschein, Aharon. "Additional Comments on Hasadran and Hamesader" [Hebrew]. *Leshonenu* 67 (2005): 331–46.

Moore, Carey A., ed. *Esther*. AB 7B. Garden City, NY: Doubleday, 1971.

——. *Judith: A New Translation with Introduction and Commentary*. AB 40. Garden City, NY: Doubleday, 1985.

——. "Esther, Additions to." *ABD* 2:626–33.

——. "Esther, Book of." *ABD* 2:633–43.

Mulin, Jacob. *Sefer Maharil: Minhagim*. Edited by Shlomo Spitzer. Jerusalem: Machon Yerushalayim, 1989.

——. *Shut Maharil (Responsa of Rabbi Yaacov Molin-Maharil)*. Edited by Yitzchok Satz. Jerusalem: Machon Yerushalayim, 1979.

Münz-Manor, Ophir. "All about Sarah: Questions of Gender in Yannai's Poems on Sarah's (and Abraham's) Barrenness." *Prooftexts* 26.3 (2006): 344–74.

Narkiss, Bezalel. *Hebrew Illuminated Manuscripts*. Jerusalem: Keter, 1969.

——. *The Golden Haggadah: A Fourteenth-Century Illuminated Hebrew Manuscript in the British Museum*. London: Eugrammia, 1970.

Narkiss, Bezalel, Aliza Cohen-Mushlin, and Anat Tcherikover. *Hebrew Illuminated Manuscripts in the British Isles*. Vol. 1: *Spanish and Portuguese Manuscripts*. Jerusalem: Israeli Academy of Sciences; Oxford: Oxford University Press, 1982.

Neusner, Jacob. *Genesis Rabbah: The Judaic Commentary of the Book of Genesis: A New American Translation*. Atlanta: Scholars Press, 1985.

——, ed. *The Talmud of the Land of Israel*. Chicago: University of Chicago Press, 1987.

Neusner, Jacob, and Alan Avery-Peck, eds. *Encyclopedia of Midrash: Biblical Interpretation in Formative Judaism*. 2 vols. Leiden: Brill, 2005.

Noam, Vered. *Megillat Taanit: Versions, Interpretations, History. With a Critical Edition* [Hebrew]. Jerusalem: Yad Ben-Zvi Press, 2003.

O'Bryan, Robin. "Carnal Desire and Conflicted Sexual Identity in a 'Dominican' Chapel." Pages 41–60 in *Images of Sex and Desire in Renaissance Art and Modern Historiography*. Edited by Angeliki Pollali and Berthold Hub. New York: Routledge, 2018.

Offenberg, Sara. "Expressions of Meeting the Challenges of the Christian Milieu in Medieval Jewish Art and Literature" [Hebrew]." PhD diss. The Ben-Gurion University of the Negev, 2008.

Otzen, Benedikt. *Tobit and Judith*. Sheffield: Sheffield Academic, 2002.

Pagis, Dan. *Innovation and Tradition in Secular Poetry: Spain and Italy* [Hebrew]. Jerusalem: Keter Publishing, 1976.

———. *Secular Poetry and Poetic Theory: Moshe Ibn Ezra and His Contemporaries* [Hebrew]. Jerusalem: Bialik Institute, 1970.
Patai, Raphael. *The Hebrew Goddess*. Detroit: Wayne State University Press, 1990.
———. *The Seed of Abraham*. New York: Charles Scribner's Sons, 1986.
Perez Castro, Federico. *Poesía secular hispano-hebrea*. Madrid: CSIC, 1989.
Pessin, Sarah. "Loss, Presence, and Gabirol's Desire: Medieval Jewish Philosophy and the Possibility of a Feminist Ground." Pages 27–50 in *Women and Gender in Jewish Philosophy*. Edited by Hava Tirosh-Samuelson. Bloomington: Indiana University Press, 2004.
Pierce, Joanne M. "Holy Week and Easter in the Middle Ages." Pages 161–85 in *Passover and Easter: Origin and History to Modern Times*. Edited by Paul Bradshaw and Lawrence Hoffman. Notre Dame: University of Notre Dame Press, 1999.
Polzer, Natalie C. "Misogyny Revisited: The Eve Traditions in Avot de Rabbi Natan, Versions A and B." *AJSR* 36 (2012): 207–55.
Porsche, Monika. "Speyer: The Medieval Synagogue." Pages 421–34 in *The Jews of Europe in the Middle Ages (Tenth to Fifteenth Centuries: Proceedings of the International Symposium Held at Speyer, 20–25 October 2002*. Edited by Christoph Cluse. Turnhout: Brepols, 2004.
Priebatsch, Hans Yohanan. "Das Buch Judith und seine hellenistischen Quellen." *Zeitschrift des Deutschen Palästina-Vereins* 90 (1974): 50–60.
Pritchard, James B. ed., *The Ancient Near East: An Anthology of Texts and Pictures*. Princeton: Princeton University Press, 2010.
Radford Ruether, Rosemary. *Goddesses and the Divine Feminine: A Western Religious History*. Berkeley: University of California Press, 2005.
Rakel, Claudia. *Judit—Über Schönheit, Macht und Widerstand im Krieg: Eine feministische-intertextuelle Lektüre*. Berlin: de Gruyter, 2003.
Ray, Jonathan. "The Jew in the Text: What Christian Charters Tell Us about Medieval Jewish Society." *Medieval Encounters* 16 (2010): 246–48.
Recanati, Menachem. *Perush 'al ha-Torah* [Hebrew]. Lemberg, 1880.
Regev, Shaul. "'Woman of Valor' אשת חיל: The Character and Status of Women in Jewish Philosophy of the Sixteenth Century." *European Journal of Jewish Studies* 4 (2010): 241–54.
Reinhartz, Adele, and Miriam-Simma Walfish. "Conflict and Coexistence in Jewish Interpretation." Pages 101–26 in *Hagar, Sarah and Their Children: Jewish, Christian and Muslim Perspectives*. Edited by Phyllis Trible and Letty M. Russell. Louisville: Westminster John Knox, 2006.

Roi, Biti. "Divine Qualities and Real Women: the Feminine Image in Kabbalah." *Havruta* 5 (2010): 62–69.
Rosen, Tova. *Unveiling Eve: Reading Gender in Medieval Hebrew Literature*. Philadelphia: University of Pennsylvania Press, 2003.
Rosen-Tzvi, Ishay. *Demonic Desires: "Yetzer Hara" and the Problem of Evil in Late Antiquity*. Philadelphia: University of Pennsylvania Press, 2011.
Rosman, Moshe. *How Jewish Is Jewish History?* Portland: Littman Library, 2007.
Sabar, Shalom. "'The Fathers Slaughter their Sons': Depictions of the Binding of Isaac in the Art of Medieval Ashkenaz." *Images* 3 (2009): 9–28.
——. "'The Right Path for an Artist': The Approach of Leone da Modena to Visual Art." *Hebraica hereditas* (2005): 255–90.
Samely, Alexander. *Forms of Rabbinic Literature and Thought*. Oxford: Oxford University Press, 2007.
——. *Rabbinic Interpretation of Scripture in the Mishnah*. Oxford: Oxford University Press, 2002.
Sáenz-Badillos, Ángel. "Philologians and Poets in Search of the Hebrew Language." Pages 49–75 in *Languages of Power in Islamic Spain*. Edited by Ross Brann. Bethesda, MD: CDL, 1997.
Sáenz-Badillos, Ángel, and Judit Targarona-Borrás. *Samuel ha-Nagid. Poemas I. Desde el campo de batalla. Granada 1038–1056. Edición del texto hebreo, introducción, traducción y notas*. Córdoba: El Almendro 1988.
——. *Yehudah ha-Levi. Poemas*. Madrid: Editorial Alfaguara, 1994.
Salvatierra Ossorio, Aurora. *Cantos de boda hispanohebreos. Antología*. Córdoba: El Almendro, 1998.
Sänger, Dieter, ed. *Psalm 22 und die Passionsgeschichten der Evangelien*. Neukirchen-Vluyn: Neukirchener Verlag, 2007.
Sapir Abulafia, Anna. "The Interrelationship between the Hebrew Chronicles of the First Crusade." *JSS* 27 (1982): 221–39.
Schäfer, Peter. *Mirror of His Beauty: Feminine Images of God from the Bible to the Early Kabbalah*. Princeton: Princeton University Press, 2002.
Scheindlin, Raymond. *The Gazelle: Medieval Poems on God, Israel, and the Soul*. Oxford: Oxford University Press, 1991.
——. "La situación social y el mundo de valores de los poetas hebreos." Pages 53–70 in *La sociedad medieval a través de la literatura hispano-judía: VI Curso de cultura hispano-judía y sefardí de la Universidad de Castilla-La Mancha*. Edited by Ricardo Izquierdo Benito and Ángel Sáenz-Badillos. Cuenca: Universidad Castilla-La Mancha, 1998.

———. "Merchants and Intellectuals, Rabbis and Poets: Judeo-Arabic Culture in the Golden Age of Islam." Pages 315–86 in *Culture of the Jews: A New History*. Edited by David Biale. New York: Schocken, 2002.

———. *The Song of the Distant Dove: Judah Halevi's Pilgrimage*. Oxford: Oxford University Press, 2008.

———. *Wine, Women and Death: Medieval Hebrew Poetry on the Good Life*. Philadelphia: Jewish Publications Society, 1986.

Schippers, Arie. *Spanish Hebrew Poetry and the Arabic Literary Tradition: Themes in Hebrew Andalusian Poetry*. Leiden: Brill, 1994.

Schirmann, Hayyim. *Hebrew Poetry in Spain and Provence* [Hebrew]. Vol. 1. Jerusalem: Bialik Institute, 1954.

———. *The History of Hebrew Poetry in Muslim Spain* [Hebrew]. Edited by Ezra Fleisher. Jerusalem: Magnes, 1995.

Schlosser, Julius von, and David Heinrich Müller. *Die Haggadah von Sarajevo: Eine spanisch-jüdische Bilderhandschrift des Mittelalters*. Vienna: Hölder, 1898.

Schmitz, Barbara. "Holofernes's Canopy." Pages 71–80 in *The Sword of Judith: Judith Studies across the Disciplines*. Edited by Kevin R. Brine, Elena Ciletti, and Henrike Lähnemann. Cambridge: Open Book, 2010.

———. "Ιουδιθ and Iudith: Überlegungen zum Verhältnis der Judit-Erzählungen in der LXX and der Vulgata." Pages 358–80 in *Textcritical and Hermeneutical Studies in the Septuagint*. Edited by Johann Cook and Hermann-Josef Stipp. Leiden: Brill, 2012.

———. "Zwischen Achikar und Demaratos—Die Bedeutung Achiors in der Juditerzählung." *Biblische Zeitschrift* 48 (2004): 19–38.

Scholem, Gershom. *Die jüdische Mystik in ihren Hauptströmungen*. Frankfurt am Main: Suhrkamp, 1980.

———. *Kabbalah*. New York: New American Library, 1974.

———. *Major Trends in Jewish Mysticism*. New York: Schocken, 1946.

———. *On the Kabbalah and Its Symbolism*. New York: Schocken, 1965.

———. *On the Mystical Shape of the Godhead: Basic Concepts of the Kabbalah*. New York: Schocken, 1991.

———. *Origins of the Kabbalah*. Philadelphia: Jewish Publication Society, 1987.

Schroer, Silvia. "Altorientalische Bilder als Schlüssel zu biblischen Metaphern." Pages 123–52 in *Hebräische Bibel—Altes Testament: Schriften und spätere Weisheitsbücher*. Edited by Christl Maier and Nuria Calduch-Benages. Stuttgart: Kohlhammer, 2013.

Schwartzmann, Julia. "Gender Concepts of Medieval Jewish Thinkers and the Book of Proverbs." *JSQ* 7.3 (2000): 183–202.

———. "The Medieval Philosophical Interpretation of the Creation of Woman" [Hebrew]. *Da'at* 39 (1997): 69–87.

Shepkaru, Shmuel. *Jewish Martyrs in the Pagan and the Christian Worlds.* Cambridge: Cambridge University Press, 2005.

Shoham-Steiner, Ephraim. "The Virgin Mary, Miriam, and Jewish Reactions to Marian Devotion in the High Middle Ages." *AJSR* 37 (2013): 75–91.

Signer, Michael A. "God's Love for Israel: Apologetic and Hermeneutical Strategies in Twelfth-Century Biblical Exegesis." Pages 123–49 in *Jews and Christians in Twelfth Century Europe.* Edited by Michael A Signer and John Van Engen. Notre Dame: University of Notre Dame Press, 2001.

Sijarić, Mirsad, ed. *The Sarajevo Haggadah: History and Art.* With a commentary volume by Shalom Sabar. Sarajevo: The National Museum of Bosnia and Herzegovina, 2018.

Simon, Maurice. *Midrash Rabbah IX.* London: Soncino, 1939.

Sneed, Mark R. *The Social World of the Sages: An Introduction to Israelite and Jewish Wisdom Literature.* Minneapolis: Fortress, 2015.

Soloveitchik, Haym. "Three Themes in the *Sefer Hasidim.*" *AJSR* 1 (1976): 311–57.

Spiegel, Shalom. "*Aggadot* on the Binding of Isaac: A *Piyyut* about the Slaughter of Isaac and His Resurrection by R. Ephraim of Bonn" [Hebrew]. Pages 471–547 in *Alexander Marx Jubilee Volume on the Occasion of His Seventieth Birthday.* New York: Jewish Theological Seminary of America, 1950.

———. *The Last Trial: On the Legends and Lore of the Command to Abraham to Offer Isaac as a Sacrifice—The Akedah.* Philadelphia: The Jewish Publication Society, 1967.

Spiegel, Yaakov S. "Woman as Ritual Circumciser: The Halakhah and Its Development" [Hebrew]. *Sidra* 5 (1989): 149–57.

Steiner, Richard C. "A Jewish Theory of Biblical Redaction from Byzantium: Its Rabbinic Roots, Its Diffusion and Its Encounter with the Muslim Doctrine of Falsification." *Jewish Studies Internet Journal* 2 (2003): 123–67.

Stemberger, Günter. *Einleitung in Talmud und Midrash.* Munich: Beck, 2011.

———. "Midrasch in Babylonien, am Beispiel von Sota 9b–14a." *Henoch* 10 (1988): 183–203.

Stern, David, and Mark Jay Mirsky. *Rabbinic Fantasies: Imaginative Narratives from Classical Hebrew Literature*. Philadelphia: Jewish Publication Society, 1990.

Stienstra, Nelly. *Yhwh Is the Husband of His People: Analysis of a Biblical Metaphor with Special Reference to Translation*. Kampen: Peeters, 1993.

Stow, Kenneth R. *Alienated Minority: The Jews of Medieval Latin Europe*. Cambridge: Harvard University Press, 1992.

———. "The Jewish Family in the Rhineland: Form and Function." *American Historical Review* 92 (1987): 1085–110.

Stuard, Susan Mosher. "Brideprice, Dowry, and Other Marital Assigns." Pages 148–62 in *The Oxford Handbook of Women and Gender in Medieval Europe*. Edited by Judith Bennett and Ruth Mazo Karras. Oxford: Oxford University Press, 2012.

Sukenik, Eliezer L. *The Synagogue of Dura Europos and Its Wall Paintings* [Hebrew]. Jerusalem: Bialik Institute, 1947.

Swartz, Michael D., and Joseph Yahalom, eds. and trans. *Avodah: An Anthology of Ancient Poetry for Yom Kippur*. University Park: Pennsylvania State University Press, 2005.

Tabory, Joseph, and Arnon Atzmon, eds. *Midrash Esther Rabbah*. Jerusalem: Schechter Institute of Jewish Studies, 2014.

Thompson, John L. *Writing the Wrongs: Women of the Old Testament among Biblical Commentators from Philo through the Reformation*. Oxford: Oxford University Press, 2001.

Tishby, Isaiah. *The Doctrine of Evil and the Kelippah in Lurianic Kabbalism* [Hebrew]. Jerusalem: Schocken, 1984.

Tishby, Isaiah, and Fischel Lachower, eds. *The Wisdom of the Zohar: An Anthology of Texts*. Vol. 2. Translated by David Goldstein. Oxford: Oxford University Press, 1989.

Tobi, Yosef. "'Maimonides' Attitude towards Secular Poetry, Secular Arab and Hebrew Literature, Liturgical Poetry and Towards their Cultural Environment." Pages 422–66 in *Between Hebrew and Arabic Poetry: Studies in Spanish Medieval Poetry*. Edited by Yosef Tobi. Leiden: Brill 2010.

Toch, Michael. "Jewish Peasants in the Middle Ages? Agriculture and Jewish Land Ownership in Eighth-Twelfth Centuries" [Hebrew]. *Zion* 75 (2010): 291–312.

Touitou, Elazar. *Exegesis in Perpetual Motion: Studies in the Pentateuchal Commentary of Rabbi Samuel Ben Meir* [Hebrew]. Ramat Gan: Bar Ilan University Press, 2003.

Transier, Werner. "Speyer: The Jewish Community in the Middle Ages." Pages 435–47 in *The Jews of Europe in the Middle Ages (Tenth to Fifteenth Centuries): Proceedings of the International Symposium Held at Speyer, 20–25 October 2002*. Edited by Christoph Cluse. Turnhout: Brepols, 2004.

Trible, Phyllis. *Texts of Terror*. Philadelphia: Fortress, 1984.

Tuttle, Virginia. "Lilith in Bosch's 'Garden of Earthly Delights.'" *Simiolus: Netherlands Quarterly for the History of Art* 15.2 (1985): 119–30.

Urbach, Ephraim. *The Sages: Their Concepts and Beliefs*. Jerusalem: Magnes, 1979.

Valler, Shulamit. "Who is *ēšet hayil* in Rabbinic Literature?" Pages 85–97 in *A Feminist Companion to Wisdom Literature*. Edited by Athalya Brenner. Sheffield: Sheffield Academic, 1995.

VanderKam, James C., ed. *"No One Spoke Ill of Her": Essays on Judith*. EJL 2. Atlanta: Scholars Press, 1992.

Vardi, Yonatan. "Poems of Salvation by Shemuel Hanagid." *Hispania Judaica Bulletin* 14 (2019): 1–14.

Waldman, Felicia. "Edenic Paradise and Paradisal Eden: Moshe Idel's Reading of the Talmudic Legend of the Four Sages who Entered the Pardes." *Journal for the Study of Religion and Ideology* 6.18 (2007): 79–87.

Walfish, Barry Dov. *Esther in Medieval Garb: Jewish Interpretation of the Book of Esther in the Middle Ages*. Albany: State University of New York Press, 1993.

———. "An Introduction to Medieval Jewish Biblical Interpretation." Pages 3–9 in *With Reverence for the Word: Medieval Scriptural Exegesis in Judaism, Christianity and Islam*. Edited by Jane Dammen McAuliffe, Barry Walfish, and Joseph Ward Goering. Oxford: Oxford University Press, 2010.

———. "The Mordecai-Esther-Ahasuerus Triangle in Midrash and Exegesis." *Prooftexts* 22 (2002): 305–33.

Wasserstrom, Steven M. *Between Muslim and Jew: The Problem of Symbiosis under Early Islam*. Princeton: Princeton University Press, 1995.

Weinberger, Leon. *Jewish Hymnography: A Literary History*. London: Littman Library of Jewish Civilization, 1998.

Weingarten, Susan. "Food, Sex, and Redemption in Megillat Yehudit." Pages 81–95 in *The Sword of Judith: Judith Studies across the Disciplines*. Edited by Kevin R. Brine, Elena Ciletti, and Henrike Lähnemann. Cambridge: Open Book, 2010.
Werblowsky, R. J. Zwi. *Joseph Karo, Lawyer and Mystic*. Philadelphia: Jewish Publication Society, 1977.
Wertheimer, Joseph Chaim. *Midrash Shir Ha-Shirim: Printed From a Geniza Manuscript* [Hebrew]. Jerusalem: Ketav-Yad va-Sefer Institute, 1981.
West, Gerald. "Judith." Pages 748–62 in *Eerdmans Commentary to the Hebrew Bible*. Edited by James D. G. Dunn and John W. Rogerson. Grand Rapids: Eerdmans, 2003.
Wharton, Annabel J. "Good and Bad Images from the Synagogue of Dura Europos: Contexts, Subtexts Intertexts." *Art History* 17.1 (1994): 1–25.
Whybray, R. N. *The Composition of the Book of Proverbs*. Sheffield: Sheffield Academic, 1994.
Wilhelm, Jakob David. "Sidre Tiqqunim" [Hebrew]. Pages 125–46 in *Alei Ayin: The Salman Schocken Jubilee Volume. Contributions on Biblical and Post-Biblical Hebrew Literature, Poetry and Belles-lettres. Issued on the Occasion of His Seventieth Birthday by a Circle of his Friends*. Jerusalem: Schocken, 1952.
Wistinetzki, Judah, ed. *Sefer Hasidim*. With an introduction by Jacob Freimann. Frankfurt am Main: Vahrmann, 1924.
Wolfson, Elliot. *Circle in the Square: Studies in the Use of Gender in Kabbalistic Symbolism*. Albany: State University of New York Press, 1995.
———. "The Mystical Significance of Torah Study in German Pietism." *JQR* 84.1 (1993): 43–77.
Wolfthal, Diane. *Picturing Yiddish: Gender, Identity, and Memory in the Illustrated Yiddish Books of Renaissance Italy*. Leiden: Brill, 2004.
Wolters, Al. *The Song of the Valiant Woman: Studies in the Interpretation of Proverbs 31:10–31*. Carlisle: Paternoster, 2001.
Wright, L. M. "Misconceptions Concerning the Troubadours, Trouvères and Minstrels." *Music & Letters* 48 (1967): 35–39.
Wünsche, August. *Aus Israels Lehrhallen: Kleine Midraschim zur späteren legendarischen Literatur des Alten Testaments*. 5 vols. Repr., Hildesheim: Olms, 1967.
Yahalom, Joseph. *Yehuda Halevi: Poetry and Pilgrimage*. Jerusalem: Magnes, 2009.

Yuval, Israel J. "Monetary Arrangements and Marriage in Medieval Ashkenaz" [Hebrew]. Pages 191–208 in *Religion and Economy: Connections and Interactions*. Edited by Menahem Ben-Sasson. Jerusalem: Merkaz Shazar, 1995.

———. *Two Nations in Your Womb: Perceptions of Jews and Christians in Late Antiquity and the Middle Ages*. Berkeley: University of California Press, 2006.

———. *Zwei Völker in deinem Leib: Gegenseitige Wahrnehmung von Juden und Christen in Spätantike und Mittelalter*. Göttingen: Vandenhoeck & Ruprecht, 2007.

Zakovitch, Yair. "'A Woman of Valor,' *'eshet hayil* (Proverbs 31.10–31): A Conservative Response to the Song of Songs." Pages 401–13 in *A Critical Engagement: Essays on the Hebrew Bible in Honour of J. Cheryl Exum*. Edited by David J. A. Clines and Ellen van Wolde. Sheffield: Sheffield Phoenix, 2011.

———. "The Books of Esther and Judith: A Parallel." Pages 1–37 in *The Book of Judith: Greek Text with English Translation, Commentary and Critical Notes*. Edited by Morton Scott Enslin. Leiden: Brill, 1972.

Zenger, Erich. *Das Buch Judit. Historische und legendarische Erzählungen*. JSHRZ 1.6 Gütersloh: Gütersloher Verlagshaus, 1981.

Contributors

Carol Bakhos is Professor of Near Eastern Languages and Cultures and of Study of Religion at the University of California, Los Angeles (UCLA). She works at the intersection of religion, culture, literature, and history and is the author of several monographs and edited volumes, including *The Family of Abraham* (Harvard University Press, 2014), *Ishmael on the Border* (SUNY, 2006), *Islam and Its Past*, edited with Michael Cook (Oxford, 2017), the coedited work, *The Talmud in Its Iranian Context* (Mohr Siebeck, 2010), *Judaism in Its Hellenistic Context* (Brill, 2004), and *Current Trends in the Study of Midrash* (Brill, 2006). Since 2012 she has served as Chair of the Study of Religion program and Director of the Center for the Study of Religion at UCLA.

Judith R. Baskin, who received a PhD in Medieval Studies from Yale University, is Philip H. Knight Professor of Humanities Emerita at the University of Oregon. The author of numerous scholarly articles, her books include *Pharaoh's Counsellors: Job, Jethro, and Balaam in Rabbinic and Patristic Tradition*, *Midrashic Women: Formations of the Feminine in Rabbinic Literature*, and the edited collections *Jewish Women in Historical Perspective*, *Women of the Word: Jewish Women and Jewish Writing*, and *The Cambridge Dictionary of Judaism and Jewish Culture*. With Kenneth Seeskin of Northwestern University, she coedited *The Cambridge Guide to Jewish Religion, History, and Culture*, a 2011 National Jewish Book Award winner.

Elisheva Baumgarten, Yitzhak Becker Professor of Jewish Studies, Departments of Jewish History and History, Hebrew University of Jerusalem, is a social historian who studies the Jews of medieval Ashkenaz. Her books include *Mothers and Children: Jewish Family Life in Medieval Europe* (Princeton University Press, 2004), *Practicing Piety in Medieval Ashkenaz* (University of Pennsylvania Press, 2014), and *Biblical Women and Daily Life in Medieval Ashkenaz* (University of Pennsylvania Press, 2022), and she has published many edited volumes and articles. She directed the research group Beyond the Elite: Jewish Daily Life in Medieval Europe (2016–2022).

Dagmar Börner-Klein is a professor of Jewish Studies at the Heinrich Heine University Düsseldorf, Germany. Her main field of research encompasses rabbinic literature and its interpretations and perception throughout the centuries. Her publications include many topics on the exegesis of the Hebrew Bible, Esther, Judith, Sefer Josippon, Pirke Rabbi Eliezer, the Alphabet Ben Sira, and on the literary contributions of the "Wissenschaft des Judentums." She is the chief editor of the series Jewish Biblical Interpretation in the Middle Ages (Jüdische Bibelauslegung im Mittelalter), which includes the ground-breaking first translation of the Jalkut Shimoni into German. Currently, she is working on a comprehensive introduction to the Jalkut Shimoni that revisits the question of its dating.

Constanza Cordoni is visiting professor at the Department of Jewish Studies of the Freie Universität Berlin. She teaches at the University of Vienna from which she received the *venia legendi* in Jewish Studies in 2021. She has conducted research at the University of Utrecht and the Austrian Academy of the Sciences and is the author of *Barlaam und Josaphat in der europäischen Literatur des Mittelalters: Darstellung der Stofftraditionen, Bibliographie, Studien* (Berlin: De Gruyter, 2014) and *Seder Eliyahu: A Narratological Reading* (Berlin: De Gruyter, 2018).

Rachel Elior is professor emerita of the Hebrew University in Jerusalem, in the Department of Jewish Thought and a Senior Research Fellow at Van Leer Jerusalem Institute. She has written nine books on various periods of Jewish mystical creativity. She has edited ten books, transcribed from manuscripts, and edited and annotated three books. She has received many awards, among them the Friedenberg Award of Excellence of the Israel National Academy of Sciences and Humanities, the Beracha-Yigal Alon Prize for Academic Excellence, and in 2006 the Israel Academy of Sciences and Humanities awarded her the Gershom Scholem Prize for Research in Kabbalah. In 2016 she was awarded an honorary doctorate by the Hebrew Union College in Cincinnati and Jerusalem.

Meret Gutmann-Grün, a literary historian and philologist, combines the field of Latin and Greek literature with Jewish studies. After studying in

Basel, Lucerne, and the Hebrew University of Jerusalem, she received her doctorate in 2006 from the University of Basel. In 2008 she published *Zion als Frau: Das Frauenbild Zions in der Poesie von al-Andalus auf dem Hintergrund des klassischen Piyyuts*. She teaches Latin, Greek, and Hebrew, and her main interests are literary and theological questions, which continue to grow on the ground of the Hebrew Bible, opening new points of view on the ancient biblical traditions, especially modern Israel. Her current project is the Juedisch-Christliche Akademie in Basel (https://juedisch-christliche-akademie.ch), which she colaunched in 2018.

Robert A. Harris is Professor of Bible at The Jewish Theological Seminary, teaching courses in biblical literature and commentary, particularly medieval Jewish biblical exegesis, and is Chair of the Bible Department. He has written several books and has published many studies in the history of medieval biblical exegesis in both American and Israeli journals. He also lectures on biblical narrative and Jewish liturgy in congregations and adult education institutes around the country. He has lectured as a visiting professor at universities in Europe, Canada, and Israel and has served as a rabbi in several congregations in the United States and Israel.

Yuval Katz-Wilfing is Executive Director of the Coordinating Committee for Christian-Jewish Cooperation and research fellow at the Department of Religious Studies, University of Vienna, where he received his PhD. He also holds an MA from the Hebrew University in Jerusalem in religious studies. His main areas of research include conversion to Judaism, reception history in rabbinic texts, history of ideas, Jewish identity, current life in Austria and beyond, halakhah, and interreligious dialogue.

Sheila Tuller Keiter received a PhD from the Department of Near Eastern Languages and Cultures at UCLA and a JD from Harvard Law School. She teaches on the Judaic Studies faculty at Shalhevet in Los Angeles. In 2021, she published *Perils of Wisdom: The Scriptural Solomon in Jewish Tradition*. She also has written for the *Jewish Review of Books* and is a regular contributor to the *Jewish Journal*'s "Table for Five" Torah column.

Katrin Kogman-Appel has published work on Hebrew manuscript painting, Jewish book culture, and the relationship of Jewish visual cultures to Christian and Islamicate arts. Among her books is *A Mahzor from Worms: Art and Religion in a Medieval Jewish Community* (Harvard University

Press, 2012) and *Catalan Maps and Jewish Books* (Brepols, 2020). Formerly affiliated with the Ben-Gurion University of the Negev, in 2015 she assumed an Alexander von Humboldt Professorship at the University of Münster.

Gerhard Langer is a professor at the Institute for Jewish Studies at the University of Vienna. He studied Catholic theology, Jewish studies, and ancient Semitic philology. His main scholarly interests are Jewish cultural history, interreligious dialogue, and biblical reception history (especially in midrash). Langer is member of the interdisciplinary research center Religion and Transformation and Vice-Chair of the Vienna Doctoral School of Theology and Research on Religion. In his spare time he writes crime novels. His recent book publications are *Midrasch* (Mohr Siebeck, 2016) and *Judentum für Dummies* (Wiley, 2022).

Aurora Salvatierra Ossorio, PhD (1992) in Hebrew Literature, University of Granada (Spain), is Associate Professor of Hebrew Literature in the Department of Semitic Studies at the Granada University. Her research fields are focused on the Hebrew poetry and narrative in al-Andalus and in the Christian Iberia. In this area, she has published different articles in academic journals and collective volumes on medieval Jewish literature. She is author of a monograph about the poetic collections of Selomoh ibn Gabirol and Yehudah ha-Levi (Granada, 1994) and an anthology of Hebrew wedding songs (Córdoba, 1998). She has also published, in collaboration with O. Ruiz Morell, several books about rabbinic literature (Estella, 2001; Barcelona, 2005; Estella, 2010). She is a member of a research project focused on the edition and study of medieval texts.

Felicia Waldman (PhD 2001) is Associate Professor at the Center for Hebrew Studies of the University of Bucharest. She coordinates the Center and its Goldstein Goren MA program in Hebrew Culture and Civilization. She is also Deputy Head of the Romanian Delegation to the International Holocaust Remembrance Alliance and former Chair of its Education Working Group. She served as visiting professor at the State University of Milan, Paul Valery University of Montpellier and Al. I. Cuza University of Iasi, and as guest professor at the Romanian Diplomatic Institute of Bucharest. Her research interests include Jewish mysticism, Holocaust education and remembrance, and Romanian Jewish history and heritage. She has published four books, coedited four volumes, curated four exhibition, and served as consultant for four documentary films.

Ancient Sources Index

Hebrew Bible/Old Testament

Genesis
Ref	Pages
1	249
1:27	75, 249, 254
2	249
2:8	75
2:18	75–76, 84, 254
2:22	77–78
3:21	79, 83
4:23	86
5:2	76
9:6	76
9:7	76
12:11	178
16:1–3	92
16:4	94
16:5	97
16:6	96, 99
16:11	94, 96, 98
16:12	205
16:14	93
17:19–21	93
18	162
18:6	115, 164
18:15	162
21:9	214
21:9–10	94
21:9–13	95
21:14	94, 97
22	162, 292
23	162
24:16	178
24:49	164
24:59	165
24:63	290
25:1–2	92
25:13	204
25:21	292, 294
25:22	295
25:23	299
25:27	294
27:1–29	296
27:3	165
27:11	214
28:9	212
33:19	277
36:20–21	205
37:27	87
38	161

Exodus
Ref	Pages
2:15–20	301
2:21	301
4:20	302
4:25	302
4:28	109
19:18	213
21:6	278
23:9	268
25:18	205
26:20	77
28:35	193–94

Leviticus
Ref	Pages
16:11	76
19:14	88
26:42	60

Numbers
7:89	238
12:8	117
15:39	109

Deuteronomy
2:19	60
6:4	63
6:5	156, 271
7:3	159
10:17	115
11:19	221
14:26	76
17:16–17	147
21:22–23	60
23:4	271–72, 280
25:5–10	21
28:30	64

Joshua
1:8	274
2	161
6:25	161

Judges
3	272
3:15–30	272
3:20	272
16:19	65

Ruth
1:14	274
1:16	273
2:4	277
3:7	279
3:14	274
4:10	274

1 Samuel
2:92	222
4:4	205
12:11	60, 86
15:33	39
16:12	205–6
25	159

25:3	179
25:6	76
25:14–42	178
25:31	159
25:39	178

2 Samuel
7:5–16	148
7:12–13	148
11	159
11:2	178
12:29	194
13	161, 180
16:11	161
16:22	161
18:28	60

1 Kings
1:3–4	178
1:11–31	147
1:40	61
3:5–12	150
3:9	148
3:12	148
3:16–28	147
5:6	147
5:12	127
5:17	148
5:27–30	147
10:23	147
10:26	147
10:27	147
11:1–3	147
11:1–10	159
11:3	146
11:4	146, 149
11:4–8	147, 149
11:7	149, 212
16:31	179
21:25	163

2 Kings
7:1	115

Ancient Sources Index

1 Chronicles		22:1	48–49
22:7–10	148	22:2–11	48
29:23	273	22:7	49, 233
		22:10	48–49
Esther		22:14	48–49
1:1	42	33:6	243
1:8	40	37:15	66
1:14	52	55:20	113
1:20	50	56:1	192, 202, 209
2:1	40	62:12	110
2:6	43	87	224
2:7	43–44, 48, 50, 180	90:1	116
2:9–11	50	102	201
2:10	44	102:7–8	200
2:15	44, 51, 61	126:1–2	216
2:19	51	128:3	180
2:20	44, 51	133:3	194
2:21	52	137	215–16
3:8	51	137:5–6	214
4:3–4	45	139:5	78
4:8	51	145:1	116
4:14	39, 51		
4:14–15	45	Proverbs	
4:17	39, 45, 51	1:1	115, 126
5:1	46, 51	2:16	159
5:1–5	47	3:4	44
5:2	61	4:2	49
5:4	52	5:19	185, 205–6
5:6	51	5:20	159
5:9	51	6:24	159
7:1	51	11:30	278
7:8	117	18:22	135
9:1–2	36	22:29	104
9:16–19	35	25:11	114
9:20–22	35	30:1	113
9:21–22	36	30:1–4	150
9:26–28	35	30:2	146
9:28	52	30:30	167
9:29	36, 181	31	3, 7, 169
9:31	35–36	31:1	146
10:4	40	31:1–4	148
		31:1–9	135, 146, 150
		31:3	136, 146
Psalms		31:10–31	4, 8, 13, 133, 135, 153, 168–70
12:7	271		
22	47–49		

Proverbs (cont.)

31:10	13, 135–36
31:13	25
31:14	16
31:19	23
31:23	167

Ecclesiastes

1:1	115, 126
2:22	83
4:2	274
7:26	269
9:9	76
12:8	126
12:13	148

Song of Songs

1:2	116, 126–28, 182
1:4	203
1:5	184, 204
1:6	118
1:7	184
1:14	213
1:15–2:3	118
2:4	183, 211
2:5	198
2:5–6	119
2:6	129
2:7	193
2:9–13	120
2:12	207
2:14	125, 192, 197, 199, 207
2:16	206
2:17	211
3:1	200
3:2	199–200
3:5	121
3:9–11	120
4:3	182, 192–93
4:5	108–9
4:7	182
4:8	205
4:8–9	204
4:9	204–5
4:12	192
4:13	205
4:16	183, 204–5, 207
5:1	193
5:2	206
5:2–7	122
5:4	211
5:5	182
5:6	203
5:7	189, 199, 210–11
5:8–9	200, 210
5:8–6:3	124
5:10	193
5:13	181
6:2	183
6:3	183
6:4–7:11	125
6:8–9	127
6:11	215
7:2	192
7:3	186
7:12–13	204
7:12–8:4	121
7:14	198
8:2	205
8:3	211
8:6	111, 129, 201
8:11	208
8:13–14	125
8:14	211

Isaiah

5:1–7	208
5:7	204
5:12	117
10:17	48
11:12	197
19:1	213
21:3	45
24:9	117
29:8	82
34:14	254, 260
50:1	109
50:6	214
54:2	209
54:11	202–3

Ancient Sources Index

54:11–55:5	203	10:3	58
60:14	99		

Pseudepigrapha

Jeremiah

2:2	211	4 Ezra	
3:1–13	109	8	224
9:9–10	198		
21:9	61	### New Testament	
25:10	64		
31:14	165	Matthew	
31:15	198, 212	1:1–17	161
31:35–36	165	27:46	47
50:19	204		

Mark

Lamentations		15:34	47
1:1	194, 200		
1:2	200–1	### Prerabbinic and Rabbinic Writings	
1:12–22	194		
1:20	194	Avot of Rabbi Nathan	
4:5	239	A1	82
5:16	239	B9	82
		B42	82

Ezekiel

1:4	126	b. ʿAvodah Zarah	
16	109	27a	306
23:17	129		
44:30	76	b. Bava Metziʾa	
		59a	164
Hosea		84b	141
1–3	109	87a	164
2:9	110		
		b. Bekhorot	
Micah		8a	81
4:10	204		
		b. Berakhot	
Zechariah		6a	222
1:8	43, 48	10a	141
9:9	233	61a	77–78
9:12	216		
		b. ʿEruvin	
### Deuterocanonical Books		18a	77
		18b	255
Judith		100b	81–82, 88
8:1	57		
8:7–8	58		

b. Hagigah		b. Sotah	
5b	155	13	224
		14a	83
b. Hullin		21b	74
42a	167		
		b. Sotah	
b. Horayot		47a	272
10b	272		
		b. Sukkah	
b. Megillah		29a	165
4a	67	49b	141
10b–17b	37		
12b	40	b. Ta'anit	
13a	43–44	26b	142
13b	51		
14a	159	b. Yebamot	
14b	159	61a	85
17a	296	63a	76, 79
29a	222, 251		
		Esther Rabbah	
b. Nazir		1–5	42
23b	272	6:5	43
		6:6	45
b. Niddah		6:9	44
24b	255	6:12	44
31a	79	8:3	45
		8:6	46
b. Pesaḥim		9:1	47
22b	88		
50b	142	Exodus Rabbah	
		6:1	141
b. Sanhedrin		29:9	239
20a	141		
21b	159	Genesis Rabbah	
37a	187	8	78
39a	77	8:1	77
57b	79	9:5	83
70b	141–42, 146, 148	17:2	76
105b	272	17:4	77
		18:4	79
b. Shabbat		19:4	80
23a	67–69		
35b	115	Genesis Rabbah (cont.)	
145b–146a	269	19:5	80
		20:5	81

Ancient Sources Index

20:6	81	Pesiqta Rabbati	
20:12	83	26	224
21:5	83	34 §8	233
45:6	96	37 §3	233
58:5	162		
60:16	290	Pirqe Rabbi Eliezer	
63:6	294	12	
63:10	296	75	
		13	80
Leviticus Rabbah		14	82
14:1	77	29	310
		31	292
m. Avot		32	162
3:6	222–23	45	166
		49	39
m. Sabb.			
2:6	82	Qoheleth Rabbah	
		1:1	141
m. Sotah			
3:4	74	Ruth Rabbah	
		2:9	272
m. Yad.		2:14	160
3:5		4	271, 280
		4:9	160
Megillat Taanit			
17 Elul	64–66	Seder Eliyahu Rabbah	
		1:3–4	39
Midrash Psalms			
22	47, 49	Seder Olam Rabbah	
22:3	48	15	141
22:6	49		
22:7	49	Sifre Deuteronomy	
22:14	48–49	§355	224
22:16	48	103	
22:19	49		
22:23	48	*Hasidei Ashkenaz*	
22:24	49		
22:25	49	Sefer ha-Rokeach ha-Gadol	
22:27	49	Hilkhot Teshuvah, no. 1	160
		Hilkhot Teshuvah, no. 14	156
		Hilkhot Teshuvah, no. 20	156
Midrash Ruth Zuta			
1:1	160	Sefer Hasidim manuscript in Bologna	
		§14	156
Numbers Rabbah		§29	155
10:4	141, 148		

Ancient Sources Index

Sefer Hasidim ... Bologna (*cont.*)		2:20	51
§102	162	2:21	52
§135	163–64	3:1	52
§158	167	3:8	51
§161	159	4:1	51–52
§183	161	4:8	51
§222	155	4:14	51
§336	165	4:17	51
§509	156	5:1	51
§514	165	5:4	52
§619	158, 160	5:6	51
§872–73	155	5:9	51
§1148	165–66	6:1	51
		7:1	51
Sefer Hasidim manuscript in Parma		9:28	52
§15	160		
§984	155	Moses ibn Ezra	
§989	155	no. 37	198
§669	155		
§670	155	Shlomo ibn Gabirol	
§1715	155	no. 95	204
		no. 96	193
Medieval Writings		no. 131	205
		no. 133	207, 214
Judah Halevi		no. 163	212
no. 152	213		
no. 159	208	Shmuel Hanagid	
no. 181	213	no. 9	215
no. 206	203	no. 180	189
no. 208	212		
no. 251	214	**Medieval Midrashim and Collections**	
no. 272	213		
no. 324	204, 209	Jacob ben Nissim ibn Shahin 59–60	
no. 326	200, 209		
no. 357	202, 209	Kol Bo b. Shab. 23a	68–69
no. 379	203, 210–11		
no. 390	212	Ma'ase Yehudit	61
no. 401	215–16		
		Megillat Yehudit	63–64
Leqach Tov on Esther			
1:14	52	Midrash Aggadah Gen 25:21	294
1:20	50		
2:7	50	Sefer Yosippon (Josippon)	40–42
2:15	51		
2:19	51	Yalqut Shimoni No. 115	299

Ancient Sources Index 363

Medieval Writings and Aggadot

British Library Oriental
BL MS Oriental 2737   289
BL Or. 2884 (fol. 4v)   296
Or. 1404   288, 302–3, 307

Golden Haggadah   287, 296, 298, 302

Regensburg Pentateuch   310–11, 313

Rylands Haggadah   193, 287, 302, 304, 307

Sarajevo Haggadah   287, 290–91, 294, 299, 300–1

Second Nuremberg Haggadah   288, 292, 297, 301, 305, 310

Yahudah Haggadah 288, 292–93, 295–96, 301

Medieval Commentaries

Abraham ibn Ezra
   on Prov 31:1   146

Ben Asher, Bahye
   on Exod 4:24   307

Gersonides (Ralbag)
   on Gen 16   99
   on 1 Kgs 11:4   149

Ibn Kathir, *Al-Bidāyah wa-al-nihāyah fi al-ta'rīkh*   101

Kimchi, David
   on Gen 16:5–6   96–97
   on Gen 21:11, 14   97
   on 1 Kgs 11:7   149

Kimchi, Joseph
   on Prov 31:1   146

Kimchi, Moses
   on Prov 31   146

Nachmanides (Ramban)
   on Gen 2:18   84
   on Gen 2:19   85
   on Gen 16:2   98
   on Gen 16:6–11   98

Rabbi Eliezer of Beaugency
   on Ezek 1:4   126

Rabbi Samuel ben Meir (Rashbam)
   on Song 1:2–8:14   115–124

Rashi
   on Gen 2:8   75
   on Gen 2:18   75
   on Gen 2:20   76
   on Gen 2:22   77
   on Gen 2:23   78
   on Gen 2:25   79
   on Gen 3:1   79
   on Gen 3:8   110, 113
   on Gen 3:14–15   81
   on Gen 3:20–22   83
   on Gen 23:2   162
   on Exod 4:24   307
   on Ps 55:20   113
   on m. Sotah 3:4   74
   on b. ʿAbod. Zar. 18b   75
   on b. Shabb. 23a   67

Tosafot
   on b. Meg. 4a   67

Mysticism and Hasidism

Dov Baer of Mesritsch, *Maggid devarav le-Yaʿakov*   243

Joseph Karo, *Maggid Mesharim* 18–19   240

Menachem Recanati
  35b   266

Midrash Ha-Nelam Ruth, ZH
  78b   270
  82a   275
  82b   269
  85c   275

Pardes Rimmonim
  186d   259

Rabbi Israel Baal Shem Tov (the Besht)
  ʾIgeret Haqodesh   242

Sefer Habahir
  29   226
  33   226
  119   210

Shlomo Alqabez
  Lekha Dodi   238

Saba de-Mishpatim
  98b   268
  100a   268

Sefer Yetzirah   221, 226, 231–32

Sitrei Torah
  1:147b–148a   259

Zohar
  Bereshit 34b–35a   77
  Vayera 1:111a   274
  Vayeshev 1:188b   279
  Vayaqhel 2:217b   276
  Shemot 55a, 231a   77

Modern Authors Index

Adler, Elkan Nathan	58	Buber, Salomon	49, 294
Agus, Irving	16–17	Caponigro, Mark	56
Alexander, Philip	187	Castelli, Elizabeth	91–92
Alfonso, Esperanza	175, 209	Chavel, Charles B	84
Alster, Baruch	108	Chavel, Haim D.	307
Ansberry, Christopher B.	135–37, 141, 148	Chazan, Robert	15, 158, 227, 316–18
Astell, Ann W.	104, 131	Clines, David J. A.	43, 135
Atzmon, Arnon	38, 42	Cluse, Christoph	17, 24, 26
Baer, Yitzhak	156, 317	Cohen, Esther	20
Bakhos, Carol	92	Cohen, Gerson	104
Baldwin, John W.	122	Cohen, Jeremy	317
Baskin, Judith R.	13, 16, 18, 20, 31, 82, 155, 157, 161, 163, 166–69	Cohen, Mark	247
		Cohen, Menachem	105–6
Baumgarten, Elisheva	18, 23, 25–26, 28, 157, 286, 306–7, 313–16	Cohen, Naomi	75
		Cohen, Shaye J. D.	74, 310
		Cole, Peter	3, 178
Bebe, Paulina	269	Cordoni, Constanza	38, 50
Bercher, Léon	211	Crenshaw, James L.	134, 141, 147
Berliner, Abraham	27	Dahan, Alon	225
Bernstein, Marc S.	3	Dahood, Mitchell J.	47
Bernstein, Shimon	198	Dan, Joseph	154, 157, 225, 257
Biale, David	2, 156	David, Yonah	180
Bickerman, Elias J.	62	DeFranza, Megan K.	135–37, 139
Bloom, Harold	257–58	Delcor, Mathias	56
Bodendorfer, Gerhard	37	Dell, Katharine J.	134–37, 141, 148
Bonnen, Gerald	17	Dobbs-Weinstein, Idit	4
Börner-Klein, Dagmar	37, 58–67	Dönitz, Saskia	40
Bossong, Georg	190	Drory, Rina	196
Boyd-Taylor, Cameron	56	Dubarle, Marie-André	57–59, 61–63, 65–66
Brann, Ross	174, 190, 192		
Braude, William G.	48	Dunsky, Samson	104
Brin, Gerson	126	Eidelberg, Shlomo	316
Brine, Kevin R.	58–59, 63, 73	Einbinder, Susan L.	318–19
Brinner, William	101	Eisenstein, Jehuda Dov	58
Brody, Hayyim	178–79, 181, 197	Elhadad-Aroshas, Deborah	313

Elior, Rachel	224, 234, 237, 242	Halkin, Abraham S.	191–92, 195
Elizur, Shulamit	4, 194, 317	Hallamish, Moshe	264–68
Elsner, Jas	286, 289	Hanhart, Robert	56–57
Elukin, Jonathan	15	Harris, Julie A.	289
Engel, Helmut	57	Harris, Robert A.	105, 111, 130
Epstein, Marc M.	288–89, 296, 301–2, 306,	Harris, Tracy K.	2
		Har-Shefi, Bitkha	28
Exum, J. Cheryl	92	Haverkamp, Eva	316–17
Falk, Zeev W.	20–21	Hecker, Joel	264–66, 269–73, 279–80
Fine, Steven	286	Heiman, Dov	292
Firth, David G.	43	Henten, Jan Willem van	56, 59
Fishbane, Eitan P.	251, 253	Hirshman, Marc	104
Fishbane, Michael	108, 125	Hoffman, Lawrence	15, 310
Fisher, Charles Dennis	64	Hollender, Elisabeth	37, 317
Fleischer, Ezra	4	Horovitz, Haim Shaul	210
Flusser, David	40–41	Horowitz, Elliott E.	19–20, 313
Fonrobert, Charlotte E.	78	Hossfeld, Frank-Lothar	47
Fox, Michael V.	134–146	Humphreys, W. Lee	43
Friedlander, Gerald	39, 75, 292	Hurovits, Avigdor	134–38, 141–48
Frisch, Amos	149	Hüsch, Adolf	107
Frojmovic, Eva	306–7, 309, 312–14	Huss, Matti	190
Frymer-Kensky, Tikva	137–39	Iancu-Agou, Daniele	17
Gafni, Isaiah	43	Idel, Moshe	77, 224, 247, 253
Gaster, Moses	62	Ilan, Tal	56, 59, 74–75
Georges, Karl Ernst	58	Jakobi, Renate	197
Goitein, Shlomo Dov	16, 36–37–40	Japhet, Sara	105–8, 111–13, 122, 126–29
Goldberg, Arnold Maria	233	Jellinek, Adolf	58–59
Goldin, Simha	317, 319	Jordan, William C.	24
Graves, Robert	255	Kamin, Sarah	104–5, 111–12
Gray, Alyssa	25	Kanarfogel, Ephraim	18, 154
Grayzel, Solomon	29–30	Kaplan, Aryeh	226
Green, Arthur	131, 224, 265, 309	Kaplan, Debra	25
Greenspahn, Frederick E.	138–40, 147	Katz, Jacob	19, 21, 29
Grintz, Jehosua M.	56	Keil, Martha	24
Grossman, Avraham	16, 19–21, 23–24, 26–27, 106, 157, 306, 309, 314, 317–19	Kimmelman, Reuben	104
		Kogman-Appel, Katrin	287–89, 299, 302, 307, 313
Gruber, Mayer I.	113		
Grundmann, Regina	67	Koller, Aaron	36–38, 44
Gutmann-Grün, Meret	189, 192, 194–95, 197–98	Kraeling, Carl	286
		Krautheimer, Richard	26
Gutwirth, Israel	257	Krakowski, Eve	4
Haberman, Bona Devorah	310	LaCocque, André	56
Hackett, Jo Ann	92	Langer, Gerhard	38, 73, 80, 265
Haider, Peter W	59	Lassner, Jacob	3
Ha-Kohen, Isaac b. Jacob	257	Lerner, Myron Bialik	37, 42

Modern Authors Index

Levenson, Jon D. 95
Levine Gera, Deborah 5, 58–59
Lieber, Laura 4
Lipsius, Richard Adelbert 59, 68
Liss, Hanna 107
Lockshin, Martin 106
Lodahl, Michael E. 252
Loewe, Raphael 193, 288
Lotter, Friedrich 317
Lowin, Shari 175, 177, 180
Luzzato, Shmuel David 209
Lyke, Larry 94
Malter, Henry 36
Manix, Pam 17
Marcus, Ivan G. 2, 13–14, 18, 25, 154, 158, 160, 167, 316–18
Margaliot, Reuven 154, 225–26
Mathews, Henry J. 107, 128
Matter, E. Ann 104, 131
Meir, Tamar 160
Metzger, Mendel 313
Meyers, Carol 36, 43
Michels, Evi 52
Mintz, Alan 318
Mireaux, Émile 56
Mirsky, Aron 4
Mondschein, Aharon 127
Moore, Carey A. 35, 36, 41, 43, 45, 56
Münz-Manor, Ophir 4
Narkiss, Bezalel 287–88, 302
Neusner, Jacob 266, 290, 300
Noam, Vered 64
O'Bryan, Robin 262
Offenberg, Sara 301
Otzen, Benedikt 55
Pagis, Dan 195
Patai, Raphael 255, 259–62
Perez Castro, Federico 178
Pessin, Sarah 4
Pierce, Joanne M. 15
Polzer, Natalie C. 82
Porsche, Monika 26
Priebatsch, Hans Yohanan 56
Pritchard, James B. 93
Radford Ruether, Rosemary 249

Rakel, Claudia 57
Ray, Jonathan 17
Regev, Shaul 145
Reinhartz, Adele 95, 100
Roi, Biti 249
Rosen, Tova 183, 199
Rosen-Tzvi, Ishay 80
Rosman, Moshe 26
Sabar, Shalom 286–87, 292
Samely, Alexander 38
Sáenz-Badillos, Ángel 174, 178, 181, 183
Salvatierra Ossorio, Aurora 176–77, 180–81
Sänger, Dieter 47
Sapir Abulafia, Anna 317
Schäfer, Peter 309
Scheindlin, Raymond 2–3, 173, 176, 179–80, 185, 198, 202, 205, 207, 209, 216
Schippers, Arie 3, 174, 177, 191–92, 195
Schirmann, Hayyim 178–79, 185, 191, 195
Schlosser, Julius von 287
Schmitz, Barbara 55–57
Scholem, Gershom 224, 226–27, 231, 248, 251, 255, 258–59, 265
Schroer, Silvia 208
Schwartzmann, Julia 84, 138, 143–44
Shepkaru, Shmuel 317–19
Shoham-Steiner, Ephraim 309
Signer, Michael A. 111
Sijarić, Mirsad 287
Simon, Maurice 44, 186
Sneed, Mark R. 134–36, 138–39, 141
Soloveitchik, Haym 154
Spiegel, Shalom 292, 317
Spiegel, Yaakov S. 306
Steiner, Richard C. 126–27
Stemberger, Günter 37, 49, 104
Stern, David 107, 256
Stienstra, Nelly 109
Stow, Kenneth R. 14, 16, 154, 158
Stuard, Susan Mosher 20
Sukenik, Eliezer L. 288
Swartz, Michael D. 4

Tabory, Joseph	42
Thompson, John L.	92
Tishby, Isaiah	227–29, 231, 234
Tobi, Yosef	175
Toch, Michael	17
Touitou, Elazar	106
Transier, Werner	117
Trible, Phyllis	92, 95
Tuttle, Virginia	262
Urbach, Ephraim	253
Valler, Shulamit	138, 141–42
VanderKam, James C.	56
Vardi, Yonatan	189
Waldman, Felicia	253
Walfish, Barry Dov	36, 44, 98, 103, 106–7, 126, 128
Walfish, Miriam-Simma	95, 100
Wasserstrom, Steven M.	3
Weinberger, Leon	177–78, 201
Weingarten, Susan	63
Werblowsky, R. J. Zwi	237
Wertheimer, Joseph Chaim	104, 109
West, Gerald	55
Wharton, Annabel J.	286, 289
Whybray, Roger N.	134–38, 140–41
Wilhelm, Jakob David	229
Wistinetzki, Judah	154
Wolfson, Elliot	247, 252, 256, 280
Wolfthal, Diane	306, 314
Wolters, Al	134–37, 139–43
Wright, L. M.	122
Wünsche, August	58–59
Yahalom, Joseph	4, 195–96, 200, 209, 215
Yuval, Israel J.	14, 23, 300
Zakovitch, Yair	135, 140
Zenger, Erich	47, 57

www.ingramcontent.com/pod-product-compliance
Lightning Source LLC
Chambersburg PA
CBHW032148010526
44111CB00035B/1251